W9-DDG-593

The Economics of
Environmental Quality

Second Edition

The Economics of Environmental Quality

Second Edition

EDWIN S. MILLS
PRINCETON UNIVERSITY

PHILIP E. GRAVES
UNIVERSITY OF COLORADO

W · W · Norton & Company · Inc · *New York*

Copyright © 1986 by W. W. Norton & Company, Inc.
Printed in the United States of America.

All Rights Reserved

ISBN 0-393-95270-3

Library of Congress Cataloging in Publication Data
Mills, Edwin S. and Philip E. Graves
   The economics of environmental quality.
   Includes bibliographies.
   1. Environmental policy.   2. Pollution—Economic
aspects.   3. Environmental policy—United States.
I. Title.

FOR MARGARET, JESSICA, AND WENDY

Contents

*Part II. Discharges and Environmental Quality in
the United States*

Preface

This is a textbook on environmental economics intended for undergraduates who have had at least one semester of introductory microeconomics. While in no way lowering the level of the first edition, the second edition adds additional material designed to appeal to a broader range of interests. By substituting the new Chapter 2 for Chapters 3 and 4 (Chapters 2 and 3 of the first edition), *The Economics of Environmental Quality* may be successfully used in environmental economics classes composed not only of economics majors but also of students with a diverse background (environmental design, minerals and land management, biology, ecology, and so on). Full comprehension of Chapters 3 and 4 will, as with the earlier edition, require readers to know the elementary theories of the firm and the consumer, as well as suppy and demand. Some of the exposition is abstract, but no mathematics beyond high school algebra is used in the text. No knowledge of welfare economics is assumed; and the reader need have no prior acquaintance with environmental problems.

As with any applied subject in economics, some knowledge of the subject matter will increase the depth of understanding gained from reading this book. However, the second edition does contain much more institutional material and more on the "nuts and bolts" of benefit/cost analysis. This is because we have encountered a particular difficulty in our teaching of environmental economics: students appear to learn (temporarily) that one should control pollutants up to the point where marginal benefits equal marginal costs; unfortunately, they soon realize that they have no idea where either of the marginal curves actually lies! Moreover, the usual text does not give them any idea how one might go about acquiring the needed information. We feel that an important strength of the second edition of *The Economics of Environmental Quality* is the solid feel that a student will get for how environmental analysis is actually conducted.

The intent of the second edition, as with the first, is to present a coherent thread of theoretical and empirical analysis. Part I presents the basic theoretical tools necessary to understand the subject. The new Chapter 2 discusses the supply and demand for ordinary goods and for environmental goods, emphasizing both similarities and differences. Also market failure, public goods, property rights, the "free rider" problem, and other topics treated only implicitly in the first edition are incorporated into Chapter 2. This new chapter closes with a revisitation of the resource-allocation problem, discussing the inevitability of choice, selection of convenient units, and approaches to the difficult problem of determining the optimal environmental quality. A brief discussion of efficiency and equity is also included in this new chapter. The remainder of Part I retains the detailed presentation of the neoclassical theories of the firm and consumer, tying the environmental concepts introduced in Chapter 2 into the mainstream of economic theory. These chapters may be omitted in courses taken principally by non-majors in economics.

Part II presents basic technical data on water, air, and solid-waste discharges, and the resulting environmental degradation. Sources, amounts, damages, abatement techniques, and benefit/cost calculations are discussed successively for each environmental medium. The second edition provides much more information on discharges and their effect on environmental quality than did the first edition, although it remains the case that less information exists than would be ideal.

Part III is concerned with the American pollution-control programs. This part begins, in Chapter 8, with a historical sketch of environmental policy in the United States. Water quality is discussed first (reversing the order of Part II) since water legislation predated laws to control air quality. The spate of recent laws dealing with hazardous substances is also considered in detail. Chapter 9 provides a critical evaluation of the environmental policy enacted in the United States, leading into Chapter 10's discussion of how to best restructure environmental programs. While advocating the economic incentive approach as in the first edition, greater emphasis is given in the second edition to some alternative reforms that are receiving current attention. Many of these reforms deal with the spatial dimension of pollution problems, a dimension that has long received too little attention.

Foreign and global problems are taken up in Part IV. Chapter 11 deals with the approaches to environmental quality that have been taken in several other countries and contrasts these approaches to the United States program. The diversity of cultures and of environmental problems among these countries has led to varied policy responses reflecting these differences. Global environmental problems are considered in Chapter 12, which first places the subject in the framework of neoclassical growth theory. Case studies of global problems resulting from heat, carbon dioxide, hydrocarbon, and chlorofluorocarbon discharges are then examined. Part IV closes with a new chapter, Chapter 13, that brings together our speculations about the future of environmental economics.

No one should learn environmental economics from only one book. To do so imparts an upward bias to one's sense of the unity of the subject. Although this edition contains much empirical material and government policy analysis, some description has been sacrificed to the goal of developing systematic theoretical and empirical analysis. Our justification is that the richness and complexity of the subject can be learned from other sources, but the systematic analysis cannot. Readers wishing to supplement this book will find readings listed at the ends of chapters. Most important, readers should apply the tools of analysis to environmental problems of their choice. It is nearly impossible to appreciate the complexity of environmental economics without undertaking a case study.

One cannot write sensibly on environmental economics without incurring a large debt to Allen Kneese, whose published work has largely structured the subject during more than twenty years. Robert Socalow, Daniel Feenberg, and Richard Price read parts of the manuscript. The book has benefited greatly from the comments of A. Myrick Freeman III, of Bowdoin College, Dale Lehman of Fort Lewis College, Ed Morey of the University of Colorado, and George

Tolley of the University of Chicago. Drafts of most chapters were originally typed with great skill and energy by Annmarie Ritz; others in the second edition were similarly treated by Gladys Bloedow. Last but not least, Donald Lamm first suggested that this book be written; he showed uncommon patience during the writing of both editions.

E.S.M. and P.E.G.

Part I

BASIC THEORETICAL ANALYSIS

There are many points of view from which environmental problems can be studied. A meteorologist might be concerned with the ways pollutants move through the atmosphere. A biologist might analyze the effects of pollutants on living things. An engineer would be concerned with the design of devices to prevent pollutants from entering the environment. The economist is concerned with pollution as a problem in resource allocation, a problem involving how much environmental quality we want to have in light of the other goods that must be given up to obtain it. Information from the meteorologist, the biologist, the engineer, the economist,—indeed information from a great many professionals—is necessary before wise decisions can be made about environmental quality. For that reason, environmental problems are frequently said to be multidisciplinary.

In environmental economics, the fundamental point of departure is this observation: If pollution is an appropriate area for government intervention, it must be because, in the absence of government intervention, resources are misallocated in ways that pollute the environment excessively. Why does economic activity, unconstrained by government pollution-control programs, lead to excessive pollution? How can the appropriate amount of pollution be calculated? What can governments do to ensure that resources are allocated to produce no more pollution than is appropriate? It is in the answers to the preceding questions that the economic way of thinking is seen to be vitally important. Part I lays out carefully a systematic analytical framework, devised by economists over many decades, for analyzing pollution problems and appropriate programs to control environmental degradation.

Chapter 1

Resources, Production, Consumption, and Pollution

Like other sciences, economics started by gradual separation from people's broad speculative thought about themselves, society, and the world around them. Each new intellectual discipline—physics, psychology, sociology, economics—emerged slowly during many decades. Identification of a birthday for economics is thus arbitrary, but the publication of Adam Smith's *Wealth of Nations* in 1776 is as good a date as any.

It is no exaggeration to say that economics originated in the deep concern among eighteenth-century thinkers about the relationship between people's living standards and their physical environment. Much early speculation among economists was about the most basic aspects of the relationship, that between food production and growth of the population to be fed. The physiocrats, who preceded Smith, could hardly recognize commodities other than food as genuine wealth and output. Smith greatly broadened the concepts of wealth and output to include other goods produced to satisfy people's needs and wants. Gradually, services—such as haircuts, teaching, and legal advice—came to be recognized as part of society's total production. Marxists have never recognized services to be socially valuable output and to this day Communist countries do not include them in their measures of national output. The physiocrats, and classical economists such as Smith, Thomas Malthus, David Ricardo, and Karl Marx, spent most of their lives studying whether and, if so, how people could produce enough goods with the labor and materials available to rise above a subsistence living standard.

Today it would be said that the classical economists were concerned mostly with resource, in contrast with environmental, economics. In part, the reason is that resource problems were more pressing than environmental problems during the eighteenth and nineteenth centuries. In part, the reason is also that environmental economics requires tools of analysis that were unavailable to the classical economics. The neoclassical economists, writing during a period centered on the turn of the twentieth century, placed great emphasis on developing tools of analysis. Much of the modern theory of the firm, the consumer, and market equilibrium was developed by neoclassical writers such as Alfred Marshall, Knut Wicksell, Léon Walras, and A. C. Pigou. Marshall and Pigou, in particular, developed the concepts of external economies and diseconomies, which are crucial in understanding environmental problems.

After World War II, tools of economic theory and statistical methods, and data concerning resources and the environment, have improved steadily. In addition, society rapidly became conscious of environmental problems in the 1960s and of shortages of fuels and resources in the 1970s. The result has been rapid growth in research by natural scientists, engineers, and economists on resource and environmental problems. Although serious inadequacies remain in the analysis and the data, environmental economics can now be treated in a unified and comprehensive way that was impossible as recently as the 1960s.

If one reviews the two-hundred-year history of economic thought about the relationship between people's living standards and their environment, one is impressed that progress in understanding has been painfully slow, but that it has been definite and quite steady.

Resource and Environmental Economics

Economic activity consists of the application of energy to materials to transform them from their natural forms into forms in which they are useful to people. Behind this simple statement lies all the complexity of modern industrial society. Every commodity that you use—the house you live in, the food you eat, and the book you are reading—is made by applying energy to materials extracted from the earth's crust, surface, atmosphere, or waters. Although it is less obvious, the same is true of the economic activities usually classified as services. A doctor providing patient care uses the hospital building, fuel to heat or cool it, and complex equipment as inputs to provide the service. In addition, the food he eats provides his energy used in providing his services. (Food is classified as a final or consumption good instead of an input in the national income accounts, but it is clearly necessary to enable people to produce services.)

All these materials have been extracted from the environment and processed with the use of energy. The natural forms of materials are their forms before people process them. Some are metals, fossil fuels, and other elements and compounds in the ground; some are living organisms on the earth's surface or in its waters; and some are gases in the atmosphere. When the energy used to transform materials is human or animal energy, food is the fuel. Only since the Industrial Revolution have human and animal work ceased to be society's major energy sources. Some energy is obtained by directly harnessing natural forces, such as hydroelectric power, tidal power, solar energy, and geothermal energy. A small but growing amount of energy is generated by atomic fission world-wide, although cancellations have been exceeding new applications for nuclear power plants in the United States since the Three Mile Island accident. In the United States, more than 90 percent of the energy generated comes from combustion of fossil fuels—petroleum, coal, and natural gas.

Materials are transformed by many complex mechanical, biological, and chemical processes to make useful products. Metals are mined with large amounts of unwanted materials. The materials are separated, refined, combined with other materials, and fabricated into useful products. Food is extracted in the agricultural and fisheries industries and then processed in factories, stores, and homes before consumption. Petroleum is pumped from the ground and then refined and processed into fuel, chemicals, plastics, and many other products.

As technology progresses and living standards rise, materials are subjected to more and more complex processing between their extraction from the environment and their consumption by people. The manufacture of a steam shovel requires much more, and much more complex, processing than the manufacture of enough hand shovels to move the same amount of earth. In fact, the period since the Industrial Revolution can be characterized by the discovery of new materials, increasingly complex products and fabrication methods, and new sources of energy and ways to use it. The result has been that common people, at least in industrialized countries, have achieved living standards far above the subsistence level for the first time in history. Industrialization has in the past resulted in dramatic increases in materials and fuels extracted from the environment, although this trend may not continue in the future.

Unfortunately, no comprehensive historical data exist on materials extracted from the environment. We do know that currently materials extraction is on a truly massive scale, with many *billions* of tons of materials being extracted annually in recent years in the United States. To put the matter in more meaningful human terms, this is roughly 130 pounds per day per person! The presumption is strong that total materials extraction has grown somewhat less rapidly than total national output in the course of American history. One reason is that services, which presumably require less materials extraction per dollar of output than do commodities, have been an increasing share of total output as income and output have risen. Another reason is that commodity output per unit of materials extraction grows as technology improves and processing becomes more efficient.

It is also known that extractive industries have become a much smaller part of the American economy since the beginning of rapid industrialization in the early nineteenth century. Harold Barnett and Chandler Morse show that value added, or income earned, in extractive industries—agriculture, fisheries, lumbering, and mining—fell from 44 percent of gross national product (GNP) in 1870 to 10 percent in 1954. This dramatic decrease resulted in part from the reasons given in the last paragraph for gradual increases in output per unit of materials extraction and in part from large decreases in the prices of materials relative to prices of other inputs. Thus, for at least a century and possibly continuing at the present time materials have become increasingly plentiful despite rapid growth in worldwide demand.[1]

The basic reason for the long-term decline in the relative price of materials was that technology continually found ways of using plentiful and previously unused materials. Oil was not valuable until

1. See among the references Johnson, Bell, and Bennett, who support Barnett and Morse, but also Slade, who presents evidence of a recent turnabout.

technology enabled people to refine it and to make fuels and many other products from it. Likewise, plutonium was not a valuable fuel until science and technology enabled people to generate electricity from atomic fission.

The first half of the 1970s was a period of shortages and rapidly rising prices for certain materials, while the early 1980s experience appears to indicate a return to earlier declines in real prices of many materials. Some people suggest (for example Margaret Slade in the *Journal of Environmental Economics and Management*) that the period of increasingly plentiful materials has ended and that growth of demand has caught up with the ability of technology and of extractive industries to increase supply. That is far from certain, but it is wise to be aware that declining relative prices of materials may not continue indefinitely. We shall return to this topic in Chapter 13.

There have also been dramatic increases in energy use in the American economy. Data are much better on energy use than on use of total materials, lending confidence to the observations that follow. Danielsen, in *The Evolution of OPEC*, a book with a much broader scope than is suggested by its title, compiled and analyzed this (and other) information: From 1960 to 1973, the pre-embargo period, the Gross Domestic Product of the United States grew at an annual rate of 4.0 percent, while both total primary energy used and oil consumption grew at a 4.3 percent annual rate. In the post-embargo period of 1973–78, the GDP growth rate was only 1.7 percent, total primary energy used grew at 1.2 percent, and oil usage grew at 2.4 percent. The United States in 1980 used 39 percent of the free world's primary energy consumption and 27 percent of the world total.[2] In spite of early 1980s gluts of oil, energy use should be expected to grow somewhat more slowly than total output because of the shift to services in total output and because of gradual increases in efficiency of energy conversion. Services typically require less energy per unit of output than commodities. And each form of energy conversion—thermal electric generation, transportation, space heating, and others—is subject to gradual improvements in efficiency as technology progresses. It is likely that the increases in fuel costs during

2. The data of the text were taken from tables presented in Albert L. Danielsen's *The Evolution of OPEC*, 1982. Another useful reference for those interested in energy issues is James M. Griffin and Henry B. Steele's *Energy Economics and Policy*, 1980. Annual data may be obtained, additionally, from recent *Statistical Abstracts of the United States* and from various *Economic Reports of the President*.

the 1970s will result in further reductions in energy use per unit of total output. Except for direct harnessing of natural forces, such as hydroelectric generation, all energy consumption requires extraction of fuels from the environment. In fact, about half of all materials extraction consists of fuels in the United States.

An obvious question to ask, and the subject of environmental economics presented in this book, is what happens to the materials extracted from the environment for use in the economic system? Many details of the answer are complex and poorly understood. But the basic fact is that economic activity neither creates nor destroys matter; it merely transforms it. Economic activity cannot violate the laws of conservation of matter and energy. All materials extracted from the environment and inserted into the economic system continue to exist in some form. This notion has led to a concept called the materials balance, which is simply a set of accounts that show the source, use, and disposition of all materials extracted. In its simplest form it says: All the materials in the economic system at the beginning of a year plus those extracted during the year must equal those in the system at the end of the year plus those returned to the environment during the year. Put slightly differently, the increase in the stock of materials in the economic system during a year must equal the excess of withdrawals from over discharges to the environment during the year. The increase in the stock of materials in the system is another expression for capital accumulation, and includes increases in fixed capital, business inventories, and goods in the hands of consumers. The terms *withdrawals* and *extractions* are synonymous, as are *returns* and *discharges*.

The materials balance is an identity that plays exactly the role in resource and environmental economics that the identity between sources and dispositions of income plays in national income analysis. Both are simple and intuitively persuasive ideas once explained, but both lead to important insights and both help to avoid mistakes frequently made by those who do not understand them. Equally important, both have limitations. Complete economic theories consist not only of identities but also of relationships that represent technology and the behavior of people in the system to be analyzed. Production functions are examples of technological relationships and demand and supply functions are examples of behavioral relationships. Identities are not substitutes for carefully specified technological and behavioral relations. Much of this chapter is about the materials balance. Subsequent chapters are mostly about behavioral and technological relationships.

Resource economics is about the extraction and use of natural resources. Environmental economics is about the return of materials to the environment and about alternatives to their return, such as reuse. The materials balance provides the link between the two subjects. It is unfortunate that we do not have a complete set of materials accounts for any year in the United States. A beginning has been made by Allen Kneese and a team at Resources for the Future, a Washington research institution at which much good work on environmental economics has been carried out.

It is important to understand that the materials balance, like all identities, holds because its terms are defined so that it must hold. The environment must be defined to include all places from which materials are obtained and all places to which they are discharged by people. The economic system must be defined to include all activities that use materials to contribute to people's living standards. For the most part, one's intuitive notion of the environment is appropriate for the materials balance—the crust of the earth, its land and water surfaces, and its surrounding atmosphere. In fact, most withdrawals are of materials on or just under the earth's land surface. Relatively small amounts are extracted from water and the atmosphere. Also, most materials are discharged on or just under the land surface. But more is discharged to than is withdrawn from water and air, and discharges to those media give rise to most environmental problems. Note that the definition of the environment does not distinguish among private, government, and no ownership, although that distinction is important in understanding most environmental problems.

For the most part, one's intuitive notion of what constitutes the economic system and economic activity is also clear. Economic activity includes extraction of materials, production and consumption of goods and services, and the disposal of materials when they are not wanted in the economic system. By no means all economic activity, and by no means all polluting discharges, take place in the profit-seeking sector. Much economic activity is in the private nonprofit and government sectors.

Like all social-science concepts that cover a great variety of human activities, including the concepts of income and wealth, the terms in the materials balance are fuzzy at the edges of the subject. Strip mining digs up enormous quantities of earth to get at the coal underneath. Once the coal is removed, the earth is put back more or less in place, and without being processed in any way. The earth so removed is an extraction in that it is removed in an important economic activity which causes a serious environmental problem. But there is no way of knowing the volume of such extractions. The same analysis applies to the top of a hill that is cut away in building a road and to material taken from the middle of a river and deposited at the edge in dredging a ship channel. Large amounts of materials are extracted in the sense of merely being moved around in the course of economic activity, although no one knows exactly how much. What about human respiration? Inspiration withdraws the mixture of gases in the atmosphere, and expiration discharges a different mixture containing more carbon dioxide and less oxygen. Respiration certainly contributes to people's well-being, and it alters the atmospheric environment; but it is quantitatively unimportant.

The basic notion behind the materials balance is that the distinction between the economic system and the environment is important. People and their activities are as much a part of nature as are animals and plants. The point of the materials balance is not to make an artificial distinction between people and nature. Instead, the point is that people and their activity can have important and controllable effects on the environment. Understanding the distinction between the economic system and the environment is the first step in learning to make rational decisions affecting both.

The materials balance says that except for capital accumulation, all materials withdrawn from the environment are returned. Two additional notions are needed to complete the panoramic view of resource and environmental economics.

First, people's welfare or utility is affected not only by the goods and services they consume, but also by the quality of the environment in which they live. Breathing badly polluted air or drinking badly polluted water can make people ill and in extreme cases, kill them. Less dramatically, the enjoyment of a day at the beach depends on the quality of the water and on the quantity of litter on the sand. There are many dimensions to environmental quality, and they will be explored in subsequent chapters. But it would be uninteresting were it not that people's welfare is affected not only by goods and services consumption, but also by environmental pollution caused by economic activity.

Second, every discharge to the environment alters its quality in some way. Discharges intended mainly to dispose of unwanted materials cheaply almost always impair the environment's quality, sometimes very seriously indeed. There are many less damaging ways to return materials to the environment, but virtually all require energy and other valuable resources. The relationships between discharges and environmental quality are complex and will also be explored in subsequent chapters. The main point is that emissions are not of interest *per se*, but rather become of interest because of their impact on environmental quality.

Uses of the Materials Balance

The first use of the materials balance is to state carefully how the familiar economic notions of production and consumption fit into a materials framework. In the usual microeconomics textbook, resources first appear in conjunction with input-supply equations and they disappear as the products in which they are incorporated are consumed. There is nothing wrong with this picture. But it needs to be embellished and clarified for the important purposes of this book, which are to analyze where the materials come from and go to.

It was said in the last section that production and consumption do not create or destroy matter, but that they change its form. Iron ore in the ground cannot satisfy human needs and wants. For that purpose, it must be removed from the ground, processed, and fabricated, along with many additional materials, into cars, buildings, and other products. Production consists of conversion of materials from their natural forms into forms in which they satisfy human needs and wants.

Consumption is the reverse process. It consists of use of products, thereby converting materials from forms that satisfy human needs and wants to forms that cannot do so. Food is a nondurable commodity and is changed from useful to nonuseful form in a single act of consumption. An aluminum frying pan is a durable good and can be used to cook food for many years. But eventually a hole burns through it or the handle comes off and it is no longer useful. It has been gradually consumed. But the same amount of aluminum exists in the world before it is removed from the ground, while it is in the form of frying pans and after it has become unusable and been discarded. No consumption activity changes the total amount of matter. Of course, the amount of consumption, or utility, obtained from a product may depend on how it is made or used. If a TV set is poorly made or abused in use, it will be consumed after a few uses and will therefore yield little consumption or utility. A well-cared-for work of art may last hundreds of years, but it too deteriorates eventually. It is possible to economize on the materials needed to satisfy a given need or want by making and using products carefully, but it does not change the fact that neither creation nor destruction of matter occurs in production or consumption.

The foregoing implies that the notion of resource exhaustion is somewhat fanciful. All of human activity has not exhausted one ounce of the stock of aluminum, iron, or copper in the world. The same amounts of these elements are in and on the earth as were there a million years ago. Although economic activity does not affect the total amounts of materials, it does affect their availability. Some uses of materials make them more easily available for further use and some make them less easily available. It depends on the extent to which processing and consumption concentrate or disperse the materials. And that in turn depends on how materials are processed, what is made of them, how products are used, and what happens to them after they have been consumed. Resource exhaustion and availability are determined by the detailed performance of the economic system and not merely by the rate of extraction. The current performance of the economic system makes it easy to reuse some materials and hard to reuse others. But *ways will be found to reuse most materials if it is expensive either to extract materials from the environment or to return materials to the environment.*

The term *resource exhaustion* may be used to mean that materials are processed and discharged to the environment in ways that make it difficult to reuse or re-extract them. Modern products are complex and combine many materials in physical and chemical ways that may make it difficult or impossible to separate the materials.

Alternatively, the term *resource depletion* may be used to mean that all of a material that can be easily extracted is already incorporated in products in the economic system. All the world's copper or aluminum might someday be contained in wires, frying pans, and other products in use. Then the only source of the material would be its reuse from existing products. In that case, the material would be exhausted in the sense that there was no more to be extracted from the environment. A less extreme form of the same situation would occur if such a large fraction of some material were in products that the cost of obtaining it from used products were less than the cost of further extraction from the environment. Then there would be no extraction and it might be useful to say that the material was exhausted, at least in an economic sense. Although there is probably no material whose entire supply now comes from used products, there are many materials whose supply is partly from reuse. Increasing percentages of expensive metals such as copper are in this latter category.

Fuels are somewhat different. Fuels are not incorporated in products. Instead, energy is extracted from them by combustion. This energy is eventually dissipated into outer space in the form of heat, along with a much larger volume of heat that is radiated by the earth after having been absorbed from the sun. Once that heat leaves contained areas such as pipes and buildings, it is mostly irretrievable. Thus fuels are exhaustible in an almost literal sense in which other materials are not. Of course, the source of all energy stored in fossil fuels, the sun, is itself exhaustible in that it contains only a finite amount of energy that will eventually be dissipated. As with all environmental questions, the important issues are quantitative: How much and how soon? These questions will be discussed in a later chapter.

Another use of the materials balance is to clarify the notion of *replenishable resources*. Fresh water, wood, and food are sometimes classified as replenishable resources, in contrast with metals and other resources that are referred to as exhaustible. The term is useful provided it is properly interpreted. It does not mean that the creation of replenishable resources violates the laws of conservation of matter and energy. Instead, it means that there are natural processes that do just what economic activity does: apply energy to materials to change their form. Trees grow because energy from the sun is used to extract materials from the earth's crust and to combine them in the form of trees; there is a continuing supply of fresh water because the sun provides energy to evaporate water from oceans and to deposit it as fresh water on land masses. Gathering and hunting societies depend on the natural production of food. Agricultural societies organize the process of food production as part of economic activity. Thus natural processes replenish certain resources without man's intervention. People can and do intervene to alter and augment natural processes. People began to cultivate crops only a relatively few thousand years ago. Forests have been increasingly cultivated the same way in recent years. People are just beginning to produce fresh water by desalting salt or brackish water.

The final use to be made of the materials balance in this chapter is to classify methods of improving environmental quality. The basic message of this book is that a wealthy society like ours has a wide range of options as to the kinds, amounts, and locations of pollution it wishes to accept. And it is important to understand at the start that some pollution will be preferred to none since all but the most trivial improvements in environmental quality involve costs that must be borne by all or part of society. Some environmental protection and improvement measures are cheap and bestow large benefits. Others are expensive and entail dubious benefits. Sorting these issues out is the nuts and bolts of environmental economics. The materials balance can help with the first steps along the way.

The materials balance says that discharges equal the excess of withdrawals over capital accumulation. Thus, by definition, the only ways to reduce discharges are to withdraw less or to accumulate more. Increasing the rate of capital accumulation can be dismissed out of hand as a way of solving environmental problems. Capital should be accumulated to the extent justified by its contribution to the production of goods and services. To accumulate otherwise unwanted capital as a means of material disposal would rightly be regarded as itself a form of pollution.[3] It would be better not to withdraw the materials in the first place. In this book, it will be assumed that capital accumulation is not a viable means of environmental protection. That does not preclude the possibility that other environmental protection measures might affect the rate of capital accumulation or the kind of capital that is accumulated.

Thus the only practical way *to reduce discharges*, one of several approaches leading to improved environmental quality, is *to reduce material withdrawals* from the environment. One way to reduce withdrawals is simply to produce less output, that is, to lower living standards. The dismantling of industrial society and the return to a simpler economy which withdraws less material from the environ-

---

3. Radioactive wastes from atomic electric plants are an exception to this statement. There appears to be no safe way to return them to the environment. Practice in the United States has therefore been to store them in concrete drums. This must be interpreted as capital accumulation to avoid polluting discharges.

ment has indeed been suggested by some writers. It is a drastic solution and is a counsel of despair in that it explicitly abandons the goal of improving living standards by goods and services production, which is what economics has been about for two centuries and what most human effort has been about since people appeared on earth. Furthermore, although total returns are proportional to total withdrawals, the common dimensions of pollution are not proportional to living standards. Most poor countries have much less good quality environments that do rich countries. For example, many have badly polluted public water supplies. Nevertheless, intentional reduction of production would be justifiable if the alternative were to so damage the environment that human life was impossible or possible only at a lower level of welfare than would result from reduced production of goods and services. Fortunately, it is likely that such drastic cures are unnecessary. As with capital accumulation, other environmental protection measures than direct reduction of output may have the indirect effect that goods and services production is reduced. Productive resources are scarce and devoting more to environmental protection leaves less to devote to goods and services production. For example, if a large part of the construction industry is employed building sewage-treatment plants, it is necessary to restrict construction of houses, offices, factories, and roads. Likewise, if we produce chemicals to treat wastes, we must restrict production of chemicals for other purposes.

A second way *to reduce withdrawals and discharges* is *to increase the reuse or recycling of materials*, that is, to retain and reuse materials within the economic system once the consumption value of the products they are contained in is gone. A given rate of goods and services production can be maintained while reducing both withdrawals and discharges by reusing materials. For example, trees are felled to manufacture newspapers and petroleum is pumped from the ground to be used as a fuel in thermal electric generation. Newspapers are mostly returned to the environment by placing them in dumps and landfills. A day or two after publication, a newspaper's consumption value is gone although its physical condition is virtually unchanged by consumption. Petroleum is returned to the environment partly by wastes generated in refining, but mostly by discharge of gases and heat to the air during combustion. The production and consumption of newspapers and electricity could be maintained, while reducing the withdrawal and discharge of petroleum, if used newspapers were used as fuel in thermal electric plants. The amount of newspaper produced and returned to the environment would be unchanged, but less petroleum would be needed. Of course, the time, place, and form of the return of newspapers would be altered by burning them in a thermal electric plant instead of burying them in a landfill, but the amount of newspaper returned would be unchanged. None of this proves that burning newspapers in thermal electric plants is advantageous, only that it is possible. Indeed, it is possible to burn most organic wastes in power plants, although whether this is advantageous is an economic question, discussed later in the book.

As a second example, glass bottles can be collected, cleaned, and reused for their original purposes, thus reducing by equal amounts the materials withdrawn to make glass and the discharge of glass to the environment. Reuse of bottles would leave unchanged the number of bottles available to be used as containers. Glass is made from inexpensive and widely available substances that are innocuous in the environment in their natural state. As is common, processing these materials to make glass transforms them into a form in which they become annoying and dangerous if not returned to the environment with care. As always, whether recycling is or is not desirable is an economic issue, and such issues are seldom immediately clear. Moreover, recycling may be undesirable at one time and desirable at another: for example, rising fossil-fuel prices might raise the cost of producing new aluminum cans relative to the cost of recycling, which is much less energy intensive. Many materials are reused in the normal course of production and consumption. Many more could be reused, all at some cost. Despite the enthusiasm for recycling in recent years, the evidence is that the amount of materials reuse still depends mostly on what it has always depended on: relative costs of new and used materials and the technology of materials reuse.

A third way *to reduce withdrawals and discharges* is *to increase the technical efficiency with which materials are used*, thereby increasing production of commodities per unit of materials withdrawn from the environment. A pervasive element of technological progress for a century or more has been a gradual improvement in the efficiency of materials use. Technological progress increases the efficiency of materials use by subjecting them to more and more careful processing and by finding uses for previously discarded materials. In the early years of the century, much of the content of crude oil was returned to the environment after fuel was refined out. Now a wide range of other products—plastics, chemicals, medicines, and many others—is made from materials previously discarded. A different example is that better layout of patterns on fabrics and metals reduces the waste when the material is cut. As a third example, better combustion has increased the amount of usable energy obtained per pound of fuel burned for many purposes. Most improvements in materials use come about as a by-product of the search for better products and cheaper means of production. The reasons that technological change is successfully pursued in one direction instead of another are poorly understood, and little is known about the likelihood of success in trying to turn technological change more in the direction of increased efficiency in materials use. But materials use does respond to economic incentives. When fuel becomes expensive, buildings are insulated and fuel-efficient vehicles are demanded and produced. When a metal becomes expensive, industries spend money to avoid its waste and to find less costly substitutes.

Efficiency in materials use includes efficiency in construction, maintenance, and use of capital goods and consumer durables. Materials withdrawals and returns can be reduced by making capital goods that are more durable, by better maintenance of capital goods, and by more care in their use. The services yielded by structures and machinery depend very much on how they are built, maintained, and used. Although there is widespread belief that products are less well made and durable than formerly, there is almost no evidence to support the claim. Also, it is possible to invest excessive materials and other inputs in making products durable. The important question is whether competition among firms results in optimally durable products. Diversity is likely to characterize the optimal durability since uses will vary (as for example the paper plate—certainly the extreme case of "planned obsolescence") and tastes or incomes will vary (e.g., the Mercedes versus the Chevrolet).

Technology also creates environmental problems. Persistent pesticides, such as DDT, or atomic energy are products of modern technological progress whose environmental effects are of great concern. These effects were not anticipated during development of the products, but some writers tend to assume that most new technology is likely to do more harm than good. This is a badly distorted view. Technological advance has generally favored the environment. That is, homes are heated largely by electricity or natural gas now, rather than with coal, horses (while rustic in small numbers) would be much more polluting than cars as the sole means of transportation in New York City, and so on. Moreover, technological progress has been extremely important in raising living standards during the last century or two. It will continue to be important and will be crucial in finding alternatives to dwindling supplies of some materials.

Thus several options are available to society to alter the amounts of materials it withdraws from and returns to the environment. But the one option that is not available is a policy of no returns or no discharges. It is impossible to reuse all materials and economically infeasible to reuse large amounts. A zero-discharge economy would be a zero-withdrawal economy; a zero-withdrawal economy would be a zero-production economy and a zero-production economy would be a zero-people economy. A zero-discharge economy is a figment of dreamers' imaginations.

Other Environmental Protection Measures

Fortunately, reducing the total volume of discharges is by no means the only way to reduce pollution and other means are often more desirable. Pollution is damage to the environment that impairs its usefulness to people. Environmental damage depends not only, or even mainly, on the volume of discharges, but also on the kinds of discharges and the locations of discharges. Thus pollution depends on the details of resource allocation in the economy; and much of this book is concerned with exploration of these issues.

Almost all material withdrawals from the environment are from the crust and land surface of the earth, including almost all metals, fuels, and food. Only small amounts are from its waters and its atmosphere. In principle, large amounts of materials could be returned to the land after use in more or less their form before withdrawal, although it would be extremely expensive in some instances. Such returns would hardly be classified as polluting. In fact, large amounts of materials are returned to the air and water environments, and they cause most of the pollution problems of great concern. Thus one way to reduce pollution, although not total discharges, is to abate discharges to the air and water environments and to increase amounts of materials returned to the land. For example, sewage consists of organic material most of which was extracted from the earth's crust before its consumption generated sewage. Most cities collect the sewage in pipes and some discharge it raw to the nearest water body.

In that case the organic material withdrawn from the land is discharged to the water environment. Most American cities treat sewage in a treatment plant, in which case most of the organic material is converted into a solid waste called sludge. With further processing, sludge can be returned to the land and used as high-quality fertilizer. Then most of the organic material is returned to the land and is nonpolluting. Of course, the fact that the sewage is treated does not guarantee that it is nonpolluting. New York City treats most, but not all, of its sewage, and then dumps the sludge in the water just a few miles farther out than it dumps its untreated sewage.

Thus the most important way to abate pollution is to reduce residual discharges to the air and water environments and instead to discharge materials to the land. But that is not the entire story. In the first place, it is neither possible nor economical to eliminate all discharges to air and water. The air and water environments, as well as the land, can absorb limited amounts of most discharges without impairment of their quality. Even when abused by excessive discharges, the environment usually regenerates itself, although sometimes only slowly. Discharge of limited amounts of wastes is a legitimate use of the absorptive capacity of each environmental medium. The damage done by discharges to the environment depends greatly—a point we will emphasize again and again throughout the book—on the time, form, and place of such discharges. The damage depends to a much smaller extent on the sheer volume or tonnage of discharges. A large part of this book is about the ways society should ration discharges to air and water. In the second place, discharges to the land can also entail severe environmental damage. One need only look at the town dump, an abandoned strip mine, or a slag heap to appreciate the posibility of such damage. But it is of a lesser order of magnitude than air and water pollution.

It is common to refer to air, water, and land as sinks into which materials are discharged. The notion of a sink suggests a long residence time of the material in the place identified. But there are important connections between environmental sinks. Ashes discharged to the air eventually fall onto land or water. Soil disturbed in strip mining may wash into streams. Heat discharged to water passes to the atmosphere as water evaporates. Frequently materials do the most damage in the medium to which they are discharged. But it is important to ask about movements of pollutants among enviromental media. For example, if the ocean is the ultimate sink for airborne fuels and fuel by-products, then the magnitude of damages to ocean life from oil-tanker spills, drilling accidents, and other marine discharges would be dwarfed in comparison.

There is a basic difference between land on the one hand and air and water on the other which accounts for their different positions in environmental problems. It is technically relatively easy to define property rights in land. The result is that most land is privately owned and traded on markets. Individual owners benefit when the land is productive and attractive and suffer when it is abused and ugly. Thus private owners limit the amounts, kinds, and forms of materials they discharge or permit to be discharged on their land. Air and water are in large part fugitive substances whose movements are difficult to control and predict. It is difficult to establish property rights in air and water and they are part of what is usually referred to as the public domain. This means that everyone can use them more or less freely. It is extremely cheap to dispose of unwanted materials by washing them into the nearest stream or sending them up the chimney. It is much more expensive to collect and transport residuals to open land that they can be deposited on or under, especially from urban centers where most materials are used. Wastes discharged to air and water are widely dispersed by natural forces. The harmful effects of each discharge are therefore felt by many people, albeit only slightly. Everyone thus finds it easy to discharge materials to the air and water environments, and everyone suffers. The importance of property rights and public goods to an understanding of environmental quality will be further clarified in the next chapter.

Location of discharges, both in the time and in the spatial dimensions, has already been indicated to be of critical importance to proper environmental policy. The damages resulting from any given quantity of emissions to the air or water can be orders of magnitude larger or smaller depending on where and when they are discharged. Considering air, emissions in downtown areas of major cities where densities of fifteen thousand people per square mile are not uncommon will be, roughly, a thousand times more damaging than those same emissions in a rural area with fifteen people per square mile. Emissions during periods of stagnant meteorological conditions (air inversions) are, similarly, much more damaging than those same emissions at other times.

In the case of water, an urban lake might have far more recreational, fishing, and other users than a rural lake, hence emissions into the former are (other things equal) much more damaging and undesirable. During the late summer, stream flow is normally low and water temperatures high—emissions at this time are much more damaging to stream biota than at other times of the year. As will be seen, these considerations—where and when emissions occur—are largely ignored or mishandled in current environmental policy, at great disservice to mankind.

Pollutants: Categories, Sources, Trends

For each environmental medium there are many different types of pollutants, with each having diverse sources. Some of these pollutants are of increasing concern while others are becoming of less concern with the passage of time. This section briefly introduces some environmental jargon, but it is useful jargon and will additionally give more of a "real-world" feel to the study of environmental economics. Additional detail, by environmental media categories, is presented in later chapters.

Air   Air pollution was synonymous, up until about 1950, with "smoke"—what would now be referred to as Total Suspended Particulates (TSP). This pollutant, along with various sulfur oxides (SO_2, SO_3, and SO_4), comes predominantly from fossil-fuel combustion and industrial processes. Particulates (diverse in chemical structure) and sulfur oxides (especially the non-SO_2 forms) were the pollutants implicated in the health damages resulting from air inversions in the 1940s, 1950s, and 1960s in Donora (Pennsylvania), London, New York, and elsewhere. Among the commonly monitored pollutants, TSP and SO_x continue to be of principal concern from the perspective of human health.

Fortunately, during the 1970s air quality improved with respect to these pollutants. In part, that improvement was due to environmental controls enacted during this period, but part was due to voluntary conversions from coal, which is messy and bulky, to alternative energy sources for residential heating. As these alternative fuels rose in price in the 1970s due to OPEC oil price increases, this long-standing trend may be reversed, eliminating much of the past decade's environmental progress. Already one is seeing greatly increased use of wood-burning stoves—among the most environmentally damaging residential-heating alternatives—in many parts of the United States. Even lovely resort areas, such as Aspen, Colorado, are currently experiencing severe local pollution problems, and it is estimated that a substantial portion of the winter pollution haze in Denver and parts of the Northeast is due to stoves and fireplaces.

In terms of tonnage of emissions, the transportation sector, primarily the automobile, is now the largest polluting sector. Carbon monoxide (CO), hydrocarbons (HC), nitrogen oxides (NO_x), and lead are the principal pollutants emitted by the automobile. Additionally, ozone (O_3) is formed, in complicated photochemical reactions in the atmosphere, from HC and NO_x, which operate as so-called precursors. Lead and carbon monoxide have very serious health consequences in high concentrations, although such concentrations are unlikely to occur under ordinary circumstances in ambient air. Ozone and NO_x have very weak health impacts, while HC appears to have no shortrun health effects at concentrations near those actually observed in urban atmospheres. However, acute health effects may not be as important as health problems associated with chronic, long-term exposures. Hydrocarbons, HC, are actually composed of at least 200 different chemical compounds, several of which might be carcinogenic (cancer-causing), and lead is so impervious to degradation that even low-level exposures can accumulate in the environment in adverse ways. The lack of information about such long-term effects makes environmental analysis live and exciting. But it greatly complicates rational environmental decision-making.

Trends in atmospheric concentrations of transportation-related pollutants are mixed. On the positive side, add-on control devices (for example, exhaust gas recirculation systems, catalytic converters) have reduced emissions substantially of hydrocarbons, HC, and carbon monoxide, CO. However, the more complete burning associated with the higher temperatures and better oxygen supplies of such emission systems, while converting HC and CO to relatively harmless water and carbon dioxide, tends to also create more nitrogen oxides, NO_x, from the normally inert and harmless nitrogen gas which comprises four-fifths of the atmosphere. Hence, CO and HC emissions have been declining, while NO_x has increased. Atmospheric lead concentrations appear to be falling in very recent years, due mainly to the larger number of catalytic-converter-equipped cars, which require lead-free gasoline.

Overall, most dimensions of air quality affected by automobile emissions appear to be improving somewhat. However, the larger number of vehicles in the rapidly growing sunbelt cities has caused photochemical-smog (mostly ozone) problems to worsen in some areas. Continued general improvement is expected as the automobile population ages, with newer cleaner vehicles replacing their older more polluting counterparts. Partially offsetting this expectation is the fact that substantial percentages (2 to 13 percent according to one estimate[4]) of catalytic-converter-equipped cars are being fueled by leaded gas; such cars are as much as 100 times dirtier than they would have otherwise been.

The measures of the preceding air contaminants, and standards applicable to them, are increasingly given in terms of micrograms per cubic meter (μ/m^3) of air. Other measures sometimes used are parts per million (ppm), parts per hundred million (pphm) or, rarely, parts per billion (ppb). Larger numbers indicate lower quality of air from the perspective of the specific measured pollutant.

Overall, and in spite of delays and confrontation between states and the federal government, the 1970–1980 decade was one of progress in air quality. During the 1940–1970 period, air pollution emissions grew 40 percent, while in the more recent decade particulate emissions are down 50 percent, leading to a 20 percent improvement in ambient particulate levels. Similar progress has been noted for sulfur dioxide, SO_2, and carbon monoxide, CO. This progress has not come cheaply: 90 percent of the 68 percent increase between 1971 and 1978 in the real capital costs of providing coal-fired electricity was for pollution control. P. R. Portney estimates, in 1978 dollars, that the real cost of efforts to improve air quality between 1978 and 1987 will be about $280 billion ($111 billion for mobile source control, $83 billion for industrial control, $66 billion for utility control, and $20 billion for governmental sources of pollution).

Water   Interest in water pollution predates interest in air pollution both historically in the United States and in the context of

---

4. This figure, and a great many others throughout the book in discussions about air quality, come from articles in the *Journal of the Air Pollution Control Association* (in this case, *JAPCA*, November 1980, p. 1232). To avoid numerous lengthy citations, we shall merely note here that much of the information presented here comes from various monthly issues of this journal dating from the early 1980s.

developing countries today. However, the study of water quality shares two difficulties with the study of air quality. First, how to define "quality" is not easy since water quality, like air quality, has many dimensions. Second, the hydrological mechanism that converts effluent discharges along a stream into in-stream water quality is, like the meteorological mechanism converting emissions into air quality, poorly understood. Yet the hydrological mechanism is vital to the conduct of rational water quality policy: *benefits* of clean-up relate to water quality changes resulting from a policy action, while *costs* of clean-up relate to discharges. Hence to compare benefits with costs of a policy response (we will see in the following chapter why this comparison is desirable), we must be able to convert changes in discharges to changes in water quality.

The most common measures of water quality relate to the presence of either dissolved oxygen (DO) or deoxygenating wastes, for example, biochemical oxygen demand (BOD). This water-quality parameter—oxygen—has an important bearing on the quality and diversity of stream life, with rainbow trout, for example, being unable to survive in water that can support carp quite nicely.

Other less frequently monitored measures of water quality are microbiological content (total coliform, fecal coliform), acidity or alkalinity (pH, total alkalinity), and presence of solids (total hardness, total dissolved solids, "conductivity," suspended solids, "turbidity"). Conductivity measures how easily electricity passes through water and turbidity is a measure of the clarity of the water. Water that "looks clean" may, like air, be highly polluted—for example, the water is much clearer in acid-rain-polluted lakes than in lakes with a normal pH.

Specific sources of water pollution will be discussed in detail in a later chapter, but some observations may usefully be made now. First, in terms of bulk, the largest single "point-source" polluter category is governmentally owned wastewater treatment plants. Second, point sources (easily identified sources discharging piped or channeled effluent which may be, or not be, toxic) have generally become sufficienctly highly controlled that *non*-point sources, such as runoff from agriculture, construction, and urban land uses, would in many cases violate existing water-quality standards *even if* point sources had zero discharges. The policy implication is that other approaches (water-absorbent parking lots, earth barriers to retain runoff, and so on) should at least be examined as an alternative to additional, very costly point-source controls. Finally, as with the automobile in the case of air, trade-offs in attempts to control pollution emerge in unanticipated ways: using hypochlorides to kill fecal coliform in sewage also destroys nitrogen-oxidizing organisms in a stream, reducing its natural waste-assimilative capacity.

Trends in water quality are mixed, as was the case with air. DO levels appear to be increasing generally, on the positive side, but nutrient levels have also been growing, with resulting undesirable algae blooms in stagnant water bodies. As with air, positive or negative trends have a strong spatial component, with some rivers or lakes improving (for example, the Great Lakes, Hudson River, Thames River, among others) while continuing deterioration characterizes rivers and lakes in other locations.

The measures of water quality are, as was true with air, of many types and somewhat confusing. Not only are ppm, pphm, or ppb used as with air, but also milliliters per liter (ml/l), milligrams per liter (mg/l), and, for dissolved oxygen, percent of saturation.

Other Environmental-Quality Dimensions   Thermal pollution, while not of great significance for air, is a major water pollutant and is associated almost exclusively with energy production. Water is used as a coolant (as in the large cooling towers one sees in the air case) and returned to a stream or lake. The heat rise can harm some species directly or can affect the aquatic system indirectly since warmer water contains less DO.

Similarly noise pollution, while not important for water (as far as we know), is a major air pollutant, one that despite being non-chemical is frequently cited in urban surveys as the most irritating neightborhood disamenity.

Pollution of the land, while much less of an environmental problem than air or water pollution, is of considerable concern in that large numbers of people may be damaged by aesthetically loathsome urban blight, dumps, strip mines, and the like. Emissions to the land are growing, as we know they must if overall material use increases: improvements in overall air or water quality must involve increases in materials discharged to land. As noted earlier, *daily* discharges into all environmental media must approximately equal daily materials extraction, the latter being the weight of the entire U.S. population.

Only one hazardous material (lead, emitted into the atmosphere by vehicles) has been mentioned thus far. This is not because hazardous materials are environmentally unimportant. Quite the opposite is the case. Hazardous materials such as PCB, arsenic, lead, asbestos, mercury, beryllium, sulfuric acid, vinyl chloride, fluoride, hydrogen sulfide, reduced sulfur, and radioactive substances, while exceedingly small in bulk when compared to pollutants already discussed, are very damaging and also poorly understood. Moreover, the number and variety of such pollutants are increasing, as is the amount discharged of each.

Damages from hazardous substances take the form of cancer, mutation, brain damage, and sterility, to name only a few impacts. It can confidently be predicted that, to the extent that future environmental policy is rational, hazardous substances will receive far greater attention and control resources than they have in the past. Recent political concerns also suggest that this change in relative emphasis is likely to occur.

The bare bones of the environmental problem have now been laid out. Enough has been said to indicate that pollution of the air, water, and land is a problem of resource allocation. Why do we have these resource-allocation problems? What policy responses to these problems will lead to their solution in the most desirable way? Understanding the answers to these questions is to clothe the bare bones of the environment with solid economic analysis. Chapters 2, 3, and 4 show how the economic theory of resource allocation can be used to shed light on the causes and solutions of pollution problems.

DISCUSSION QUESTIONS AND PROBLEMS

1. How would you modify the materials balance to account for international trade and for discharge of residuals across international boundaries?

2. Suppose birth rates fell so low that population declined. What would be the effect on each term in the materials balance? Is that a desirable way to improve environmental quality?

3. If pollution is caused by production and consumption, why do poor countries, which have less production and consumption than rich countries, have more pollution?

4. Some argue that continued economic growth will lead to environmental collapse, while others feel that greater economic growth will enhance environmental quality. What might the arguments be in support of such conflicting opinions?

5. Has history clearly indicated that economic growth results in inevitably increasing environmental degradation?

6. How would you handle a pollution problem such as that at Times Beach, Missouri, or the Love Canal?

REFERENCES AND FURTHER READING

Barnett, Harold, and Morse, Chandler. *Scarcity and Growth: The Economics of Natural Resource Availability*. Baltimore: Johns Hopkins University Press, for Resources for the Future, Inc., 1963.

Baumol, William, and Oates, Wallace. *Economics, Environmental Policy and the Quality of Life*. Englewood Cliffs, N.J.: Prentice-Hall, 1979.

Council on Environmental Quality. *Environmental Quality*. Washington, D.C.: U.S. Government Printing Office, published annually.

Danielsen, Albert L. *The Evolution of OPEC*. New York: Harcourt Brace Jovanovich, 1982.

Enthoven, Alain C., and Freeman, A. Myrick, eds. *Pollution, Resources and the Environment*. New York: Norton, 1973.

Griffin, James M., and Steele, Henry B. *Energy Economics and Policy*. New York: Academic Press, 1980.

Johnson, Manuel H.; Bell, Frederick W.; and Bennett, James T. "Natural Resource Scarcity: Empirical Evidence and Public Policy." *Journal of Environmental Economics and Management* 7, no. 3 (September 1980): 256–71.

Journal of the Air Pollution Control Association, A Monthly Journal Devoted to Air Quality Management.

Kneese, Allen; Ayres, Robert; and d'Arge, Ralph. *Economics and the Environment*. Baltimore: Johns Hopkins University Press, for Resources for the Future, Inc., 1970.

Meier, Richard. *Science and Economic Development*. Cambridge, Mass.: MIT Press, 1966.

Schumpeter, Joseph. *A History of Economic Analyses*. New York: Oxford University Press, 1954.

Slade, Margaret E. "Trends in Natural-Resource Commodity Prices: An Analysis of the Time Domain." *Journal of Environmental Economics and Management* 9, no. 2 (June 1982): 122–37.

Tolley, George S.; Blomquist, G. C.; and Yaron, D. *Environmental Policy: Water Quality*, Cambridge, Mass.: Ballinger, 1983.

Tolley, George S.; Graves, Philip E.; and Cohen, Alan S. *Environmental Policy: Air Quality*. Cambridge, Mass.: Ballinger, 1982.

Tolley, George S.; Graves, Phillip E.; and Blomquist, Glenn C. *Environmental Policy: Elements of Environmental Analysis*. Cambridge, Mass.: Ballinger, 1981.

Chapter 2

Economics and Environmental Quality: The Basics

Environmental quality is like any ordinary economic good in that one can have either too little or too much of it. The former case of insufficient environmental quality is perhaps most obvious: at totally uncontrolled discharge levels, environmental quality would be so low (for example, the smelly anaerobic stream) that the health, property, and aesthetic benefits of efforts to improve quality would greatly exceed the resource costs (labor, capital, energy, and so on) associated with those efforts. But the less intuitively obvious point is equally true, namely that we can have environmental quality that is too high. This case occurs when the scarce resources used to produce environmental quality have more highly valued uses in producing other goods that people also care about.

Why do we tend to get too little environmental quality in the unconstrained free market setting? What is the nature of environmental goods that cause this failure of the market in providing the "right" amount? What would the answers to the preceding questions suggest about the proper design of environmental policy? To pursue these questions further we must first understand how ordinary goods are provided in free markets, drawing parallels to environmental goods.

Supply and Demand for Ordinary Goods and for Environmental Goods

The notion of equilibrium between the forces of supply and demand, with price rising in the presence of excess demand and falling with excess supply, is explained in all introductory economics courses. What often receive insufficient emphasis in the midst of the many supply-and-demand applications are the desirable features of the equilibrium quantity.[1] If one takes the income distribution as given,[2] the outputs resulting from competitive markets are socially optimal.

Before the preceding strong assertion can be clarified, one must get behind the veil of dollars that obscures the real meaning of demand and supply curves. The demand curve for a good represents how much society would pay for various quantities of that good, in comparison with other available goods. This "willingness-to-pay" for various quantities represents the value to society of those quantities:

1. In part this stems from the stress, in the simple Keynesian demand-driven aggregate models, on the fact that there is nothing particularly "good" or "bad" about the equilibrium income level. This is, of course, misleading when one considers aggregate supply. If this footnote is unclear to the reader, do not be unduly concerned as the main point is merely that equilibrium is a balancing of forces that often has desirable properties.

2. This is not so stringent as one might suspect; first, one may argue that the existing distribution is "best" from the perspective of the typical voter, for otherwise it would be changed via the political process. Since the income distribution is a "public good" (discussed later in this chapter) about which each individual will have different and irreconcilable differences of opinion, the political consensus is the best guide we have. A second, and more sophisticated, argument is that the errors in optimal provision resulting even from an improper income distribution may not matter. Since all income is allocated in some way, the income elasticity of demand is one for all goods collectively (including savings). Lacking other information, the best-guess income elasticity for any good would be one. If the income elasticity of demand for environmental quality were in fact exactly one, the demand curve would be *unaffected* by income redistribution among people with similar tastes. The demand for environmental quality would fall for the rich (if income was transferred from them), but the demand for environmental quality of the income-receiving poor would rise by exactly the same amount. Ironically, if environmental quality is a superior good, as evidence suggests, and if one feels that income should be distributed more equally, then the socially best environmental quality would be *lower* than if income were not redistributed. These points relating to equity will be further clarified in the text, after we have discussed efficiency more fully.

at a higher price a given quantity of a good would no longer be desired, while at a lower price people would want more of the good relative to other goods available. Note that "value" as this term is (properly) used in resource allocation discussions is a *marginal* concept. Marginal valuations of large quantities of a particular good can be quite low, regardless of the *total* value of that good to society. This insight resolves paradoxes that used to trouble economists (and that still trouble non-economists): many nonessential items of a frivolous nature have high values (e.g., diamonds) while goods with great "intrinsic" value (e.g., water, which is essential to life) often have very low value. The so-called "value-in-use" (area under the demand curve up to a particular quantity) may bear no relation, in other words, to the value in exchange of that quantity. Yet the (marginal) value in exchange is the more useful value, since resource-allocation decisions usually involve questions of whether a little bit more or less of a commodity should be produced. In short, the demand curve for a good represents, in dollar terms, the marginal trade-off between the good and other real goods that people care about.

The supply curve of a good similarly represents the real cost, in terms of forgone other goods, of producing various quantities. If inputs must be paid more to produce larger quantities, it is because the opportunity costs of forgone other uses for these inputs (perhaps leisure in the case of labor) are higher than at smaller quantities.[3] Hence, costs of production of various quantities—points on the supply curve in the competitive case—represent not just "dollars" but rather the value of other outputs which must be forgone if more of the good under consideration is produced.

Consider now Figure 2.1, which depicts the supply-and-demand equilibrium for some ordinary good, say steak. The market-equilibrium quantity is given, by Q^*, this quantity selling for price P^*. Suppose now that either a higher (Q_H) or lower (Q_L) quantity were, for some reason, to be produced. At Q_L, the low quantity, the value to steak-buyers[4] of additional steak is high relative to the social cost

3. The reader may recall (although this is not critical to the text discussion) from elementary economics courses that the supply curve for a good results from the horizontal summation of the marginal cost curves (above the minimum of the average variable cost curves) of all firms in the industry.

4. One can substitute "society" for steak-buyer if the income distribution is deemed proper—otherwise the social marginal value of steak will be below steak-buyers' marginal values (if steak-buyers are viewed as the privileged group), or conversely.

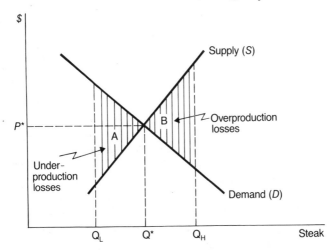

Figure 2.1

Supply, Demand, and Optimal Goods Provision

of providing additional steak—scarce resources have a higher value in producing steak than in producing other goods, hence more steak should be produced. The damage to society from underproduction of steak is depicted by area A in Figure 2.1.

Society can have too much of any good, even a good such as environmental quality, if the costs of providing the last units exceed the benefits of those units. At Q_H in Figure 2.1 this case is shown, with area B representing the loss to society resulting from overproduction.

Market Failure: Externalities

The free-market outcome, discussed above, would always be socially desirable, *if* both the demand and supply curves accurately represented social benefits and social costs. The demand curve is likely to be "wrong" only if people systematically don't know what is good for themselves.[5] Perhaps some limited role in the misallocation of resources is played by ignorance on the part of consumers,

5. Or if the income distribution is wrong and the income elasticities are nonunitary, as discussed in earlier footnotes.

but this source of misallocation is not likely to be a major problem. First, general improvements in consumer education and information transfer are occurring over time as technological advance occurs in the mass media. Also, people "learn by doing"—if a product doesn't satisfy consumers, they will shift their expenditures to other goods. Finally, the world is imperfect—and consumer information is no exception—but interference with the free market can only improve matters if some non-consumer authority, such as government, has superior information to that possessed by consumers.

Another source of resource misallocation occurs in the presence of monopoly on the supply side: the information in the demand curve (average revenue) represents social benefits, but that information is not viewed as relevant by the monopolist. The monopolist cares about the marginal revenue curve, which lies below a declining average revenue curve, in the same way that a declining average grade point implies that a student's marginal grade is below the average. Hence, in comparing marginal revenue with marginal cost, the monopolist underproduces from society's perspective.[6]

By far the most important, enduring, and systematic source of resource misallocation is on the cost side. Suppose, for reasons considered shortly, that firms in an industry do not have to pay all of their production costs. For specificity, consider steel production or a power plant generating electricity from a primary fossil fuel, say coal. Since firms must pay for labor and capital (including ingredient inputs), the social cost that steel plants or utilities do not pay will largely take the form of environmental damages to people who are not compensated for those damages. This leads to an important definition: *externalities* are said to occur when the actions of one economic agent affect the welfare of another economic agent and the latter is not compensated for the damages (or benefits[7]). Externalities may then be referred to, alternatively, as "uncompensated spillovers." Another way to think about externalities is to regard them as exchanges occurring outside the economic system that leave at least one party to the exchange worse (or better) off.

6. The discussion here is deliberately terse, since most environmental problems involve overproduction rather than underproduction.

7. Positive cost externalities, such as a beekeeper's benefits to nearby apple orchards, and conversely, are less common and not so closely related to the study of the environment as are negative externalities. Similarly, external effects on the demand side, such as external positive effects associated with education, will receive little emphasis here.

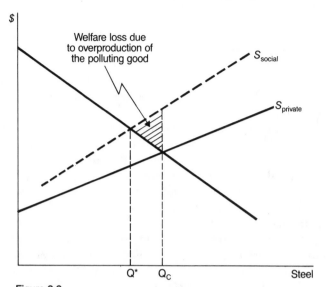

Figure 2.2

Negative Externalities and Resource Misallocation

These ideas, and their resource-misallocation implications, can be illustrated through a modified version of Figure 2.1. In Figure 2.2, Q_C represents the competitive supply-and-demand equilibrium outcome. At Q_C, however, uncompensated damages are occurring to some people in society. These damages are represented, in dollar terms, by the vertical distance between the private and social supply curves in Figure 2.2. Since the true social costs are reflected by S_{social}, the socially desirable outcome is Q^*; society overproduces steel or electricity and the social loss associated with this resource misallocation is shown by the shaded area in Figure 2.2. *Why* does this happen? Why does the private market outcome lead, in some cases, to externalities and resource misallocation while in other cases externalities appear not to be present?

Property Rights, Public Goods, and the Free Rider

The reason why externalities emerge at some times in production and not at other times or places is that certain inputs into production are scarce but not always priced to appropriately reflect that scarcity.[8] For most inputs this is not the case; if a firm wishes to use more labor or capital, that firm must compensate owners of those inputs for their use. Moreover, the compensation must be at least enough to make resource owners willingly supply the additional inputs—that is, the input owners must receive in dollar payment at least as much as they value alternative uses of these inputs, for example leisure.

For inputs into production like air, water, or solid materials, positive prices may not be charged.[9] Hence, a rational producer will tend to use these inputs until their marginal benefit is zero, since their marginal cost is zero. The input will be overused by firms in exactly the way that they would overuse labor if it were for some reason priced at zero; firms would substitute labor for capital anywhere they could, digging ditches, for example, by hand rather than using backhoes or even shovels (if shovels have positive prices).

Why do owners of labor get compensated, providing an automatic check on overuse, when owners of air, water, and so on do not? The answer is that for technological reasons, some inputs are difficult to "own" in a meaningful way. The air and water are constantly moving around, hence can't be "fenced in," and other environmental goods (lack of congestion, freedom from blight or noise) are equally slippery in terms of meaningfully defining ownership.

This problem is worsened, in a political setting, by issues of who *should* own the environmental inputs. When naturally clean air and water are very abundant as they once were in this country, the true marginal social cost of using environmental resources may well be close to zero; on the frontier nobody is damaged by air or water pollution, and the private and social costs of production are the same. As population and income increase, damages rise because more people are there to be damaged and because environmental quality is a normal or superior good. The appropriate price to charge for using environmental resources becomes positive, but who should pay it?

8. Sometimes firms do have to pay for all of their social costs. This subtlety is discussed in detail in Chapter 4; for present purposes the so-called "Coase Theorem" represents an unnecessary potential for confusion.

9. The "inputs" may be like other material inputs (e.g., air mixed with coal to produce energy; water used for cooling), but the reader should note that the real issue is the use of the air, water, or land as a waste disposal medium (whether or not the media are directly an input into production). Wastes are discharged freely into the environment, damaging other users, and it is the lack of compensation for these damages that is reflected in the zero price facing discharges.

Firms, historically able to use the resources without charge, will feel unfairly persecuted by demands (in the form of regulations, taxes, and so on) that they switch to more expensive production methods. People exposed to environmental pollution, on the other hand, will feel that they should not have to bribe firms to clean up—they have the right to breathe clean air. These are issues of equity: who should have property rights to the environmental good?

Viewed slightly differently, most environmental goods are closely akin to so-called "public goods." That is, they have the property that they exist in a given quantity that is available indivisibly to all, with individual use not affecting (or, in less extreme cases, negligibly affecting) the amount available to others. Classic examples of public goods are national defense or lighthouses. Once they exist, the marginal cost to an additional user becomes zero. Similarly, in the environmental context, if air quality is improved, it is improved for everyone. This has very important implications for desirable environmental policy, as will become increasingly evident. For ordinary goods, if more is produced, only those willing to pay for the good get it and others do not benefit. Hence, in going from individual to market demand one adds *horizontally* how much each individual demands at any price to arrive at total demand at that price.

A different way of arriving at total demand is required for a public good. Envision the decision of whether to build or not build a lighthouse on a particularly dangerous rocky ocean location. If the lighthouse is built, it benefits, unlike the private-good case, many consumers. The appropriate question now is, How much are all consumers together willing to pay for one lighthouse? This amounts to *vertical* summation of individual willingness to pay, where perhaps the rich yacht-owners and commercial fisherman would each be willing to pay $1,000 per year, moderate-income rowboat owners might be willing to pay $100, and the poor might have zero willingness to pay. If there are enough rich and moderate-income individuals living near the dangerous rocks, the (vertical) sum of willingness-to-pay for one lighthouse may well exceed the cost of building and running a lighthouse. A similar calculation at another location may have costs greater than benefits, because either the rocks are less dangerous or fewer people live near them.

Several observations make the preceding discussion controversial. First, there are the obvious equity issues: society is allocating scarce resources to lighthouses, which have no value to the poor. The labor, capital, and other inputs used to produce the lighthouse could have been used to produce low-income housing. That benefits exceed costs for a project does not always imply that the project should be undertaken—however, if the benefits *do* exceed the costs, we know that the winners from the project *could* compensate the losers, making everyone better off, including the poor.

Equity issues inevitably emerge for environmental goods as well; we do not all benefit equally from environmental improvement. Equity implications of current environmental policy will be discussed further below.

There are important efficiency implications of the required vertical summation of individual demands for public goods. First, it is difficult to observe directly individual demands for a public good. (For private goods the problem doesn't exist; you reveal your willingness-to-pay for the good or you don't get the good.) Individuals may have incentives to *understate* their preferences for the public good, reasoning as follows: I am one of many boat-owners, so what I say a lighthouse is "worth" to me will have little impact on the aggregate valuation. I may, in other words, be able to be a "free rider," getting a valuable good without having to pay for it. Unfortunately, since everyone thinks they can take a free ride, the aggregate valuation falls short of costs and even projects having true benefits greatly in excess of costs do not get undertaken.

An additional implication of vertical demand curve summation is important in that it explains the frequent controversy and strong pro or con feelings regarding public goods. *Even at the socially optimal quantity of a public good, almost everybody may feel that there is either too much or too little of it!* The rich yacht-owner will feel that there are too few lighthouses; the poor will feel that there are too many. One doesn't have this particular problem for ordinary private goods— rich and poor alike can buy exactly as much as they wish, respectively, at the market-clearing price. Disagreement and polarization among groups, each becoming progressively more militant in pressing their demands, are the natural result. Lawyers and consultants will benefit from controversy about even the optimal quantity of a public good, but their time might be better spent in other pursuits from a social perspective. This is, unfortunately, a problem having no obvious solution.[10]

10. One possibility, not usually recognized by non-economists, is to note that many "public goods" really aren't: one can "buy" different amounts of clean air by moving to different locations. This may involve greater commuting cost or higher rents, but to the extent that variation in public-good consumption can occur by "voting with

The preceding observations may be summarized with reference to Figure 2.3, which may be compared to Figure 2.1:

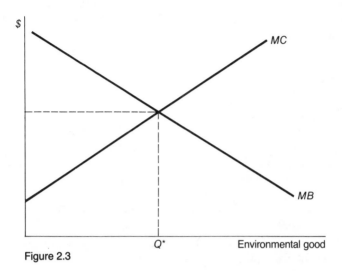

Figure 2.3

The optimal environmental quality is where marginal benefits and marginal costs are equal, though very few people may actually agree that the $Q*$ is "right" even if they have *identical* information.

Notice that best provision of public goods occurs when government effectively attempts to replicate the desirable features of the competitive price system. This should be clear from the fact that the *MC* and *MB* curves in Figure 2.3 correspond in meaning exactly to the supply-and-demand curves of Figure 2.1. The difference and the difficulty—for reasons already discussed—are that the comparison of benefits and costs is hard to make for the environmental good since markets don't exist to automatically coordinate supplies and demands.

We now see, then, that the common man-on-the-street notion that an undesirably degraded environment is somehow a fault of the price system is completely wrong. Exactly the opposite is the truth: the problem is not with pricing or the capitalist system but rather with the *lack* of prices.[11] Chickens and cows are *not* endangered species,

one's feet," the environmental problem becomes less severe (in that a government policy dealing with the "problem" may not be necessary or desirable).

11. As we shall see later, environmental quality in socialist or communist countries is no better, at equivalent levels of development, than their capitalist counterparts.

because they are owned and priced. Eagles and blue whales, on the other hand, are in danger of disappearing from the earth precisely because nobody owns them. If they were owned, a positive price reflecting supply (cost) and demand (benefit) considerations would eliminate the scramble to "get 'em before somebody else does" at a zero price.

The Resource-Allocation Problem Revisited

The preceding discussion establishes that benefit-cost analysis is likely to be a desirable tool in forging socially desirable environmental policy. Benefit-cost analysis is nothing more, stripped to its logical essentials, than arguing that one should compare the advantages with the disadvantages of alternative courses of action. Since failing to do so will result in decisions that are systematically unwise, why has there been so much controversy surrounding use of benefit-cost analysis in decisions about the level of environmental quality?

A number of reasons can be identified for dislike and mistrust of the benefit-cost approach to environmental quality and to resource allocation more generally. First, the public-good nature of environmental quality implies that for many—probably most—people, even a properly-conducted benefit-cost analysis will result in what will be perceived as the "wrong" level of environmental quality. To further clarify, suppose for a moment that steak were a public good and some socially determined quantity, Q^*, would be distributed to n people in society, with each person receiving $(1/n)Q^*$. That is, each person receives the same proportional share.[12] Clearly, if costs were also distributed evenly, the poor and vegetarians would be receiving more steak than they want (for them, costs are greater than benefits), while rich or highly carnivorous individuals will feel shortchanged (for them, benefits are greater than costs). These reactions would be present even if the socially optimal overall quantity of steak were to result from a careful benefit-cost analysis. We are indeed fortunate that steak is not a public good!

Partly, then, as a result of the frequently public-good nature of

Indeed, there are reasons for suspecting lower environmental quality due to the more widespread philosophy of "free use for all."

12. There is a logical problem here in that if steak were *really* a public good, each person would get Q^*, not $(1/n)Q^*$. However, the fundamental point is unaffected by scale: the point is that proportional distribution ignores variation in tastes and income that will make people unhappy with Q^*.

environmental quality, many environmentalists don't want to accept trade-offs, since even correct analysis of benefit-cost trade-offs is likely to give them less environmental quality than they want. At the same time, others won't want to accept benefit-cost analysis because they will perceive the resulting environmental quality as too costly for the benefits they receive. Yet any policy, ranging from doing nothing to imposing extremely stringent environmental standards, will inevitably have benefits and costs; the benefit-cost analyst merely makes these benefits and costs explicit.

Another reason benefit-cost analysis is disliked is that there are still some people who fail to accept the fact of scarcity. If we could have greater environmental quality without having to give up other things that we also care about, it would of course be irrational not to have perfect environmental quality. Unfortunately, there is "no free lunch" in environmental quality: the amount of capital and labor required to generate a pristine environment would be immense, implying an immense loss of other goods.

Some of this apparent irrationality is due to the choice of accounting unit by the benefit-cost analyst. Typically, the benefit and cost comparisons are conducted using dollars. The use of "base" dollars is often taken to imply a crass inhumanity on the part of the analyst: "How can one compare the lives saved ('priceless' benefits) from an environmental improvement with the rising utility bills necessary to obtain the improvement (dollar cost)?"

Three points are noteworthy about the argument that environmental trade-offs are inherently not comparable. First, any policy implicitly makes such comparisons: people will in fact die or become sick to a greater or lesser degree depending on the extent to which scarce resources are not or are devoted to environmental quality. Such comparisons are *inevitably* made, with benefit-cost analysis just bringing these comparisons out into the open, to help decision-makers. Second, the choice of unit of account is quite fundamentally immaterial: one could use "life-equivalent units" or apple units, or indeed, Michael Jackson concert-ticket units rather than dollars. The benefit-cost ratio will be *unaffected* by choice of unit, the point being that since the comparisons must inevitably be made, they might as well be made in convenient units.[13] On the third point, analysts,

13. Many of the costs, and some of the benefits, of environmental clean-up automatically come in the form of dollars, making dollars a convenient choice for unit of account. For example, a wet limestone scrubber or electrostatic precipitator costs a

recognizing that conversion of all trade-offs into common units (whether dollars or barrels of oil) is fraught with weighting difficulties, are increasingly leaving this work to the decision-maker via something called *multi-objective optimization modeling* or *multi-criteria analysis*. Roughly speaking, these approaches take responsibility for weighting the effects of environmental policy away from benefit-cost analysts and give that power to the decision-maker. Rather than receiving a single number as the informational basis for a decision, the decision-maker receives a vector of effects (health damages, soiling, energy costs, and so on) which he or she then internally weights in arriving at a decision. Whether this is better or worse in terms of the social desirability of the resulting decision is difficult to say. Indeed, it is not even clear that the choice between benefit-cost analysis and multi-criteria analysis makes any difference, although it might;[14] difficult comparisons must be made in either case.

The preceding reasons why benefit-cost analysis is often disliked do not depend on whether the analysis is good or bad. The analysis is bad if it is so incomplete as to give a biased impression and/or if the analyst is biased and deliberately misleads the decision-maker.

Consider first an incomplete analysis in which only a few effects of a policy are quantified. If what is omitted from analysis is also clearly indicated to the decision-maker, bias is not introduced. The decision-maker is merely thrust back in the realm of multi-criteria analysis, in which he must compare the net dollar value of the quantified effects with a vector of unquantified effects. Realistically, it is our human nature to downplay the shortcomings of our efforts, and benefit-cost analysts are no different from anyone else in this regard. Even the unbiased researcher has time and money limitations on what can be well quantified. It is sometimes argued that these limitations result in understating benefits and overstating costs of environmental improvement. The argument is that many subtle benefit categories for a control policy are ignored (for example, aesthetics or

certain amount to purchase and maintain, with those dollar costs representing the scarce labor, capital, and materials used in environmental clean-up.

14. If the decision-maker is an elected official, the weighting might involve vote-maximization, which is seldom equivalent to weightings arrived at through benefit-cost analysis. The motivations, hence weightings, applied by a nonelected civil servant are even more unclear. It is far from obvious whether the environment would be cleaner or dirtier if multi-criteria analysis became widely preferred to benefit-cost analysis.

subtle ecological impacts) because they are so difficult to estimate with precision. Costs are at the same time relatively overstated because they are more completely available and because evaluators fail to allow for technological improvements that would stem from introduction of the control policy.

These arguments are apparently sensible in theory, but have been criticized in practice, since actual costs for particular control options have tended to be much higher than anticipated and benefits lower, for two reasons. First, the devices commonly used to reduce emissions (scrubbers, catalytic converters in automobiles, and so on) have tended to not work as reliably as expected from purely engineering design considerations. The reason for this is largely economic and will be clarified later in the book. Hence, environmental-improvement benefits have been smaller than anticipated. Second, in estimating health benefits of cleaning the environment, the benefit-cost analyst often uses the results of studies showing important air-pollution damages (premature death, bronchitis, and the like) while ignoring a body of literature showing no statistically significant damages at relevant air-quality levels.

The issue of deliberate bias on the part of benefit-cost analysts, in the benefits and costs they consider and in their techniques of analysis, is more serious. Given *identical* data, for example on air or water quality and hospital admissions over some time period, two researchers can publish quite different results. One may find no effect while another may report a pronounced health effect of the air or water pollutant. In part, this is understandable in that theoretical guidance for empirical studies is lacking, hence there are few compelling reasons for preferring the empirical results from one assumed relationship over other possibilities. In any event, controversies of this sort are likely to become less significant over time as universally accepted approaches to data analysis become more commonplace.[15] In the meantime, court and other advocacy proceedings, although time-consuming, are desirable in that they will expose decision-makers to both sides of important issues.

The final reason why benefit-cost analysis is sometimes disliked relates to issues of equity. If one attempts an explicit accounting of

15. See R. Krumm and P. Graves, "Morbidity and Pollution," *Journal of Environmental Economics and Management*, December 1982, for more detail on appropriate handling of data when theoretical guidance is weak.

the benefits and costs of alternative environmental policies, an inevitable question arises: Who receives the benefits and who has to pay the costs? The answer to this distributional question is very critical politically and yet surprisingly few studies have discussed who are the winners and losers from current environmental policy.[16]

We will go on record a bit more strongly than most authors on this issue: the net impact of environmental policy has been *regressive*. That is, the poor receive a smaller proportion of their income in environmental benefits, but pay a higher proportion of their income for costs of abatement. A more typical conclusion is that the benefits appear to be roughly proportional to income while the overall regressivity stems from a regressive nature of costs. We shall see presently why benefits as well as costs are likely to be regressively distributed.

What are the arguments? Consider first who receives the benefits of environmental policy. There is clearly theoretical ambiguity on the benefit side. If one views environmental quality as a pure public good (for example, uniform air quality in some air basin), abatement effects are received equally by all, rich and poor. However, *valuations* of those effects are unlikely to be equal. The rich have, by definition, many more ordinary goods relative to the fixed quantity of environmental good. Hence, the marginal willingness-to-pay for environmental quality is expected to be quite high for the rich. The poor, on the other hand, have few ordinary goods relative to the fixed amount of environmental good. Their marginal valuation of the environmental good is likely to be very low, in that they would be willing to give up much more environmental quality to, say, get a new car than would a rich person. These arguments become even stronger if environmental quality is a superior good (income elasticity of demand greater than unity), as many authors believe.

But what of the non-public-good nature of environmental quality? It is commonly noted that the poor live in the dirtier parts of urban areas. These areas will, in order to meet federally mandated environmental-quality standards, be cleaned up relatively more than will the already-clean suburbs. Hence, it is often argued that the poor may receive more of the clean-up effects, possibly offsetting their lower marginal valuations of those effects. If this were true, the degree of regressivity on the benefit side would remain, as many believe, ambiguous.

16. Several exceptions to this rule are given at the close of this chapter as suggestions for further reading.

But there is another argument, which is usually ignored. Even if the poor do receive the bulk of the clean-up effort, do they, ultimately, receive benefits—or do they have to pay, in higher rents, for the health and aesthetic benefits received? If dirty areas are cleaned up, they become relatively more attractive places to live, hence will rent and sell for more. The "gentrification" observed in many American cities, in which young, affluent couples are outbidding the poor for downtown locations, may be (in part) due to environmental clean-up occurring during the 1970s. In a competitive housing market, those receiving health and other benefits of a clean-up effort must pay to the landowner the full value of the environmental improvement or they will be unable to continue to occupy the cleaner locations. Since poor people are more likely to rent than to own, the benefits of clean-up are likely to be regressive.

When one considers that national parks, wilderness areas, and other recreational facilities are used predominantly by the relatively well-off, the final conclusion becomes fairly clear: the rich benefit relatively more than the poor from the package of environmental controls currently in use.

On the cost side of efforts to clean up the environment, the case is more clear. The rich spend a smaller proportion of their income on manufactured goods, whose price is most affected by environmental controls. Services, indulged in proportionately more by the rich, become relatively less expensive as compared to manufactured goods. Even in cases where expenditures might be the same (for example, the rich buying a proportionately more expensive car than the poor), environmental controls harm the poor relatively more: a catalytic converter and exhaust gas recirculation (EGR) system lead to a higher-percentage price increase on a Chevy than they do on a Porsche or Mercedes.

Taken together, the preceding discussion suggests that environmental policy in the United States is pro-rich. This analysis is moreover consistent with attitudes toward the environment expressed in surveys of both rich and poor. If further progress in environmental clean-up is deemed to have benefits exceeding costs, greater attention than in the past will need to be given to issues of equity (perhaps financing from general tax revenue) to avoid social conflicts among classes.

An Interdisciplinary Approach[17]

A five-step procedure can usefully bring together all of the elements necessary for rational environmental policy. These steps are:

1. Specifying a policy option, its costs, and the impact in terms of reduced emissions (volume, timing, and location) into the environment.

2. Specifying what the likely impact of the reduced emissions will be on improving environmental quality.

3. Specifying the benefits that stem from the improved environmental quality.

4. Specifying the spatial impact of both the costs and benefits, and in turn noting that the spatial impact will affect the costs and benefits.

5. Specifying the incidence of the policy option: who is helped and hurt by the policy?

The above procedure can give the reader a real-world flavor of how to conduct environmental policy analysis that cannot be achieved by simply saying "equate marginal benefits of control to marginal costs of control"—a statement that is accurate but not very illuminating. The value of the five-step approach becomes most clear when one discusses the problems and possibilities encountered in each of the five steps. Suppose we are concerned about automobile pollution and wish to think about the implications of various environmental-control strategies. What kinds of issues would emerge in each step of the analysis? What kinds of information would be required at each step to formulate rational policy?

17. This approach is paraphrased from G. S. Tolley, P. E. Graves, and G. C. Blomquist, *Environmental Policy: Elements of Environmental Analysis*, Cambridge: Ballinger Publishing Co., 1981. This volume is the first of a five-volume series on environmental policy under the general editorship of G. S. Tolley of the University of Chicago. Other volumes of particular interest to readers seeking hands-on environmental expertise are: G. S. Tolley, P. E. Graves, and A. S. Cohen, *Environmental Policy: Air Quality*, Cambridge: Ballinger, 1982; and G. S. Tolley, G. C. Blomquist, and D. Yaron, *Environmental Policy: Water Quality*, Cambridge: Ballinger, 1983.

In Step 1, a policy option or range of options would need to be specified. Suppose we consider, as a first possibility, a policy of requiring installation of a catalytic converter on all new passenger cars. Engineers could be consulted to estimate the cost per car and also the impact on emissions per car.[18] Economists could then be asked to estimate the share of the stock of automobiles that would be of the newer, low-polluting type in each future year.[19] From this information emission reductions could be calculated.

In Step 2, experts on air dispersion could be called in to estimate the impact of the emission reductions on air quality. Reductions might be substantial in some locations (intersections, shopping malls, and the like) and not important in other locations. If air-dispersion studies were viewed as too expensive in a particular policy setting (say, for a local government decision-maker operating with a small budget), the simpler (but generally less accurate) approach of assuming air-quality improvements proportional to emission reductions could be taken.

In Step 3, benefits of the air-quality improvement would be estimated. These benefits take the form of *reduced damages* to health, property, and the aesthetic environment. Consulting medical experts can lead to estimates of health impacts: lessened heart pains, dizziness, headaches, bronchitis, perhaps fewer deaths, and so on. Property benefits would, in this illustration, be most closely related to reduced damages from the smaller amount of ozone.[20] These benefits might take the form of less damage to crops or ornamental plantings such as roses and other flowers. Finally, aesthetic considerations must be examined. Perhaps evidence from surveys could be used to gain insights on how people in, say, Denver or Los Angeles value the ability to see more distant objects and to see closer objects more clearly. All of the physical impacts would be, ideally, quantified and weighted in relative importance with a common unit of account,

18. There are uncertainties in the impact of the policy even at this stage. Some emissions such as lead, CO, and HC would be expected, because of more complete burning and changes in fuel, to go down. However, others such as NO_x might go up under such a policy. since higher burning temperatures and greater oxygen oxidize the normally inert nitrogen gas, N_2. This latter impact is unlikely to be anticipated during the policy-formulation stage.

19. The higher cost of the newer cars with control devices would presumably keep older, more polluting cars in use longer than would otherwise be the case.

20. For other policies, more frequent painting, damage to statuary, soiling of structures, and so on might need to be considered.

perhaps dollars. Or, if one wished to let others perform this function, as with multi-criteria analysis, the benefits of the environmental improvement could be left as a list of health, property, and aesthetic effects.

Turning in Step 4 to spatial effects, one may wish to think about whether dense central-city locations will be favored relative to the suburban fringe. Or, since automobile-related environmental problems are primarily urban will cities gain population from rural areas as they become cleaner? Indeed, examining the spatial effects may suggest alternative policies: why require cars registered in rural areas to have costly control equipment when benefits to rural residents may be zero or close to zero? This change in the policy could reduce costs by about one-third without a corresponding reduction in benefits.[21] Other purposes for analyzing the spatical impacts are that benefits (and generally costs) are affected: if the cleaner city lures more people to it, then the benefits of a still cleaner city are larger than would otherwise have been estimated.

In Step 5, equity issues are raised. Here, also, important revisions to a particular policy may suggest themselves. Suppose the catalytic converter is viewed as too burdensome to the poor in their efforts to buy or maintain a car. In this case explicit tax relief could be given those below a certain income level who purchase a new, cleaner car, offsetting the inequitable features of the policy. Or, consideration of equity may occasionally even suggest a more efficient policy. The poor are usually viewed as having relatively less money and relatively more time (or a lower opportunity cost of time). If so, then perhaps an inspection-maintenance program to require cars to meet factory emission standards might be fairer than requiring catalytic converters and exhaust gas recirculation systems. If one program turned out also to be more efficient (have greater excess of benefits over costs), a clearly preferred social policy might emerge.

Our example illustrates the great potential value of the five-step approach in leading to logical, sound environmental policy. But the

---

21. Similarly, for a broad range of pollutants whose primary damage is to local populations, the policy implications of the spatial setting are immense: as a first approximation, if urban population densities are a hundred or a thousand times higher than in rural areas, then the benefits of greater controls are a hundred or a thousand times greater. There should be, in other words, great spatial variation in the stringency of controls since there is great spatial variation in the marginal benefits (and costs) of control.

example also illustrates the difficulties and uncertainties in the conduct of environmental analysis.[22]

With this glimpse of the approach the economists brings to environmental analysis behind us, we turn to more detailed microeconomic considerations in the two chapters that follow.

DISCUSSION QUESTIONS AND PROBLEMS

1. History makes very clear that pollution is not a modern invention. Can you think of examples of improvements in environmental quality? Of worsening environmental quality? Of environmental damage that is due not to man's activities but to natural phenomena?

2. Many different types of pollutants have received attention in the standards-setting process (CO, HC, TSP, NO_x, Ozone, lead). Cities are sometimes ranked in terms of the total number of days in which any such standards are violated. How significant are such rankings? What alternatives might you suggest?

3. The public, collectively, can often *benefit* from a rise in price. Think about some cases where this is true and about the distributional effects of that price rise—who is helped and who is harmed?

4. Private control of scarce natural resources, such as oil, is often felt by the man in the street to lead to undesirably rapid depletion because of greedy profit-taking on the part of resource owners. What arguments might suggest that, on the contrary, the profit motive leads to optimal intertemporal resource allocation? How likely is it that public control of resources by individuals facing elections every four years would lead to more desirable results?

5. Discuss the difference between the following two statements:
a) We should attempt to eliminate all forms of environmental damage.
b) We should attempt to eliminate externalities.

6. Since marginal benefits and marginal costs of environmental control policies vary greatly over space, uniform federal environmental standards would seem inappropriate. What are some arguments that support the opposite view?

7. What would be the most important drawback to using a referendum approach to determine the best level of environmental quality (letting people vote for various policies)?

22. We feel that the bulk of the uncertainty relates to specifying the physical effects of the policy (for example, How many will die? What will air quality effects be?) with a smaller relative amount of uncertainty surrounding the weighting of those effects. This is another reason we tend to favor cost-benefit analysis, in which a single number is presented to the decision-maker, over multi-criteria analysis. This view comes from extensive experience with the health (and other damage) literature in which variation in estimated physical effects is very large indeed.

REFERENCES AND FURTHER READING

Asch, P., and Seneca, J. J. "Some Evidence on the Distribution of Air Quality." *Land Economics* 54, no. 3 (August 1978).

Baumol, W. J. "Environmental Protection and Income Distribution." In H. Hochman and G. Peterson, eds. *Redistribution Through Public Choice.* New York: Columbia University Press, 1974.

Becker, L. *Property Rights.* London: Routledge and Kegan Paul, 1977.

Burdach, E., and Pugliaresi, L. "The Environmental Impact Statement and the Real World." *Public Interest* 49 (Fall 1977).

Council on Environmental Quality. *Environmental Quality.* Washington, D.C.: U.S. Government Printing Office, published annually.

Council on Environmental Quality. *The Global 2000 Report to the President: Entering the 21st Century.* Washington, D.C.: U.S. Government Printing Office, 1980.

Dorfman, N. S., and Snow, A. "Who Will Pay for Pollution Control." *National Tax Journal* 28, no. 1 (March 1975).

Dorfman, R. "Incidence of the Benefits and Costs of Environmental Programs." *American Economic Review* 67, no. 1 (February 1977).

Dorfman, R., and Dorfman, N. S., eds. *Economics of the Environment*, 2d ed. New York: Norton, 1977.

Fischer, A. C., and Peterson, F. M. "The Environment in Economics: A Survey." *Journal of Economic Literature* 14 (March 1976).

Freeman, A. M., III. "The Distribution of Environmental Quality." In A. V. Kneese and B. T. Bower, eds. *Environmental Quality Analysis.* Baltimore: Johns Hopkins University Press, 1972.

Graves, P. E., and Krumm, R. J. *Health and Air Quality: Evaluating the Effects of Policy.* Washington, D.C.: American Enterprise Institute, 1981.

Hanke, S., and Anwyll, J. "On the Discount Rate Controversy." *Public Policy* (Spring 1980).

Hardin, G. "The Tragedy of the Commons." *Science* 162, no. 3059 (December 13, 1968).

Harrison, D. *Who Pays for Clean Air: The Costs and Benefit Distribution of Federal Automotive Emission Controls.* Cambridge, Mass.: Ballinger, 1975.

Herfindahl, O. C., and Kneese, A. V. *Quality of the Environment: An Economic Approach to Some Problems in Using Land, Water and Air.* Baltimore: Johns Hopkins University Press, 1965.

Howe, C. W. *Natural Resource Economics.* New York: Wiley, 1979.

Kneese, A. V., and Schultze, C. L. *Pollution, Prices and Public Policy.* Washington, D.C.: The Brookings Institution, 1975.

Krumm, R. J., and Graves, P. E. "Morbidity and Pollution." *Journal of Environmental Economics and Management* 9, no. 4 (December 1982).

Lave, L., and Seskin, E. "Epidemiology, Causality, and Public Policy." *American Scientist* 67 (March–April 1979).

Mishan, E. J. *Cost-Benefit Analysis*. New York: Praeger, 1976.

Mishan, E. J. *Technology and Growth: The Price We Pay*. New York: Praeger, 1970.

Morey, E. R. "Fishery Economics: An Introduction and Review." *Natural Resources Journal* 20 (October 1980).

Olson, M., and Landsberg, H. H., eds. *The No-Growth Society*. New York: Norton, 1974.

Portney, P. R., *et al.*, eds. *Current Issues in U.S. Environmental Policy*. Baltimore: Johns Hopkins University Press, 1978.

Rosenberg, N. *Perspectives on Technology*. Cambridge: Cambridge University Press, 1976.

Stokey, E., and Zeckhauser, R. *A Primer for Policy Analysis*. New York: Norton, 1978.

Tolley, G. S.; Blomquist, G. C.; and Yaron, D., eds. *Environmental Policy: Water Quality* (Vol. 3). Cambridge, Mass.: Ballinger, 1983.

Tolley, G. S.; Graves, P. E.; and Cohen, A. S., eds. *Environmental Policy: Air Quality* (Vol. 2). Cambridge, Mass.: Ballinger, 1982.

Tolley, G. S.; Graves, P. E.; and Blomquist, G. C., eds. *Environmental Policy: Elements of Environmental Analysis* (Vol. 1). Cambridge, Mass.: Ballinger, 1981.

Tolley, G. S., and Havlicek, J., Jr., eds. *Environmental Policy: Solid Wastes* (Vol. 4). Cambridge Mass.: Ballinger, forthcoming.

Tolley, G. S., and Vaughn, R. J., eds. *Environmental Policy: Recreation and Aesthetics* (Vol. 5). Cambridge, Mass.: Ballinger, forthcoming.

Wolf, C., Jr. "A Theory of Non-market Failures." *Public Interest* 55 (Spring 1979).

Chapter 3

The Microeconomic Theory of Discharges and Environmental Quality

Microeconomic theory deals with the production, exchange, and consumption of goods and services. The basic building block of production theory is the production function or isoquant map, which shows input combinations with which a firm can produce each of many output volumes. The basic building block of consumer theory is the utility function or indifference map, which shows a consumer's preferences among bundles of goods and services. These building blocks are combined with a variety of assumptions about market organization to generate theories of the ways market economies allocate scarce resources among competing uses.[1] Almost all the analysis in this book will be carried out on the assumption that firms and consumers buy and sell goods and services in perfectly competitive markets, the key characteristic of which is that people can buy and sell as much as they want without affecting prices. One reason for the assumption of competitive markets is that it greatly simplifies the analysis, thus increasing the number of definite conclusions and testable hypotheses that can be derived. A much more important reason is that it is a good approximation for most environmental

1. These theories are presented in any good price-theory text, such as Mansfield, *Microeconomics: Theory and Applications.*

problems. Many students find this hard to accept, believing that pollution must be the work of greedy monopolists with no sense of social responsibility. In fact, the opposite is more nearly true. Not only is most of the economy more competitive than is commonly believed, but also the need for government intervention to solve pollution problems is greatest when large numbers of polluters and victims are involved and markets therefore approximate the competitive model. This issue will be analyzed in detail in Chapter 4. There is no need to take the usefulness of the competitive market assumption on faith. The justification for and implications of the competitive assumption will be indicated at appropriate places throughout the book. The reader can evaluate the persuasiveness of the analysis, modify it where the assumptions are found to be objectionable, and compare it with analyses based on other assumptions.

In Chapters 1 and 2 it was indicated that economic activity affects environmental quality in many complex ways in an industrialized economy. Some of the most important of these effects will be explored in realistic detail in subsequent chapters. In this chapter the focus will be on ways to incorporate discharge decisions into microeconomic theory. The goal will be to show more formally than in Chapter 2 how discharge decisions are affected by the price, cost, profit, and utility considerations that govern ordinary market transactions. In all applied studies it is found that the textbook theory must be elaborated and modified to account for the complexity of real-world phenomena; it is no less true in environmental economics than in other specialties in microeconomics. Thus the abstract models presented in this chapter are not literally realistic, but they should provide a framework within which to begin to think systematically about the real and complex issues.

Materials are discharged at every stage of economic activity: extraction, processing, distribution, and consumption. The first three activities are mostly carried on by firms and the first task of this chapter is to extend the theory of the firm to include discharges. Consumption takes place in households, and the second task is to extend the theory of consumer behavior to include discharges. Both firms and households discharge residuals, directly and indirectly. *Direct discharges* are materials returned to the environment by those who generate them. Examples of direct discharges to the air are emissions from factory and household chimneys, from motor vehicles, and, indeed, from human respiration. Examples of direct waterborne discharges are factory processing wastes and household sewage discharged directly to water bodies. Examples of direct solid-waste discharges are deposits by firms of refuse in private or public dumps and households that litter streets and the landscape with cans, bottles, waste paper, and junk autos. *Indirect discharges* are those by organizations to which residuals have been handed over for disposal. Most such organizations are agencies of local governments, but some are private firms. By far the most important indirect-discharge organizations are local sewage-treatment plants and trash-collection agencies. Such institutions discharge and sometimes process materials from both firms and households. Sewage-treatment and trash-collection agencies dispose of waterborne and solid wastes. There is no significant example of indirect disposal of air pollutants.

In the next two sections firm and household discharges are assumed to include both direct and indirect discharges. It will be shown that similar extensions of the theories of producer and consumer behavior cover both direct and indirect discharges. But the environmental effects of all discharges—direct and indirect—depend on the ways that materials are processed and discharged, not on who does the processing and discharging. Analyzing the behavior of indirect dischargers is the third task of the chapter.

The final task of the chapter is to formalize the materials balance and to present an abstract analysis of the ways discharges affect the environment and people's welfare. Then the abstract positive model of environmental economics will be complete.

Production Theory

Firms discharge large amounts of many materials during production. Most extractive industries remove massive quantities of unwanted materials from the environment in order to obtain materials wanted for processing. Unwanted materials are separated and usually returned to the environment without processing. Mining firms often store slag on open ground. Agricultural, forestry, and fishing firms usually return unwanted organic materials by permitting them to decay where they are separated from wanted materials. Remaining materials are processed in many ways by manufacturing firms and materials are discharged at almost every stage. Likewise, each stage of production in both extractive and manufacturing industries uses energy to process materials, so heat, gases, and solids are discharged as wastes to the environment.

The elementary theory of the firm starts with a production function showing the amounts of a commodity or service that can be produced with various combinations of input quantities. The first step in incorporating environmental considerations into microeconomic theory is to include materials and discharges in the account of the production process. The key to a correct representation of materials and discharges in production theory is that firms face a materials balance similar to that faced by the entire economy. All the materials purchased or extracted by a firm must go somewhere. They must be used to increase the firm's inventory of materials, but that is a small part of the total and will be ignored in this book. Otherwise, all the materials that enter the firm must leave it either as part of products which are sold or as discharges.

The simplest production function that incorporates materials can be written

$$y = f(m,x) \tag{3.1}$$

where y is the quantity of output produced, m is the quantity of material input, and x is the quantity of another input, say labor. Of course, firms typically produce many products and use many materials and other inputs. Attention is focused on the one-output, two-input case because it illustrates most of the basic ideas and most results can be generalized easily. m is materials purchased by the firm. Ignoring capital accumulation, all materials leave the firm either incorporated in products or as wastes to be returned directly or indirectly to the environment. Furthermore, the only way the firm can obtain materials to incorporate in products is by purchasing m. Thus m equals materials incorporated in products plus those discharged,

$$y + r = m \tag{3.2}$$

where r is materials returned or discharged to the environment.

The careful reader will notice that there is a potentially confusing distinction between the y terms in equations (3.1) and (3.2). In equation (3.1), y is normally thought of as, for example, "number of TVs," while in (3.2) we are interpreting the y as being "pounds of TVs." While it would be possible to produce more output in the first sense without doing so in the latter sense, as long as the nature of the product being produced does not change, the use of output measured in pounds will be equivalent to what one normally thinks of as output.

The easiest interpretation of equation (3.2) is the case in which a firm purchases a material out of which it manufactures a product. Then the firm can produce more from a fixed purchase of m by applying more of the input x to the production process. For example, if the firm purchases sheet metal from which it stamps patterns, more patterns can be produced per ton of sheet metal purchased by applying more labor to arrange irregular patterns carefully on the sheet metal. If the firm makes canned tomatoes from raw tomatoes, more canned tomatoes can be produced from given purchases of tomatoes by employing more labor to avoid waste. Of course, firms do not produce just one product with just one material and one nonmaterial input. The reader should write out equations (3.1) and (3.2) for cases in which there are more outputs and inputs.

Many firms sell some services in conjunction with products they produce. For example, a firm may agree to repair machinery purchased from it for a stipulated time. Equations (3.1) and (3.2) can represent that case by interpreting y to be units of the product produced and sold, but including the value of the services provided in the price of y. If services are provided in proportion to products sold, nothing is lost by the suggested interpretation.

What about a firm that produces only services? For example, a college may produce only educational services or a law firm only legal services. Material inputs may nevertheless be used, for example, fuel to heat buildings, but there is no physical product in which materials are incorporated. In that case, all material inputs are discharged and equation (3.2) must be modified accordingly. The reader can follow through the analysis with the modified equation.

The production function represented by equation (3.1) can be shown as an isoquant map as in Figure 3.1. Each isoquant shows the combinations of m and x quantities that can produce an amount of y such as y^0 or y^1. The isoquants are drawn with conventional shapes; they slope down to the right, are convex, do not intersect or touch, and movements to the northeast represent greater outputs, that is, $y^1 > y^0$. These properties represent the economic assumptions that both inputs have positive marginal products, that there are diminishing returns to input proportions, and that the production function is single-valued, in other words, that each input combination is associated with a unique output quantity. The fact that one input is a material and the other is labor provides no justification for changing conventional assumptions about isoquant properties. For fuels or materials incorporated in products it is normally possible to economize on the material input by increasing the labor input. If there are many material

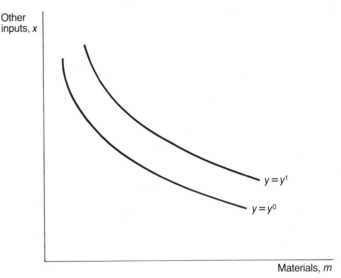

Figure 3.1

inputs, substitution between pairs of material inputs is also possible.[2] Isoquant properties have been chosen to be applicable to a great variety of production technologies, and the emphasis here on material inputs fits easily into the conventional textbook assumptions.

Although material discharges are not shown explicitly in Figure 3.1, they can be calculated easily using equation (3.2). The production function, equation (3.1), shows the output y that results from input quantities m and x. Then the discharge quantity is simply $r = m - y$, that is, whatever materials are not incorporated in the product must be discharged. r cannot be negative, so y can be no greater than m. Isoquants that satisfy the materials balance for the firm must be drawn with some care, as shown in Figure 3.2. Consider the output quantity $y = y^0$, whose isoquant is shown in Figure 3.2. Only input combinations such that $m > y^0$ can be used to produce y_0 units of y. $m < y_0$ would imply negative discharges.[3] There-

---

2. An important environmental example would be the substitution of a low-polluting input (for example, low-sulfur Western coal) for a more polluting input (for example, high-sulfur Eastern coal).

3. In the education example, y^0 would be the education output *in terms of pounds;* hence $y^0 = 0$ in this case, although the economic value of the good may be very great in spite of its intangible nature.

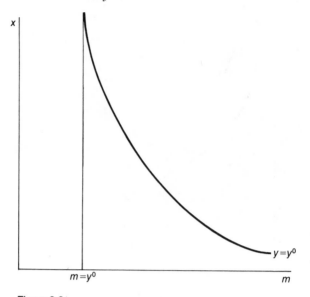

Figure 3.2

fore, only the part of the isoquant to the right of $m = y^0$ is relevant to realistic production possibilities.

The reader will recall from the previous chapter, although full incorporation of the points would greatly complicate the present analysis, that the *form* of r is likely to be far more critical than its tonnage. That form can be air, water, or solid, and (in whatever form) the timing and location of the emissions can make an immense difference to the resulting environmental damage.

There are no significant examples of production processes in which only two inputs are used, but the flavor of the analysis can be conveyed by some examples. Almost every product can be made using various combinations of capital and labor. Ditches can be dug by people with shovels or by operators using mechanized ditchdiggers. Bowling pins can be set up by workers or by automatic pinsetters. And cars can be assembled using various combinations of workers and automated machinery. Every substitution of machinery for labor is in part a substitution of fuel for human work, since all machines require fuel. Likewise, in almost every process in which products are fabricated from materials, given amounts of product can be fabricated with smaller material inputs by applying more labor to the process. Dress patterns can be cut from bolts of cloth or metal patterns can be cut from sheet metal in ways that waste little of the material if large amounts of labor are employed to place patterns and cut materials carefully. In almost every production process, workers and machinery can be used to retrieve scrap materials that can be reused and, at least partially, be incorporated in products.

The next step in production theory is to ascertain the combinations of inputs and outputs chosen by the firm. It will be assumed here that firms maximize profits and that they buy inputs and sell outputs in competitive markets. In competitive markets, firms maximize profits by choosing input quantities such that the value of the marginal product of each input equals its price or, in the case of labor, its wage. The value of the marginal product in turn is defined as the price of the output times the marginal product of the input. These equations can be written

$$p_y MP_m = p_m \qquad (3.3)$$

and

$$p_y MP_x = p_x \qquad (3.4)$$

where p_y is the price of the output y, p_m and p_x are the prices of the inputs m and x, and the MPs are their marginal products. Although each MP is the marginal product of the input indicated by its subscript, each is a function of both input quantities. Written in full, that for x would be $MP_x(m,x)$. Thus equations (3.3) and (3.4) are two simultaneous equations for the two variables m and x. Their solution gives profit-maximizing input quantities.[4] Having found the values of m and x by solving equations (3.3) and (3.4), y is determined by equation (3.1) and r by equation (3.2).[5]

What can be said about the discharge quantities that result from

4. Although reasonable restrictions on the properties of equation (3.1) guarantee the existence of solutions to equations (3.3) and (3.4), they do not guarantee unique solutions. If equation (3.1) has constant returns to scale, then equations (3.3) and (3.4) can be solved only for input ratios. This means that in a competitive industry with constant returns, the size of the firm is indeterminate, although the industry's total output is determinate.

5. Arguing that r is determined by equation (3.2) implicitly presumes a fixed relationship between output measured in economic units (such as number of TVs) and output in pounds—this need not always be the case, as discussed earlier. Keep this in mind in the text discussion for the next few pages.

the above solution? As is shown in price-theory texts, the solution of equations (3.3) and (3.4) can be expressed as a point of tangency between an isoquant and an iso-outlay line representing the combinations of m and x that can be bought for a given expenditure of money S, as in Figure 3.3. The iso-outlay curve touches the m and x axes at S/p_m and S/p_x respectively, and has a slope equal to $-p_m/p_x$. m^0 and x^0 are the profit-maximizing quantities of inputs m and x if y^0 is the profit-maximizing output level. They represent the least-cost combination of m and x that can produce y^0 units of output. Having found the input and output quantities, the discharge quantity is calculated using (3.2), as shown above.

In Figure 3.3, the higher is p_x relative to p_m, the flatter is the iso-outlay curve and the more m is used to produce a given y. As equation (3.2) shows, a larger m for a fixed y means a larger r. Thus, if materials are cheap relative to other inputs, large material inputs are used to produce given output volumes and discharges from the firm are correspondingly large. This illustrates a proposition that is much more general than this specific model: Circumstances that make materials scarce or expensive relative to other inputs induce firms to reduce discharges.

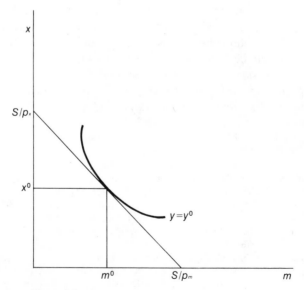

Figure 3.3

It is also possible to express discharge quantities explicitly as a function of the two input prices, without holding output constant. If equations (3.3) and (3.4) are solved, the result is to express m and x as functions of p_m, p_x, and p_y. These are input demand equations. Figure 3.4 shows the input demand equation for m and there is of course a similar equation for x. Input demand curves normally slope downward, as shown in the figure. If the market price of m is p_m^0, then m^0 units of m are purchased by the firm. The input of m increases as p_m decreases because m is substituted for x as m becomes relatively cheap and because the fall in p_m represents a decrease in the firm's costs, which induces it to increase output.

Thus, as p_m decreases, both y and m increase. Therefore, it is not immediately obvious whether the discharge r, which is the difference $y - m$, increases or decreases. The normal case is that in which a decrease in p_m leads to a larger increase in m than in y, and therefore to an increase in discharge r. Therefore it should be expected that discharges will be greater the cheaper are material inputs relative to other inputs. Figure 3.5 is a discharge demand curve, showing r as a function of p_m. It is derived from Figure 3.4 and equation (3.2). Figure 3.5 shows the normal case in which discharges increase as material price decreases. Discharge quantity r^0 corresponds to materials price p_m^0. Of course r could also be expressed as a function of p_x. The reader should work out the likely shape of that curve.

Price-theory texts also derive the expansion path, which shows how input quantities vary as output varies. The expansion path consists of a set of tangencies between isoquants and parallel iso-outlay curves, since the slope of the iso-outlay curve is constant if input prices are constant. Divide equation (3.3) by equation (3.4) to get

$$\frac{MP_m}{MP_x} = \frac{p_m}{p_x} \tag{3.5}$$

which is the tangency condition: the ratio of MPs equals the ratio of input prices. Holding input prices constant, the left side of equation (3.5) gives a value of m corresponding to each value of x. Each (m,x) pair corresponds to a value of output y.

If the production function has constant returns, the MPs are unchanged by an equiproportionate change in all inputs. Then the left side of equation (3.5), the marginal rate of technical substitution, is kept equal to the right side by equiproportionate changes in the two inputs. But if the inputs remain in fixed proportion at each output level, the expansion path is a straight line through the origin. Constant returns also implies that an equiproportionate change in inputs leads to the same proportionate change in output. But if m and y change in constant proportion, then r must also. Thus, with constant returns, fixed input prices lead to a fixed ratio of each input and of discharges to output. Doubling output leads to doubling each input and discharges. With constant returns, discharges per unit of output depend only on input prices and not on the scale of production.

Until now it has been assumed that discharges are unconstrained by government policies. But an important task of this book is to analyze ways that governments do and should restrict polluting discharges. Various policies that governments could adopt to restrict discharges will be described and evaluated in detail in later chapters. Here some technical tools for that evaluation will be introduced.

The government policy that has been used to control discharges in the United States is direct regulation. Although such policies are remarkably complicated, their essence is that a government agency decides how much each firm should be allowed to discharge in the public interest and forbids discharges in excess of those amounts,

Figure 3.4

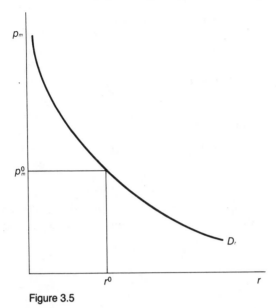

Figure 3.5

subject to civil and criminal penalties. In later chapters, the ways government might choose permissible discharge quantities will be analyzed. Suppose that p_m is at the level p_m^0 shown in Figure 3.5 and the profit-maximizing discharge quantity is r^0. Suppose the discharge permitted by the government is $\bar{r}$ units. If $\bar{r}$ is at least as great as r^0, the firm's behavior is unaffected and the government need not have bothered to regulate the discharge. If $\bar{r}$ is less than r^0, the constraint is effective and the firm reduces its discharge volume to $\bar{r}$. The effect on input and output quantities depends on the production function. The required reduction in r raises the total, average, and marginal cost curves. The result is to reduce the profit-maximizing output below its level before discharges were constrained.[6] The

6. If the regulation is in terms of allowed discharges per unit of output, it is possible (in some cases likely) that the total and average cost curves would rise, but the marginal cost curve would fall. For example, imposing such a regulation on a firm with constant returns to scale might lead the firm to select a much larger output level if there are substantial economies of scale in the control devices required. Hence the average costs could rise but the marginal cost curve fall—the firm would produce a larger output level, but the industry would produce less, as there would be fewer firms in long-run equilibrium.

attraction of regulation as a pollution-control policy lies in its apparent definiteness. If the government agency decides what discharge volume is in the public interest, it can set that volume as an upper limit to the firm's discharge and be sure that no more will be discharged provided only that enforcement is severe enough.

The most important alternative to discharge regulation as a pollution-control policy is a fee or charge on discharges, usually referred to as an effluent fee. Under an effluent-fee policy, the government sets a price, p_r, which the firm must pay the government for each unit of material discharged, and permits the firm to decide how much to discharge.

It is worthwhile to analyze the firm's response to the effluent fee in detail. Although it will not be demonstrated formally, an effluent fee leads the firm to choose input quantities that satisfy

$$(p_y + p_r)MP_m = p_m + p_r \qquad (3.6)$$

and

$$(p_y + p_r)MP_x = p_x \qquad (3.7)$$

Both equilibrium conditions are different from those in the absence of government pollution-control policy, equations (3.3) and (3.4). The rationale for equations (3.6) and (3.7) can be shown as follows: At a given amount of m, a unit increase in input x increases output by MP_x. But equation (3.2) shows that, for a given m, an increase in y by MP_x decreases r by the same amount, and each unit decrease in r saves the firm p_r. Hence a unit increase in x increases the firm's revenues by $p_y MP_x$, the value of the marginal product, plus $p_r MP_x$, the saving in effluent-fee payments. Thus equation (3.7) indicates an input of x which equates the increments in revenue and in factor payments from an increment in x. An increment in m increases output by MP_m, and sales revenue by $p_y MP_m$. But a unit increase in m increases discharges by $(1 - MP_m)$, and hence effluent-fee payments by $p_r(1 - MP_m)$. The addition to sales revenue is $p_y MP_m$ and the addition to input payments is p_m. Equation (3.6) indicates an input of m which equates the increment in revenues $p_y MP_m$ to the increment in outlays $p_m + p_r(1 - MP_m)$.

The attraction of effluent fees to economists is that they introduce market incentives into pollution-control programs. The government merely sets the price at which discharges are permitted and firms decide how much to discharge. Most economists are impressed by the strength of the incentive that markets provide to economize on scarce resources. The ambient environment is a scarce resource and economists want public policies to provide firms with incentives to economize on its use, that is, on discharges to it. Unfortunately, the choice between direct regulation and effluent fees as public policies to control discharges cannot be settled with the simple model developed in this section. But it is important to begin to construct a careful framework for understanding the issues in this important debate.

With the theoretical model developed in this section, it is possible to answer one important question concerning the choice between effluent fees and direct regulation as government pollution-control policies. Suppose an effluent fee is set at a level $p_r = \bar{p}_r$ such that the firm's resulting discharge level is $\bar{r}$ units. As an alternative, consider a government policy of direct regulation which limits the firm's discharge to the same $\bar{r}$ units. Using some intermediate calculus, it is shown in the Appendix to this chapter that the marginal conditions for profit maximization imply the same input and output levels for the firm under both policies. Thus profit is maximized by producing the same output level under both policies. But the profit level is lower under the effluent fee than under direct regulation. Under both policies, the firm buys the same input quantities, and therefore has the same production costs. It produces the same output level, so it has the same sales revenue under both policies. But under the effluent fee, it must pay the government $\bar{p}_r\bar{r}$ for the materials it discharges. Although the same quantity is discharged under direct regulation, there is no payment analogous to $\bar{p}_r\bar{r}$ under the effluent-fee policy. Therefore, the resulting profit level is less under the effluent-fee policy than under the analogous direct-regulation policy.

The result is paradoxical. Using the marginal conditions, an effluent fee and a direct control have been found that have the same effect on inputs, output, and discharge. But the fee reduces profit by more than the direct control. If so, more resources should be expected to leave the industry under the fee than under direct controls, thus reducing output by a greater amount under the fee than under the controls. The resolution of the paradox lies in the fact that the equivalence between the two policies was demonstrated using only the marginal conditions for profit maximization. The statement that the larger reduction of profits under the fee than under controls induces more resources to leave the industry refers to its overall profitability. Price theory texts show that the long-run equilibrium of the firm requires not only the marginal conditions, but also the "total" condition that the firm's total profit (valuing owners' resources at rates they could earn elsewhere) be nonnegative.

In the short run, the firm produces whatever output level maximizes profit, and that level is the same under the two policies. But in the long run, the profit level also matters. The effluent fee lowers profits more than does direct regulation. In the long run, some resources will move to other industries where profits are higher. The result is a reduction in the supply of y at the previous equilibrium price p_y. This can be illustrated in Figure 3.6. Y is the industry total of the commodity in question. S_Y and D_Y are industry supply and demand curves before imposition of a pollution-control program, and p^0_Y and Y^0 are the equilibrium price and quantity. The direct-regulation policy shifts the industry supply curve back to S'_Y, raising the equilibrium price to p'_Y and reducing the quantity to Y'. The effluent-fee policy shifts the industry supply curve back further, to S''_Y, raising the equilibrium price to p''_Y and reducing the quantity to Y''. The analysis in the last two paragraphs shows that $p''_Y > p'_Y > p^0_Y$ and $Y'' < Y' < Y^0$, that is, the effluent fee raises the price and lowers the quantity more than direct regulation.

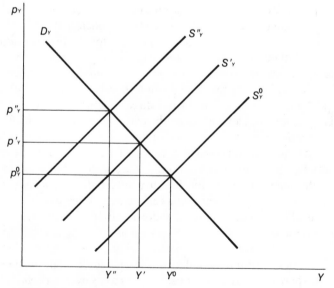

Figure 3.6

Elementary texts show that the amount by which price goes up and quantity down under the two policies depends on the elasticities of demand and supply. The more inelastic the demand curve, the more the price goes up and the less the quantity goes down as the result of the pollution-control program, and the greater the excess price increase under the effluent fee compared with direct regulation. Likewise, the more inelastic the supply curve, the smaller the price increase and the less the quantity decrease as a result of the pollution-control program.

What can be learned about the relative desirability of regulations and effluent fees as pollution-control measures from the preceding analysis? It has been shown that an effluent fee that results in the same discharge abatement lowers profits and hence output more than direct controls. In a world in which the government did not need to levy taxes to finance government services and transfers, effluent fees would be a bad policy in that they lower short-run living standards more than necessary to achieve the desired pollution abatement. But in the world of the 1980s, governments in the U.S. and most other countries tax away a third or so of national income to finance their activities. Many important taxes have serious distorting effects on the economy. Thus a possible government policy is to control pollution by an effluent fee and to lower other taxes to offset revenues from the fee. Then effluent-fee payments by firms would be instead of other taxes and there would be no net higher payments associated with the fee than with direct controls. Of course the particular residents who paid the effluent fee might not be the same as those whose other taxes were reduced, and that might be beneficial or harmful. Even if each firm and resident had other taxes, say, income taxes, reduced by amounts that left purchasing power unchanged because of introduction of the effluent fee, the fee would nevertheless have the desired effect. Firms would economize on material inputs and discharges since they would become relatively expensive compared with nonmaterial inputs. And households would economize on products whose production was polluting because they would become expensive relative to nonpolluting products. In fact, these relative price effects are the fundamental desirable characteristic of effluent fees. But the complete analysis cannot be presented until Chapter 4.

To test understanding of the analysis, the reader should carry it through with a third policy sometimes proposed to control pollution, an abatement subsidy. Under an abatement subsidy, the government makes a payment to the firm proportionate to the firm's reduction in discharges below the unconstrained equilibrium level r^0. For a given set of input and output prices, the marginal conditions are satisfied at the same input and output levels under a subsidy of p_r per unit of abatement as under an effluent fee of the same amount. But the total conditions show that profit is greater under the subsidy than under direct regulation, and therefore also greater than under the effluent fee. Therefore the subsidy induces expansion of the industry's output unless accompanied by increases in other taxes.

The model developed in this section is elementary. To be realistic it must be extended in several directions. First, firms use many material and nonmaterial inputs. Second, some inputs can be employed specifically to convert harmful materials into innocuous ones before discharge. Third, it is not always realistic to assume that firms start from long-run competitive equilibrium. Fourth, in some cases quite specific information is available about properties of production functions, and such information can be used to derive more precise results than those derived here.

Consumer Theory

The extension of the theory of consumer behavior to include discharges is analogous to the extension of production theory for the same purpose, just as the two theories are themselves closely parallel. Thus the presentation in this section can be more abbreviated than that in the last section.

The theory of consumer behavior assumes that consumers have preferences among bundles of commodities and services they might buy. A bundle is a set of specific amounts of each comodity or service. A utility function is a rule for attaching numbers to bundles so that, as between any pair of bundles, the preferred one is assigned a larger number. If the consumer is indifferent between two bundles, they are assigned the same utility number. In a world of certainty, a consumer need only rank bundles in order to make choices among them. Thus any set of utility numbers that ranks bundles in the same order as the consumer's preferences is as good as any other, and no significance attaches to the specific numbers chosen. For that reason, utility functions in this theory are said to be ordinal, in contrast to cardinal utility functions that are relevant in making choices in uncertain situations. If there are two commodities consumed in amounts y_1 and y_2, a consumer's utility function can be written

$$u = u(y_1, y_2) \tag{3.8}$$

As with the theory of the firm, equation (3.8) is easy to generalize to an arbitrarily large number of commodities.

An indifference map is a diagram of contours, or indifference curves, of a utility function. Each indifference curve consists of the set of bundles that have a given rank in the consumer's preferences, and all such bundles are therefore assigned a single number by the utility function. Although each consumer may have a unique or even eccentric set of preferences, the theory assumes that all preferences have certain properties that ensure rational or consistent market behavior. These properties, discussed in price-theory texts, ensure that indifference curves slope downward and that exactly one indifference curve passes through each bundle or point on the indifference map. Less fundamental, but common, is the assumption that the consumer's preferences display diminishing marginal rates of substitution between pairs of commodities, which ensures that indifference curves are convex.

Consumers face a materials balance similar to that faced by firms. Materials purchased by the household in the form of consumer goods are either added to the household's physical assets or leave the household in some way. Some, such as used cars and pianos, are sold or given to others for further use, possibly after processing. The remainder are returned directly or indirectly to the environment. Direct returns include solid, waterborne, and airborne wastes. Examples are litter strewn on picnic grounds, drainage from a household septic tank, and the emissions from the household's chimney or automobile tail pipe. Indirect returns are solids and liquids. By far the most important examples are the trash put out for the local collection agency and the sewage pumped to the local treatment plant.

The simplest and most common situation is that in which the consumer buys products on the market and, after a delay, discharges all the materials contained in the products without additional charge or regulation. Most direct discharges are of this type. Indirect discharges are paid for by households, but normally by taxes instead of by charges closely related to volumes discharged. Thus, as a good approximation, most indirect discharges are free at the margin. In this situation, quantity consumed is identical to quantity discharged and it can be determined by the conventional diagram. Although production of services entails discharges of materials, consumption of services normally does not. Discharge decisions in connection with consumer services are mostly made by producers, not by consumers. Service production by doctors, lawyers, barbers, and teachers generates wastes, but they are mostly discharged by producers. Therefore waste discharges by consumers can be ignored. Of course, transportation to the doctor's office generates waste discharged by the consumer, but that is another matter.

Continuing with the two-good case, suppose the consumer has income I to spend and must choose purchase quantities y_1 and y_2 at fixed prices p_1 and p_2. Figure 3.7 shows the consumer's budget constraint and three indifference curves labeled by their utility numbers where $u^3 > u^2 > u^1$. Then a rational consumer buys the bundle preferred among those that cost no more than I. In the figure the bundle (y_1^0, y_2^0) is purchased. It satisfies the budget constraint and the equilibrium condition that the marginal rate of substitution or slope of an indifference curve equals the ratio of product prices or slope of the budget constraint. The budget constraint can be written

$$p_1 y_1 + p_2 y_2 = I \tag{3.9}$$

and the equilibrium condition

$$MRS(y_1, y_2) = -p_1/p_2 \tag{3.10}$$

where MRS is the slope of the indifference curve and the notation shows that it is a function of both y_1 and y_2. Equations (3.9) and (3.10) are two equations in the two unknowns y_1 and y_2. Their solutions

$$y_1 = g_1(p_1, p_2, I) \tag{3.11a}$$

and

$$y_2 = g_2(p_1, p_2, I) \tag{3.11b}$$

are the consumer's demand equations for the two commodities.

To be specific, suppose y_1 represents not only the quantity of commodity one bought but also the quantity of waste eventually discharged, whereas y_2 is a service that results in no discharge by the consumer.[7] Then y_1^0 in Figure 3.7 represents not only the quantity

---

7. As with the discussion of production theory, we assume a fixed relationship between number of units consumed and the poundage consumed. It is not, in other words, "number of hamburgers" but rather "number of quarter-pound hamburgers."

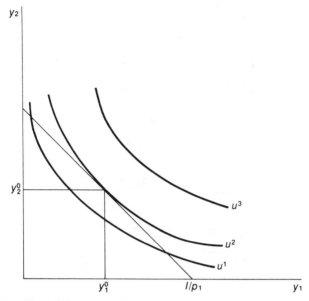

Figure 3.7

demanded, but also the quantity of waste discharged at the prices and income shown, and equation (3.11a) represents not only the product-demand equation but also the quantity discharged as a function of prices and income.

It is remarkable how few government restrictions there are on discharges from households. Of all the government regulations that have been imposed on discharges in recent years, almost none applies to households. Even the national auto-emission-control laws place most responsibility on producers and little on car-owners. Nuisance laws that prohibit litter have always applied to consumers as well as to firms. In recent years, open-burning laws have restricted outdoor leaf-burning in many communities. But these are about the only examples that can be found. Undoubtedly, an important reason for the paucity of discharge regulations on households is that households are so numerous that enforcement is difficult. But it is likely that another reason is that household members vote whereas business firms do not.

Nevertheless, it is easy to analyze how discharge controls, similar to those discussed in the previous section for firms, would work for households. The effect of direct regulation is shown in Figure 3.8.

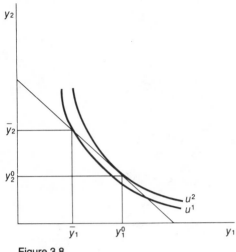

Figure 3.8

If the consumer initially buys the bundle (y_1^0, y_2) and the government imposes a maximum discharge $\bar{y}_1$ units of y_1, it would have no effect if $\bar{y}_1$ were at least as large as y_1^0. If, as shown in the figure, $\bar{y}_1 < y_1^0$, then the consumer would buy and discharge only the permitted amount and would buy the bundle $(\bar{y}_1, \bar{y}_2)$. This would, of course, put the consumer on a lower indifference curve, u^1 instead of u^2 in the figure, and he would not be at a point of tangency between an indifference curve and the budget line.[8]

The effect of an effluent fee is shown in Figure 3.9. Since purchases, consumption, and discharges of y_1 are all equal to each other, an effluent fee on discharges of commodity one is exactly like a tax on the purchase of the commodity. Thus the fee simply raises the price per unit of y_1 from p_1 to $p_1 + p_r$ where p_r is the effluent fee. Then, instead of equations (3.9) and (3.10), the consumer's equilibrium conditions become

$$(p_1 + p_r)y_1 + p_2 y_2 = I \tag{3.9a}$$

8. Actually, this is a partial analysis which ignores the benefits of the discharge controls. If the controls are socially desirable, it must be the case that utility goes up for the typical consumer—the marginal value of the environmental goods gained by the controls (not shown in Figure 3.8) would be greater than the costs in terms of forgone consumption value of the original bundle.

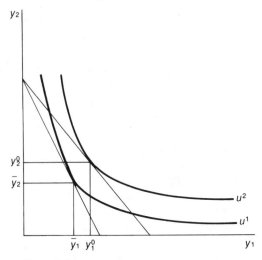

Figure 3.9

and

$$MRS(y_1, y_2) = -\frac{p_1 + p_r}{p_2} \qquad (3.10a)$$

and the consumer chooses the bundle $(\bar{y}_1, \bar{y}_2)$ in Figure 3.9. The reader can easily show that an effluent fee can be found that achieves any discharge volume achieved by direct regulation.[9]

As with the model of the firm presented in the last section, this model of consumer discharges is too simple to reflect important elements of reality. It is straightforward to introduce into the model an arbitrarily large number of commodities and services and alternative means of disposal, each with its peculiar environmental effects. It is then easy to show the effects on discharges of direct regulations and effluent fees. The formal analysis is left to the reader.

As an example, there are two frequently used methods of disposing of kitchen food wastes. One is to grind them in a disposal and wash them down the drain. Then they must be treated in the local

---

9. Notice also that there is an income effect analogous to the profit effect in the production theory. As in the former case, the revenue could be returned to the consumer in the form of a tax cut elsewhere; if the polluting good is normal, however, this will reduce the effectiveness of the fee in improving environmental quality.

sewage plant and the resulting sludge disposed of in some way. The other way is to place them in the trash can, in which case they are collected by the local trash collector and disposed of by returning them directly to the land in a dump or sanitary landfill. If the first disposal method is environmentally more damaging than the second, households can be induced to use the second by regulations or an effluent fee on the first. In this example, as in most realistic examples, the regulation or fee must be on the disposal method and not simply a regulation or fee on food purchases. Incidentally, this example illustrates that many wastes can be returned to the environment as liquids or solids depending on how they are handled.

As a second example, consider used automobiles. Some are abandoned in city streets, in streams, and in fields. But most are eventually recycled back into metals-processing industries. Suppose the government wanted to increase the number recycled. How would you design a regulation or fee for the purpose? Taxes on new cars do not affect owners' incentives to dispose of them in desirable ways. The obvious government policy is a tax or regulation on the return of old cars to the environment. The danger is that, if disposing of old cars in dumps, fields, and streams is taxed or regulated, then people may dispose of them surreptitiously to avoid the tax or regulation. Since it is harder to produce new cars surreptitiously than to dispose of old cars surreptitiously, some people have proposed a tax on new cars that would be refunded in whole or in part to anyone who recycled the materials or who disposed of the hulk properly. The availability of the refund would deter surreptitious disposal. Do you think this would be workable? To whom would the refund be given? Is there an analogous regulatory scheme?

These two examples, and many others that could be presented, illustrate that there are many economic incentives and regulatory programs that can be proposed to solve an environmental problem. There is a strong tendency in government to accept proposals which sound plausible without careful comparison with a wide range of alternative proposals and without careful consideration of administrative feasibility and costs.

Indirect Discharges

At the beginning of the chapter, the distinction was made between direct discharges to the environment and indirect discharges made to an agency that may process materials before discharging them to the environment. Until now, firm and household discharges have been analyzed in the absence of government restrictions and under government regulations or effluent fees, but without paying much attention to whether the discharges were direct or indirect.

If indirect dischargers were profit-making firms, their analysis would be covered by the models in the section on firms' discharges. Indeed, some indirect dischargers are commercial firms. Private collection and disposal of refuse from homes, commercial establishments, and factories is a large and growing business. Sometimes commercial refuse firms contract with a local government for the work in the jurisdiction, but sometimes they contract directly with households and businesses, usually under regulations laid out by state or local governments. Of course, a household or business has no incentive to pay an indirect discharger to collect and dispose of its waste unless there are regulations or fees that limit direct discharges. It is perfectly possible that most wastes might be discharged by commercial indirect dischargers established for the purpose. Undoubtedly, the main reason for the recent rapid growth of such firms has been increasingly stringent controls on direct discharges. If we had a comprehensive set of regulations or fees on direct discharges, it is possible that a variety of specialized waste-processing and disposal firms would arise. They would accept materials for a fee, process and recycle them, or discharge them to the environment under the applicable regulations or fees.

However, the vast bulk of indirect discharges is made through government agencies instead of through private firms. Most are agencies of local governments and have responsibility for collection and disposal of refuse and sewage from households, businesses, and other organizations. Mostly they are financed by appropriations from local governments. Some sewage collection and treatment agencies are financed at least in part by water charges, but it is rare that they charge fees that depend on the quantity and strength of sewage. Such agencies have a wide range of technical options as to the kinds and amounts of wastes they collect, the ways they process or treat wastes, and the means of disposal. Yet they have no shareholders and are not motivated by profit. Thus it is important to ask what theoretical model can be used to analyze their activities. Realistic comments about the operations of such agencies will be made in the empirical chapters concerned with the residuals they are responsible for. Here the concern is with an abstract model of their behavior. Unfortunately, social scientists have undertaken little theoretical or empirical research on such models.[10] But the purposes of this chapter require only a few basic ideas which are readily acceptable.

The tradition among economists is to assume that government agencies are motivated to maximize a measure of social welfare. In fact, each government organization has its structure, clientele, and resulting incentives. Just as profit maximization by private firms may or may not lead to social welfare maximization, depending on market characteristics, so a political system may or may not lead government agencies to maximize social welfare. In both cases, the issues must be studied on their merits. The obvious substitute for profit maximization is the assumption that in a democracy, public agencies act to further the interests of the electorate to which they are responsible. There are of course as many exceptions to this rule as there are to the assumption that firms maximize profits, but its implications are plausible in the concerns of this chapter.

If a community is located along a river into which it discharges its sewage and in which many of its electorate like to swim, fish, and boat, it can vote to tax itself enough to build a high-quality sewage-treatment plant to protect the river from pollution. Likewise, if a town disposes of its garbage in an open dump and becomes tired of the ugliness and vermin, it can vote to tax itself to build a sanitary landfill or a modern incinerator in which to dispose of its refuse. These decisions are made frequently in communities everywhere and the assumption that they reflect the interests of the electorate is not implausible.

These examples suggest that the behavior of indirect dischargers can be analyzed with a model analogous to the theory of consumer behavior. To pursue this idea, think of the community as having a set of preferences similar to those of an individual consumer. To be specific, simplify the sewage example by supposing that residents' preferences are between a commodity, called goods or G for short, and water-based recreation, called joy or J for short. Figure 3.10 shows some indifference curves of the community between J and G. If the community spends all its money on G it cannot build a treatment plant and much of G will be dumped into the river, polluting

10. See the paper by Haefele in Kneese and Bower, *Environmental Quality Analysis*, for a survey of such research.

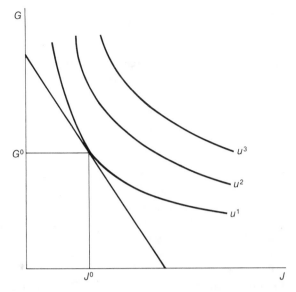

Figure 3.10

it and preventing the community from having any J. If it spends only part of its money on G, it can spend the rest on the treatment of its sewage, leaving the river clean enough to have some J. The more money it spends on treatment, the cleaner the river will be and the more J can be consumed. This constraint on the use of the community's funds is represented by the straight-line budget constraint in Figure 3.10. The slope of the budget constraint is the ratio of the price of G to that of J. The price of J is the cost of enough more treatment to improve the quality of the water so residents can have another unit of J. Then, of course, a rational community chooses to consume J^0 units of J and G^0 units of G.

This model should not be taken too seriously. There are no natural units in which to measure recreational activity. More important, communities do not have preferences, only individuals do. Thus the indifference curves must represent an average of residents' preferences. The appropriate average depends on the nature of the political process. And the model says nothing about the resolution of conflicts between, for example, swimmers and nonswimmers. But communities must make choices of the kind represented in the model. And most of the model's qualitiative implications are plausible. For example, it implies that if both *J* and *G* are superior goods, the community will buy more of each as average income rises. In addition, the same assumption implies that the community will buy more *J* if its price falls, for example because treatment plants become cheaper. The model can also be used to make qualitative predictions about the community's response to regulations or effluent fees imposed on its discharges by higher levels of government.

Perhaps the most important implication of the assumption that local governments represent the interests of their electorates is that the community is unconcerned about damage its activities may do to nonresidents. Modify the sewage example by assuming that residents can swim upstream of their sewage outlet and that the flow is such that the discharge of raw sewage pollutes the beaches of only downstream communities. Then the model predicts that the community will not treat its wastes even if a small expenditure would result in a large increase in badly wanted recreation for downstream residents. Once again, the implication may not be literally true in that communities undoubtedly do sometimes incur costs for the benefit of nonresidents. But it helps to understand why basic air- and water-pollution-abatement policies are formulated by national instead of state and local governments.[11] And it helps to understand why international pollution-control programs are so hard to obtain agreement on, fund, and enforce.

Demand Functions and the Effect of Pollution on Welfare

This section presents the final steps in incorporating materials, discharges, and pollution into microeconomic theory.

Building on the notation introduced in the last three sections, it is now possible to state the materials balance in careful algebraic fashion. The variables that have been introduced have referred to individual firms and consumers or to totals in individual markets. They

11. In an ideal world, the pollution-control jurisdiction would correspond exactly to the extent of the externality. Just as the local jurisdiction is too small for externalities spilling across local boundaries, so also it is the case that federal or state jurisdictions can be *too large*. Uniform national standards, for example, prevent individuals from choosing various levels of goods *(G)* and environmental quality *(J)*, in much the same way that a uniform national standard for hamburgers would prevent individuals from consuming a smaller or larger (for example, double-patty cheese) amount of the controlled good.

now must be aggregated to obtain totals for the entire economy. For many purposes it is desirable to aggregate different materials separately. Here it will be assumed that only one material is involved. The operations can be generalized by simply introducing subscripts that distinguish materials and repeating the operations for each material.

In the section on the firm it was shown that equation (3.2) determines the firm's discharges depending on the technology used. Suppose now that m is used in many production processes and that varying amounts, including none and all, are incorporated in the products made. Then total material input, production, and discarges by all the firms satisfy the following identity:

$$M = Y + \Delta K + R_1 \qquad (3.12)$$

where $M = \Sigma m$, $Y = \Sigma y$, $R_1 = \Sigma r$, and $\Delta K = \Sigma \Delta k$, each summation being taken over all firms. M is total material input, Y equals material incorporated in consumer goods, ΔK is material incorporated in net new capital formation, and R_1 is discharges. The subscript 1 on R means it refers to the production sector. Capital letters refer to economy-wide totals, whereas lower-case letters continue to refer to individual firms and consumers. Equation (3.12) says that total material input of firms equals that incorporated in consumer goods plus that incorporated in capital goods plus that returned by firms to the environment. In equation (3.12), Y refers to material output of firms. Production of services is excluded. This is a more restrictive definition of y than that used in the section on firms, where it included services as well.

Consumer goods are sold to the household sector, which consumes the output and returns the materials to the environment or to firms for reuse:

$$Y = R_2 + M_2 \qquad (3.13)$$

where $R_2 = \Sigma r_2$ and $M_2 = \Sigma m_2$, the summations being taken over all consumers. The subscript 2 refers to the household sector and r_2 refers to a household's discharges. m_2, a symbol not used before, refers to materials returned by a household to firms for reuse in production.

Of course firms recycle their wastes as well as those of households. That could be introduced in the above identities, but they are restricted to transfers of materials between sectors in order to keep the notation simple. Thus, if a firm generates scrap metal which it collects and reuses, it is simply counted as metal incorporated in products in equation (3.12).

Two additional identities complete the accounts:

$$R = R_1 + R_2 \qquad (3.14)$$

and

$$M = M_1 + M_2 \qquad (3.15)$$

Equation (3.14) says that total discharges, R, are those from firms plus those from households. Equation (3.15) says that total material inputs of firms, M, equal those that firms extract from the environment, M_1, plus those reused from the household sector, M_2.

It is easy to see that equations (3.12) through (3.15) imply that withdrawals equal discharges plus capital accumulation, $M_1 = R + \Delta K$. This follows by starting with equation (3.14), substituting $M - Y - \Delta K$ for R_1 from equation (3.12), substituting $Y - M_2$ for R_2 from equation (3.13), canceling the terms in Y, and substituting M_1 for $M - M_2$ from equation (3.15). This is an algebraic statement of the fact, discussed in Chapter 1, that economic activity transforms materials but neither creates nor destroys them.

It was stated in Chapter 1 that almost all discharges have more or less adverse effects on the environment, and that discharges to air and water almost always have serious adverse effects. The nature and severity of such effects depend greatly on the time, form, and place of discharges, and the effects of many discharges are poorly understood. In our simple one-material model, such effects can be represented by the equation

$$E = D(R) \qquad (3.16)$$

where E is an index of environmental quality and R, as before, is total discharges. The function $D(R)$ is the physical dispersion function, which converts emissions into environmental quality, the latter being what damages people when it is worsened by human activity. As with the other models introduced in this chapter, equation (3.16) is meant to place environmental problems within a broad and consistent framework, but not to be correct in detail. A first step in making equation (3.16) more accurate would be to disaggregate R by kinds of materials, such as organic wastes, metals, and the like. A second step would be to disaggregate E by the dimensions of air, water, and land destinations of discharges. A final disaggregation of the dispersion function would be to distinguish discharges by the time interval during which they have deleterious effects. Carbon monoxide discharged to the urban air by cars mostly disappears in a few hours. Organic wastes take several days to decay in aerobic streams. DDT may remain one or two decades in the ambient environment. Some radioactive wastes release deadly materials for centuries. Mercury discharged to a stream by a chemical plant remains there permanently unless removed, since it is an element. The point of these examples is that physical, chemical, and biological processes occur in the natural environment and most such processes gradually reduce the harmfulness to people of their material discharges.

The reader should rewrite the dispersion function, equation (3.16), to take account of some of the complexities just indicated.

The final step is to rewrite the utility function, equation (3.8), to indicate that people have preferences among environmental qualities as well as among bundles of commodities and services. The simplest such utility function can be written

$$u = u(y, E) \tag{3.8a}$$

In equation (3.8a) it is assumed that there are only one good and one dimension of environmental quality. The important property of equation (3.8a), and the key to understanding the economic problem of environmental quality, is the appearance of the lower-case variable for the produced good y and the captial letter for environmental quality E. This reflects the assumption that the important effect of goods and services on a person's welfare comes through the amounts he or she consumes, not through amounts consumed by others, whereas the quality of the environment that affects each person's preferences or welfare is the result of discharges by many people and firms. Furthermore, a given environmental quality E is shared by many people—the public-good feature discussed in the last chpater.

As with theoretical relationships introduced previously, equation (3.8a) is too aggregated to be realistic. Not only should E be disaggregated by its important dimensions, but also the environmental quality of a given person is affected mostly by discharges in his city or region, not by those in the entire economy. Garbage dumped in San Diego Harbor has no effect on the quality of the water in Lake Michigan off Chicago. And automotive emissions in New Orleans have no effect on the air breathed in Boston. Some environmental problems are national or even global, but the vast majority are local and regional. The point of equation (3.8a) is that the effect of goods and services on a person's welfare depends on commodities and services the person chooses to purchase and consume, whereas the effect of environmental quality on a person's welfare depends on discharge decisions by many people, over most of whom an individual has no direct control.

Many people question whether consumers really have consistent preferences among bundles of commodities and services. The evidence is that they do not if faced with a large number of complex choices, but that the theory of consumer behavior provides a valuable framework for describing choices averaged over the many buyers in a market. Such doubts should be much greater concerning effects of environmental quality. Everybody knows whether he or she is bothered by litter on a picnic ground and may be able to state roughly how much it would be worth to picnic in a litter-free area. And people whose residences are downwind from a factory react rather consistently if its smoke bothers them. But few consumers know how much sulfur dioxide is in the air they breathe, how much harm it does them, or how much it would be worth to have the sulfur-dioxide level in the air reduced. The best scientific analysis of such issues leaves experts uncertain and divided. Intelligent consumers are at least as uncertain. The implication of this paragraph is neither that pollution should be ignored nor that no risks of any uncertain harm should be taken. Both are foolish attitudes. Nor is the implication that consumer attitudes toward pollution abatement should be ignored. The implication is that in the present state of knowledge almost any action must take some chance of being judged wrong in the light of subsequent evidence.

The positive theory of the economics of environmental quality is now complete. Most important, the theory presented in this chapter suggests that pollution is a government policy issue because markets are unable to establish salable property rights in environmental quality. Markets are able to allocate labor and TV sets efficiently because private parties are free to make the best transactions they can in their self-interest, and competition ensures that the terms reflect the important social costs and benefits of each transaction. But the social advantage of self-interest and competitive markets breaks down with environmental quality. Although environmental quality may have as much effect on people's welfare as their consumption of TV, they cannot bargain for environmental quality in competitive markets. The implication is that government regulation is desirable to improve resource allocation as it affects the environment. This issue is the subject of Chapter 4.

DISCUSSION QUESTIONS AND PROBLEMS

1. Opponents of effluent fees often claim that firms will "just pass them on to consumers and not abate discharges." What does the claim imply about the shape of the firm's isoquant map? Do you think it likely in practice?

2. Why are there indirect-discharge agencies for waterborne and solid wastes, but not for airborne wastes?

3. How would you rewrite the materials balance for a country to take account of imports and exports of materials?

4. Many city governments are running out of land for solid-waste disposal. A local government proposes to charge residents per pound of trash put out for collection in order to induce residents to recycle more materials. What would be the effects? Is it a good idea? If so, why is it not done?

5. Some people have proposed, as an alternative to direct regulation or effluent fees, that governments calculate optimum discharges, say to a river, and sell rights to discharge the optimum amount at whatever price the market will bear. Analyze this proposal as an alternative to other government programs.

6. The material presented in this chapter is very closely related to the discussion of the five steps toward improved environmental analysis given in the preceding chapter. It would be a good idea for the reader to return to the discussion in Chapter 2 at this point. In particular, what is the relation between Step 3 (specifying the benefits of control) and equation (3.8a)?

REFERENCES AND FURTHER READING

Baumol, William, and Oates, Wallace. *The Theory of Environmental Policy.* Englewood Cliffs, N.J.: Prentice-Hall, 1975.

Dorfman, Robert, and Dorfman, Nancy, eds. *Economics of the Environment.* 2d ed. New York: Norton, 1977.

Journal of Environmental Economics and Management. Published quarterly by Academic Press, this journal (edited by Ralph C. d'Arge and Allen V. Kneese) provides a forum for recent advances in the theory and practice of environmental policy.

Kneese, Allen; Ayres, Robert; and d'Arge, Ralph. *Economics and the Environment.* Baltimore: Johns Hopkins University Press, for Resources for the Future, Inc., 1970.

Kneese, Allen, and Bower, Blair. *Environmental Quality Analysis.* Baltimore: Johns Hopkins University Press, for Resources for the Future, Inc., 1972.

Mäler, Karl-Göran. *Environmental Economics.* Baltimore: Johns Hopkins University Press, for Resources for the Future, Inc., 1974.

Mansfield, Edwin. *Microeconomics: Theory and Applications.* 4th ed. New York: Norton, 1982.

Appendix

The purpose of this appendix is to prove that a discharge regulation leads to identical short-run profit-maximizing input and output levels as an effluent fee that results in the same discharge quantity.

First, consider direct regulation. The firm is told it can discharge no more than $\bar{r}$ units of materials. $\bar{r}$ must be binding, that is, less than profit-maximizing discharges in the absence of regulation. Then equation (3.2)in the text will be satisfied as

$$\bar{r} = m - y \tag{A.1}$$

Given the constraint in equation (A.1), the firm maximizes profit, equal to total revenue minus total cost. Form the Lagrangian expression

$$L = p_y f(m,x) - p_m m - p_x x - \lambda[\bar{r} - m + f(m,x)] \tag{A.2}$$

where y has been eliminated using the production function, equation (3.1).

The necessary conditions for constrainted profit maximization are

$$\frac{\partial L}{\partial m} = p_y f_m - p_m + \lambda(1 - f_m) = 0 \tag{A.2m}$$

and

$$\frac{\partial L}{\partial x} = p_y f_x - p_x - \lambda f_x = 0 \tag{A.2x}$$

where f_m and f_x are partial derivatives of equation (3.1) with respect to m and x, that is, the marginal products of m and x. Rearrange equations (A.2m) and (A.2x) so that terms in λ appear on the left sides. Then take the ratio of equation (A.2m) to equation (A.2x), resulting in

$$\frac{1 - f_m}{f_x} = \frac{p_m - p_y f_m}{p_y f_x - p_x}$$

Clearing of fractions and rearranging terms gives

$$p_y f_x + p_x f_m = p_x - p_m f_x \qquad (A.3)$$

Next, consider the effluent-fee policy. Under it, total profit is

$$\pi = p_y f(m,x) - p_m m - p_x x - p_r [m - f(m,x)]$$

The necessary conditions for profit maximization are

$$\frac{\partial \pi}{\partial m} = {}_y f_m - p_m - p_r + p_r f_m = 0 \qquad (A.4m)$$

and

$$\frac{\partial \pi}{\partial x} = p_y f_x - p_x + p_r f_x = 0 \qquad (A.4x)$$

which are the same as equations (3.6) and (3.7). Rearranging equations (A.4*m*) and (A.4*x*) to put terms containing p_r on the left-hand side, dividing equation (A.4*m*) by equation (A.4*x*), and again clearing of fractions leads to equation (A.3).

Thus both the direct-regulation and effluent-fee policies lead to the same relationship between input and output prices and marginal products. In addition to equation (3.3), equations (3.1) and (A.1) must be satisfied. By assumption, p_r is set so as to make $\bar{r}$ the same under the effluent-fee policy as under direct regulation. Therefore, the same three equations determine y, m, and x under both policies, and the solution is the same.

Chapter 4

Welfare Economics and Environmental Policy

Welfare economics is that branch of economic theory concerned with evaluation of the performance of the economic system. This chapter shows, more formally than Chapter 2, how welfare economics can be used to analyze government programs to protect the environment. Some basic assumptions and ideas of welfare economics are explained first. Then, in the next section, some key analytical results are derived.[1] The chapter then proceeds to show how polluting discharges can be incorporated into the framework of welfare economics and how the theory can be used to evaluate government pollution-control policies.

To evaluate the performance of the economic system, a yardstick with which to measure performance is needed. Such a yardstick is called a value judgment. The value judgment almost always used by economists is that an economic system's performance is to be judged by its ability to satisfy the needs and wants of people as they perceive them. People's needs and wants enter the analysis in two ways. First, and most analyzed, is the consumption of goods and services, given consumer income. As has been shown in Chapter 3, people

---

1. A more detailed development of the subject is found in good price-theory texts, such as Mansfield, *Microeconomics: Theory and Applications.*

have preferences among bundles of consumer goods and services. The utility function measures how well these preferences are satisfied for various combinations of goods and services. Second is the production of goods and services, which gives rise to consumer income.[2] People evaluate the desirability of jobs by how much they pay and by the conditions of work. All of us are willing to sacrifice some pay for better working conditions and vice versa. Although the effects of working conditions on people's welfare have received relatively little attention in formal welfare economics, they fit into the framework easily.

A key part of the value judgment is the notion that each individual's needs and wants are to be judged by the individual's perception of them. Almost everybody accepts this value judgment in principle although, like acceptance of the principle of free speech, it is often honored in the breach. Everyone makes at least some exceptions to the principle. Most people believe that children and mental defectives are poor judges of their best interests. Many people believe that government transfers to the poor must be constrained in various ways because the poor are unable to judge their needs and wants. Food stamps are a good example. Environmental quality is another example of a situation in which people may be unable to judge their best interests. It has already been suggested that many people have only crude perceptions of the effects of pollution on their health and property.

In fact, the notion that people cannot perceive correctly their needs and wants is almost never a good argument for governments to decide for them what people need and want. In the first place, although people make plenty of mistakes in pursuing their self-interest, there is no reason to believe governments make fewer mistakes on behalf of constituents. More important, whatever information governments may have that would enable them to estimate people's needs and wants better than the people can themselves, governments can give to people so they can use it to estimate their needs and wants. For example, it is not appropriate for governments to ban smoking or saccharin because people may underestimate the harm these activites may cause them. Instead of banning the products, governments can provide people with the evidence of harm and people can decide for

2. Recall the circular flow of economic activity from macroeconomic principles texts.

themselves whether to take the risk.[3]

Although the possibility that people may not percieve their self-interest is a poor reason for government intervention in private transactions, intervention may be justified on other grounds. There may be circumstances that governments can alter that prevent people from realizing their self-interest. In fact, the subject of this chapter is how pollution may result from a breakdown in the ability of people to further their self-interest by private transactions. The reason for the breakdown will be explored carefully in later sections. But it is not that people do not know what is good for them.

In summary, it will be said that the economic system better satisfies an individual's wants, or improves the individual's welfare (hence "welfare economics"), in situation A than in B if the allocation of resources in A places the individual on a higher indifference curve than in B. *Almost every change in government programs and policies makes some individuals better off and some worse off.* As discussed in Chapter 2, choices must inevitably be made in a world of limited resources relative to wants: such choices have costs and benefits to society which are never uniformly distributed. To make progress in evaluating the desirability or undesirability of such programs and policies, economists distinguish between the social efficiency and the equity of the economic system. An allocation of resources is said to be *socially efficient* if no reallocation could improve the welfare of one or more people without making others worse off. Resource allocation is said to be *equitable* if income and wealth are fairly distributed among people. Although there is no unique socially efficient allocation of resources, the criterion for judging social efficiency is clear in principle and sometimes in practice. But people have a variety of standards as to what distribution of wealth or income is equitable. And people differ in the extent to which they believe governments should intervene to alter income distribution.

As discussed in Chapter 2, income distribution is a public good and disagreement about appropriate levels of such goods is persistent (even at the "right" amounts). These are important and divisive issues, but their importance can be overestimated. Most Americans believe that extreme inequality is undesirable and that government should

3. For an interesting and readable discussion of the saccharin issue, which contains insights into a much broader range of regulatory programs, see William R. Havender, "Ruminations on a Rat: Saccharin and Human Risk," *Regulation*, March-April 1979: 17–24.

reduce the inequality of incomes that results from unequal earnings, savings, and inheritances. In fact, little will be said in this book about equity beyond the discussion in Chapter 2, which suggested that environmental control is on net regressive. In part, the reason is that pollution-control policies are unlikely to have substantial effects on income distribution. In part, however, the reason is that pollution-control policies are a poor means of redistributing income and the adverse equity effects they might have can be offset by tax and other policies designed for the purpose, provided the political will is there.

The term *socially efficient resource allocation* is to be contrasted with *privately efficient resource allocation*. A firm is privately efficient if it produces so as to minimize costs or maximize profit. A consumer is privately efficient if utility is maximized given the market conditions faced by the consumer. The issue of social efficiency concerns conditions under which markets are such that privately efficient maximizing behavior leads to a socially efficient use of resources.

Simple Analytical Models of Welfare Economics

The most important ideas in welfare economics can be presented in simple models. Some of these ideas will be presented in this section, ignoring polluting discharges and their effects on people. The complications resulting from pollution will be introduced in subsequent sections.

Start with the simplest model in which a problem of socially efficient resource allocation can arise, the pure consumption model. The model is based on the theory of consumer behavior outlined in Chapter 3. Like the theory of consumer behavior, the model presented here can easily be generalized to many commodities and people, yet the basic insights can be obtained in the two-commodity, two-person case.[4] Suppose that fixed total amounts Y_1 and Y_2 of commodities one and two are available and must be allocated between two consumers, A and B. Suppose each individual has a set of indifference curves showing the individual's preference among bundles of the two commodities. The allocation problem can be shown in Figure 4.1. The length of the horizontal sides of the rectangle represents

---

4. Actually the two-person case is *more* complicated than the many-person case, since issues of bargaining are more important in the two-person case, while with many people competition results in simpler price-taking behavior.

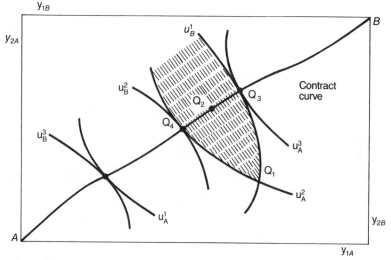

Figure 4.1

the quantity of Y_1 and the vertical sides represent the quantity of Y_2. Lower-case letters indicate amounts of the two commodities consumed by the two individuals.

Notice that $y_{1A} + y_{1B} = Y_1$ and $y_{2A} + y_{2B} = Y_2$, hence any point in, or on, the box in Figure 4.1 represents an allocation of the goods among A and B. The origin for A's consumption is at the lower left corner of the rectangle in Figure 4.1, designated A. B's origin is at the upper right corner, designated B. A's consumption of commodities one and two increases with horizontal and vertical movements away from A's origin. B's consumption increases with similar movements away from B's origin. Thus y_{1B} increases with left movement along the top horizontal side and y_{2B} movement down the right side. A few indifference curves are shown for each of the consumers. A's have their origin in the lower left corner, so A is made better off by movements upward and to the right, whereas B's have their origin in the upper right corner, so B is made better off by movements downward and to the left. In each case, higher-numbered indifference curves represent greater welfare.

Finding a socially efficient allocation of Y_1 and Y_2 between A and B is equivalent to finding a point in the diagram such that no other point lies on a higher indifference curve of one individual without lying on a lower indifference curve for the other. Viewed this way, it is clear that efficiency is desirable: it would be irrational to be unwilling to move from a point such as Q_1 to Q_2 in Figure 4.1. Both individuals are better off at Q_2, although A would prefer Q_3 still more, while B would strongly prefer Q_4.[5] Reflection reveals that all points (such as Q_2, Q_3, and Q_4) at which one of A's indifference curves is tangent to one of B's are socially efficient allocations, provided that the indifference curves have the usual shape and that such tangencies exist. Starting at an allocation such as Q_1, not a point of tangency, it is possible to make at least one person better off, leaving the other no worse off, by any reallocation into the shaded lens-shaped area between the two indifference curves passing through Q_1. Reallocation can continue, each time making one or both people better off and neither worse off, provided the starting point is not a point of tangency between two indifference curves. It follows that the complete set of socially efficient allocations is the set of points on the line connecting the points of tangency. The set of socially efficient points is sometimes called a contract curve.[6] Points of tangency satisfy the equation

$$MRS_A(y_{1A}, y_{2A}) = MRS_B(y_{1B}, y_{2B}) \qquad (4.1)$$

which simply says that A's and B's indifference curves have the same slope at the point in question.

The social-efficiency criterion narrows the allocation problem from the set of all points in the rectangle to the set of points on the contract curve. Further progress in narrowing the choice among allocations requires an equity criterion. It is hardly possible that all points on the contract curve would be considered equitable since A gets all of both commodities at one end and B gets all of both at the other. Toward the center of the contract curve A's and B's living standards are more nearly equal. Which point on the curve is chosen depends on the equity criterion used.

5. Note that some individuals would argue that if the gains from trade (moving from Q_1 to any of Q_2, Q_3, or Q_4) are distributed very unevenly (as at Q_3 or Q_4), such "exploitation" is unfair. This equity position suggests that the appropriate outcome, among efficient outcomes, may be greatly limited by equity considerations.

6. Kenneth Boulding refers to the efficient points as a "conflict" curve, since any effort by A to improve his or her relative position, once on the curve, will make B worse off, hence will lead to conflict. Another way to put the matter is that voluntary exchanges will get society on the contract curve—further exchange is likely to be involuntary!

Until now, nothing has been said about institutions that might allocate the two commodities. The discussion has been entirely in terms of the characteristics of the resulting allocation. Of course, with only two people and two commodities, no institutions to allocate resources are needed or even possible. Strength, cunning, and other traits affecting relative bargaining power will determine where on the contract curve one will end up. But interest in the problem looks toward generalization to many people and many commodities. One institution that could solve the allocation problem would be a government agency that knew the amounts of goods available, the two utility functions, and the equity criterion to be used. Then it could compute the set of efficient allocations and the subset of efficient allocations thought to be equitable. Of course no government agency has or could obtain the required information when the numbers of people and commodities are large. Suppose, instead, that the goods are sold to consumers by profit-maximizing firms at prices that are the same to each buyer and do not depend on quantities bought. Then, as was seen in the last chapter, each consumer buys quantities of goods that equate his or her *MRS* to the ratio of product prices p_1 and p_2:

$$MRS_A(y_{1A}, y_{2A}) = -\frac{p_1}{p_2} = MRS_B(y_{1B}, y_{2B}) \qquad (4.2)$$

Since each person buys quantities that equate his or her *MRS* to the same product price ratio, the *MRS*s are equated to each other and the allocation satisfies equation (4.1) and is socially efficient. Equilibrium competitive prices certainly produce a socially efficient allocation, but the only requirements for social efficiency in this simple market are that prices clear the markets and that each consumer pays the same price for a given commodity. If the price is not a market-clearing equilibrium price, total quantities demanded and supplied will not equal the quantities in existence; price will have to change (perhaps after some trades have occurred). Competitive markets are not, however, necessary. Although the model is extremely simple, it is remarkable that social efficiency can be achieved even though suppliers neither know nor care about consumers' welfare or anything but their profits, each consumer cares only about his welfare, and the consumers' preferences may be quite different from each other.

There is of course no guarantee that the socially efficient allocation the market provides will also be equitable. Which point on the contract curve results from market transactions depends on the distribution of income or purchasing power. In fact, it is possible to find a purchasing power distribution that results in each socially efficient allocation, and they cannot all be equitable.

The model can now be enriched by adding a production side to it. Suppose each of the two commodities is produced with a production function like equation (3.1) in which there are two inputs. To continue the notation previously developed, write the production functions

$$Y_1 = f_1(x_1, m_1) \text{ and } Y_2 = f_2(x_2, m_2) \qquad (4.3)$$

where Y_1 and Y_2 are amounts of goods one and two produced using the indicated input quantities of x and m. Suppose further that fixed total input quantities X and M are available to be allocated to the production of commodities one and two. Then the problem of allocating X and M to the production of commodities one and two can be solved with the diagram shown in Figure 4.2, which is analogous to Figure 4.1. The dimensions of the rectangle in Figure 4.2 are total input quantities X and M and the interior shows isoquants of the production functions, equation (4.3). The origin for the production of commodity one is the lower left corner and that for the production of commodity two in the upper right corner.

Social efficiency requires an allocation of X and M between pro-

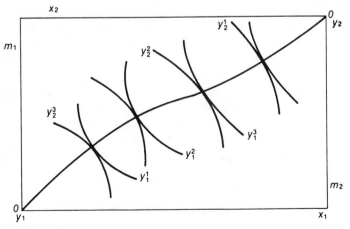

Figure 4.2

duction of commodities one and two such that no reallocation would permit an increase in the output of one commodity without decreasing the output of the other. If such a reallocation were possible, at least one person's consumption of one of the commodities could be increased without decreasing the amount of either commodity consumed by either person. If that were possible, the original allocation could not have been socially efficient. An argument analogous to that used in the pure consumption model shows that the set of socially efficient allocations of X and M consists of the set of points of tangency between isoquants of the two production functions. Starting at an allocation that is not a point of tangency, any movement between the isoquants passing through the point permits an increase in the production of one or both commodities with no decrease in either. Only when the allocation is at a point of tangency between an isoquant for each firm is no such movement possible. As in Figure 4.1, the tangency points have been connected by a smooth line in Figure 4.2, and it also will be referred to as a contract curve. Since the slope of an isoquant is the ratio of the marginal products of the two inputs, the social-efficiency condition just derived can be written

$$\frac{MP_{m1}}{MP_{x1}} = \frac{MP_{m2}}{MP_{x2}} \tag{4.4}$$

As with equation (4.1), equation (4.4) specifies the condition for social efficiency entirely in resource uses and without reference to the institutions using them. In the consumption model it was shown that the allocation of the commodities would be socially efficient if they were sold to consumers at market-clearing, nondiscriminatory prices. A similar result can be demonstrated on the production side. Specifically, suppose that the two commodities are produced by firms that do not affect either input or output prices by their individual decisions (that is, like competitive consumers, firms are price-takers). Then, as was indicated in the last chapter, each firm maximizes profit by using input quantities that equate the value of the marginal product of each input to its price or wage:

$$MP_{m1}p_1 = p_m, \; MP_{x1}p_1 = p_x \tag{4.5}$$

for a commodity-one producer, and

$$MP_{m2}p_2 = p_m, \; MP_{x2}p_2 = p_x \tag{4.6}$$

for a commodity-two producer.

The final step is to show that equations (4.5) and (4.6) imply equation (4.4), that is, resource allocation by competitive profit-maximizing firms is socially efficient. Divide the first equation by the second in equation (4.5) and in equation (4.6). The result is

$$\frac{MP_{m1}}{MP_{x1}} = \frac{p_m}{p_x} = \frac{MP_{m2}}{MP_{x2}} \tag{4.7}$$

Thus a commodity-one producer and a commodity-two producer equate the ratios of the marginal products to the same input-price ratio and hence the ratios of marginal products are equated to each other, so the resource allocation satisfies equation (4.4).

The model now encompasses the allocation of both inputs and outputs. Social efficiency requires output and input allocations that satisfy both equations (4.1) and (4.4). And it has been shown that market allocation at equilibrium prices faced in common by all consumers provides a socially efficient allocation.

The implications of equations (4.5) and (4.6) can be stated another way. In equation (4.5) divide the first equation by MP_{m1} and the second by MP_{x1}. The result is

$$\frac{p_m}{MP_{m1}} = p_1 = \frac{p_x}{MP_{x1}} \tag{4.8}$$

Equation (4.8) can be interpreted as follows: Suppose the commodity-one producer decides to increase output by a one-unit increase in input m_1. The denominator MP_{m1} gives the additional output that results, and the numerator p_m gives the additional expenditure on the input. The ratio is increased input cost per unit of increased output, or marginal cost. For example, if an additional worker receives a wage of $100 per week and produces 20 additional units of output, then the increased cost per unit of additional output is $100/20 = 5$, or a marginal cost of $5 per unit of output. The second equality in equation (4.8) says that to maximize profit, the firm should employ input quantities such that the marginal cost of increased output is the same regardless of which input it increases by a small amount. Equation (4.6) has the same implication for commodity two. *Marginal cost equals price is a necessary condition for profit maximization by a competitive firm, but it is also an implication of the conditions for socially efficient production.* The intuition is that the *quest* for profit causes firms to produce what people want and produce it as cheaply as possible. In long-run equilibrium, there are in fact no profits: short-run profit possibilities encourage resources to be reallocated in such a way as to achieve socially efficient production.

The model is far from complete, but it is now sufficiently complex to convey the flavor of modern welfare economics. Instead of further complicating the model, the technical analysis will stop here and the remainder of this section will concentrate on interpretations and verbal statements of additional results.[7]

None of the above results depends on there being only two consumers, two commodities, two inputs, or two firms. All the results carry over easily to arbitrary numbers of people, commodities, inputs, and firms. For example, if there are many consumers and many commodities, then social efficiency requires that an equation like (4.1) holds for each pair of consumers and each pair of commodities. And the argument that led to equation (4.2) shows that equilibrium single-price markets provide an efficient allocation of all commodities to all consumers. Likewise, if there are many inputs and outputs, social efficiency requires equations like (4.4) for each pair of inputs and outputs. And the argument that led to equation (4.7) shows that competitive markets allocate all inputs efficiently.

The arguments that led to equations (4.2) and (4.7) show that competitive markets provide a socially efficient allocation of resources, but they do not show that competitive markets are the only means of socially efficient resource allocation. In fact, in the model presented, both monopolies and competitive firms provide a socially efficient resource allocation. If the commodity-one producer were a monopolist, marginal revenue would replace product price in condition (4.5) for profit maximization. The reader should be able to show that the resulting resource allocation nevertheless satisfies equation (4.4) and is therefore socially efficient. However, if the model is extended to include variable input supplies, it can be shown that the only market allocation that is efficient is that of competitive markets. Monopoly prices are too high relative to those in competitive markets and place the economic system off the contract curve. There may, of course, be nonmarket allocations that are efficient.

The discussion has included only the marginal conditions for market equilibrium. It was seen in the last chapter that the total condi-

---

7. The reader is referred to Dorfman and Dorfman, *Economics of the Environment*, and Mansfield, *Microeconomics: Theory and Applications*, for further technical analysis.

tion of zero long-run competitive equilibrium profits is also important. In the present context, the total condition can shed light on technical conditions required for social efficiency of markets. The important result is that if one of the production functions in equation (4.3) has increasing returns to scale at each output level, then no set of input and output quantities and prices can satisfy the marginal productivity conditions (4.5) or (4.6) and also the zero-profit condition. Increasing returns means that average cost falls as output increases at fixed input prices. If average cost decreases, marginal cost is less than average cost and price equals marginal cost implies a price less than average cost. Therefore the firm makes losses. A firm with increasing returns is called a natural monopoly. If there is a natural monopoly, total cost is least if the entire industry's output is produced by a single firm. Natural monopolies must be subsidized if they are to satisfy the social-efficiency conditions.

An enlarged model could shed further light on the equity issue. In a model with variable input supplies, the condition for an efficient labor supply is that each worker's marginal rate of substitution between goods and leisure equal his marginal product. In such a model, competitive markets elicit a socially efficient labor supply and generate a corresponding socially efficient distribution of earned income, which depends on tastes for goods and leisure, skills, product demands, and so forth. Competitive markets also induce workers to supply labor so that the best combination of working conditions and pay is achieved. A similar model generates socially efficient supplies of property inputs. The corresponding socially efficient property income distribution depends on the productivity of capital and on savings and inheritance patterns. A complete set of competitive markets generates a socially efficient income distribution, but it may involve great inequality and may not be equitable. If so, the task of public policy is to find and reach an equitable income distribution that is nevertheless socially efficient. It should achieve this goal by seeking redistributive programs that do not impair social efficiency of markets.

External Diseconomies and Environmental Quality

Pollution is probably the most widely studied source of economic inefficiency. It is certainly the most widely discussed external diseconomy, having motivated much of the theoretical research on the subject of externalities for more than half a century.

The terms *external economy* and *diseconomy*, already introduced in Chapter 2, refer to economic activities that affect people's welfare in ways that are outside or external to the market system. Suppose a refinery produces gasoline and emits wastes that pollute the air in a downwind residential neighborhood. Suppose the refinery buys its inputs and sells its gasoline in competitive markets. Then the results in the previous section show that its output level just balances the value to consumers of extra gasoline against the value of other products that could be produced with inputs freed by a reduction in gasoline production. In other words, the last gallon of gasoline production is just worth the other products forgone in order to produce it. But an additional gallon of gasoline production entails additional discharges and thus additional damages to downwind residents. The pollution damage is a social cost of gasoline production that does not show up in the accounts of the refinery owners. Make the usual assumption that the refinery owners maximize profits equal to revenues from gasoline sales minus expenditures on inputs used to produce the gasoline. Then the full marginal social cost of an additional gallon of gasoline production, including both the extra inputs purchased and the extra pollution damage, exceeds the value to consumers of the extra gasoline (recall Figure 2.2 in Chapter 2 and the discussion surrounding it). It would be possible to make some people better off without making others worse off by reducing gasoline production somewhat and using the inputs saved to produce nonpolluting products. In economists' jargon, it is said that an external diseconomy causes a competitive industry to overproduce gasoline, as concluded in Chapter 2. The term *external diseconomy* refers to the cost of gasoline production borne by downwind residents that is external to the firm's decision calculus. The firm is motivated to take account of the social cost of its other scarce inputs because it must pay competitive prices for them. But it has no incentive to take account of the costs its waste discharges impose on downwind residents. Thus the external diseconomy of gasoline production causes the refinery to violate the conditions for social efficiency.

This much has been well known for decades and has recently been subject only to relatively minor technical debate. But there is still deep disagreement and great uncertainty about the conditions that prevent certain costs or benefits from being brought into the market framework. Many economists formerly believed that externalities were mostly determined by technological conditions of production and, indeed, the term *technological externalities* was common. But largely as the result of the work of Ronald Coase,[8] it is now realized that the issue is much more complex than it seemed in the discussion of Chapter 2. The basic point is that, if the economy is off the contract curve, then there must be potential transactions that would make some people better off without making anyone worse off. This follows from the definition of the contract curve. But potential gainers have incentive to seek each other and to negotiate mutually advantageous transactions. Viewed in this light, the study of externalities becomes the study of the reasons that potentially advantageous transactions are not made. Whether a particular economic activity is the subject of agreement between two or more parties depends on whether mutually advantageous terms can be found and not merely on technological considerations.

Return to the refinery example. Suppose the downwind residents form a neghborhood association to try to solve their pollution problem. One possible strategy would be for the association to try to negotiate an agreement with the refinery which would limit the kinds, amounts, and times of emissions from the refinery. If the pollution is excessive, there must be some abatement that would be worth more to the residents than it would cost the refinery. In the next section ways to measure benefits of abatement will be discussed. For now, assume that after investigation and discussion it is concluded that a means of abatement costing $1,000 would provide benefits worth $1,500 to the residents. Then clearly a transaction can be found that will make everyone better off. Any payment by the association to the refinery between $1,000 and $1,500, in exchange for an agreement to abate discharges, must make at least some people better off without making any worse off.

An alternative strategy for the neighborhood association would be to threaten to sue the refinery for pollution damages if the refinery did not abate its emissions at its expense. Whether it could win such a suit would depend in part on the precise wording of laws or on judicial interpretation of common law.

The two strategies would probably not have precisely the same resource-allocation effects. They would have different effects on the refinery's profits and it was shown in the last section that that would affect its resource allocation. Likewise, the two strategies would have

8. See his paper reprinted in Dorfman and Dorfman, *Economics of the Environment*.

different effects on residents' incomes, which would affect their demands for goods and services, possibly including their demand for the refinery's gasoline. But the most important difference between the two strategies is one of equity. Under the assumptions made, both would get to the contract curve, but at different points. The second strategy would favor the residents, and the first the refinery's owners, customers, and employees. In this example, as in many, the content of the statute or common law affects equity rather than efficiency. It is now common to say that in this example the law determines the distribution of property rights. If it makes the success of a suit likely, it assigns property rights in clean air to residents, and the refinery can pollute the air only if it compensates residents. If the law makes the success of a suit unlikely, it assigns to the refinery property rights to discharge waste to the air and residents can stop the refinery from polluting the air only if they compensate it.

Why are all inefficiencies resulting from pollution not solved by these and other kinds of private negotiations? There seem to be three primary answers.[9]

First, there may be considerable ambiguity about the property rights in air quality, leading to a breakdown in private negotiations. If the firm has historically been able to pollute, it may feel that it has that right and will only give up that right if it is bribed to do so. If, on the other hand, consumers feel they have the right to breathe clean air, they will feel that the firm should compensate them for damages. Whoever has property rights in air quality is, of course, wealthier and the courts must make the judgment on that equity issue. The court system is, however, not costless; and there must exist enough basic contract and tort law and enforcement that the consumers and firms can deal with one another.[10]

Second, and more commonly noted, are numbers and transactions costs. Transactions costs refer to the costs of negotiating and execut-

9. In some circumstancs, the Coase theorem appears to have experimental validity, although the numbers of economic agents are small or informational assumptions are restrictive. See Elizabeth Hoffman and Matthew Spitzer, "The Coase Theorem: Some Experimental Tests," *Journal of Law and Economics* 25, no. 2 (April 1982): 73–98 and Yves Coffi Prudencio, "The Voluntary Approach to Externality Problems: An Experimental Test," *Journal of Environmental Economics and Management* 9, no. 3 (September, 1982): 213–28.

10. See David W. Carroll, "Two Games That Illustrate Some Problems Concerning Economic Aanlysis of Legal Problems," *S. Cal. L. Rev.* 53: 1371 (1980).

ing an exchange, excluding the cost of the commodity or service bought. The transactions costs of buying a car are the time and other costs of finding the car you want and of negotiating a purchase agreement. Transactions costs often depend greatly on the number of parties to a transaction, but normally not much on the amount of the transaction itself. Complicate the air-pollution example by supposing the relevant set of residents to be all the residents of a metropolitan area. They are affected, in varying amounts, by pollution from thousands of automobiles, thousands of residential chimneys, and dozens of factories, office buildings, and the like. It is easy to see that the transactions costs of contacting residents, estimating damages to each from each source, and conducting the appropriate negotiations or legal suits would be prohibitive since the transactions costs would exceed the net benefits of the resulting discharge abatement. For this reason, most pollution problems not resolved by private agreements involve large numbers of discharge sources and people damaged. A single firm that was the sole source of a polluting discharge affecting only a few people or firms would be a pollution problem in which private negotiation would be relatively easy, once the law had assigned property rights.

The third answer is that air quality is to a large extent a public good, a technical term that the reader will recall was described in Chapter 2 as a good or service that has two characteristics: its benefits can be enjoyed by additional people at no extra cost, once it has been produced; and it is costly or impossible to exclude people from its use or consumption if it has been produced. The classic example is national defense. Once it has been decided to produce a military establishment capable of defending most of the country from foreign attack, it probably costs no more to defend Mississippi as well. Furthermore, it might be costly to arrange the military system so that it excluded Mississippi. The border of Mississippi with other states is longer and more difficult to defend than is its border on the Gulf of Mexico. Much the same is true of pollution. If air pollutants pervade the atmosphere over a metropolitan area, it costs no more, and probably costs less, to clean the air over the entire metropolitan area than over a large part of it. Of course, pollutants are not completely pervasive over a substantial area either in air or water. But they are sufficiently pervasive that the pure public-good model provides important insight into the problem of private antipollution agreements.

Return again to the refinery example and suppose that the neighborhood association must raise money from residents to pay the refinery to abate its discharges or to pay legal fees for a suit. If there are many residents, each knows that his contribution will be a small part of the total and will therefore hardly affect the success of the association's efforts. But if the association is successful, he will benefit from the improved air whether or not he contributes, because it is not possible to clean others' air without cleaning his. Therefore, even though he stands to receive substantial benefits from the association's efforts, he has no incentive to admit to any interest in cleaner air or to agree to pay part of the association's costs. This motivation applies to all residents and all lack incentive to contribute to the association. Therefore the association cannot raise the needed money even though the resulting benefits would exceed the costs. This is the free-rider problem introduced in Chapter 2.

It is no answer to this argument to say that each person contributes because each knows that if all took a negative attitude the benefits would not be forthcoming. It is not the fact that person *A* fails to contribute that causes person *B* to fail to contribute. If *A* knew that his contribution would induce others to contribute, it would be worth his while to contribute. The reason that *B* does not contribute is that, like *A*, he knows that he will either get the cleaner air or not, pretty much regardless of whether he contributes. Therefore both have the same motivation to withhold contributions, but neither does so because the other does. Instead, both withhold contributions because both have similar motivations. Both behave rationally. Thus, because of both transactions costs and the public-good nature of pollution abatement, private agreements are unlikely to solve many pollution problems.

This conclusion leads to the obvious suggestion that governments must take responsibility for pollution-abatement programs. It is an easy jump from the premise that private actions cannot solve a problem to the conclusion that governments should solve it. The jump is sometimes unjustified because the reason private agreements do not solve a problem may be that no solution is possible or that all solutions entail costs that exceed the benefits of the solution. In the pollution-abatement case, the justification for government action must be that government can formulate and implement abatement programs more cheaply than can private organizations that depend on voluntary participation. Nobody knows exactly why or under what circumstances government public-good provision is more economical than private provision. But the case is probably stronger regarding pollution abatement than almost any other domestic program.

Benefits and Costs of Pollution Abatement

The conclusion of the last section was that private agreements are unlikely to be able to achieve social efficiency of resource allocation in protecting the environment. If government is to intervene to protect the environment, it must have a systematic method of measuring the effects of its intervention. It is possible, as the supply-and-demand analysis of Chapter 2 indicated, for government to do too little, too much, or merely the wrong things to protect the environment. Benefit-cost analysis is an important technique for measuring the effects of government programs on peoples' welfare.[11] It is an elaborate and highly developed subject. It has been used and abused by governments for many decades, and has been studied intensively by welfare economists since World War II. Many issues are still subjects of professional controversy; areas of disagreement will be indicated at the end of the section. But there is widespread agreement among academic economists on basic issues.

The basic idea of benefit-cost analysis is simple: it is an attempt to replicate for publicly-provided goods the desirable features of a perfectly functioning private market. It leads governments to choose programs that will improve the social efficiency of resource allocation. It suggests techniques for calculating the benefits and costs of proposed programs, and it makes clear that social efficiency cannot be increased by programs whose benefits are less than their costs. Among all programs that are alternatives to each other and whose benefits exceed their costs, the one should be chosen that has the greatest ratio of benefits to costs. The analysis will be developed here in the context of environmental improvement, but the techniques apply to any government program.

Suppose we start from a situation in which there is no government program to protect the environment. Discharges to the environment are determined by profit and utility maximization, as shown in Chapter 3. Suppose, using the notation introduced in Chapter 3, that the

11. The discussion in this chapter ignores alternatives, such as multi-criteria analysis, to benefit-cost analysis. See Chapter 2 for a brief discussion of these alternatives.

resulting environmental quality is a value E^0 of the environmental index E, say in a community. E might be the concentration of a pollutant in the air or water, or it might be a broad index of environmental quality. For the purposes of this section, it does not matter. Since environmental quality can be measured in any units, we can put $E^0 = 0$. This is simply a notational convenience; it does not imply that the environment could not be worse.

What are the benefits of improving environmental quality, that is, of government programs that will make $E > 0$? In Chapter 3 it was shown how demand equations for two commodities y_1 and y_2 could be derived from the budget constraint and the conditions for tangency between the budget constraint and an indifference curve for y_1 and y_2. Equation (3.9) is the budget constraint and equation (3.10) is the tangency condition. Equations (3.11a) and (3.11b) are the resulting demand equations. At the end of Chapter 3, in equation (3.8a), it was shown that environmental quality E can be included in the utility function. It has value to consumers, as do commodities sold on markets.

For a moment, suppose that E can be sold on a market. A unit of E can be bought at price p_E and each consumer decides how much to buy. Using the utility function, equation (3.8a), the two conditions for consumer utility maximization, analogous to equations (3.9) and (3.10), are

$$p_y y + p_E E = I \tag{4.9}$$

and

$$MRS(y,E) = -p_y/p_E \tag{4.10}$$

Analogously to equations (3.11a) and (3.11b), the demand equations for y and E are the solutions of equations (4.9) and (4.10) for y and E,

$$y = g_y(p_y, p_E, I) \tag{4.11}$$

and

$$E = g_E(p_y, p_E, I) \tag{4.12}$$

Equation (4.12) shows how much E the consumer demands, that is, how high quality an environment he is willing to buy, as a function of its price, and of course of the price of y and of the consumer's income I.

Next, remember that E is a public good, that is, that a given quantity of E is enjoyed by all members of the community (which is the reason it appears as a capital letter in the individual function). Then there is a demand equation like (4.12) for each consumer. These demand equations show the price each consumer is willing to pay for each value of E. At a given E, the prices vary among consumers because they have different incomes and different utility functions. But the prices can be added (vertically) together for all members of the community who benefit from an improved environment. The sum of the prices shows the total willingness of the community to pay for a cleaner environment. The addition can be undertaken for each value of E, yielding the curve shown in Figure 4.3. It is called a marginal benefit *MB)* curve because it shows, for each E, the amount of money community members are willing to pay for a slight increase in E, that is, for a small improvement in the environment.

The reader can test understanding of the *MB* curve by comparing it with an ordinary market demand curve as discussed less formally in Chapter 2. The market demand curve for a marketed commodity is the sum of amounts demanded by consumers at each price. Unlike

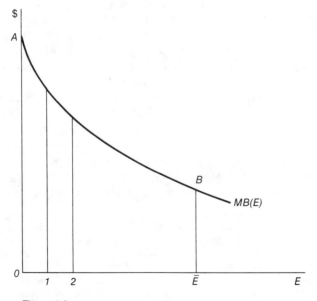

Figure 4.3

a marketed commodity, the environment is enjoyed in common by many people; in other words, it is a public good. Therefore, what is relevant is the total payment that beneficiaries are willing to make for an improvement in environmental quality. As argued in Chapter 2, the *MB* curve is thus a vertical sum of individual demand curves for environmental quality, whereas a market demand curve is a horizontal sum of individual demand curves for the marketable commodity.

The *MB* curve is the key to measuring benefits from government programs to improve the environment. Just as an ordinary demand curve measures the value to the consumer of an additional unit of the commodity, so the environmental demand curve, equation (4.12), from which the MB curve is calculated, measures the value to the consumer of an additional unit of environmental quality. *MB* measures the sum of values of additional units of environmental quality to all those who benefit from the improvement.[12]

Now suppose the government proposes a program to improve the environment from $E = 0$ to $E = \tilde{E}$. As with any commodity, the first unit of environmental improvement is worth more than subsequent units. The first unit is worth to consumers the area under the *MB* curve and to the left of the vertical line above $E = 1$. For a small improvement, the area is approximately the height of the curve times the size of the environmental improvement. Likewise, the second unit of improvement is worth the area under the *MB* curve and between the lines above $E = 1$ and $E = 2$. Continuing this reasoning, the conclusion is that the total benefit of a program that raises environmental quality from $E = 0$ to $E = \tilde{E}$ is the area under the *MB* curve and to the left of the line above $E = \tilde{E}$.

Suppose, for example, that E is a measure of air quality. Starting from an initial situation of low-quality air, the first units of improvement might cause substantial improvements in health by reducing the incidence and severity of emphysema, lung cancer, and so forth. This improvement would be worth a great deal to people. The next

12. The *MB* curve, as defined here, is an approximation which has engendered much controversy in the technical literature. The issue is beyond the scope and level of this book. The best evidence is that the approximation is nearly accurate in practical cases. A technical analysis is in Robert Willig, "Consumer's Surplus without Apology," *American Economic Review* 66 (September 1976): 589–97. For further clarification of the meaning (and non-meaning) of consumer surplus, see Ed Morey, "Confuser Surplus," *American Economic Review* 74, no. 1 (March 1984): 163–73.

improvements might improve the health of those who smoked a great deal. Those people apparently care less about their health than do others, so the second improvement is not worth as much. The third improvement might reduce cleaning and painting costs of buildings. Subsequent units of improvement might have aesthetic benefits in that they made the air clearer. Each subsequent improvement has smaller benefits than earlier improvements. In actuality each improvement in environmental quality has impacts on virtually all dimensions of human behavior: such improvements do not have the hierarchical nature suggested above, although the intuitive appeal of this notion accounts for its popularity.

The area under the *MB* curve is called consumers' surplus. More specifically, the area $0AB\bar{E}$ is the consumers' surplus of an improvement in environmental quality from 0 to $\bar{E}$. It is a measure of the benefit from pollution abatement in the precise sense that it is the maximum amount of money consumers would be willing to pay in order to obtain the improvement in the environment.[13]

Consumers' surplus is also defined for marketable commodities. It is the area under the usual market demand curve defined as the horizontal sum of individual demand curves. It measures, as with environmental quality, the maximum amount of money consumers would pay to avoid doing without a given quantity of the commodity.

Some students are shocked to know that economists use a measure of benefits from government programs that depends on the level and distribution of income. It should not surprise anyone to be told that high-income recipients are willing to pay more for a clean environment than low-income recipients. But some find it hard to accept the implication that it may be a bigger improvement in social efficiency to spend $100 to clean up the air in a rich than in a poor town.

One can feel either way about the substantive issue. The point to remember is that made in the introduction to the chapter, that benefit-cost analysis deals only with the social efficiency of resource allocation, not with equity. On efficiency grounds, the $100 should be spent where it will do the most good, and it may well be in the rich town. The rational reason for wanting it to be spent in the poor

13. It is *not* more than this. Specifically, even with cardinal utility functions, the dollar figure thus arrived at is nonunique: a linear (or affine) transformation of the utility function will affect the level of marginal utility, hence the area under it. However, dollar *rankings* of alternative projects will correspond to utility rankings, which is all that matters in choosing among alternatives.

town, contrary to the dictates of benefit-cost analysis, is that one wants to use the pollution-control program to alter the income distribution.

Now turn to the cost side, which is much easier to analyze. In order to maximize social efficiency, pollution-control programs must be carried out with the least-cost combination of inputs. The analysis of socially efficient production earlier in the chapter applies as well to public as to private goods. Suppose that, analogously to equation (3.1), there is a production function that shows environmental improvements that can be obtained by using inputs for the purpose,

$$E = f_E(x_E, m_E) \qquad (4.13)$$

Then social efficiency is obtained on the production side if the inputs x and m are sold in competitive markets and are used to produce a given E at minimum cost. For this, inputs must be combined to produce E so as to satisfy equation (4.7),

$$\frac{MP_{m_E}}{MP_{x_E}} = \frac{p_m}{p_x} \qquad (4.14)$$

where the *MPs* are the marginal products of inputs in equation (4.13), and the *ps* are the input prices.

Equations (4.13) and (4.14) show the input combination that minimizes the cost of producing each level of E. The sum of the resulting input quantities, each multiplied by its price, gives the total cost of producing each level of E in socially efficient fashion. The set of such total costs for all levels of E constitutes the total cost function $C(E)$.

The change in total cost resulting from a small change in E is marginal cost, designated *MC(E)*.

It is now possible to show how to find the environmental quality that maximizes social efficiency. Figure 4.4 shows the *MB* and *MC* curves for environmental quality. The socially efficient environmental quality is the value E^* of E that equates marginal beneifts to marginal cost,

$$MB(E^*) = MC(E^*) \qquad (4.15)$$

If E were less than E^*, an increase in E would increase benefits more than costs, and would therefore be worthwhile, as discussed less formally in Chapter 2. Similarly if E were greater than E^*, a decrease

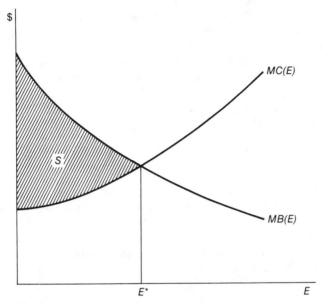

Figure 4.4

in E would decrease benefits less than costs, and would therefore be worthwhile.

Another way to state the same conclusion is to say that the socially efficient value of E is that which maximizes net surplus S, equal to the excess of benefits over costs. As has been shown, total benefit is the area under the MB curve. Likewise, total cost is the area under the MC curve. Thus S is the difference between the two areas, the shaded area in Figure 4.4. S is maximized at the E that equates MB to MC, just as a firm's profit is maximized at the output that equates its marginal revenue to its marginal cost.

It can now be seen more clearly than in Chapter 2 that there is a precise analogy between the equality of MB and MC for a public good and the equality of price and marginal cost in a competitive industry producing a marketable commodity. It was shown earlier in the chapter that $p = MC$ is the the condition for social efficiency for a marketable good in the absence of externalities. The usual industry demand curve is a marginal benefit curve for a marketable commodity. Government programs to equate MB and MC for public goods are analogous to private markets in which profit and utility maximization generate socially efficient resource allocation for marketable commodities. The difference is that there is no private market for a public good like environmental quality.

Until now E has been assumed continuously variable. Then the issue is how much government programs should provide. But many proposed government projects are discrete or lumpy. For example, there may be two possible sites for a bridge across a river, and the issue is which, if either, should be used. For each site, the surplus is

$$S = B - C \qquad (4.16)$$

where B is the total benefit of a bridge at the site and C its total cost. Neither bridge should be built if $S<0$, that is, $B<C$ or $B/C<1$ at both sites. If $B/C>1$ for at least one site, then the bridge should be built at the site at which B/C is larger. This is the benefit-cost test. To take an environmental example, two ways to clean up a river might be to treat wastes before they are discharged into it or to increase low flow in the river by building a dam and reservoir. The method should be chosen for which B/C is larger, provided $B/C>1$ for at least one method.

Expressed in terms of benefit-cost analysis, it is now easy to see, for discrete choices, that one can have too little or too much environmental quality, as argued in Chapter 2. Consider discrete policies which would result in, respectively, $E^* + \triangle E$ or $E^* - \triangle E$ in Figure 4.4. Both policies are worse than one yielding E^*, but a policy yielding E^* may not be available. It is clear, relative to area S, that either policy option will have fewer net benefits; but of more interest for present purposes is the observation that society may prefer over-control ($E^* + \triangle E$) or under control ($E^* - \triangle E$) or may indeed be indifferent (if the loss of benefits in excess of costs at $E^* - \triangle E$ is exactly equal to the excess of costs over benefits at $E^* + \triangle E$).

Another characteristic of many government projects is that some benefits result long after the project is undertaken. A bridge or dam may last fifty or one hundred years. Dumping sludge in the ocean may pollute the water years later. It is theoretically straightforward to extend benefit-cost analysis to include benefits and costs at different times. What is needed is a forecast of benefits and costs associated with the project during each year of its life. It is clear that $100 worth of net benefits *next* year is not worth $100 now. The reason is that some smaller amount can be invested now at the going interest rate to yield $100 next year (for example, $90.91 now will become worth $100 in one year at an interest rate of 10 percent). If the $100 return occurs two years from now it has a still lower current value (for example, $82.64 will cumulate to $100 in two years at a 10 percent interest rate). It is the *current* values (so-called "present values") of all future benefits and costs which are to be compared to examine the efficiency of a particular policy.

More formally, write $S_t = B_t - C_t$ for the net surplus from the project in the tth year of its life. Then $S_t/(1+p)^t$ is the present value of S_t dollars t years hence using a discount factor $1/(1+p)$, where p is the interest rate. The present value of future net surpluses from a project whose initial cost is K dollars, is V where

$$V = \sum_t \frac{S_t}{(1+\rho)^t} - K = B - K \tag{4.17}$$

where the sum is over all years of the project's life and B is the present value of future net surpluses. Among alternative projects, the one for which B/K is largest should be undertaken provided its V is positive.

This completes the basic statement of benefit-cost analysis. Except for some relatively minor technicalities, almost all of it is accepted by academic economists. It has been studied and perfected for half a century by some of the best minds among economists. Yet it remains controversial in application. One reason is recurring misunderstanding of its relationship to equity issues. But much of the controversy concerns estimation of appropriate numbers to use in the analysis. Sources of dispute can be discussed under two headings.

First is how to estimate *MB* curves. Demand curves, the analogue of marginal benefit curves for marketable commodities, can be estimated with more or less difficulty by econometric methods because markets provide price, quantity, and other data needed for the purpose. But the precise justification for government intervention regarding public goods is the absence of markets on which to register demand. Therefore other data must be used to estimate *MB* curves for public goods such as environmental quality. Some ingenious procedures have been derived to estimate *MB* curves, and they will be described in later chapters. But there is no single method that can be certified as appropriate to all problems.

The second issue is distortions in market data. Competitive equilibrium prices are appropriate market data to use in estimating costs because, as has been shown, they represent benefits foregone by using inputs for environmental improvement. But actual market prices differ from such opportunity-cost values for several reasons. The most commonly discussed distortion is from monopolies and oligopolies. Although noncompetitive pricing is important in some product and labor markets, the best evidence is that the resulting distortions are slight. The most serious distortion results from taxes levied by governments. For example, sales taxes prevent competitive prices from equaling marginal cost. Personal income taxes prevent workers from equating marginal utilities of leisure and of goods obtained by more work. High taxes on corporate profits distort corporate capital costs. Both inflation and high taxes on income from property distort market interest rates from levels that would measure the opportunity cost of using capital for pollution abatement. There has been much controversy about the correct interest rate to use in discounting surpluses from government investment projects.[14]

Alternative Pollution-Abatement Policies

In Chapter 3, preliminary analysis was presented of alternative pollution-control policies. Attention was focused on effluent fees and direct controls on discharges. In this section, the analysis can be carried further, using the concepts of welfare economics.

The first thing to show is that a set of appropriate effluent fees can induce discharges that result in a socially efficient use of resources to protect the environment. The demonstration is easy.[15]

Suppose the government has calculated the optimum value E^* of E from equation (4.15). Then, as shown in equation (3.16), an optimum total discharge R^* corresponds to the optimum environmental quality. Then the government must choose the optimum effluent fee, the value p_r^* of p_r in Chapter 3, that induces dischargers to discharge a total of R^* units. The result becomes plausible if one thinks of environmental damage as a cost of production, just like employing workers. If labor is competitively priced, each firm uses the quantity of labor that minimizes its total production cost, so labor is allocated

14. All these topics are discussed in greater detail in more advanced books, such as Mishan, *Cost-Benefit Analysis*.

15. This and other results presented in this section are proven rigorously in Baumol and Oates, *The Theory of Environmental Policy*.

efficiently among firms. In addition, total employment is such that workers balance the desire for more market goods against the desire for more leisure. Likewise, if environmental quality is appropriately priced, at a value p_r^* of p_r set by the government, firms minimize the total cost of pollution abatement in the process of profit maximization, since each equates the marginal cost of abatement to the same value p_r^* of p_r. Furthermore, the socially efficient discharge volume is achieved, since p_r^* was chosen (perhaps by "trial and error") to equate *MB* to *MC*.

Can a system of direct-discharge regulation also achieve socially efficient resource allocation? The answer is no. Suppose the government correctly calculates E^* from equation (4.15); as before, suppose they calculate R^* from equation (3.16); and that they calculate r^*, the socially efficient discharge for each firm. Of course, r^* differs among firms, since marginal costs vary according to the nature of what is being produced and the age of the firm and since marginal benefits vary spatially (depending importantly, for example, on population density). The direct-discharge policy consists of preventing each firm from discharging more than its quota r^* by civil and criminal penalties under the law. It was shown in Chapter 3 that this system of direct regulation leads to greater output by polluting firms than does an effluent policy that results in the same discharge quantities. The reason is that under direct regulation, firms pay nothing for discharges under the quota given them. Therefore their production costs are lower than those of firms subject to effluent fees, and they produce more. *In summary, direct regulation leads to overproduction by polluting firms.*

This is the fundamental argument for effluent fees. It refutes the common argument against them that fees will "merely" be passed on to consumers. It is the fact that they will, in part, be passed on that provides their major justification. The argument is like a claim that valuable labor should not be allocated by high wages because wage costs will merely be passed on to consumers. In large part they will, and one of their purposes is to discourage consumption of commodities whose production requires large amounts of such a valuable resource. If a clean environment is valuable, a goal of government should be to discourage consumption of commodities whose production causes pollution.

A curious argument against effluent fees is that government does not know the *MB* curve accurately. It is curious because it is really an argument against any form of pollution control, not merely against effluent fees. Direct regulation places no less a burden on the knowledge of the *MB* curve than does a program of effluent fees. However, it is a fact that *MB* curves are known only approximately. Suppose that, somehow, the political process has chosen a target value of *E*, whether it is the socially efficient value or not. Then an important advantage of effluent fees is that the government need only experiment to find the value of p_r that achieves the target value of *E*. It can be sure that dischargers, in their self-interest, will allocate the resulting discharges among themselves so as to minimize the cost of the abatement achieved. Under a policy of direct regulation, the government needs to know each firm's abatement cost schedule in order to assign discharge quotas to dischargers.

The preceding point regarding allocation of abatement effort among dischargers is important and merits further consideration. Consider Figure 4.5 in which marginal costs of various levels of abatement effort are depicted for two polluting firms. The marginal cost of any given percentage emission reduction is higher for Firm 2, perhaps because it is an older firm or because the good it produces involves a different technology from that of Firm 1. Suppose a policy of uni-

Figure 4.5

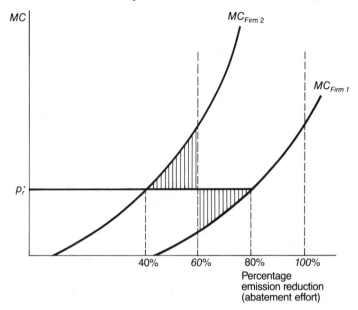

Figure 4.6

form direct control (a typical policy approach) is now imposed, for example requiring each firm to eliminate 60 percent of its emissions. Firm 2 has a very high marginal cost of control at the 60 percent emission reduction level, while Firm 1 has a much lower marginal abatement cost at that level of control. By merely relaxing controls on Firm 2 and at the same time increasing controls on Firm 1, scarce resources (labor, capital, and so on) can be saved *without* any reduction in environmental quality. These resource savings will continue to occur as control effort is reduced by Firm 2 and increased by Firm 1 until their marginal control costs are equal.

In Figure 4.6 the real resource savings associated with a tax that results in the same overall 60 percent emissions reduction are shown as the shaded areas. Note that with the tax, each firm will control until the marginal benefits of control (the tax savings) equal the marginal costs of control. The firm that can control relatively easily (Firm 1) will have the incentive to do so, while the high-cost firm is better off (as is society, since less scarce resources having high value elsewhere are used) controlling relatively less. The shaded areas in Figure 4.6—the real resource savings associated with the proper allocation of pollution-abatement effort among firms—will automatically be realized with a pollution tax p_r^*. Suppose that the tax is accidentally set at the wrong level (either too high or too low) to achieve the socially desired abatement effort and resulting environmental quality, E.* It is still possible, and indeed likely, that the cost savings associated with improved abatement allocation will more than offset the inefficiencies resulting from the wrong overall abatement effort. And, of course, the pollution tax can be changed so as to achieve the proper abatement effort when it is realized that the target value of E has not been achieved.

The foregoing is a powerful argument for effluent fees. It is made even more powerful by taking two additional elements of reality into account. First, what happens if conditions change? Suppose someone wants to build a new factory in the metropolitan area or to expand or modernize an old one? If an effluent fee is in effect, the owner is informed of the fee and builds and operates his plant accordingly. Of course, the new or expanded plant may require that the fee be raised to meet the environmental quality target, and the owner can be informed of that possibility, if he does not figure it out himself. If direct regulations are used, the government must calculate the discharges that would have resulted from the new or expanded source if there had been no regulations, and then assign a discharge quota to the source equal to the appropriate percentage of unregulated discharges. This calculation is very difficult because it requires the government to discover how the factory would have been built and operated had there been no regulations. And of course the owner's incentive is to persuade the government that the polluting discharge would have been large. Thus direct regulations inevitably require the government to learn a great deal about the products and processes of the plant's technology. It is inevitable in such situations that the government is forced to impose standards on firms for the design and operation of plants. For example, it is common to require that a new or expanded food-processing plant install a secondary waste-treatment process for its biological wastes, even though that may be a very inefficient way to abate the plant's discharges. Thus direct regulation of discharges inevitably leads to direct regulation of many aspects of plant design and operation. In fact, intrusion of government officials into every aspect of private company operations has been increasingly important in the direct regulations on which governments have relied for pollution abatement in the United States.

Second, there is always uncertainty about the costs and efficacy of new technology for pollution abatement. As the economy grows, antipollution policies inevitably become more stringent. That means that dischargers must continuously try unproven technology for pollution abatement. Thus there is always uncertainty on the part of governments and firms about how quickly new technology will be ready, how much new devices will cost, and how effective they will be. In this situation, the advantages are all on the side of effluent fees. A goal of public policy should be to provide dischargers with continuing incentives to seek economical means of discharge abatement as long as any pollutants are discharged. An effluent fee provides that incentive since the fee is paid on all discharges, however small. Under direct regulation, however, dischargers have no incentive to institute even inexpensive means of abatement once the standard is met. The situation is worse if regulations lead the government to require specific devices. Once required devices are installed, dischargers are not even motivated to be sure that they are operated efficiently, let alone to seek further means of discharge abatement. This problem has been especially serious with municipal sewage-treatment plants. Typically federal regulations require communities to build secondary treatment plants, and most of the cost is paid by federal subsidies in order to soften political opposition. But once the plant is built, the regulation has been met and the local government can save operating costs by operating the plant well below maximum efficiency, and most of the damage is borne by downstream water users.

It should be pointed out that the problem dealt with in this section is not as complex as are real environmental problems, but that none of the additional complexity affects the relative advantages of effluent fees over direct regulations. The most important complexity so far ignored is that discharges from various sources have various effects on environmental quality. A thermal electric plant on the windward side of a metropolitan area does much more damage to the metropolitan area's air quality than one on its leeward side. Likewise, a ton of organic material discharged one hundred miles upstream does less damage to water quality in the estuary than does a ton discharged just above the estuary. In such cases, the optimum discharge from each source is that which equates the source's marginal abatement cost to the marginal benefits of abatement from that source. Such calculations can be very complex and have never been made with much accuracy. Neither a uniform effluent fee nor a direct regulation that requires uniform percentage abatement can be optimum in this complex situation. Any information the government has about the variability of marginal abatement benefits among dischargers can be used to establish an appropriate set of effluent fees. Such a set of fees makes it possible to achieve a given level of environmental quality at less cost than it can be achieved with a set of rules for direct regulation, if the rules are based on the same information.

Before concluding this chapter, it is worth mentioning briefly a couple of common misunderstandings about effluent fees. A formerly common objection to effluent fees was that they "sell the right to pollute," but this argument has become less common as environmental discussion has become more sophisticated. Economists find it hard to know what to make of this claim. The literal answer to it is, "Yes, that is exactly what effluent fees do. Direct regulations give away the right to pollute and we think selling it is a big improvement." But many who make the argument really want to say that pollution should be prohibited, not rationed. Interpreted as a plea for zero discharges, it was shown in earlier chapters to be both impossible and undesirable. But if discharges are not to be prohibited, then some pollution is to be permitted, since all discharges are polluting in some degree. The economist's claim is that effluent fees are a more efficient way to allocate scarce "rights" to pollute than direct regulation. Sometimes the argument is meant to imply that it is immoral to use market incentives to allocate something as important as environmental quality. The argument seems to be that it is permissible to allocate unimportant things by market incentives, but not important things. That suggests that there is a much more effective allocative mechanism than markets. If so, it has not been found. Certainly, experience in the United States with direct regulations or, indeed, with market controls generally does not suggest that they are more effective allocation devices than markets.

A second objection to effluent fees is that they require metering of discharges, which may be expensive or impossible. The claim is correct, but it applies equally to most direct regulations or other programs to limit polluting discharges. Any government program to limit discharges requires that discharges be measured, and any policy is more effective the more accurately discharges are metered. To be sure, it is often easier to determine that a required control device (for example, a catalytic converter on new cars) is in place than it is to monitor emissions from that device. Some regulations are, as a consequence, stated in terms of required abatement equipment, but these regulations tend to have fewer environmental benefits since the users have no incentive to be certain that the equipment works. Advances in monitoring technology are occurring rapidly that should reduce our dependence on such inefficient regulations. There are, however, many problems concerned with the metering of some discharges, and some will be discussed in subsequent chapters. But any inaccuracy in metering discharges affects all government programs to improve the environment about equally and seldom makes one policy more desirable than another.

DISCUSSION QUESTIONS AND PROBLEMS

1. It has been proposed that governments control environmental quality by choosing a permissible discharge quantity R^g and then auctioning off discharge permits for a total discharge of R^g. How would you evaluate the desirability of this proposal relative to effluent fees and direct regulation?

2. Evaluate the claim that effluent fees are undesirable because they reduce the competitiveness of American products in international trade.

3. Automobile effluents are regulated by limiting all automobiles to the same number of grams of pollutants discharged per mile driven. Do you think that is efficient?

4. Since it is so difficult to estimate *MB* curves from behavioral data, why not just ask people how much they would be willing to pay for a clean environment?

5. Would it be a good way to set effluent fees to put them on a public referendum?

6. The welfare discussion reflected in Figure 4.1 suggests that only the preferences of mankind matter, since the indifference curves relate only to people. Should other species have property rights in environmental quality? If so, which species? (Be careful! If you say intelligent, furry things, but not cockroaches and spiders, you are guilty of "speciesism.") Do you feed your pet dog or cat correctly from his or her standpoint? Would environmental quality be optimally higher or lower if other species were considered, apart from how they enter mankind's utility functions? Does focusing on merely human benefits and costs have implications for the future of our ecological system? (Hint: Suppose the optimal environmental damage leads to loss of species diversity in the food chain.)

7. Do you believe there are systematic biases in measuring the benefits and costs of environmental control policies? If so, what do you think is the direction of that bias?

8. Do you think it is fair to future generations to discount to the present benefits that are received in the distant future? Would you favor a lower or a higher discount rate than the interest rate?

REFERENCES AND FURTHER READING

Baumol, William, and Oates, Wallace. *The Theory of Environmental Policy.* Englewood Cliffs, N.J.: Prentice-Hall, 1975

Carroll, David W. "Two Games That Illustrate Some Problems Concerning Economic Analysis of Legal Problems." *S. Cal. L. Rev.* 53: 1371 (1980).

Dorfman, Robert, and Dorfman, Nancy, eds. *Economics of the Environment.* 2d ed. New York: Norton, 1977.

Havender, William R. "Ruminations on a Rat: Saccharin and Human Risk." *Regulation* (March-April 1979): 17–24.

Hoffman, Elizabeth, and Spitzer, Matthew. "The Coase Theorem: Some Experimental Tests." *Journal of Law and Economics* 25, no. 2 (April 1982): 73–98.

Mäler, Karl-Gören, and Wyzga, Ronald. *Economic Measurement of Environmental Damage.* Washington, D.C.: Organization of Economic Cooperation and Development, 1976.

Mansfield, Edwin. *Microeconomics: Theory and Applications.* 2d ed. New York: Norton, 1975.

Mishan, E. J. *Cost-Benefit Analysis.* New York: Praeger, 1976.

Morey, Ed. "Confuser Surplus." *American Economic Review* 74, no. 1 (March 1984): 163–73.

Prudencio, Yves Coffi. "The Voluntary Approach to Externality Problems: An Experimental Test." *Journal of Environmental Economics and Management* 9, no. 3 (September 1982): 213–28.

Willig, Robert. "Consumer's Surplus without Apology." *American Economic Review* 66 (September 1976): 589–97.

Part II

DISCHARGES AND ENVIRONMENTAL QUALITY IN THE UNITED STATES

Part I presented the basic positive and normative economic theory of materials use and polluting discharges. In Part II, flesh is placed on the bare bones of theory by presenting technical information regarding water, air, and solid-waste pollution. The following three chapters summarize information regarding the kinds, amounts, sources, and effects of pollutants and techniques of pollution abatement. This will permit specific substances to be identified with the theoretical variables of Part I, and will indicate what is, and what is not, known about physical and dollar magnitudes regarding pollution.

The formulation and evaluation of government pollution-abatement policies require understanding of both the appropriate economic analysis and the biological, physical, and chemical relationships involved. The economic analysis was presented in Part I. The technical background will be presented in Part II. In Part III, both building blocks will be used in a critical evaluation of American pollution-abatement policies.

It would be desirable to have a complete set of materials accounts for the United States economy. Such accounts would include materials withdrawals each year classified by material; uses classified by material and industry; and returns to the environment classifed by material, industry, and whether the return was waterbone, airborne, or solid waste. An important beginning at compilation of materials accounts has been made at Resources for the Future (RFF), but large gaps remain, and the data have not been updated.

Table II.1 shows the RFF estimates of materials production in the United States two decades ago. The growth of these numbers began to slow around 1968, in part because of slower secular growth of the economy and in part because the rate of population growth began to decline. The rate of growth of mineral fuels in particular (half of the total weight) is now very small compared to this earlier period. The total of 2,640 million tons for 1965 was about 70 pounds per person per day; more recent data, were it available, would be closer to 100 pounds per person per day. Even these staggering figures ignore large volumes of construction and other materials that are moved from one place to another without important chemical or physical changes.

TABLE II.1

Weight of Basic Materials Production in the United States
plus Net Imports, 1963–65 (10^6 tons)

Material	1963	1964	1965
Agricultural (incl. fishery and wildlife and forest) products			
Food and fiber			
Crops	350	358	364
Livestock and dairy	23	24	23.5
Fishery	2	2	2
Forest products (85% dry wt. basis)			
Sawlogs	107	116	120
Pulpwood	53	55	56
Other	41	41	42
TOTAL	576	596	607.5
Mineral fuels	1,337	1,399	1,448
Other minerals			
Iron ore	204	237	245
Other metal ores	161	171	191
Other nonmetals	125	133	149
TOTAL	490	541	585
GRAND TOTAL[a]	2,403	2,536	2,640.5

[a]Excluding construction materials, stone, sand, gravel, and other minerals used for structural purposes, ballast, fillers, insulation, etc.

SOURCE: A. V. Kneese, R. U. Ayres, and R. C. D'Arge, *Economics and the Environment* (Baltimore: Johns Hopkins Press, for Resources for the Future, Inc., 1970), p. 10.

All the materials in Table II.1 are returned to the environment in one way or another. Although the data are badly incomplete, it is certain that most materials are returned to the environment as solid wastes. Amounts returned to water bodies and to the atmosphere are smaller by weight but more important by the pollution they cause. The purpose of Part II is to trace the returns of materials to the environment and to analyze the effects of pollution discharges on the environment and on people and property.

Chapter 5

Air Quality

People have much less choice about the air they breathe than about the water they drink or about other dimensions of environmental quality. We must be able to breathe the air almost everywhere we go, whereas we can be selective about the water we drink, swim in, and use for many other purposes. The fact that we live in the air makes the formulation of national air-pollution policy simpler than the formulation of water-pollution policy. All the ambient air must be fit to breathe, whereas water bodies can be classified in complex ways by the kinds of uses for which their quality is appropriate.

In almost all other respects, however, acquiring an understanding of air quality and its impact on mankind is at least as complicated as for water quality, which we will turn to in Chapter 6. A large variety of complex and poorly understood chemical and physical processes takes place in the air, both among pollutants discharged to it and between pollutants and substances found naturally in the atmosphere. There are still mysteries about the exact fate of many substances discharged to the air. Furthermore, air circulates in complicated ways. Substances discharged to the air diffuse in patterns peculiar to locations, seasons, and heights, and subject to important random effects. Vertical diffusion especially is poorly understood. Substances discharged at the earth's surface appear in the stratosphere years later, and they may remain there many years. Finally, there is great uncertainty about the effects of pollutants on people and property. It is simply not known, to a degree of accuracy that can provide a basis for rational government programs, what harm is done by many airbone pollutants.

All uncertainties about air pollution are made more serious by the fact that people and animals are extremely sensitive to even low concentrations of certain pollutants. Concentrations of most airbone pollutants are a few parts per million. It is difficult and expensive to design and manufacture devices that can meter accurately such low concentrations, although technological advance is occurring rapidly in the air-pollution-monitoring industry. And it is often uncertain which parameters of ambient concentrations are most critical. Average concentrations are recorded most frequently, but peak exposures may be more critical.

As with water pollutants, society has many options as to what it discharges to the air. For almost every economic activity, there are important ways to limit airborne discharges. Some are cheap and some are expensive, some are effective and some are ineffective. Almost none is free. Even more than with water pollution, zero discharge of airborne pollutants is not an option. The very act of breathing changes the composition of the air. But much more important is the relationship between combustion of fuels and airborne discharges. Virtually all the energy released by combustion ends up as heat that must be dissipated to the atmosphere. The only way to reduce heat discharges without lowering living standards is to increase production of commodities and services per unit of fuel burned. For example, automobile engines can be made so they burn less fuel per mile driven and waste heat from thermal electric plants can be used to heat and cool buildings. In fuel combustion and in many other production processes, materials are released to the atmosphere unless specific, and sometimes costly, measures are taken to capture them. A high-quality atmosphere is among our options if we want to pay the price in reduced production of commodities and services, but a pollution-free atmosphere is not.

Atmospheric Discharges

Many substances are discharged to the atmosphere in at least small volumes. Data are incomplete regarding substances discharged in small amounts. In some cases, there is little awareness of discharges until someone hypothesizes that the substance does harm. But government data on airborne discharges have improved greatly since the early 1970s, and comprehensive data are now available regarding substances discharged to the atmosphere in substantial quantities.

Table 5.1 presents national data on airborne discharges for the 1970s and early 1980s, with comparisons to earlier periods. The total of all the airborne discharges is but a small portion of total discharges, much smaller than solid-waste discharges, which will be discussed in Chapter 7.

Measured by weight, the five substances in Table 5.1 account for almost all airborne discharges in the United States. There is, of course, no assurance that damages are proportionate to weight of discharges, and in some cases the evidence is to the contrary.[1] Damages will be discussed in the next section; here weight will be used to make discharge measures commensurate. Of total discharges in the table, carbon monoxide represents about half. Of roughly equal importance are sulfur oxides, nitrogen oxides, and hydrocarbons (the later term replaced by a less common expression, "volatile organic compounds," in Table 5.1), with particulates representing smaller amounts.

Most airborne discharges result from the burning of fuels, but significant amounts also result from a variety of industrial processes. Particulates, or particles, are small pieces of materials discharged to the air by burning fuel, and by industrial processes. When fuel is burned, small pieces of unburned material pass to the atmosphere. Large particulate discharges result from the burning of a ton of coal or wood, whereas petroleum products and, especially, natural gas generate only small amounts of particulates per ton. Wood is burned in only small quantities in the American economy.[2] Any coal-fired combustion system, whether for space heating or thermal electric

1. Hazardous substances' impact on air, water, and land quality will be discussed in Chapter 7.

2. While small in use when compared to alternative sources of energy, wood use involves not only erosion, siltation of dams and streams, loss of wilderness habitat, and decreased aesthetics, but can also lead to several local pollution problems: since the mid-1970s wood-burning in Aspen, Colorado, has resulted in dramatic increases in airborne particulates (from 30 micrograms per cubic meter to approximately 75 micrograms in succeeding years). These figures are from *Colorado: Air-Quality Data Report: 1981*, State of Colorado, Dept. of Health, 1982.

TABLE 5.1

National Air Pollutant Emissions Estimates, by Pollutant, 1940–1982 (million metric tons per year)

Year	Partic-ulates	Percent of 1974	Sulfur oxides	Percent of 1974	Nitrogen oxides	Percent of 1974	Volatile organic compounds	Percent of 1974	Carbon monoxide	Percent of 1974
1940	22.4	182	18.1	67	6.7	34	17.1	76	79.8	92
1950	24.2	197	20.4	76	9.2	47	19.3	86	85.3	99
1960	20.9	170	20.1	74	12.7	64	21.9	97	87.9	102
1970	18.0	146	28.4	105	18.1	92	25.3	112	100.2	116
1971	16.8	137	26.9	100	18.5	94	24.5	109	98.6	114
1972	15.0	122	27.6	102	19.7	100	24.5	109	95.7	111
1973	13.9	113	28.9	107	20.2	103	24.0	107	91.6	106
1974	12.3	100	27.0	100	19.7	100	22.5	100	86.5	100
1975	10.3	84	25.7	95	19.2	97	21.0	93	82.4	95
1976	9.6	78	26.3	97	20.4	104	22.1	98	87.2	101
1977	9.0	73	26.3	97	21.0	107	21.9	97	83.0	96
1978	8.9	72	24.6	91	21.2	108	22.4	100	82.3	95
1979	9.0	73	24.6	91	21.3	108	21.9	97	79.5	92
1980	8.6	70	23.3	86	20.7	105	20.8	92	77.6	90
1981	8.1	66	22.5	83	20.9	106	19.4	86	75.3	87
1982	7.5	61	21.4	79	20.2	103	18.2	81	73.6	85
Changes 1970–1982	−58%		−25%		+12%		−28%		−27%	

SOURCE: Council or Environmental Quality, *Environmental Quality*, 1983 (14th Annual Report), Table A-57, p. 316.

generation, discharges particulates. Diesel engines in large trucks, buses, and some cars discharge small amounts of particulates, but internal-combustion engines discharge almost none. After discharge to the atmosphere, particulates disperse according to the wind pattern. Eventually, they fall to earth, mostly within a few miles of the point of discharge. Particulates vary greatly in size, which strongly affects their dispersion, the speed with which they settle out of the atmosphere, and the harm they do to people and property.[3]

Natural processes such as volcanic action discharge substantial amounts of sulfur to the atmosphere. But most sulfur in the air over urban areas results from human activities, particularly the burning of coal and oil, but also from a variety of industrial processes, especially smelting and refining. Some kinds of coal and oil contain much more sulfur than others. All the sulfur in the fuel at the time of combustion is released during combustion and enters the atmosphere unless captured beforehand. Sulfur oxidizes in the atmosphere and most falls back to earth either as dilute sulfuric acid during precipitation or as a dry deposit. Heating oil used for space heating is a major source of sulfur discharges, as is the heavy oil used in thermal electric generation and in large space-heating units in apartment houses and other large buildings. Almost no sulfur is discharged from internal-combustion engines and little from diesel engines. Some results from train and subway systems, in generating electricity to run them. Sulfur discharges recorded in Table 5.1 are several times as great as the amount mined for industrial and commercial use in the United States. Once discharged from chimneys and smokestacks, sulfur disperses according to the wind pattern, height of discharge, and weather conditions. Some sulfur returns to earth within a few miles of the discharge point, but some appears in other metropolitan areas. There is increasing evidence that much sulfur is transported long distances in aerosol form after discharge to the air and may increase the acidity of lakes and soil hundreds of miles from the point of discharge.

Virtually all the carbon monoxide in the atmosphere is discharged

---

3. Particulates range in size from about .001 microns to 1,000 microns (a micron is one-millionth of a meter, with for reference human hair ranging from 5 to 600 microns in diameter), although particles over about 100 microns settle fairly rapidly to earth. Particles less than .1 micron move with Brownian motion like gas molecules, not settling at all; it is the smaller particles (.5 to 5 microns in diameter) that cause most lung damage. Particles larger than about 10 microns can be seen with the naked eye.

by human activities. Most results from burning gasoline in internal-combustion engines, but some results from many industrial processes. Carbon monoxide results from incomplete combustion in internal-combustion engines, and less is discharged the more complete the combustion. Carbon monoxide is an apparently inert gas in the atmosphere; it does not react with other substances there. Yet much of the massive discharge of carbon monoxide in metropolitan areas disappears within a few hours, at a rate apparently not explainable by the circulation of air. It is still something of a mystery what happens to it, although carbon monoxide is slightly lighter than air.

Hydrocarbons, which include the volatile organic compounds of Table 5.1, are discharged from the combustion of fossil fuels, from industrial processes, and from a variety of miscellaneous sources. Among the latter are evaporation of industrial solvents and the wearing of motor vehicle tires from driving. Like carbon monoxide, hydrocarbons are the products of incomplete combustion in internal-combustion engines, the largest single source of hydrocarbons. Important natural processes also discharge hydrocarbons, and in much larger quantities than human activities on a worldwide basis. As with sulfur oxides, human activities account for most hydrocarbons in the atmosphere over urban areas. Hydrocarbons are reactive in the atmosphere. Along with nitrogen oxides, they result in the formation of photochemical smog in appropriate climatic conditions.

Nitrogen oxides are naturally present in the atmosphere in large volumes. Most nitrogen discharges from human activity are in the form of nitrogen dioxide, but human activity accounts for only a minor part of all atmospheric nitrogen dioxide. Virtually all nitrogen discharges from human activity result from combustion of fossil fuels in motor vehicles, space-heating systems, and thermal electric plants. Whereas carbon monoxide and hydrocarbons are the products of incomplete combustion, nitrogen oxides are the natural products of combustion. Therefore procedures to improve the effeciency of combustion reduce carbon monoxide and hydrocarbon discharges, but increase nitrogen oxide discharges. In the atmosphere, nitrogen dioxide is an ingredient in the formation of photochemical smog. Photochemical reactions take place within a few hours of discharge. Nitrogen dioxide that does not take part in photochemical reactions is removed from the atmosphere as aerosols by settling on the earth and by rain, mostly within days of discharge.

Table 5.1 shows a gradual reduction of airborne discharges, during the decade of the 1970s and early 1980s. These reductions ranged from 58 percent for total suspended particulates to 25 percent for sulfur oxides, with only nitrogen oxides showing an increase (12 percent).

The downward trend in particulate discharges is part of a long-term trend of at least twenty-five years, resulting in large part from substitution of oil for coal for economic, not environmental, reasons. In the early 1970s, substitution of oil for coal was encouraged by the EPA for environmental reasons. Since the oil embargo in 1973, the government has stopped encouraging such fuel substitution and a debate has ensued whether national policy should encourage a return to use of coal in order to conserve scarce and expensive petroleum. Reductions in discharges of other substances have resulted mostly from the program of air-pollution abatement. In the mid-1970s, the energy crisis induced the EPA to permit delays in meeting the most stringent sulfur-emissions standards. Similar rule changes have occurred, and no doubt will continue to occur, as a response to changed priorities and political considerations; for example, in 1982 the EPA rescinded rules about hydrocarbon standards set more than a decade earlier.

Air Quality

The discharge data just discussed are inportant because they are a guide to ambient pollution levels, because they inform us about sources of pollutants, and because the data are plentiful and of at least moderately high quality. But damages to people and property result from ambient pollution concentrations, and discharge data are valuable in assessing damages only insofar as they are a guide to ambient concentrations. The relationship between discharges and ambient concentrations is complex, depending on the substance in question, on weather conditions, and on detailed discharge characteristics. It is therefore important to study ambient air-quality measures carefully.

For reference, and to provide an insight into the magnitude of the cleansing power of the natural environment, the chemical composition of unpolluted air is given in Table 5.2. The amount of pollutants, even in heavily polluted air, is small relative to the total diluting capacity of the atmosphere: the total amounts, in terms of parts per million, of pollutants present will lie between the amount of carbon dioxide and neon. This is not to downplay the importance of envi-

TABLE 5.2

*The Gaseous Composition of Unpolluted Air (Wet Basis).**

	ppm (vol)	$\mu g/m^3$
Nitrogen	756,500	8.67×10^8
Oxygen	202,900	2.65×10^8
Water	31,200	2.30×10^7
Argon	9,000	1.47×10^7
Carbon dioxide	305	5.49×10^5
Neon	17.4	1.44×10^4
Helium	5.0	8.25×10^2
Methane	0.97–1.16	$6.35 – 7.63 \times 10^2$
Krypton	0.97	3.32×10^3
Nitrous oxide	0.49	8.73×10^2
Hydrogen	0.49	4.00×10^1
Xenon	0.08	4.17×10^2
Organic vapors	ca. 0.02	—

SOURCE: A. C. Stern, H. C. Wohlers, R. W. Boubel, and W. P. Lowry, *Fundamentals of Air Pollution* (New York: Academic Press, 1973).

ronmental quality, as some pollutants are damaging even in very small quantities. Rather, it is to stress the assimilative capacity of the natural environment. We now turn to the nature of the actual air quality around us, since unpolluted air is rare and of little interest for our purposes.

Unfortunately, ambient air-quality measurement is an inherently difficult task. Ambient concentrations are frequently very low and strain the capability of monitoring devices. Most important, measurements depend greatly on where and when they are taken, and on how they are averaged.

Table 5.3 shows summary ambient air-quality data for many of the recent years for which Table 5.1 shows discharge data. Monitoring stations are gradually being established in metropolitan areas throughout the country. The number of stations reporting varies by pollutant and by year, although more stations reported for later than for earlier years. The first stations tend to be located in the most critical areas. In spite of these difficulties, substantial improvement has been observed in air quality during the 1975–1982 period (except for nitrogen dioxide, a pattern roughly consistent with the emissions data). However, the national data are not terribly useful in that substantial local variations in air quality exist and "micrograms per cubic meter" and "parts per million" and other measures of pollution con-

TABLE 5.3

National Ambient Air Pollutant Concentrations, 1975–1982[1]

Pollutant	Measurement units[2]	No. of sites[3]	1975	1976	1977	1978	1979	1980	1981	1982
Total suspended particulate: Annual geometric mean[4]	$\mu g/m^3$	1,768	60.0	60.8	60.2	59.6	60.0	61.6	58.0	50.8
Sulfur dioxide: Annual arithmetic mean	ppm	351	0.015	0.015	0.014	0.012	0.012	0.011	0.010	0.010
Carbon monoxide: Annual 2nd maximum nonoverlapping 8-hour average	ppm	196	11.68	11.09	10.37	9.84	9.38	8.68	8.64	8.01
Nitrogen dioxide: Annual arithmetic mean	ppm	276	0.26	0.26	0.26	0.28	0.28	0.27	0.26	0.26
Ozone: Annual 2nd daily maximum 1-hour average	ppm	193	0.154	0.154	0.153	0.154	0.139	0.143	0.129	0.127
Lead: Annual maximum quarterly		46	0.88	0.80	0.88	0.84	0.69	0.44	0.44	0.32
averages[5]	$\mu g/m^3$	214	—	—	—	—	0.74	0.57	0.45	0.42

[1] The air quality statistics used in this report relate directly to the appropriate National Ambient Air Quality Standards.

[2] $\mu g/m^3$ = microgram per cubic meter; ppm = parts per million.

[3] For a monitoring site to be included in this analysis, the site had to contain at least 6 out of the 8 years of data in the period 1975 to 1982 and each of these years had to satisfy annual data completeness criteria.

[4] The trend in TSP is complicated by the fact that the glass fiber filters used to collect TSP data have been manufactured by different vendors. The filters used in 1979, 1980, and 1981 were found to record higher values than the filters used in 1978 and 1982, because of higher filter alkalinity, which is related to artifact error. The alkalinity of the 1978 and 1982 filters were found to be similar, so that TSP data for these years should be comparable.

[5] In order to increase the number of lead sites available for trend analysis, both an 8-year and 4-year time period are presented.

SOURCE: Council on Environment Quality, *Environmental Quality*, 1984, Table A-55, p. 315.

centration are not very intuitively meaningful. The typical reader of this book will be much more familiar with the Pollution Standards Index—it appears along with the local weather on most evening television newscasts. Yet few people really know what the Pollution Standards Index (PSI) is.

The PSI converts the pollutant concentrations measured in a community's air into a simple number on a scale of 0 to 500. These intervals are related to the potential health effects of five major pollutants: carbon monoxide, photochemical oxidants, nitrogen dioxide, sulfur dioxide, and particulate matter. The index of 100 corresponds, for each pollutant considered separately, to the thresh-

TABLE 5.4

Health Effects Associated with Levels of Pollutant Standards Index (PSI)

PSI value	Descriptor	Health effects	Warning
400 and above	Hazardous	Premature death of ill and elderly. Healthy people will experience adverse symptoms that affect their normal activity.	All persons should remain indoors, keeping windows and doors closed. All persons should minimize physical exertion and avoid traffic.
300–399	Hazardous	Premature onset of certain diseases in addition to significant aggravation of symptoms and decreased exercise tolerance in healthy persons.	Elderly and persons with existing diseases should stay indoors and avoid physical exertion. General population should avoid outdoor activity.
200–299	Very un-healthful	Significant aggravation of symptoms and decreased exercise tolerance in persons with heart or lung disease, with widespread symptoms in the healthy population.	Elderly and persons with existing heart or lung disease should stay indoors and reduce physical activity.
100–199	Unhealthful	Mild aggravation of symptoms in susceptible persons, with irritation symptoms in the healthy population.	Persons with existing heart or respiratory ailments should reduce physical exertion and outdoor activity.
50–99	Moderate		
0–49	Good		

SOURCE: Council on Environmental Quality, *Environmental Quality*, 1981, p. 31.

old level of the pollutant below which health effects have not been observed. Hence, for any pollutant, an index value greater than 100 corresponds to a violation of the National Ambient Air Quality Standard (NAAQS). The PSI reports the index value for the maximum subindex pollutant; on days when more than one pollutant violates its health-related standard, each pollutant is reported. This approach is somewhat imperfect in that the scientific base for comparing relative health effects, and the nature of those effects themselves for each pollutant, is scant.

Table 5.4 depicts the official meaning of various PSI readings. How much variation is there in these readings, depending on which part of the country you live in? This question, very important in that there is much variation in pollution exposure, can be at least partly answered by referring to Table 5.5, which ranks forty Stan-

TABLE 5.5

Ranking of 40 Standard Metropolitan Statistical Areas (SMSAs) Using the Pollutant Standards Index (PSI), 1978–80.

Severity level (days with PSI greater than 100)	SMSA	3-Year average of number of days "Unhealthful," "very unhealthful," and "hazardous" (PSI > 100)	"Very unhealthful," and "hazardous" (PSI > 200)
More than 150 days	Los Angeles	231	113
	San Bernardino, Riverside, Ontario	174	89
100–150 days	New York	139	6
	Denver	130	36
	Pittsburgh	119	18
	Houston	104	23
50–99 days	Chicago	93	14
	St. Louis	89	19
	Philadelphia	74	6
	San Diego	72[b]	8[b]
	Louisville	70	4
	Phoenix	70[b]	6[b]
	Gary	68	33
	Portland	62	11
	Washington	62	3
	Jersey City	58[a]	0[a]
	Salt Lake City	58	18

TABLE 5.5 *(Continued)*

Severity level (days with PSI greater than 100)	SMSA	3-Year average of number of days "Unhealthful," "very unhealthful," and "hazardous" (PSI > 100)	"Very unhealthful," and "hazardous" (PSI > 200)
	Seattle	52	3
	Birmingham	50[a]	8[a]
25–49 days	Cleveland	46	11
	Detroit	39	4
	Memphis	37[a]	3[a]
	Baltimore	36	2
	Indianapolis	34	2
	Cincinnati	28	1
	Milwaukee	28	2
	Kansas City	28[a]	1[a]
0–24 days	Sacramento	22	1
	Dallas	21	1
	Allentown	21	2
	Buffalo	20[b]	4[b]
	San Francisco	18	0
	Toledo	15	2
	Dayton	15	1
	Tampa	8	1
	Syracuse	7	1
	Norfolk	6[b]	0[b]
	Grand Rapids	6[a]	0[a]
	Rochester	5	0
	Akron	4	0

[a]Based on 1 year of data.
[a]Based on 2 years of data.
SOURCE: Council on Environmental Quality, *Environmental Quality*, 1981, p. 33.

dard Metropolitan Statistical Areas (SMSAs) using the PSI. Note that while Los Angeles appears to be far more polluted than other cities, according to the PSI, the ambiguities mentioned earlier are present: auto-related pollutants are more prevalent in the West and are giving rise to the high PSI numbers, yet a long history of studies has pinpointed particulates and SO_x as being of principal health concern. In other words, the index values must be interpreted with caution, when one's interest is in the health damages associated with locating at various places. Individual city data, for twenty-three representative cities considered annually from 1973 to 1980, confirm the national trend toward cleaner air.[4]

Damages from Air Pollution

It is convenient to classify damages from air pollution as human health and property damages. Like any simple classification of a complex subject, it leaves some aspects hard to classify. For example, some damages from air pollution may be purely aesthetic. People may simply dislike the look of smog, or they may dislike the loss of atmospheric clarity caused by some kinds of air pollution. As a second example, some people are concerned about damage from pollution to wildlife, which is no one's property. Little is known or could easily be discovered about these and similar damages. It is unlikely that air pollution abatement that was optimum taking account of human health and property damages would entail significant aesthetic or wildlife damages. Thus the discussion will be largely confined to human health and property damages.

Beyond doubt, the greatest concern regarding air pollution pertains to its possible effect on human health. Such concern is not irrational. Health is not priceless, but it is precious, and it is rational for society to devote large amounts of scarce resources to its preservation and improvement. Even in narrow economic terms, forgone production and income from poor health can be great in an economy in which wages are high in absolute terms and in which labor's share of national income is about 80 percent.

Although concern about the health effects of air pollution is rational, the state of knowledge on the subject is decidedly unsatisfactory. The subject is intrinsically difficult to study scientifically because ambient concentrations are mostly low and difficult to meter, because low concentrations mostly have chronic health effects which are difficult to distinguish from other causes of health changes, and because many kinds of people—old, young, healthy, sick—are exposed in many different ways. In addition, studies of the health effects of air pollution are of recent origin. Few were done before 1960. There

4. To conserve space, these data are not presented here. They are available in Table A-51, pp. 244–45 of the 1981 edition of *Environmental Quality*.

has been a gradual improvement in the quantity and quality of data, in statistical and laboratory techniques of estimating causal relationships, and in the underlying base of biological knowledge.

It is useful to distinguish four kinds of studies that shed light on the health effects of air pollution.

First is laboratory experiments. Most are performed on animals. For example, a scientist might experiment on one hundred rats, selecting at random ten groups of ten rats each. The rats in each group would be subjected to a carefully chosen dosage of carbon monoxide. The number of rats in each group that displayed specific symptoms—such as death, loss of consciousness, loss of ability to negotiate a maze, and so forth—would be observed and recorded. Such data permit the scientist to estimate a damage function showing the frequency of a specified kind of damage to the rats as a function of the dosage of the pollutant received. Of course the clearest evidence of damage appears at high dosage levels. The scientist must then extrapolate the damage function back to the low dosages typical in the ambient atmosphere. Such extrapolation is uncertain and depends on the experimental design, the statistical techniques employed, and the functional form of the damage function imposed on the data. Especially controversial is whether the data imply a threshold. A threshold means that the damage is zero at exposures below some level. A threshold might imply an ambient pollution concentration below which there was no immediate damage or one below which there was no chronic damage from long-term exposure. The latter concept is the relevant one, but would be hard to estimate. If the threshold exists, it might constitute a basis for setting ambient standards. But it is usually not possible to identify a threshold accurately from observations at high concentrations. A second, and even more difficult, extrapolation is that from rats or other animals to humans. Small mammals may have quite different responses to pollutants from those of humans.

Some experiments are also done on humans. For example, student volunteers may be exposed to carbon monoxide concentrations similar to those observed on busy highways and they may be given mental tests, reaction tests, or simulated driving tests. Experiments on humans are usually restricted to low exposure levels to protect subjects' health and behavioral effects are therefore usually slight and difficult to measure. These experiments entail a different kind of extrapolation, that to more vulnerable groups of people. Students are mostly healthy, and scientists are reluctant to perform such experiments on infants, the aged, and others who may be much more vulnerable to pollutants.

Second is data from catastrophic pollution episodes. Killer fogs have been observed and studied on several occasions during the middle half of the twentieth century. The most famous such occasion was in Donora, Pennsylvania, in 1948. Similar episodes occurred in London in 1952 and in New York in 1966. The symptoms of such acute episodes are high rates of respiratory illnesses and death during a period of a few days. The cause is usually high ambient concentrations of sulfur oxides and particulates over a city or region. Such acute episodes can occur only where discharges are large. But the triggering mechanism is an adverse meteorological phenomenon called an inversion. An inversion is a layer of warm air a few hundred feet above the ground which traps pollutants below it and prevents normal dispersion. Sulfur oxides accumulate to high levels and people with respiratory problems become ill or die. Acute-episode data make it certain that sulfur oxides and paticulates are the pollutants that are implicated.

During acute episodes, death rates may be ten times normal. Four thousand excess deaths were reported during the two weeks of the 1952 London episode. All recorded acute episodes have occurred during adverse damp and still weather and where large amounts of high-sulfur-content coal were burned. From the point of view of estimating the relationship between air quality and health, acute episodes provide data on damage functions for humans similar to the data provided for animals by laboratory experiments described above. They are almost like controlled experiments in that illness and death rates during the episode can be compared with those in the same area at other times. This comparison holds nearly constant all characteristics of the population except ambient air quality. Studies of acute-episode data permit predictions of illness and death rates from similar episodes. But is is not easy to extrapolate from such data to the effect of much lower ambient concentrations on people exposed during their entire lifetimes.

In fact, there appears not to have been an acute episode anywhere in the industrialized world since the late 1960s. It is premature to celebrate the end of the acute-episode era, but one can at least hope that they have become less frequent because of government air-pollution-control programs. Another curiosity about acute episodes is that there has not been one in Tokyo. Discharges of sulfur oxides and particulates were certainly of the requisite magnitudes in the 1960s, and Tokyo is subject to inversions. It may be that acute episodes require a precise combination of temperature and other weather conditions which is rare or nonexistent in Tokyo.

The third source of information is studies of the effect of air quality on real-estate property values and wage rates. Economists have undertaken many studies of the determinants of property values. Typically, regression analysis[5] is used, with a dwelling's sales price or rent the dependent variable and physical characteristics of the dwelling—such as lot size, age, construction material, number of rooms, location, and so on—the independent variables. Air-quality variables have been included as independent variables in some studies. The studies show consistently that, other things equal, properties in neighborhoods with poor-quality air sell or rent for less than those in neighborhoods with high-quality air. Such studies are remarkable in that they suggest that people have at least an approximate perception of neighborhood air quality and of its harmful effects. But this conclusion is controversial in that it is possible that air quality is correlated with other neighborhood quality characteristics, such as blight or proximity to nonresidential land uses, not included in the regression equation, that people know and care about. For example, there is evidence that air quality is worse in older, more run-down, higher-crime-rate neighborhoods in most urban areas. It is difficult to be certain that it is really air quality that accounts for the effects of property values that are attributed to it.

Much the same conclusion emerges from studies that compare wage rates among urban areas. They find that workers must be paid more to induce them to live and work in urban areas that are congested or badly polluted.

One attractive characteristic of property-value and wage-rate studies is that they provide direct measures of the dollar benefits of air pollution abatement. If an apartment in a polluted area rents for $20 per month less than a similar apartment in a nonpolluted area with otherwise similar characteristics, then one can say that residents place

---

5. For readers who have not had a course in statistical methods, regression analysis is a technique for estimating the effects of a set of causal variables on a dependent variable. In the example in the text, a dwelling's physical characteristics and other variables are assumed to determine its price or rent.

a value of $20 per month on living in the neighborhood with clean air. It is then easy to calculate the benefits of improvement in air quality, as described in Chapter 4. One can use wage-rate differences in a similar fashion. Of course, some effects of air pollution on property values may result from damage to the property instead of to the health of residents. Property damage is discussed below.

Air-pollution levels and resulting damages to human health are so uncertain that one must entertain serious doubts whether property-value studies provide an adequate basis for estimating the benefits of air-pollution abatement. There is controversy and grave doubt about health effects of air pollution at the most fundamental scientific level. One needs great faith in human rationality to believe that people perceive and appropriately average the health effects of air pollution in residential neighborhoods or urban areas and then translate health effects into dollar values for housing costs and wage rates. It is likely that people have some perception of air pollution and its health effects and that these perceptions have some effects on wage rates and dwelling prices and rents. But it is unlikely that the perceptions are accurate enough to provide a reasonable basis for estimating benefits from pollution abatement.

Fourth, and perhaps most important, are cross-section studies of the determinants of mortality and morbidity. In recent years, a number of careful statistical analyses of this kind have been published. In such studies, the average death rate in a metropolitan area might be the dependent variable. Independent variables used to explain death rates are income levels, racial composition, the population age distribution, climatic variables, and other variables likely to affect death rates in the metropolitan area. To these variables, measures of air quality over the metropolitan area are added. Then the relationship is estimated using data from a sample of metropolitan areas for a particular year. The most elaborate and frequently cited study is that by Lester Lave and Eugene Seskin, *Air Pollution and Human Health*.[6] Of all the pollution-concentration variables they could find, only sulfur oxide and particulate concentrations had statistically sig-

6. Mike Chappie and Lester Lave, in "The Health Effects of Air Pollution: A Reanalysis" (*Journal of Urban Economics* 12, no. 3 [November 1982]: 346–76), address criticisms of the earlier Lave and Seskin work. An excellent review of available evidence on the benefits and costs of federal efforts to improve environmental quality may be found in A. Myrick Freeman, *Air and Water Pollution Control: A Benefit-Cost Assessment*.

nificant coefficients in the regression equations. None of the pollutants discharged in large quantities by motor vehicles appeared to affect death rates. But Lave and Seskin's best estimate is that halving the ambient concentrations of sulfer oxides and particulates over a typical metropolitan area from their 1960 levels might add about one year to life expectancy in the metropolitan area. That is a dramatic finding. It is of course a long-run conclusion. It is not the 1960 air-pollution level that shortened lives, but instead air-pollution levels during several decades. The year 1960 was chosen because data are available. The pollution level has a significant coefficient in the regression equation because pollution levels are persistent in a metropolitan area. Likewise, the effect of reducing the pollution level would show up during a period of many years.

Mortality studies are subject to many criticisms. They take no account of how long people have lived in the metropolitan area or of whether they live, work, or play in polluted parts of the metropolitan area. And, of course, one year's observations do not capture the complex history of a metropolitan area's air quality during the decades that are relevant to the population's longevity. In addition, there is no definitive list of variables that affect death rates and that vary among metropolitan areas. Finally, there is no certainty as to what pollution measure is correct. Is it the maximum or average concentration? Does the duration of a high-pollution period matter? One cannot have faith that such studies are precise. But the effects of sulfur oxides and particulates show up consistently in many variants of many studies. It is unlikely that the conclusions are illusory.

It is tempting to conclude that instead of the overall mortality rate in a metropolitan area, the dependent variable should be mortality or morbidity rates from certain diseases—such as emphysema—known to be caused by air pollution. Regressions have been estimated using disease-specific mortality and morbidity rates as dependent variables, and the conclusions are much the same as those using overall mortality rates. But disease-specific studies are also subject to criticisms. In many cases, cause of death is not known, simply because it is not important to the attending physician or to surviving relations to know it. Equally important, air pollution is not listed as a cause of death. Air pollution exacerbates other causes of death such as respiratory and circulatory diseases. But the diseases have other causes and it is difficult to estimate the contribution of air pollution to them. Although something can be learned from analysis of disease-specific mortality and morbidity rates, their use is subject to limitations.

Whereas property-value- and wage-rate-determination studies place great faith in people's rationality, mortality-rate-determination studies make the opposite assumption, that people do not change their places of residence and employment in response to pollution. If people changed metropolitan areas in response to pollution levels, it would be difficult to estimate air-pollution damages from mortality studies. Undoubtedly, the truth lies between the two extreme assumptions. Some people may choose places of residence in part on the basis of air quality. For example, retired New Yorkers with respiratory diseases may move to Florida because of the better air quality. But in general, it is difficult to believe that air quality is a major determinant of where people live and work.

The second category of air-pollution damage is to property. It is usual to classify property damages into those to materials and those to farm animals and to crops. The important component of materials damages is structures. Air pollution may increase the frequency of required painting, repairs, and replacement. But other materials, such as rubber and metals, are also damaged by air pollution. Damages to crops include reduced yields and lower-quality products resulting from air pollution. Farm animals and pets may be injured by air pollution in the same ways that humans are.

As with health damages, property damages can be studied either by laboratory experiments or by collecting data on actual damages and relating them to air pollution, among other things. Laboratory experiments are relatively more important in studying materials damages than in studying health damages. This is because there is less inhibition in experimenting with materials than with human health.

Property-damage experiments are not conceptually difficult to design, although they may be expensive to execute. For example, a set of identical painted surfaces can be exposed to varying ambient sulfur oxide concentrations, and deterioration of the paint and the material can be recorded. Then a relationship between deterioration and air quality can be estimated and it can be extrapolated to estimate effects of air-quality levels not included in the experiment. The same issues arise as in estimating human-health-damage functions, in particular whether there is a threshold effect.

Estimating property damages from field observations is inevitably complex because, unlike a controlled experiment, many things vary from one field observation to another. Some loss of property values from air pollution observed in studies of health damages may be because of damages to the property itself. If air pollution causes rapid deterioration of a structure, or its paint, then its value should be expected to be low. If property values are observed to be low where air quality is bad, it provides no indication whether the cause is damage from the pollution to the property or to the residents' health. From the viewpoint of estimating abatement benefits, it does not matter. If it is assumed that people pay less for a house in a polluted neighborhood by an amount that represents damage from the polluted air, then the reduction in the property values from polluted air is a correct measure of the benefits of abatement regardless whether the damage is to the structure or to residents' health. Alternatively, if it is assumed that residents can perceive the property, but not the health damages, then health damages must be estimated separately and added to property damages to obtain a measure of total damages. That may be a reasonable assumption.

Some studies have collected data on expenditures on house painting or clothes cleaning and related them to the presumed determinants of such expenditures, including air-pollution levels. Provided the estimation is undertaken carefully, it is an appropriate procedure. But it provides an alternative, not an additional, measure to property-value studies. If the effect of air pollution is to require that a house be repainted at three- rather than five-year intervals, then the pollution reduces the house's value by the present value[7] of the extra painting costs. It is double counting to add the extra painting costs to the reduced house values.

Much the same procedures can be followed regarding crop damages. Crop yields can be regressed on their determinants—such as measures of soil fertility, fertilizer inputs, and so forth—and air pollution measures can be included in the equations. Alternatively, the effect of air pollution on the value of farmland could be estimated. In fact, few careful studies of these kinds appear to have been under-

---

7. Present value was defined in Chapter 4. In the example given, pollution requires an extra 2/15 of a paint job per year. If a paint job costs \$1,000, the interest rate is 8 percent, and the house lasts 40 years, the loss of value to the house from pollution is

$$\sum_1^{40} \frac{(2/15)1,000}{(1.08)^t} \approx \$1,600.$$

taken, presumably because there are almost no data on ambient air quality in rural areas.[8]

It appears that the pollutants identified as the main culprits in health damage are also the main culprits in property damage. It is obvious that particulates dirty clothing and structures. And it has long been known that sulfur oxide concentrations damage paint and construction and other materials. Carbon monoxide, an inert gas, apparently does little property damage. Nitrogen oxides and oxidants damage materials and crops, but good estimates are elusive.

Abatement Techniques

Although air pollution results from a relatively small number of specific activities, there are many ways to abate airborne discharges. In this connection, it is well to remind oneself that neither combustion nor any other economic activity creates or destroys matter. All the matter in fuel must go somewhere when it is burned. What does not remain as ash and is not collected beforehand is discharged to the atmosphere. Although the total volume of matter is not altered by combustion, the amount and form of discharges to the atmosphere depend very much on the details of the combustion process.

The easiest way to reduce air pollution is to substitute nonpolluting for polluting fuels. As mentioned, such substitution has occurred on a large scale even in the absence of government environmental regulations. During the twentieth century, oil and natural gas have gradually been substituted for wood and coal as the country's main energy sources. Although oil and gas result in less air pollution per BTU of energy generated than do wood and coal, substitution occurred mostly for economic, not environmental, reasons at least until the 1960s. Oil and gas were plentiful, cheap to extract and ship, and easily usable for combustion and many other purposes. In

---

8. The few studies extant have been difficult to replicate and are fraught with difficulties. Arbitrary relations between leaf damage (in percentages) and yield reductions (in percentages) are made; in many cases air pollution damages look like mildew and may have been overstated; and depending on the nature of the soil, pollution may be beneficial to plant growth over some range of concentrations. The principal conclusion that appears beyond suspicion is that ozone and other oxidants do the majority of damage, with "ornamentals" (roses and the like) near urban areas being importantly damaged; other crops show mixed sensitivities and the relation of physical damage to economic loss is very difficult to gauge.

the 1960s and early 1970s thermal electric plants converted to oil and gas under the pressure of government environmental regulations. Intrafuel substitution is also possible. Some coal and oil contain much more sulfur than others, and low-sulfur coal and oil have been substituted for high-sulfur coal and oil. Of course, clean fuels are limited in supply, like everything else. In the 1970s, natural gas, the cleanest fuel, became scarce, in part because of dwindling reserves and in part because of excessively stringent government price controls. After the oil crisis in 1973, oil became expensive. Domestic coal supplies are still plentiful.

Similar to fuel substitution is substitution of nonfuel energy sources for fuel sources. Nonfuel sources are sources provided directly from natural processes. Solar, hydro, wind, tidal, and thermal energy are the important examples. Solar energy means capturing some of the large amount of energy that reaches the earth's surface from the sun, for example, for space heating. Hydro energy is mechanical energy from flowing streams, for example, for electricity generation. Wind energy means harnassing the force of wind, as with windmills. Tidal energy is energy from rising and falling tides, which can be used to generate electricity by the same means as flowing streams. Thermal energy means capture of heat that emerges from the interior of the earth in many places, for example, for electric generation. Interest in nonfuel energy sources has grown since the energy crisis, but it is unlikely that they will be able to replace a significant portion of energy obtained from fuels in the foreseeable future.

Although substitution of clean for dirty fuels may be expensive, it is technically simple. A second way to abate air pollution is to alter processes so they are less polluting. Process changes can be very complex, indeed. Many airborne discharges are products of incomplete combustion. Among the simplest process changes to abate air pollution are those that burn fuels more completely. Among the important measures taken after the 1952 killer fog in London was introduction of modern grates in which coal was burned in fireplaces to heat homes. Modern grates burned coal more completely resulting in reduced discharges of particulates to the atmosphere. On a technically more complex level, an important method of abating automobile emissions has been to design engines that burn fuels more completely. Carbon monoxide and hydrocarbons are products of incomplete combustion in internal-combustion engines, and their discharges are abated by better combustion. A fringe benefit is more miles of driving per gallon of fuel consumed. As has been discussed, however, nitrogen oxides are also products of combustion in internal-combustion engines, and methods to reduce carbon monoxide and hydrocarbon discharges are likely to increase nitrogen oxide discharges. Other devices, such as catalysts that reduce them to harmless substances, are needed to reduce nitrogen-oxide emissions. Basic changes in combustion processes to reduce harmful discharges may also be possible in thermal electric plants that burn coal and oil, but they are still in experimental stages.

A third way to abate air-polluting discharges is to remove harmful substances from the fuel before it is burned. Sulfur contributes nothing to the combustion of coal and oil; it is merely released by combustion and goes up the stack and into the atmosphere. Thus its removal from the fuel does not reduce the energy released by combustion. Sulfur can be and is removed from oil in the refining process, at some expense. There is no known process for removing sulfur from solid coal, but coal can be converted to sulfur-free gas, at some cost and loss of BTUs. Coal gasification processes have been known for decades, but known techniques are not economically competitive with other fuels. There is only limited potential for removing polluting substances from fuel before combustion. In many cases it is technically difficult and expensive. Some polluting substances are formed by the process of combustion itself, and therefore cannot be removed prior to combustion.

A fourth means of discharge abatement is to capture harmful substances after combustion but before they enter the atmosphere. Catalysts on automobile exhaust systems capture polluting gases and convert them to harmless gases. The most common examples under this heading, however, are proposals to capture harmful substances in smokestacks of thermal electric plants and other combustion units. Precipitators have been used for some time to capture particulates in smokestacks. They simply store the accumulated material, which eventually must be removed and disposed of, normally as a solid waste. Another conceptually simple, but not costless, means of reducing particulate emissions is to vent the smokestacks into "baghouses" which perform essentially like the bag on a vacuum cleaner. Improved technology is making this an attractive choice in many circumstances. Controversy continues over the cost and effectiveness (and the regional impacts on coal miners' incomes) of requiring thermal electric companies to install wet limestone scrubbers to remove constant percentages of sulfur oxides from stacks.

The final and most controversial way to limit air-polluting discharges is to limit directly the activities that generate emissions. Of course, any effluent standards or fees make polluting activities more expensive, which limits them indirectly. But proposals have been made for direct limits on polluting activities. The most frequent such proposal is to limit automobile driving in cities. Proposals include outright bans of cars in some areas, taxes on their use, subsidies to mass transit, taxes on parking places, and others. There are also proposals to limit thermal and atomic electric generation by taxes, direct controls, and simple refusal of regulatory agencies of permission to build generating plants. Anxiety regarding atomic electric plants stems from the possibility of accidental or intentional (by acts of war or sabotage) release of radioactivity to the air from the plants, and from the possibility of radioactive release from spent fuel that remains radioactive for thousands of years.[9]

The foregoing discussion illustrates the many ways to abate polluting discharges to the atmosphere, all more or less expensive and all more or less effective. The techniques of abatement that the discussion has concentrated on for fuel combustion also apply to other sources of air pollution. Many industrial processes generate polluting discharges. A frequent source of pollution is evaporation, for instance, of volatile solvents that are used throughout industry. Often the simplest process change, for example, keeping the solvents in contained spaces so that they cannot evaporate to the atmosphere, is the best solution. But some industrial-process emissions, such as in primary metal and chemical industries, are difficult to control, and require complex changes in processes, products, or collection devices.

Other Ways to Improve Air Quality

Air pollution is concentrated in space and time. Air quality is worse in urban than rural areas. In urban areas, air quality is worst in very hot and very cold weather when air conditioning and heating are used most, and on days when the air is still or when there is an inversion. In principle it is therefore possible to improve air quality by altering the time or place of discharges. Possibilities are discussed in this section.

9. Radioactivity will be discussed in greater detail, with hazardous substances more generally, in Chapter 7.

Altering the time of discharges appears to be less feasible for airborne than for waterborne discharges. Storage of wastes from combustion until bad weather passes appears to be infeasible at any cost comparable with benefits from doing so. In most cases, storing energy from combustion is equally infeasible. It is not feasible to generate electricity on days when air quality is good and store it for use when air quality is bad. Likewise, storage of heat generated for space heating is infeasible except in small amounts and for short times. Nor is it feasible to burn fuel for transportation on good days and store the energy to produce transportation on bad days. The only practical method of temporal changes in polluting discharges appears to be emergency measures that have been planned and tried in Los Angeles and elsewhere. When air quality is bad, industries may be ordered to cease production. This has the effect of concentrating production on days when air quality is good, and meeting demand from inventory, or not meeting it at all, on bad days. When air quality is very bad, thermal electric plants may be shut down and cars ordered off the roads. These measures simply prohibit polluting activities. But it is hard to imagine that they are justified as more than emergency steps.

Dispersing polluting discharges away from urban areas is a more promising proposal than altering their temporal pattern. The simplest example in this category has been used for decades: tall smokestacks. Tall stacks do not disperse the source of the discharge; instead they discharge the pollutants at heights where air movement is better than close to the ground and where it takes pollutants longer to return to ground or nose levels, where they do the greatest harm. Computer diffusion models make it possible to calculate the effect of high stacks on the fallout pattern of the effluents. The efficacy of high stacks depends crucially on air movement. If the air is still, pollutants return to ground level near the point of discharge regardless of the height at which they are discharged. Although high stacks can be useful in preventing intense localized concentrations of fallouts, their value is limited. They do not alter the volume of discharges, instead they merely spread them around. That is of little value in a large metropolitan area or region whose air is pervasively dirty.

More promising is the proposal to disperse pollution-generating activities away from polluted parts of metropolitan areas. The first thing to note is that economic forces have been doing that for decades without regard to environmental problems. Many studies have shown that metropolitan areas have decentralized, reducing densities of population and employment and dramatically reducing concentrations of employment near the centers of metropolitan areas. Manufacturing, which is more polluting than most urban activities, has decentralized most, so that by the early 1980s the density of manufacturing employment is greater in the suburbs than in the central cities of many metropolitan areas.

The most frequent proposal to encourage dispersion for environmental reasons is made regarding thermal electric plants. As was seen earlier in this chapter, they are major sources of the most harmful pollutants in urban areas. Furthermore, it is now possible to transport the electricity substantial distances from its place of generation to its place of consumption at nominal cost and with only modest loss of voltage. In a way, thermal electric plants are ideal candidates for dispersion. They are highly capital intensive, so it is not necessary to relocate a large labor force or to require long commuting when a plant moves twenty-five or fifty miles from an urban area. In addition, they do not need large amounts of inputs that must be shipped from other urban manufacturers. Their only important material input is fuel, which comes from rural mines, wells, and refineries.

More controversial are proposals to promote or require dispersion of manufacturing activities from urban areas. The disadvantages of dispersal of manufacturing activities away from urban areas may be great. They often require a large labor force which may be loath to relocate or commute to rural or small-town workplaces. Likewise, manufacturing plants are dependent on urban suppliers of inputs and buyers of outputs. Large-scale dispersal of manufacturing from urban areas would be costly, both in production and relocation costs. In addition, dispersal would increase the total transportation of people and goods that would be necessary. Thus, to some extent, dispersal of discharges would result in increases in total discharges because of increased transportation.

In some cases, however, the preceding drawbacks do not apply. Merely encouraging new polluting firms to locate on the east side of an urban area, rather than on the west side, can greatly reduce damages since the prevailing wind direction if from west to east. With identical emissions, air quality will not be affected where it matters most—where great concentrations of people and their materials are located.

Benefits and Costs of Air-Pollution Abatement

As was pointed out in earlier chapters, estimation of costs of pollution abatement is both conceptually and practically easier than estimation of benefits. The result is that there are more, and more reliable, studies of costs than of benefits of both air and water pollution abatement.

Social costs of air-pollution control are competitive market values of resources devoted to pollution abatement. The only important practical uncertainty in calculating such cost comes from the fact that pollution-control costs are sometimes difficult to separate from expenditures for other purposes. If a firm builds a new manufacturing plant, it is likely to differ from other plants in many ways. It is likely, for example, to contain new technology that may, incidentally, be less polluting than old technology. Indeed, federal pollution-control requirements may be one, among several, reasons for choosing the technology. It is then difficult to say how much of the cost was for pollution control.

In fact, this ambiguity has been relatively unimportant so far in air-pollution control. Most expenditures for air-pollution control are for specific devices whose purpose can be identified. Table 5.6 shows estimates of national government and private expenditures for air-pollution control made by the Council on Environmental Quality for 1979 and a forecast for 1988. These figures are in terms of 1979 dollars and the high (by historical standards) inflation of the early 1980s would make current figures substantially larger. Perhaps more important, from the perspective of those currently incurring the costs, is the fact that capital investments have been entered at their annual

TABLE 5.6

Actual and Estimated Air-Pollution-Control Costs 1979 and 1988 (billions of 1979 dollars)

	1979		1988	
Government		1.5		2.5
Private		20.8		35.1
—Mobile	8.1		14.7	
—Industrial	4.3		7.1	
—Utilities	8.4	___	13.3	___
TOTAL		22.3		37.6

SOURCE: *Environmental Quality*, December 1980, p. 394.

interest and depreciation cost, not at the amounts actually invested. This is appropriate to arrive at annualized figures (to compare to annualized control benefits), but actual control expenditures for recent years have been much larger in light of the projected long lives of some of the control equipment.

It is noteworthy that the bulk of the control costs is undertaken by the private sector. In the case of water, discussed in the following chapter, municipally owned sewage-treatment plants are an important component of control costs. However, there is a very real sense in which "who pays" is merely an administrative concern; scarce resources with opportunity costs are used either way, hence *we* are the ones that pay, not some "they," whether one considers the "they" to be private industry or government.

Another thing to note, perhaps most importantly, about Table 5.6 is that more than 40 percent of actual and projected costs is for automobile pollution abatement. These costs take the form of higher purchase prices, poorer fuel consumption, and higher maintenance costs that would be necessary in the absence of pollution-control requirements. There are, then, issues about the relative expenditures on mobile sources versus stationary sources as well as issues regarding whether the overall expenditures on emissions control have been worth their cost.

Have the benefits of greater control been worth the cost? To gain a more intuitive insight, the costs of $22.3 billion in 1979 are about $233 for each of the approximately 100 million households—much more for those who bought a new car, less for those who use few manufactured goods, including electricity. That amount of money does not seem like much, but one could think of it as a month of food, half of a new color TV, ten new shirts, or whatever. Are average benefits of this same order of magnitude? Casual inspection would suggest that benefits are not ten times larger than $223 for each family, nor are they likely to be one-tenth of that amount. So in terms of overall pollution control we are not likely to be grossly inefficient. In the most careful formal assessment to date, *Air and Water Pollution Control: A Benefit-Cost Assessment*, Rick Freeman concludes that the stationary-source air emissions control program appears to be justifiable in benefit-cost terms; neither the mobile-source air emissions control program nor the water-pollution control program are so justified. Freeman's overall estimate of annual benefits of improved air quality is $21.7 billion (with a range of $4.9 to $51.1 billion reflect-

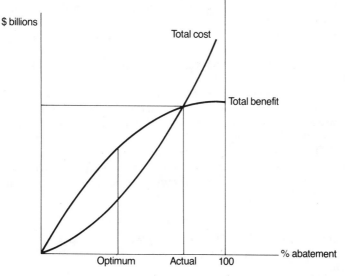

Figure 5.1

ing uncertainty). This would suggest that we are somewhere near the point "Actual" in Figure 5.1, the point at which total benefits are equal total costs. If so, the marginal costs are greater than the marginal benefits for improvements beyond the optimum, as depicted in Figure 5.1. However, since most of the benefits of air-quality improvements were associated with the stationary controls, considerable confidence can be placed in the belief that they have been worthwhile. Should the mobile-source pollution control program be scrapped, as the benefit-cost numbers found by Freeman (and by Seskin and others before him) might seem to suggest? Probably not, but there is clear potential for program improvement. Some suggestions for improved mobile-source (and, indeed, for stationary-source) emissions policies will be presented later.

DISCUSSION QUESTIONS AND PROBLEMS

1. How would you estimate the noneconomic value of increased longevity? Could you use data on cigarette smoking or other risky activities by retired people?

2. What are the important environmental damages from atomic electricity generation?

3. If environmental damages from automobiles were $5 billion per year,

it would come to about half a cent per mile driven. How do you think that would compare with congestion costs of automobile use in urban areas?

4. Would a gasoline tax be a good approximation to an automobile effluent fee?

5. Bearing in mind that most damages from pollution occur in the high-density locations where more people and materials are concentrated, do any ways of achieving proper levels of environmental quality at much lower cost occur to you? Think particularly about the automobile controls—there is a way to reduce costs by almost one-third without any notable loss of benefits by a simple administrative action!

6. The benefits and costs summarized at the end of this chapter are comprised of diverse effects where are difficult to quantify and make comparable. A review of approaches to doing this difficult task (see Chapter 2) might prove useful at this point.

REFERENCES AND FURTHER READING

Chappie, Mike, and Lave, Lester. "The Health Effects of Air Pollution: A Reanalysis." *Journal of Urban Economics* 12, no. 3 (November 1982): 346–76.

Committee on Public Works, U.S. Senate. *Air Quality and Automobile Emission Control.* Vols. 1–4. Washington, D.C.: U.S. Government Printing Office, 1974

Council on Environmental Quality. *Environmental Quality.* Washington, D.C.: U.S. Government Printing Office, published annually.

Department of Health, State of Colorado. *Colorado: Air Quality Data Report 1981,* 1982.

Freeman, A. Myrick, III. *Air and Water Pollution Control: A Benefit-Cost Assessment.* New York: Wiley, 1982.

Friedlaender, Ann, ed. *Air Pollution and Administrative Control.* Cambridge, Mass.: MIT Press, 1978

Lave, Lester, and Seskin, Eugene. *Air Pollution and Human Health.* Baltimore: John Hopkins University Press, for Resources for the Future, Inc., 1977.

Seskin, Eugene P. "Automobile Air Pollution Policy," in Paul R. Portney, ed. *Current Issues in U.S. Environmental Policy.* Baltimore: Johns Hopkins University Press, 1978.

Tolley, George, Graves, Philip, and Cohen, Alan. *Environmental Policy: Air Quality.* Cambridge, Mass.: Ballinger, 1982.

Chapter 6

Water Quality

Both air and water pollution are complex in that many substances are discharged to the media and the substances interact in complex and incompletely understood ways among themselves and with substances found naturally in the media. Air pollutants have a variety of effects on people, animals, plants, and materials. But virtually all air to which pollutants are discharged must be fit to breathe, and air that is harmless to people does little harm to other life and to materials. Water, however, is used in a much greater variety of ways and by no means all water needs to be suitable for all uses. People use only small amounts of water for purposes such as drinking that require very high quality. Since water, unlike air, flows in predictable patterns in natural channels, it is possible to permit much water to be of low quality and nevertheless to use only high-quality water for purposes for which high quality is important. The situation is aptly summarized by the statement that people are to the air as the fish are to water; they live in it. But people have much more flexibility and discretion with respect to water. Water pollution is much more complex than air pollution in the sense that society has many more options about the quality and uses of water bodies than we have about air quality.

Water is found in liquid form both on and under the surface of the earth, and is both abundant and renewable. Consider first abundance: for the continental United States alone, annual rainfall averages 30 inches per year, which is 4,200 *billion* gallons per day. Of course, much of this water (about two-thirds) is not available for use as it evaporates or is transpired by plants. The bulk of the remaining 35 percent of potential supply (91 percent of it) runs off to oceans either on the surface or from below it. Another 1 percent runs into Canada or Mexico, while 1 percent evaporates from reservoirs, leaving about 7 percent (of the 35 percent) which is actually consumed by humans in one form or another.

In spite of the losses in the so-called "hydrologic cycle," we in the United States are left with surface fresh-water reservoirs containing 150 *trillion* gallons, and aquifers (below-the-surface reservoirs in the earth's crust) are estimated to contain 200 times as much water as is in the surface reservoirs. To give a perspective on the vast amounts of water stored in aquifers, even lower bound estimates of their volume are the equivalent of two decades of *cumulative* precipitation, or, alternatively, these reservoirs contain an amount of water equal to the cumulative discharge of the Mississippi River over the past 200 years. There is clearly a lot of water out there, but this does not mean we should be complacent; as with air, there are severe local problems to be discussed in this chapter.

Surface waters are either fresh or salt, the latter being much more plentiful than the former. For most uses, salt water is much less valuable than fresh water. Salt water is unsuitable for drinking and its corrosive properties make it unsuitable for many other purposes. All natural water bodies contain some salt. A few flowing streams and interior lakes are as salty as sea water, and tidal estuaries are more or less salty. The groundwater under the surface flows downhill mostly in the direction of surface water bodies. As it flows, groundwater is largely purified by filtration. Some is "mined" as people extract it from the ground, and some feeds fresh and salt surface water bodies.

People use surface water either in its natural channels or by withdrawing it. The former are referred to as in-stream uses and the latter as withdrawal uses. Examples of in-stream uses are navigation, fishing, pleasure boating, and swimming. Examples of withdrawal uses are drinking, washing, cooling, industrial-process uses, and irrigation. Eash use has its peculiar quality requirements, which will be discussed later in the chapter. An important distinction is that in-stream uses must use water of the quality in the natural channel, whereas withdrawal uses can be preceded by processes that change its quality. For example, municipal water is mostly treated between withdrawal and use, and brackish water is sometimes desalted before use.

Almost every water use impairs its quality in some degree. The kind and amount of quality deterioration depend on the use made of the water and on the resources devoted to avoiding deterioration. Effects of various water uses on the important dimensions of water quality are discussed in the next section. Arranging water uses so as to avoid all deterioration of surface-water qualities from their natural state would be extremely expensive and probably impossible, notwithstanding the fact that this is the stated goal of the 1972 national water-quality legislation, which formulated the national water-pollution-control program through the 1970s and into the l980s. Water bodies are valuable and efficient natural mechanisms for diluting and degrading limited amounts of many wastes. But excessive discharges can do great harm to water bodies and to subsequent users.

Water quantity and quality are related in complex ways. Other things being equal, a large water body can absorb more waste, with a given quality deterioration, than a small water body. The other things include flow velocity and turbulence, because a fast, churning stream can degrade more wastes than a slow, placid stream. They also include temperature, since discharge of a given volume of organic wastes pollutes a warm stream more than a cool stream.

Because water uses affect quantity, they affect quality indirectly as well as directly. A traditional classification of water uses is between consumptive and nonconsumptive uses. Consumptive uses are those that make the water unavailable for further use, whereas nonconsumptive uses are either in-stream or return the water for further use. Consumptive uses do not affect the earth's total water volume, but they do change its location and form. The most important way people's activities make water unavailable is by vaporizing it. Irrigation causes much of the water so used to evaporate or transpire, thus making it unavailable for further use. Impoundment by dams increases the ratio of surface area to volume and hence accelerates evaporation in dry areas. Heat discharge to water bodies increases evaporation since cooling is an evaporative process. Although they perhaps should not be called consumptive, uses that change the location of water may be more important in reducing availability than are those that vaporize water. For example, most cities on estuaries withdraw water for municipal systems many miles upstream and discharge it into their saline estuaries, reducing the fresh water available downstream from the withdrawal point. Likewise, many cities withdraw water from one river basin and discharge it to another. For example, New York City withdraws much of its water from the upper reaches of the Delaware River basin and discharges it into the estuary at the mouth of the Hudson River. Los Angeles obtains most of its water from northern California and from the Colorado River,

TABLE 6.1

Water Withdrawn Per Day, by State and Puerto Rico, 1980

| State or other area | Per capita [1] (gallons) | Water withdrawn | | | | Fresh water consumed [2] (million gallons) |
		Total (billion gallons)	Surface (billion gallons)	Public supplies (billion gallons)	Irrigation (billion gallons)	
Total	1,996	460.0	360	34.0	150.0	100,000
Alabama	2,824	11.0	10	.6	(Z)	570
Alaska	546	(Z)	(Z)	.1	—	35
Arizona	2,929	8.0	4	.6	7.1	4,500
Arkansas	6,960	16.0	12	.3	5.1	3,600
California	2,272	54.0	33	4.1	37.0	25,000
Colorado	5,512	16.0	13	.6	14.0	4,000
Connecticut	1,188	3.7	4	.4	(Z)	160
Delaware	2,013	1.2	1	.1	(Z)	11
District of Columbia	—	(Z)	(Z)	.2	—	23
Florida	2,127	21.0	17	1.4	3.0	2,400
Georgia	1,259	6.9	6	.8	.6	1,000
Hawaii	2,548	2.5	2	.2	1.0	680
Idaho	19,007	18.0	12	.2	10.0	5,900
Illinois	2,187	25.0	17	1.8	.1	590
Indiana	2,551	14.0	13	.6	.2	690
Iowa	1,476	4.3	4	.3	.1	290
Kansas	2,788	6.6	1	.3	5.0	4,700
Kentucky	1,311	4.8	5	.4	(Z)	290
Louisiana	3,079	13.0	11	.6	2.2	3,500
Maine	1,421	1.6	2	.1	(Z)	53
Maryland	1,822	7.7	8	.5	(Z)	100
Massachusetts	1,027	5.9	6	.8	(Z)	90
Michigan	1,621	15.0	1	1.3	.2	460
Minnesota	759	3.1	2	.4	.2	450
Mississippi	1,387	3.5	2	.3	1.0	710

TABLE 6.1 (*continued*)

Water Withdrawn Per Day, by State and Puerto Rico, 1980

State or other area	Per capita [1] (gallons)	Water withdrawn Total (billion gallons)	Water withdrawn Surface (billion gallons)	Water withdrawn Public supplies (billion gallons)	Irrigation (billion gallons)	Fresh water consumed [2] (million gallons)
Missouri	1,401	6.9	6	.7	.1	670
Montana	13,959	11.0	11	.1	11.0	2,700
Nebraska	7,643	12.0	5	.3	9.3	7,600
Nevada	4,461	3.6	3	.2	3.1	1,700
New Hampshire	1,083	1.0	1	.1	(Z)	17
New Jersey	1,356	10.0	10	1.1	.1	380
New Mexico	2,989	3.9	2	.2	3.0	1,900
New York	967	17.0	16	2.2	(Z)	590
North Carolina	1,376	8.1	7	.6	.1	760
North Dakota	1,988	1.3	1	.1	.3	330
Ohio	1,296	14.0	13	1.4	(Z)	550
Oklahoma	592	1.8	1	.3	.9	1,000
Oregon	2,578	6.8	6	.2	5.9	3,200
Pennsylvania	1,347	16.0	15	1.5	.2	920
Rhode Island	527	.1	1	.1	(Z)	15
South Carolina	1,983	6.2	6	.4	.1	280
South Dakota	1,000	.7	(Z)	.1	.5	460
Tennessee	2,176	10.0	10	.5	(Z)	270
Texas	1,466	21.0	13	3.8	8.4	10,000
Utah	3,125	4.6	4	.8	3.2	2,900
Vermont	664	(Z)	(Z)	(Z)	(Z)	41
Virginia	2,238	12.0	9	.5	(Z)	230
Washington	2,001	8.3	8	.8	8.4	2,900
West Virginia	2,872	5.6	5	.2	(Z)	200
Wisconsin	1,227	5.8	5	.6	.1	310
Wyoming	11,368	5.4	5	.1	4.9	2,600
Puerto Rico [3]	980	3.2	3	.4	.3	300

Figures may not add due to rounding.

Withdrawal signifies water physically withdrawn from a source. Includes fresh and saline water; excludes water used for hydroelectric power.

Z = Less than 500 million.

[1] Based on population as of July 1.

[2] Evaporated transpired, or incorporated into products; excludes irrigation conveyance losses by evapotranspiration.

[3] Includes Virgin Islands.

SOURCE: Council on Environmental Quality, *Environmental Quality*, 1983, Table A-42, p. 306.

discharging it into the Pacific Ocean. Such transfers inevitably reduce the quality of the water downstream from the point of withdrawal. Thus not only do consumptive uses reduce the supply of water, but also some nonconsumptive uses move large volumes of water from one place to another. Both may cause deterioration in water quality.

Table 6.1 shows how much water is withdrawn from various sources (lakes, rivers, groundwater, and any saline sources) per day, for the United States as a whole and by state and territory. Looking first at the first column, while the average person in the United States uses almost two thousand gallons of water per day (directly or indirectly), there is huge variation among the states in per-capita water usage. In large part, this variation is due to irrigation, which varies greatly among locations, but the substantial role of pricing differences and other factors is evident from the table (for example, Wisconsin uses more than twice as much water per capita as Oklahoma in spite of the greater irrigation use in Oklahoma). Note that consumptive use is about one-fourth of the total withdrawals. Not shown from this table are the strong trends toward increased water use, and the fact that in many parts of the country, notably the Southwest, the groundwater withdrawals are exceeding recharge. Like all such trends (e.g., the 7 percent growth in energy use per year that abruptly stopped in recent years), one need not assume their continuance; if water prices were allowed to rise to reflect increasing scarcity in some locations, growth in water usage would decline and likely become negative. A great deal of water is wasted, as for example with leaky faucets, poor irrigation practices, frequent full-cycle dishwasher usage for near-empty loads, and so on, that would definitely not be wasted at higher prices.

Discharges and Water Quality

Human activities result directly or indirectly in the discharge of an enormous variety of substances to water bodies. An important distinction is between point and nonpoint discharges. Point discharges are those that send materials through pipes or other man-made channels to the water bodies. Examples are outfalls from municipal sewage systems or industrial plants. Nonpoint discharges are those that send materials to water bodies from a substantial and sometimes diffuse area. Runoff of fertilizer from ploughed farmland, runoff of rainwater from urban streets and buildings, and erosion of soil from construction sites are examples. The distinction is important because discharges from point sources are easier to meter and to abate than are those from nonpoint sources. However, the high marginal costs of control at current point source control levels suggest that it is time to examine more carefully the control of nonpoint sources.

A second important distinction is between degradable and non-degradable wastes. Natural water bodies mostly contain 2 to 10 parts per million (ppm) of dissolved oxygen (DO). Most organic materials are degraded to inorganic compounds in water bodies and deplete the water's oxygen content in the process. The rate at which degradation occurs depends on many characteristics of the water body but, most importantly, on the oxygen content of the water. In fact, a good measure of the volume of organic waste is the demand it makes on the water body's oxygen content, called biochemical oxygen demand (BOD). Organic compounds that degrade in water are said to be degradable. But some organic compounds, including phenols such as PCBs, either do not degrade or degrade only slowly.

The justification for disposing of organic wastes in water bodies stems mainly from the fact that water bodies replenish their DO by absorbing oxygen from the air and by photosynthesis in the water. Both oxygen absorption, or reaeration, and photosynthesis depend on many characteristics of the water body. For flowing streams there is a characteristic pattern by which an organic discharge lowers DO content by an amount that is a function of distance downstream from the discharge. The process is described mathematically by an oxygen-sag equation. It shows how the stream's DO level gradually sags as the polluting discharge moves downstream, followed by a gradual recovery of DO level as degradation, dilution, and reaeration take place. The oxygen-sag equation shows the dependence of the process on stream characteristics. Tidal reaches are a quite different matter. Tidal action can slosh wastes back and forth past the point of discharge for a long time before they are degraded or diluted. Lakes are the most delicate water bodies. Their water volumes are large relative to their flows, so that residence times of pollutants are long. In addition, most are relatively still, so they reaerate only slowly. Finally, deep lakes have complex diurnal and seasonal patterns of vertical water circulation, depending mainly on temperature changes. DO affects the fish and other life that can survive in the water and the uses to which it can be put. Large organic discharges deplete

DO. At that point, no fish can survive and organic degradation proceeds anaerobically, which makes the water stink.

Nondegradable wastes are those not degraded by natural processes in water. Elements such as mercury and zinc, and many inorganic chemicals such as DDT are unaffected by physical and chemical actions of water or are affected only very slowly. Nondegradable wastes can nevertheless be diluted by water and in freshwater streams their rate of discharge relative to the rate of stream flow is the key relationship. If their discharge is large relative to stream flow, their concentration can be enough to do great harm. But the greatest concern over nondegradable wastes results from the fact that the oceans are the ultimate sinks for most of them. They accumulate in oceans and in their esuarine reaches for long periods of time. That of course is why the oceans are salty and rich in many minerals. By the time evidence of harm appears, it may be difficult or impossible to reduce their concentration.

Heat discharges are between degradable and nondegradable. Most heat discharge to water bodies is dissipated by evaporation to the atmosphere and eventually to outer space. The fact that water releases its heat slowly means that a flowing stream can transport heat from places where it is excessive. As will be discussed in Chapter 12, heating of the atmosphere is of most concern in metropolitan areas. A metropolitan area on a flowing stream can remove large amounts of excess heat by discharging it to the stream. But the heat is not removed far if it is discharged to a lake or estuary in which the water moves only slowly.

What are the important materials discharged to water bodies and what volumes are discharged? Rough magnitudes of substances discharged are known, but the national government is only slowly compiling comprehensive discharge data.

The most studied discharges are those of degradable organic material. Households generate large volumes of organic wastes from human wastes, garbage disposals, and so forth. About two-thirds of households, almost all of those in urban areas, are served by municipal sewage systems. See Table 6.2 (discussed in more detail later) which shows increasing coverage and treatment level, until at least 1980. Wastes of sewered households are collected by the system, mostly treated somewhat, and discharged to water bodies. Most households not served at least minimally are in rural areas and distant suburbs and discharge their wastes to septic tanks. Anaerobic degradation

TABLE 6.2

Population Served by Municipal Wastewater Systems, by Level of Treatment, 1960–1982 (million people)

Service and degree	1960	1970	1978	1980	1982
Total U.S. population	180	203	220	224	230
Not served by wastewater systems	70	58	66	65	62
Total served by wastewater systems	110	145	154	159	168
Served, but no treatment	70	59	2	2	13
Total served and with treatment	40	86	152	157	155
Primary treatment	36	NA	211	411	37
Advanced primary treatment		NA	26		
Secondary treatment		NA	56	63	63
Advanced secondary treatment	4	NA	31	48	48
Tertiary treatment		NA	18	52	5

Data for 1960 and 1970 are not strictly comparable to 1978 and 1980 data because of different methods of data collection. Data for 1960 and 1970 were aggregated by state from the national population censuses. Data for 1978 and 1980 were compiled from the EPA inventories of municipal wastewater facilities.

In 1980, there were more than 32,000 wastewater facilities in operation throughout the country removing some 76% (9 million pounds per day) of bod5 and 80% (also 9 million pounds per day) of suspended solids. Bod5 is the amount of oxygen consumed metabolically by test microorganisms in a sample in 5 days.

NA—Not available.

[1] Primary treatment for 1978 and 1980 also includes the population served by wastewater treatment systems that have no discharges to surface waters. In 1980, this included 4 million people.

[2] Decrease in 1980 due to some tertiary plants being downgraded.

SOURCE: Council on Environmental Quality, *Environmental Quality*, 1983, Table A-61, p. 319.

occurs in septic tanks and wastes are filtered through the soil as overflow joins groundwater in flowing toward water bodies. Municipal sewage systems also collect large volumes of organic wastes from commercial institutions (restaurants, laundries, and the like) and public and semiprivate institutions (hospitals, schools, for instance). Many municipal sewage systems also collect organic wastes from industries. But industries also discharge large volumes of organic wastes to water bodies without the use of municipal sewage systems. The final important source of organic waste is agriculture. Large amounts of organic material are discarded in the harvesting of crops. Most is returned to the land, where it decomposes without affecting water bodies. But much of the waste from livestock finds its way into streams and is an important source of pollution. Processing of food off farms also generates large volumes of organic wastes, but food processing is included in the manufacturing instead of the agricultural sector.

Table 6.3 shows Environemental Protection Agency (EPA) estimates of organic-waste discharges in the United States in 1973 (more recent data are not available). In evaluating data on organic wastes it is important to know whether they refer to wastes generated or discharged. Treatment processes both remove organic wastes before discharge to waterways and convert them to inorganic compounds. About two-thirds of municipal organic wastes are removed by treatment. The percentage removed by industry is unknown. The data in Table 6.3 refer to discharges. Both the municipal and industrial totals are substantially smaller than in earlier years, because of the government's pollution-abatement program. About 90 percent of the industrial organic waste comes from four manufacturing industries: chemicals, paper, food processing, and textiles.

The striking fact about the data in Table 6.3 is the large volume of discharges from nonpoint sources. They account for more than 80 percent of organic discharges after treatment. About half is runoff from urban streets, sidewalks, and buildings. The other half is mostly agricultural wastes. If the data are accurate, elimination of all municipal and industrial sources would reduce total organic discharges by less than 20 percent.

Many kinds of nondegradable wastes are generated and discharged to waterbodies, although there are no comprehensive data, nor even widely used classifications. Most nondegradable wastes come from industrial point sources and from agricultural and mining nonpoint sources. Important nondegradable wastes include inorganic and

TABLE 6.3

Organic Waste Discharges in the United States, 1973
(billions of pounds of BOD)

Municipal sources	5.6
Industrial sources	4.3
Nonpoint sources	45.0
TOTAL	54.9

SOURCE: Council on Environmental Quality, *Environmental Quality*, 1976, p. 257.

synthetic organic chemicals, heavy metals, and suspended solids. Many salt and mineral solid wastes from industry and agriculture (in the form of runoff and irrigation return flow) also find their way into streams. The earth's crust is the source of minerals and runoff is the way the oceans have obtained their large mineral deposits. But it means that discharges cannot be estimated accurately by measuring quantities found in streams, because natural sources are sometimes large relative to amounts discharged by human activities.

With respect to human activities, there is some room for optimism, at least in terms of industrial point discharges. Since 1972 when Best Practicable Treatment (BPT) was required, the following percentage *decreases* in discharges have been recorded: biochemical oxygen demand (BOD), 71 percent; suspended solids, 80 percent; oil and grease, 71 percent; dissolved solids, 52 percent; phosphate, 74 percent; and heavy metals, 78 percent. Also on an optimistic note, since 1973 there has been a 65 percent increase in municipal sewage-treatment-plant removal of BOD and suspended solids. However, the additional 18 million people and increase of 7 billion gallons per day in wastewater flow have resulted in constant discharges in spite of greater removal.

Discharge data are important because they identify sources of pollutants, but ambient environmental quality is relevant to the effects of pollutants on people's activites. Measuring stream quality is complex. Some measures are technically difficult to obtain because small amounts of substances may be harmful and complex metering devices may be needed to obtain the desired accuracy. In addition, it is often difficult to know what measures are most useful. DO, dissolved oxygen, content of water has been metered in at least a few places for many years and accurate devices are available. But the DO reading depends on exactly where the device is placed. A wide river may be much more polluted near the edges than in the middle and just below than just above an outfall. Finally, there are issues as to how data should be reported. Average DO levels throughout a year are the most commonly available data. But stream quality has a characteristic seasonal pattern and DO levels often reach peaks in spring and troughs in late summer. A high DO level in the spring is of little comfort to those who would like to swim in a stream that is polluted in August. There are three relevant dimensions to DO content of water: level, frequency, and duration. The importance of the last two dimensions is that, if a stream is anaerobic ten days a year, it may matter whether the ten days are scattered or consecutive. For example, fish may be able to survive the former but not the latter.

Fortunately, stream-quality data are somewhat more plentiful than discharge data. EPA collects substantial amounts of data on DO levels and various indexes are published each year in *Environmental Quality*. Although inadequate to sustain a firm conclusion, the evidence suggests that *very* gradual improvement in the nation's surface waters has occured since the implementation of legislation. A 1982 National Water Quality Inventory indicated that twenty-one of thirty-five states reporting trend information said water quality was improving; fourteen states reported no trend toward either degradation or improvement. Twenty-nine states noted *localized* examples of degradation, without reporting statewide trends toward degradation.

Three areas of increasing concern, *groundwater quality, estuarine and marine water quality*, and *acid rain damage to surface waters*, deserve some additional discussion. Dramatic recent incidents of pollution in groundwater-fed public water supplies have given the impression to many that we are rapidly poisoning our huge aquifers. The fact is that very little is known with certainty about the quality of our groundwater—the supplies are enormous, slow-moving, and inaccessible. Sources of contamination are many: gas storage tanks, liquid fertilizers, chemicals and wastes, minerals leached from irrigated fields, nitrates from sewage and fertilizers, septic system organic compounds and pathogens, road salts, surface impoundments, landfills, transportation spills, illegal disposal, pesticides (e.g., aldicarb in Wisconsin, New York, Florida, Missouri, Arizona, Maine, and Virginia and ethylene dibromide [EDB] in Georgia, Hawaii, California, and other states). Toxic substances are of the greatest concern, in particular the low molecular weight chlorinated hydrocarbons, which are widespread in pesticides and cleaning agents. How far-reaching is underground water pollution? A 1981 EPA Groundwater Supply Survey sampled 945 groundwater-dependent public water supplies for volatile organic chemicals (VOC) and found that 24 percent (230) had VOCs at the detection threshold while 1 percent had VOCs in an amount greater than 50 micrograms per liter, with one-half of 1 percent having VOCs greater than 100 micrograms per liter. Unfortunately, it was the larger water supplies, those serving more than ten thousand people, that had the higher rates of contamination. Moreover, contaminated drinking-water wells have been shut down in every state (four thousand wells have been affected or shut down). In light of the preceding, the EPA is now required (by the Resource Conservation and Recovery Act, RCRA) to monitor the groundwater quality at *all* active hazardous-waste-management facilities. The perhaps surprising conclusion (from p. 93 of the 1984 *Environmental Quality*) is that, despite lack of data, "the over-whelming proportion of the nation's fresh groundwater is not believed to be contaminated." Where contamination exists, it is localized, because groundwater flows very slowly.

The case of estuarine and marine waters is less positive, in part because a huge, and growing, proportion of our population resides adjacent to such waters (the Pacific and Atlantic Oceans and the Gulf of Mexico). Part of the problem is that the marine and estuarial ecosystems are less well understood than fresh water rivers. For example, abalone fishermen would love to eliminate the sea otter, since otters compete with them in the kelp beds which are the home of the abalone. However, it turns out that sea urchins eat kelp (reducing the habitat of the abalone) and sea otters also eat sea urchins, ultimately leading to more abalone for both otter and fishermen. And this is but a simple example. The problems are many: increas-ing use of chlorine, to eliminate undesirable pests, kills desirable organisms in addition to forming trihalomethanes which are carcin-ogenic and mutagenic; sewage disposal has led to high concentra-tions of trace metals, PCBs, and DDT near dumpsites; inland changes, in for example lumbering, farming, urban or industrial practices, can have a big, poorly understood impact on coastal waters, and so on. These impacts may be very distant in terms of both time and place from their causes. Unfortunately, coastal habitats are the most productive ecosystems on earth! Over one-half of the biological pro-duction of the world's oceans is along the coasts and in estuaries, and a great many rare ecosystems are being destroyed annually as urban development encroaches on coastal wetlands. Chesapeake Bay, one of the largest and most important commercial bays in the world, has been declining in quality over the entire three-and-a-half decade period beginning in 1950. Increasingly, scientists are observing evidence of greater fish disease in the form of liver and skin cancers, skeletal and cellular abnormalities, and the like. Of particular concern in this regard are petroleum hydrocarbons, which are toxic, carcinogenic, and mutagenic and which lead to viscous smothering of certain spe-cies. High demands for oil have led to greater numbers of tanker accidents, tank washing and deballasting, refinery effluents, municipal and industrial discharges, pipeline seepage, and offshore production, and greater pollution of coastal regions from rivers and atmospheric deposition. Within this pessimistic scenario there are, however, signs of progress. Gradual improvement in shellfish breeding and harvesting areas is occurring, with a 1 to 2 percent annual increase in areas opened to harvesting since the early 1970s.

As to acid-rain damage to surface waters, the best evidence is far more mixed than one would expect from media accounts. The damage from airborne acids depends on the "buffering capacities" of the surfaces involved; that is, lakes and soils differ greatly in their ability to counteract or neutralize acid inputs. A recent study by the Fish and Wildlife Service did conclude that 220 lakes in the United States have been acified, mostly in the Adirondack Mountains. Concern also runs high in Canada, Norway, and elsewhere. However, the most recent monitoring results published by the U.S. Geological Survey in September 1983 indicate that over the 1965 to 1980 period trends in pH levels of U.S. surface waters are *mixed*. There have been small improvements in the Northeast where concern has been high and small decrements in the Southeast and West. There has been little overall trend over this period with the pattern of regional effects paralleling trends in SO_2 emissions during the same period.

Damages from Water Pollution

What difference does the ambient quality of lakes, streams, and estuaries make? The issue is complex. Many substances are discharged to water bodies and many uses are made of water. Some uses are unaffected by some discharges and some severely affected. Many effects are poorly understood because of inadequate knowledge of physical, chemical, and biological relationships and because effects are subjective and not amenable to laboratory analysis. Finally, there are interaction effects. Discharge of heat to a stream increases the polluting effects of organic discharges because the water's temperature is raised and chemical reactions proceed quickly in a warm environment.

DO level summarizes the effect on stream quality of many kinds of organic discharges. Furthermore, DO level is a crucial quality dimension for many water uses. All animals require oxygen, and fish and other aquatic life obtain their oxygen from that dissolved in the water. Each important kind of fish has its peculiar range of DO levels it can tolerate. Generally, the most desirable game fish require the highest DO levels and none can live in anaerobic water. But much more is at issue than whether particular fish can be caught in particular reaches of streams. Many fish and other water animals spawn in streams and estuaries even though they spend most of their lives in salt water. A low DO level in an estuary or tidal reach of a stream prevents spawning both there and upstream. A DO level of 4 ppm is adequate for most aquatic life.

Thus DO content of streams affects commercial and sport fishing. But it also has direct and indirect effects on people's use of water. At the extreme, an anaerobic water body has a characteristic stink which people find highly offensive. DO depletion is not uncommon in streams and estuaries near large cities where sewage, industrial wastes, and runoff are concentrated. For example, the Schuylkill, a small river flowing through Philadelphia and into the Deleware River south of the city, is frequently anaerobic. The DO level affects not only animal, but also plant life in streams. Low DO levels may stimulate growth of plants that interfere with swimming, boating, and other water activities.

Temperature also affects fish and other life in water bodies. Fishermen report catches later into the fall and winter near outfalls of thermal electric plants than elsewhere, because the discharge keeps the water warm. But in the late summer, the concentrated heat discharges, especially of large atomic electric plants, are another matter. Then water temperatures may be near the highest many kinds of fish can tolerate, organic discharges from food-processing plants are at their seasonal peak, and flow is at its seasonal low in many streams. The result is severe oxygen depletion in many streams and estuaries. High temperature may itself cause fish kills, especially near large atomic plants.

Sediment, salts, and minerals affect water in several ways. Sediment is aesthetically displeasing to swimmers, boaters, and picnickers, and it reduces the ability of streams to replenish their oxygen content. Salts are corrosive and damage pipes and water-using equipment. Salts and minerals also affect the kinds of animal and plant life that can survive in the water.

Many substances discharged to water are classified as toxic. Toxicity is a matter of degree, but the term is nevertheless useful. Radioactive discharges from atomic plants receive the most popular attention. Many chemicals are also toxic as, in lesser degree, are pesticides such as DDT. Heavy metals also fall in the toxic category. Despite periodic popular concern, there is no substantial evidence of poisoning from heavy metals discharged to water bodies in the United States. But the danger is not imaginary, and such poisoning has been documented elsewhere, especially in Japan. There people have been crippled and killed by ingestion of mercury and cadmium discharged to rivers from factories. Because mercury and cadmium are elements, their mass is conserved, and they remain in the tissues of animals that ingest them. This causes a buildup of these elements in animals up the aquatic food chain; human poisoning in the Japanese case was caused by eating poisoned fish.

Some damages from discharges are partly aesthetic, but they are not necessarily unimportant. People dislike strongly to swim in, boat on, or picnic near water that contains floating sewage, stinks, or is discolored.

In the United States, communities set stringent standards on many quality dimensions for municipal water supply. Dimensions include acidity, bacteria count, dissolved solids, as well as other measures. A mystique surrounds drinking water and popular writers frequently claim that it is a health hazard. Most such claims are figments of writers' imaginations, and the historical weight of professional public-health experts' opinions has been that our drinking-water standards are conservative, perhaps even more than is justifiable. In the mid-1970s, concern was raised about carcinogens (cancer-producing substances) in drinking water. Evidence is indirect and confounded with other likely causes. However conservative American drinking-water standards may be, they have enabled Americans to avoid for decades transmission through their public water supply of dysentery and other waterborne diseases that are still endemic in many countries. Communities tend to set the same standards for swimming pools and beaches as for drinking water. There is even less basis for swimming standards than for drinking-water standards and some medical authorities believe that the most common medical problem caused by water quality in swimming pools is earaches from chlorine added to the water to kill bacteria.

In many communities, high drinking-water standards have been met by withdrawing water from small streams well upstream from urban areas, by stringent controls on discharges and land uses upstream from withdrawal points, and by modest treatment of water before use. Some large cities, especially those on downstream reaches of large rivers, now provide extensive treatment of municipal water before use. The importance of groundwater is highlighted by the fact that half of our population, 116 million people, rely on groundwater for the primary source of drinking water. While thirty-four of the hundred largest cities depend completely or in part on groundwater, forty-eight thousand of the nation's fifty-nine thousand community-public-water systems are totally dependent on groundwater sources. That groundwater levels are falling and, at least to some extent, are becoming more polluted is clearly of great concern.

Improving Water Quality by Discharge Abatement

A wide range of options is available to society to abate polluting discharges to water bodies. The materials balance tells us that something must happen to every ounce of every substance whose discharge to water bodies is reduced. This is the most fundamental meaning of the popular saying, "There are no free lunches." The implication is that it is important to ask what will happen to substances if it is proposed to abate their discharge to water bodies. The result of an abatement program may be that the substances will be discharged in some other way that is equally harmful.

When most people think of discharge abatement they think of municipal sewage plants (see Table 6.2). These are large structures, visible downstream from every large city, which primarily treat the large organic-waste load generated in cities by households, commercial institutions, factories, hospitals, and so forth. Primary- and secondary-treatment technologies have long been standardized. Primary treatment is mainly a physical process in which solids are removed by screening and sedimentation. It removes about 30 percent of the BOD and 60 percent of suspended solids from the effluent. It produces a sludge to be disposed of, all too often by hauling it away in barges and dumping it a few miles out from the treatment plant. Secondary treatment consists of biological and chemical processes that accelerate the natural degradation process. The product is some inorganic materials and an organic sludge. Primary and secondary treatment remove a total of about 90 percent of the BOD and solids from effluent.

In recent decades, several chemical processes have been studied and become known as tertiary treatment. The technology is not standardized. Methods are available to remove additional BOD and many combinations of inorganic wastes that may be collected in municipal sewage systems. Technical progress has been substantial with tertiary-treatment systems since the early 1960s. In recent years, as seen in Table 6.2, the high cost of such systems has reduced their use. It is to the costs of attaining water quality changes that we now turn.

Average cost functions for waste-treatment systems have the conventional U-shape in price-theory texts. Examples are in Figure 6.1, where cost per person served is graphed against percent of BOD removed. The upper curve represents a small plant serving 50,000 people and the lower curve represents a large plant serving 100,000 people. Scale economies cause lower average cost up the volume normally generated by populations of 100,000 or 200,000 people. It is

Figure 6.1

usually economical to build a second plant, in a different location so as to economize on collection costs, if the population to be served exceeds a few hundred thousand. Average cost falls at low treatment levels, but rises very rapidly if the percentage of BOD removed goes above 95. In practice, costs also depend on other pollutants removed from the waste water.

Sludge disposal is always a problem for treatment plants. The easiest and most damaging disposal method is to haul it to sea and dump it. It can be burned, which converts a water-pollution problem into an air-pollution problem. It can also be disposed of by dumping it on land, which converts it into a solid-waste problem. It is safe and economical to process sludge to make high-quality organic fertilizer, which is now done in some places.

The importance of high-quality municipal treatment plants should not be underestimated, but conventional treatment plants have received excessive emphasis in the United States pollution-abatement program. In much of that program, the rule of thumb in setting discharge standards has been "secondary treatment or its equivalent." Many industrial processes generate complex combinations of waterborne wastes that are quite different from those handled by municipal treatment plants. Sometimes other treatment systems or modifed treatment systems can be used, but frequently the best abatement procedure is to modify the product or the production process so that less waste is generated. In such a case it becomes difficult to know what "secondary treatment or its equivalent" means.

The basic point is that there are many processes by which materials can be converted into products. For that reason, the theory of production outlined in Chapter 3 has been developed to emphasize input substitution. Different processes use different materials to make a given product or set of products, and the processes may generate different kinds or amounts of wastes. A second process may use some materials that are wastes in a first process and may make from them products not made by the first process. One process may extract more of a wanted material from a natural resource and therefore leave less to be discharged as waste. Often minor modifications in products permit different materials or different processes to be used, thus generating less waste, less polluting waste, or more easily treated wastes.

Until recently, these possibilities could be illustrated only by anecdotes from various industries. But in the late 1960s, Resources for the Future began to publish a series of monographs on water use in various industries. George Löf and Allen Kneese found that processes in widespread use for extracting sugar from beets generated 39.5 pounds of BOD per ton of beets processed. Process changes, each in use in at least some plants at the time, could reduce BOD generation to 11.7 pounds. Waste-treatment procedures, also in use in at least some plants, could reduce BOD discharge to 1.2 pounds. These numbers indicate that BOD discharges in the beet-sugar industry vary by a factor of more than 30 depending on the processes and treatment procedures used, with process choices accounting for most of the variation. Generally, processes that produce little waste are modern ones, and waste generation per unit of output undoubtedly falls, in this industry as in others, as modern processes are installed on profitability grounds. But many of the processes and treatment procedures are unprofitable in the absence of government policies to force or motivate reductions in discharges. Almost every beet-sugar plant could abate its BOD discharges somewhat at modest cost. The cost of a given percentage abatement would depend a great deal on the age and other characteristics of the plant. A requirement of uniform and high-percentage abatement would add substantially to the cost of producing the product.

Beet sugar is not a large industry in the United States, although it produces a large amount of organic waste per unit of output. It is part of the food-processing industry, which is in general a large source of organic wastes. There is little reason to doubt that similar possibilities for reducing organic-waste discharges are available in other areas of the food-processing industry.

Possibilities, techniques, and costs of discharge abatement vary greatly among and within industries. Discharge abatement is more complicated in the pulp and paper industry than in food processing. Furthermore, the costs and difficulties of abatement depend on the age of a plant and on details as to products produced and processes used. The implication is that rules of thumb like "secondary treatment or its equivalent" and "best practicable discharge-control technology" are useless guides to government policy. Government policy should induce large abatement in plants and industries in which abatement is cheap and modest abatement where it is expensive. Recall from Chapter 2 that "expensive" here does not importantly relate to dollar costs facing particular firms for which we may not have great sympathy. Rather, expensive refers to the large use of scarce resources having opportunity costs, in terms of forgone goods that society cares about.

The discussion so far in this section has concerned discharge abatement by altering the amount or form of substances discharged. Mention should also be made of possibilites of altering the time and place of discharges to improve stream quality. Most pollution problems are localized by time and place. Late summer is the worst season in most of the United States. Stream flow is then at its seasonal trough, water temperatures are at their peak, and discharges from some sources, notably food processing, are at their peak. All worsen pollution problems. One way to improve the situation is to alter the seasonal discharge pattern. Wastes can be stored in lagoons or in other ways until the worst season has passed. A similar problem arises on a smaller time scale for municipal treatment plants. In many cities, storm drains feed into the sewer system. The total flow in the system increases greatly after a heavy rain and often exceeds the capacity of the treatment plant. The usual procedure is to channel some of the waste into pipes that bypass the treatment plant and to discharge the untreated waste to the receiving water. This results in discharge of raw sewage and also of the wastes that rain washes off street sidewalks. It is possible, although expensive, to store this flow a few hours until the flow in the sewage system has fallen off.

Finally, it is possible to alter the place of discharge. Some cities located on rivers or estuaries have considered piping the effluent from their treatment plants away from overburdened waters to bays or to the ocean. Lake Washington in Seattle was cleaned up dramatically by piping the effluent from treatment plants to Puget Sound instead of discharging it into the lake. In fact, hauling sludge from a treatment plant out to sea is another example of the same thing. In the private sector, it is possible to move entire plants so that their wastes can be discharged elsewhere. Alternatively, their wastes can be transported in pipes or by other means. Some people have proposed zoning particular streams or stretches of streams for particular kinds of discharges. Prohibitions on discharges above municipal intakes are examples. Effluent fees or discharge standards that varied by location on a river might have the same effect. In the industrial Ruhr Valley in Germany, firms and municipalities can discharge wastes freely into a small river the entire contents of which are treated at a downstream location.

Other Ways to Improve Water Quality

The previous section was concerned with methods of reducing polluting discharges to water bodies. Discharge abatement is only one set of ways to improve water quality. Other methods that can be adopted by governments or, in a few cases, private parties are discussed in this section.

Low-flow augmentation is the most studied means of improving stream quality to be discussed in this section. As national concern with water pollution has grown, the federal government's two dam-building agencies (the Army Corps of Engineers in the East and the Bureau of Reclamation in the West) have increasingly emphasized pollution control in efforts to persuade Congress to finance dam construction. A dam is built upstream from the pollution problem and the water level in the reservoir behind the dam is raised during the season of high flow and lowered during the season of low flow, thus augmenting the low flow. The capacity of the stream to degrade organic wastes and to dilute inorganic wastes can thereby be augmented. It cannot, of course, increase annual stream flow and may in fact reduce total stream flow because of evaporation from the reservoir. Evaporation is a minor matter in the humid East, but a major matter in the dry West. Virtually all dams serve other purposes than low-flow augmentation: Flood prevention, hydroelectric power, irrigation, municipal water supply, and recreation are the most important. Some such purposes are complementary with low-flow augmentation, and some are competitive. The pattern of releases from the reservoir for flood control is likely to be similar to that desired for low-flow augmentation, that is, storage during periods of high flow and release during periods of low flow. But use of the reservoir for boating and swimming is likely to require a high water level at the time large releases are needed to augment low flows. Benefits of dams are likely to be overstated if it is not remembered that, to butcher an old saying, you cannot have your reservoir full and drain it too. In recent years, environmentalists and others have become critical of dams. Some object to the destruction of natural beauty. Inevitably, the most attractive locations for dams are upstream in hilly country where the land can enclose a large reservoir. But such places are also prized for their great natural beauty. Some object to the forced displacement of people when their land is taken by eminent domain to be flooded by the reservoir, and some are concerned that reservoirs will become polluted. A reservoir is about as delicate an ecological system as a lake and, like many lakes, reservoirs are often located near farmland where they receive agricultural runoff. The result is eutrophication in reservoirs, just as in lakes. The final comment is that although the effect of low-flow augmentation on the quality of a stream can be calculated by the oxygen-sag equation, its effect on water quality in a tidal estuary is problematical. An example is the proposed Tocks Island dam on the upper reaches of the Delware River. The river's pollution problems are concentrated in the tidal reaches of the river, starting above Philadelphia, and in the estuary below Philadelphia. No one knows how much the altered pattern of stream flow would improve water quality where it is most needed. Tidal action is too complex to be analyzed by oxygen-sag equations.

A second method of in-stream water-quality improvement that has been studied, and tried in a few places, is mechanical reaeration. Although devices differ in detail, the basic idea is simple. Pipes are laid out into the flowing stream and oxygen is pumped through them and into the water. Some oxygen is absorbed by the water, raising its DO level. Reaeration can increase the amount of organic waste a stream can receive without serious quality reduction. It is a simple mechanical process and there is no reason to think it would be technically difficult to raise the DO level of streams substantially. Although the devices may be somewhat unsightly, it is hard to imagine that as a major drawback.

A third means of improving stream quality is dredging. Sludge gradually accumulates on the bed of a stream that has received organic wastes for many years. The sludge is relatively inert and may remain for long periods of time. It degrades gradually and some experts have guessed that the buildup of sludge in some estuaries may be such that about half the BOD comes from sludge instead of from current discharges. The sludge can be removed by dredging and, in fact, dredging estuaries for other purposes, such as deepening shipping channels, brings up large amounts of sludge. A problem with dredging is where to store the sludge so that it will be less harmful than on the stream bed. Dredged material is usually dumped in marshland at the edge of the river. If so, the organic material gradually washes back into the stream and also creates aesthetic and odor problems while on the land. In addition, dredging agitates the sludge in the stream bed and can create serious pollution problems during and following the time of dredging.

The final actions to be discussed in this section are those that would improve water quality not in its natural channels but in withdrawal uses. Treatment of water before discharge was discussed in the previous section, but water can also be treated after it has been withdrawn and before it is used. In fact, municipal withdrawals are typically treated, at least minimally, before use. In a few places, especially downstream from stretches in which water is subjected to successive uses, withdrawals are treated intensively. Chlorination is the most common treatment of municipal water before use, but other chemicals are frequently added. Processes are available to bring even badly polluted water up to high quality before use. Very extensive treatment of municipal water before use is uncommon, apparently because of prejudice against "drinking other people's sewage."

Industry uses massive volumes of water. Small amounts are for cooking and sanitary purposes. Such water is usually obtained from municipal systems or from wells or other sources that meet drinking-water standards. In addition, small amounts of distilled or other very high-quality water are used for boiler feed to prevent corrosion. Much larger volumes are used as process water, which often means washing away wastes. Quality requirements for process water are minimal and water for that purpose is rarely treated before use. Other large volumes are used for cooling water, especially in thermal electric plants. If the water is not recirculated, it is simply withdrawn, passed by the heated pipes and returned to the source. Quality requirements are minimal. Increasingly, cooling water is recirculated because of legal prohibitions against excessive heating of the stream or because of possible damage to fish by massive intakes. Recirculation water is cooled, most often by a cooling tower in which evaporation cools the water, and recirculated through the cooling system. Recirculation requires much smaller withdrawals than once-through systems, and discharges most of the heat to the air instead of to the stream. Quality requirements may be somewhat higher for recirculation cooling water than for once-through cooling water.

Generally speaking, only low-quality in-stream water can be justified for the needs of industry. In the few cases in which high-quality water must be obtained by withdrawal from low-quality streams, water can be treated inexpensively by the industry to bring it to the required quality. Salt content is one of the main deterrents to industrial use of low-quality water, although most salt appears naturally in water, not as a result of human activities. Salt corrodes pipes and machinery. But much progress has been made in industrial use of brackish water since World War II, because of the development of plastic and noncorrosive materials. Availability of noncorrosive materials has undoubtedly been a cause of the rapid growth of water-using industries on estuaries.

However, mention should also be made of desalination as a treatment of withdrawn water before use. The available volume of salt and brackish water is large relative to the volume of freshwater. The idea of ending water problems by large-scale desalination of seawater has been an age-old dream. Several methods of desalination have been known for decades. All require large amounts of power, mainly in the form of electricity, which is their main cost. The United States has had a program of desalination research since the early 1950s. From that time to the early 1970s, the cost of desalting seawater fell from about \$7 per 1,000 gallons to about \$1, although it is unclear how much of this decrease resulted from the research program, how much from falling power costs, and how much from larger scale plants.

Desalting plants are now used in many special places around the world. But the current and likely future costs of desalted and brackish water are far above the cost of freshwater from alternative sources for most of the United States. Dramatic increases in fuel costs in the 1970s have undoubtedly worsened the prospects for desalination. In the United States, places where freshwater is scarcest are also mostly far from sources of seawater. Even if desalting were free, transporting water from the ocean to Arizona and New Mexico would be expensive.

The foregoing discussion shows that treating water before use can be advantageous for withdrawal uses. But treating water for in-stream uses is hardly feasible. In most cases, the volume of water to be treated makes treatment prohibitive. Moreover, the concentration of pollutants is low in natural water bodies, which makes treatment expensive. One consequence of the infeasibility of treating water for in-stream uses is that uses that were in-stream become withdrawal uses as stream quality deteriorates. The use of pools instead of natural water bodies for swimming is an example.

The discussion in this and the previous section leads to the following picture: Municipal water must be of high quality, but the amount withdrawn for municipal purposes is small relative to total withdrawals. Municipal withdrawals can be from a small number of high-quality places, or the water can be treated before use. Industrial water uses can mostly be of low quality. Industrial water that must be of high quality can be obtained from municipal supplies or can be treated before use. In-stream uses such as shipping impose only minimal requirements on water. This leaves commercial and sport fishing, pleasure boating, and other recreational and aesthetic uses of in-stream water as the main beneficiaries of high-quality water in many flowing streams and especially in the tidal estuaries around dozens of large metropolitan areas. To place the emphasis on fishing, recreation, and aesthetic benefits is not to say that water pollution abatement is or is not justified. It is merely to identify areas in which benefits to justify abatement costs must be sought.

Benefits and Costs of Water-Pollution Abatement

The previous sections have shown that many methods are available to improve water quality. Some are extremely cheap and, indeed, some have negative costs to the organizations employing them. There are examples in which firms have recovered materials that can be used to produce profitable by-products in the course of efforts to abate discharges. But firms and local governments have strong incentives to find for themselves actions which improve their economic position, and which may, incidentally, have beneficial environmental effects. Virtually all pollution-abatement methods that are not adopted by firms, households, or municipalities in their self-interest are expensive in some degree. Many are very expensive, indeed. In the 1970s real, inflation-corrected expenditures rose steadily until 1978, at which time they began a decline that left real expenditures the same in 1981 as in 1974. Still, the almost $22 billion spent annually is a great deal of money (about $100 per person or $300 annually per household) and it is important to ask whether ensuing benefits justify the costs. Remember it is *marginal* benefits that are of relevance—much water would be quite clean without any treatment whatsoever.

Most of the money spent is for projects intended to provide a pervasive increase in DO and other water-quality measures in streams and estuaries in and near cities. The conclusions of the previous section was that most of the benefits of these expenditures will be better commercial and sport fishing, improved water-based recreation, and a better aesthetic impression.

With the annual costs of water-pollution control running greater than $20 billion a year, what are the best estimates of the benefits of that expenditure? Myrick Freeman in *Air and Water Pollution Control: A Benefit-Cost Assessment* provides upper and lower bound estimates which are the most comprehensive to date. His estimates, based on a synthesis of studies, are presented here in Table 6.4. Note that these are estimates of 1985 benefits and are in 1978 dollars; the 1985 numbers might be on the order of twice as large, which would put them very close to the cost estimates presented above. At the time of his writing, Freeman believed that costs would be substantially higher in 1985 than they were in 1978 when, in fact, lower levels of control have caused real annual costs to begin falling at about that time. As a result, the benefits might be overstated since they are based on assumptions of higher levels of control than actually occurred. Hence, Freeman's conclusion, that "it is likely that on balance the benefit-cost relationship for the present water pollution control program is unfavorable" (p. 170), is probably still valid.

However, as noted by Freeman, benefits stemming from control of toxic substances to health, recreation, or ecology were not considered. The great recent concern about these chemicals and the fact that more of them will be removed with the control program than without suggest that benefits may be understated. More importantly, the existing program is not very efficient in that for the same costs, far greater environmental quality could be attained—hence greater benefits—or, alternatively, existing benefits could be attained at lower cost than at present. Various studies, referred to by Freeman, suggest that a program altering incentive structures (such as for example effluent charges, discussed in a later chapter) could lower costs as much as 25 to 50 percent while still achieving the same level of water quality.

Cost estimates of the type presented above are often used to defend the government against charges that the economy cannot afford the current pollution-control program, that it is inflationary, that it curtails investment in productive capital, and that the added product costs it entails may drive American products out of world markets. There is some truth in these charges, but they miss the main point. The issue is not whether we can afford an antipollution program; it is whether its benefits justify its costs. Because the buildup of expen-

TABLE 6.4

Benefits in 1985 From Removal of Conventional Water Pollutants
(in billions of 1978 dollars)

	Range	Most likely point estimate
Recreation	$1.8–8.7	$4.6
Nonuser Benefits		
Aesthetics, ecology, and property value	$0.5–4.0	$1.2
Commercial Fisheries	$0.4–1.2	$0.8
Diversionary Uses		
Drinking water—health	$0.0–2.0	$1.0
Municipal treatment	$0.6–1.2	$0.9
Households	$0.1–0.5	$0.3
Industrial supplies	$0.4–0.8	$0.6
Total	$3.8–18.4	$9.4

SOURCE: A. Myrick Freeman, III, *Air and Water Pollution Control: A Benefit-Cost Assessment*, Table 9.1, p. 170.

ditures has been gradual, the American economy can certainly devote $20 to 30 billion per year to pollution control without major disruptions. The issue is whether the program's benefits exceed its costs. The program is certainly inflationary in the sense that any government expenditure is inflationary. Macroeconomic theory suggests that an increase in government expenditures, whether on pollution control, defense, or welfare, stimulates the economy and might be inflationary to a degree that depends on the unemployment rate and on other factors. But, even if this argument is valid, expenditures on pollution control are neither more nor less inflationary than other expenditures and their inflationary impact can be offset by reductions in other expenditures or by tax increases. Government-mandated private expenditures add to production costs and are in large part passed on to consumers in higher product prices. It was shown in Chapter 3 that this result is entirely desirable in that it imposes the cost of pollution control on the consumers whose products cause the pollution. All product prices should reflect their full marginal social costs and justifiable pollution-control expenditures are just as much a social cost as are competitively priced inputs. One purpose of such product price increases is to deter consumption of products whose production causes pollution. Some deterred consumption is domestic and some is foreign; thus decreased exports of products whose production requires pollution-control expenditures is a natural and desirable result. Likewise, investment in waste-treatment plants or other pollution-control capital reduces the resources available for other kinds of capital formation. As with noncapital inputs, their use for pollution control is justified only if antipollution benefits exceed the value of products the inputs could otherwise have been used to make. Of course, measurement of justifiable pollution abatement is uncertain, as reflected in the large range of benefits in Table 6.4, but this is no reason not to include pollution-control costs in product prices. Government should make the best estimate of optimum pollution abatement it can, then adopt programs to ensure that the cost of achieving the estimated optimum environmental quality is included in product prices.

The answer to all these concerns is basically the same: Pollution-control expenditures are justified to the point at which marginal benefits equal marginal costs. All the above concerns are subsidiary to that rule. Sudden, large, and unpredictable changes are disruptive and undesirable in any government program. But a gradual change in either direction amounting to several billion dollars over a few years would not be disruptive.

Since the national comparisons of benefits and costs of water pollution abatement are far from perfect, it is useful to consider the small number of excellent regional benefit-cost studies of water quality. The best is a government study of the Delaware River estuary, which will be discussed in some detail.[1] The Delaware is a relatively small river which flows between New Jersey and Pennsylvania and through the heavily populated and industrialized Philadelphia metropolitan area. It has severe quality problems, although substantial improvement is being recorded as of the early 1980s. The study was restricted to the part of the river below Trenton, since this is the location of almost all the quality problems. The eighty-six mile stretch of the river was divided into thirty segments for study purposes. Each segment was treated as homogenous in the study, an assumption that can be made as accurate as desired by defining sufficiently short segments. Then a set of five quality objectives was specified. Each objective consisted of a specified valued for each of some six-

---

1. Further details are given in Kneese and Bower, *Managing Water Quality: Economics, Technology, Institutions.*

teen quality measures in each segment of the river. Examples of quality measures are DO level, coliform (bacteria) count, temperature, and toxic substances. Quality objective number one consisted of high values of each quality measure, quality objective two of somewhat lower measures, and so on. Quality objective five consisted of quality measure values at the time of the study, 1964. The next step was to ascertain the effect of discharges of various substances in each segment of the estuary on quality measures in other segments. Oxygen-sag equations can be used for this purpose for organic discharges, and dilution factors can be used for nondegradable discharges. Of course, these effects depend on the substances discharged, on stream characteristics, and on the distance between the segment in which the discharge occurs and that in which quality is measured. In this way a set of discharges in all segments can be translated into a set of quality measures in all segments. This is an example of a dispersion function, such as equation (3.16).

The cost of abating discharges of each polluting substance was then estimated. Conventional treatment costs were used for organic discharges, ignoring the possibility of process and product changes and thus overstating abatement costs. Costs of alternative means of disposal were used for inorganic discharges.

These data make it possible to calculate the costs of several government policies for achieving each quality objective. The easiest and crudest policy is to require a given percentage abatement of each discharge in all segments, with the percentage set so the objective is met in each segment. A second policy studied is to require a given percentage discharge abatement of a given pollutant in each of three zones that cover the thirty segments, with the percentages set separately in each zone so that the objective is met. The third possibility is to abate the discharge of each pollutant in each segment so that the objective is met at minimum cost. The third possibility is a sophisticated procedure and probably cannot be achieved by a realistic regulatory or effluent-fee scheme. A policy of uniform effluent fees would achieve a quality objective more cheaply than the first procedure, uniform percentage abatement. Likewise, a policy of uniform effluent fees within each zone would achieve the objective more cheaply than the second procedure, uniform percentage abatement in each zone. A policy of effluent fees that were different for each segment would achieve the minimum cost of the third procedure.

Of course, each policy can be applied to each quality objective. The result is a matrix of costs by objective level and policy employed. The total costs for the Delaware study were:

Quality objective	Uniform percentage abatement	Zoned uniform percentage abatement	Cost minimization
1	460	460	460
2	315	250	215
3	155	120	85
4	130	80	65
5	30	30	30

The numbers refer to costs (in millions of dollars) of quality objectives for the Delaware estuary from 1964 to 1980, and are of no intrinsic interest. They show, however, that pollution-abatement costs vary greatly depending on the water quality to be achieved and on the policy employed. Quality level one is 15 times as costly as quality level five, and policy one is, for quality objectives three and four, about twice as expensive as the minimum-cost method. A similar study, restricted to DO level, suggested that a policy of uniform effluent fees would achieve given quality objectives at about half the cost of achieving them by uniform percentage discharge abatement. Zone effluent fees are marginally cheaper than uniform effluent fees and achieve given quality objectives at 1.2 to 1.5 times minimum cost method.

The Delaware study also presented some estimates of the costs of in-stream reaeration, low-flow augmentation, and waste transport to achieve stream quality objectives. Although the calculations are crude, this study and others suggest that reaeration is an inexpensive method to improve stream quality, but that low-flow augmentation is much more costly than conventional treatment. Of course, reaeration and low-flow augmentation are of no help in achieving quality objectives that are not related to degradable discharges. The Delaware study made important contributions to estimation of benefits from stream quality improvements. Preliminary estimates indicate that only minimal improvements to stream quality could be justified by benefits to industry. Likewise, municipal intakes are on tributaries or are sufficiently far upstream to be little affected by most pollutants. The important intake on the main stream, for Philadelphia, is threatened mainly by salt-water intrusion when salt moves up the river at times of low flow.[2] Thus the main benefits of stream quality levels in the Delaware above those characteristic of the mid-1960s would be improved fishing and water-based recreation, as was suggested in the previous section.

The first step in estimating benefits from improved outdoor recreation opportunities is to estimate a demand equation for the relevant recreation activities. In the Delaware study, days of participation were regressed on income, family characteristics such as age of head and number of children, education, and other variables thought relevant. Recreation days were then converted to dollar benefits by using somewhat arbitrary data on the value of a recreation day.

Table 6.5, taken from Allen Kneese and Blair Bower, *Managing Water Quality*, summarizes the benefit and cost estimates from the Delaware study. The numbers give somewhat ambiguous results, but suggest that quality objective three is justified. The conclusions from the Delaware study are not to be taken seriously. Data were poor and are outdated. Techniques for analyzing the cost side were sophisticated, but those used on the demand side were defective. The entire study has been criticized, in somewhat strident terms but with considerable merit, by Bruce Ackerman et al.

One technique available to estimate recreational benefits from improved water quality is referred to as the travel-cost approach. Ordinary demand equations include the price of the commodity, but

TABLE 6.5

Benefit and Costs of Improved Water Quality in the Delaware Estuary

Quality objective	Total cost	Total benefits	Marginal cost Minimum	Marginal cost Maximum	Marginal benefit Minimum	Marginal benefit Maximum
1	460	160–350	245	145	20	30
2	215–315	140–320	130	160	10	10
3	85–155	130–310	20	25	10	30
4	65–130	120–280				

SOURCE: Kneese and Bower, *Managing Water Quality: Economics, Technology, Institutions*, p. 233.

2. There is a characteristic salt front that moves up and down estuaries with the tides and with the seasons. But salt water does not move up as far as tides reach. Salt water is heavier than fresh water and therefore the salt water pushes a body of freshwater up the stream in front of it as the tide comes in. Officials and the media show great concern anytime a salt front moves close to a municipal intake. In fact, the salt content on the salty side of the front is lower than that which some people drink routinely, and would do no harm during a drought of modest duration.

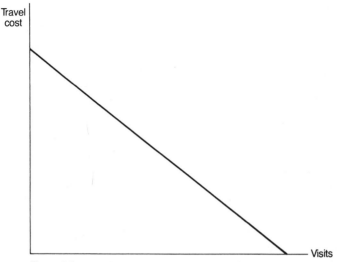

Figure 6.2

most outdoor recreation activities are free of entrance fees. Never-theless, people do devote resources to outdoor recreation, mostly the time and money costs of travel to the recreation site. People with easy access go often and those far away go seldom. Thus travel cost can be regarded as the price people pay for the recreational experi-ence. Since travel cost varies with distance, data on visits by people from various distances can be used to estimate a downward-sloping demand curve. A linear travel cost demand curve is shown in Figure 6.2. It has the properties of other demand curves and can be used to compute consumers' surplus from recreation techniques presented in Chapter 4.

It is remarkable and discouraging that neither Congress nor the executive branch showed an interest in using benefit-cost analysis in designing environmental programs until quite recently (an executive order in 1981 required that programs be justified on benefit-cost grounds). An instructive historical example concerns the Potomac estuary around Washington, D.C. In the early 1960s, the Corps of Engineers undertook a large study of water quality in the Potomac. Assuming secondary treatment of all municipal wastes, it concluded that benefits would exceed costs if a large system of sixteen major and four hundred minor dams was built upstream. The dams would have flood-control and recreational benefits, but their main purpose was to be low-flow augmentation. Dissatisfied with the Corps study,

Resources for the Future (RFF) studied alternative ways of achieving the same stream quality. It concluded that the Corps' objective of 4 ppm of DO could be achieved at a cost of $21 million by a combination of reaeration, advanced treatment, and other procedures, compared with a cost of $115 million for the dams proposed by the Corps. The moral of this story is that the Corps is authorized by law to build dams and has a long tradition of focusing on that alternative. They lack the knowledge and sophistication to consider a broad range of alternative methods of improving stream quality. Congress refused to authorize the Corps' proposed dam construction because of the RFF study and protests by environmentalists. But it has not devised a means of making a more rational attack on the problem. In fact, the problem is not conceptually difficult. Almost all the BOD in the estuary comes from municipal sewage systems that discharge effluents into the estuary. There is little industrial discharge or agricultural runoff that affects the estuary.

The few high-quality benefit-cost studies available suggest strongly that substantial improvements in stream quality over those typical in the early 1960s are justified, but that government programs have been cumbersome, costly, and slow, and have probably set excessively ambitious goals. In Part III, these conclusions will be confirmed by a detailed analysis of the program. But the most remarkable characteristic of government water-quality benefit studies is their scarcity. It is incredible that an expensive national program has been undertaken with almost no analysis of the benefits it will confer on society.

DISCUSSION QUESTIONS AND PROBLEMS

1. What are the important wastes discharged directly to the oceans, and what are their effects? What kinds of benefits would come from discharge abatement?

2. In what important ways would a benefit-cost study of stream quality differ in a very arid region from those reported in the chapter for the humid East?

3. How adequate a government policy would it be to require that discharges be abated to the point that most kinds of fish can live in streams? Might such a policy have benefits greater than costs in some locations and costs greater than benefits in other locations? What does this suggest about the appropriateness of uniform federal standards for water quality?

4. Write a proposal to study the benefits and costs of (a) abating discharges to a river so that people can swim in the estuary, and (b) building

enough swimming pools to provide the same benefits as swimming in the estuary. What groups would favor each proposal?

5. Much has been written on the "option value" of recreational facilities. For example, it is claimed that many people receive benefits from the Grand Canyon because it provides the option of going there, even though they may never go. Do you think option value is an appropriate benefit of a high-quality environment? If so, how would you measure it?

REFERENCES AND FURTHER READING

Ackerman, Bruce; Rose-Ackerman, Susan; Sawyer, James; and Henderson, Dale. *The Uncertain Search for Environmental Quality*. New York: The Free Press, 1974.

Council on Environmental Quality. *Environmental Quality*. Washington, D.C.: U.S. Government Printing Office, published annually.

Freeman, A. Myrick, III. *Air and Water Pollution Control: A Benefit-Cost Assessment*. New York: John Wiley, 1982.

Kneese, Allen, and Bower, Blair. *Managing Water Quality: Economics, Technology, Institutions*. Baltimore: John Hopkins University Press, for Resources for the Future, Inc., 1968.

Kneese, Allen, and Schultze, Charles. *Pollution, Prices and Public Policy*. Washington, D.C.: The Brookings Institution, 1975.

Löf, George, and Kneese, Allen. *Economics of Water Utilization in the Beet Sugar Industry*. Baltimore: John Hopkins University Press, for Resources for the Future, Inc., 1968.

Peskin, Henry, and Seskin, Eugene, eds. *Cost Benefit Analysis and Water Pollution Policy*. Washington, D.C.: Urban Institute, 1975.

Russell, Clifford. *Residuals Management in Industry: A Case Study of Petroleum Refining*. Baltimore: John Hopkins University Press, for Resources for the Future, Inc., 1973.

Tolley, George; Yaron, Dan; and Blomquist, Glenn. *Environmental Policy: Water Quality*. Cambridge, Mass.: Ballinger, 1983.

Chapter 7

Land Quality and Other Environmental Quality Dimensions

All materials extracted from the earth return eventually to it. Previous chapters considered discharges to the air and water and the resulting air and water quality. In this chapter we consider not only the traditional solid-waste pollutants and their impact on land quality, but also a host of other environmental-quality dimensions. Much "pollution" and resulting environmental degradation is not physical in the sense that we have been using that term; noise pollution, for example, is an externality, hence is properly an environmental problem. Moreover, although we have emphasized the point before, the environmental media interface in ways that obscure the ultimate sources of pollution. That is, dumping solid-waste pollutants into a landfill creates direct externalities in the form of visual blight, but smells from such landfills are received via the atmosphere and toxic leakages into aquifers are received via groundwater. We turn first to traditionally defined solid waste/land quality interactions.

Solid wastes are the weak sister of the environmental sciences in that little information exists and few studies have been conducted. National legislation that exists is scant and of relatively recent vintage. Although scholars and students justifiably like to have good studies and ample information available on any subject, there are some good historical reasons, related to the nature of the subject, that explain the paucity of attention that has been paid to solid-waste problems. Although the subject is by no means unimportant, solid wastes are certainly a less serious cause of pollution than are discharges to air and water.

In this book, solid wastes, like air and water discharges, are defined by the environmental medium to which they are discharged. Thus solid wastes refer to wastes discharged to land, just as air and water pollutants refer to materials discharged to air and water. It is, as already suggested, important to remember that given substances can be discharged to any of the three media, depending on circumstances. Household garbage can be ground in a kitchen disposal and then discharged to a stream through the sewage system, or it can be collected by the local refuse truck. In the latter case it may be burned in an incinerator, and hence be discharged in part to the air, or it can be placed in the local dump and hence be discharged as solid waste. Whether a waste is discharged to air, water, or land depends more on what people do with the waste than on the nature of the waste.

Solid waste is thus waste disposed of on land. The definition suggests the two basic reasons that solid wastes are less of a pollution problem than are air- and waterborne discharges.

As has been discussed in Chapters 1 and 2, first and most important, property rights in land are well defined. Land, unlike air and water, is relatively stationary and easy to identify. It is therefore possible to designate the owners of particular parcels of land and to buy and sell the parcels. Ownership includes the right to decide who can dispose of wastes on the land and under what terms. To that extent, solid wastes cannot be disposed of without the consent of the landowner. Thus effects of one person's solid-waste disposal on others' welfare are small. Put differently, solid-waste disposal is subject to much less important external diseconomies than are air- and waterborne discharges. The ambient air and most water bodies are unstable and fugitive media. Property rights in their use are difficult to define. Therefore, in the absence of legal restraints, people use them freely for waste disposal, thus imposing costs on others to whom their high quality is valuable. Waste disposal to the air and to water bodies is thus subject to important external diseconomies.

Second, solid-waste disposal better approximates the natural state from which withdrawals were made than do air and water disposal. Almost all the materials that enter the economic system are withdrawn from the land. Small amounts, such as fish, are withdrawn from water, and virtually nothing is withdrawn from the ambient air. Therefore solid-waste discharges return substances to the medium from which they were withdrawn. In that sense, solid-waste disposal is usually less of a trauma to the ambient environment than are air and water discharges.

Solid-waste disposal is fundamentally a less serious cause of resource misallocation than are air and water discharges. This is not to say that solid-waste disposal does not cause problems. It certainly does, and the problems have become increasingly insoluble for metropolitan governments in recent years. The problems are of two kinds. First, solid-waste disposal does cause external diseconomies, and they will be discussed in the next section. Second and more important, solid-waste disposal is a management problem that governments have been increasingly unsuccessful in solving. For one reason or another, governments have assumed responsibility for a large part of solid-waste disposal, sometimes with important services being provided by the private sector. Organizing this government service and providing it efficiently and reliably have been difficult for governments.

Popular literature frequently suggests that urban society will inevitably be buried in its litter. The notion is absurd. Every pound of material that ends up as solid waste was withdrawn from the environment, most of it from the land. There is thus a place to which all material could be returned, more or less in the form in which it was extracted. There is thus no possibility of running out of places to dispose of waste. Furthermore, the economic system manages to provide resources to extract and process materials, and it can certainly find resources to return them to the land in acceptable ways. The problem is not that there is no place to put solid wastes or that we cannot afford the cost of acceptable disposal. The problem is simply that we have not yet provided the institutions and incentives to do the job well.

Discharges and Environmental Damages from Solid Wastes

As used in this book, the terms *airborne*, *waterborne*, and *solid discharges* are exhaustive. Whatever discharges are not to air and water must be to land. Of course total withdrawals from and therefore discharges to the environment are not fixed. They can be altered by altering the production of commodities and services or by changing the amounts of materials reused. But for a given volume of total discharges, reduced discharges to air and water mean increased solid-waste disposal. Many proposals to reduce one form of discharges merely increase another form. Municipal sewage treatment reduces waterborne discharges but converts them to solid wastes or other discharges. That may reduce harmful pollution, but it does not alter total discharges. Solid discharges are mostly less polluting than air- and waterborne discharges, but it is important to ask what will happen to discharges that will be returned by any proposal.

Massive amounts of materials are discharged as solid wastes in the United States. Table 7.1 shows solid-waste discharges by source for 1969. The total grows steadily each year, although the annual rate of growth has halved (from about 4 percent prior to 1970 to about 2 percent since that time). The 4.3 billion tons of solid wastes in the table comes to about 120 pounds per day per inhabitant, a daily total disposal of approximately the weight of the population! The total solid-waste disposal shown in Table 7.1 exceeds the estimate of total materials withdrawn that was presented in the introduction to this section. The reason is that the estimate of total withdrawals includes only materials processed in some way, whereas Table 7.1 includes, in addition, large volumes of materials that are merely moved from one place to another in mining and agriculture. Such movements, for example in strip mining, can be polluting and the materials are therefore included in Table 7.1. In fact, the total could be made even larger by inclusion of materials moved in dredging and construction.

More than half the total wastes in Table 7.1 are in agriculture. Much of the agricultural total is crop residues on farms and animal

TABLE 7.1

Solid-Waste Discharges in the United States, 1969
(millions of tons)

Residential, commercial, institutional		250
Collected	190	
Uncollected	60	
Industrial		110
Mineral		1,700
Agricultural		2,280
TOTAL		4,340

SOURCE: Council on Environmental Quality, *Environmental Quality*, 1970, p. 107

wastes in feedlots and slaughter houses. Of the total in Table 7.1, 40 percent is mineral wastes, much of it from metal and fossil-fuel mining and processing. In many ways, the most troublesome solid wastes are the 250 (now, in the 1980s, more like 350 million tons) million tons generated by households, commercial facilities, and institutions such as hospitals and public buildings. These wastes are mostly generated in urban areas where there is little space for disposal. Households generate more than 4 pounds of solid waste per day per person. Industrial solid waste is the smallest category in the table. All manufacturing plants process materials and some inevitably appear as wastes at each processing stage. Although large volumes of materials are processed by industry, many processes generate little waste. In addition, much waste is collected and reprocessed within the manufacturing plant and therefore does not appear in the data sources. There has been a long-term trend for manufacturing processes to generate less waste per unit of output. Newer technology usually makes more efficient use of materials than does older technology. In addition, the high costs of materials and of disposal motivate businesses to reduce materials waste. However, modern technology generates some materials that are especially difficult to dispose of or are especially injurious to the environment. Plastic containers have been substituted for paper and cardboard containers. The latter degrade rapidly in the environment, whereas the former do not. Modern agricultural pesticides, such as DDT, degrade only slowly and may remain for years in the environment, perhaps moving over time into air or water where damages are much higher. We shall return to hazardous substances later in this chapter.

What happens to the solid wastes listed in Table 7.1? Much of the crop residue in agriculture is returned to the soil on the farm on which the crops are grown, thus utilizing much of the material extracted to replenish the soil. Animal wastes can be returned to the soil in limited amounts without harm. But in feedlots and slaughter houses enormous waste volumes are generated and they cause pollution unless disposed of with great care. Most mining wastes are returned to the land on the site of extraction. Most residential, commercial, and institutional solid wastes are collected by or on contract with local governments, but about 25 percent is disposed of privately. Collected solid waste is mostly that generated in urban areas. About 75 percent of solid wastes collected by municipalities is disposed of in nearby open dumps. About 13 percent is placed in sanitary landfills where each day's waste is covered with a layer of soil to prevent odors, fires, eyesores, and vermin. Some 8 percent is burned in incinerators, only some of which have satisfactory air-pollution-control devices. The remaining collected solid wastes are unaccounted for. Industrial solid wastes are disposed of in much the same variety of ways as are municipally collected solid wastes. Some are placed by the industries in municipal dumps and landfills. But much is disposed of in similar facilities owned by the industries.

What harm is done by the various means of solid-waste disposal? The question is remarkably difficult to answer. Most sources present lists of qualitative and potential damages, but quantitative evidence is almost nonexistent. As noted at the beginning of this chapter, much of the harm done by poor solid-waste disposal comes from the air and water pollution it may cause.

As indicated earlier, mining generates an enormous volume of solid waste. Traditional shaft mining inevitably removes large amounts of unwanted materials from the ground. Much of this material is stored on the ground, for instance, in slag heaps. It is an eyesore and occassionally causes harmful slides or catches fire. Mine shafts themselves cause problems in that they may collapse after they are abandoned, causing subsidence on the surface. There are famous court cases concerning mining companies' liability for damages from subsidence. In addition, abandoned coal mines frequently fill with ground water. The water and exposed sulfur in the mine form sulfuric acid which flows through the ground into nearby streams, causing water pollution. But the most serious environmental damage from shaft mining is frequently overlooked in debates about alteratives, namely, the severe air pollution in shaft mines that causes terrible damage to miners' lungs. In addition, accidents make shaft mining one of the most dangerous occupations.[1]

In the postwar period, much mineral extraction has shifted from shaft to surface mining, largely because of the availability of earth-moving machinery with great capacity. Instead of tunneling to the wanted mineral, surface mining merely removes the earth and rock

1. Note that if miners were fully aware of the likelihood of damage from pollution and accidents, they would not work in this occupation unless compensated for the expected damages; hence there would be no externality and, consequently, observed damages would not be an "environmental" problem. We doubt, however, that information is this perfect and regional employment opportunities (combined with high migration costs) may also dictate that appropriate compensation is not received.

that cover the minerals, loads the minerals onto large trucks, and hauls them away. Surface mining has long been a common technique of extracting ore and has become the most common means of extracting coal in the United States. Most of the controversy over surface mining concerns reclamation of the surface after the minerals have been removed. The land can be returned to a form in which it supports vegetation and in which it can be used in various ways, but it may be expensive and it is difficult to formulate regulations that are binding and clear. If it is not carefully reclaimed, the land remains scarred and cannot support vegetation and wildlife for years. Erosion then results, and can cause pollution in nearby streams. An additional problem, mentioned in the preceding chapter, is the potential pollution of aquifers with resulting damage to groundwater supplies. But health damages and accidents to miners are much less common in surface than in shaft mining.

Most crop residues in agriculture cause no pollution problems. They decompose on the ground and replenish organic material in soil, with little runoff. Animal wastes in slaughterhouses and feedlots sometimes cause severe problems. They are frequently near settled areas and may cause severe odors. In addition, disposal on land causes organic wastes to drain into streams, depleting the streams' DO and making them unsightly.

The most obvious problem caused by industrial wastes is the unsightliness of open dumps into which they may be put. Dumps breed vermin, which may migrate to nearby settled areas. They may burn or smolder, causing air pollution. Incineration of wastes may cause air pollution unless air-pollution-control devices are used, and it leaves an ash to be disposed of.

Local government practices in disposing of solid wastes they collect have been subject to great controversy in recent years. They spend substantial amounts of money on solid-waste disposal, but most of it is spent on remarkably inefficient systems of collecting and transporting wastes. Relatively little is spent on acquisition and operation of disposal sites. Most local governments, including many governments of large cities, still operate public dumps. Local governments seem to be incapable of contracting with each other for solid-waste disposal, with the result that even most large central-city governments operate disposal facilities within their borders. Many facilities are thus inevitably close to settled areas. Dumps are certainly ugly and odorous, they breed vermin, and they may smolder, but it is not known how many people are affected, and in what ways, by such nuisances. Well-operated landfills avoid most of the problems with dumps. They are of course considerably more expensive to operate than dumps. Much has been made in recent years of the possibility of reducing landfill costs by selecting low-quality sites and using them for development or recreation, for instance, parks or golf courses, after their use as landfills. A swamp or ravine, for example, can be selected and can be used for some years as a landfill. Then the surface can be covered and graded and the site can be used for another purpose. The landfill may have raised the site's value, so the local government can offset some landfill costs by capital gains made on the site's resale. But landfills are subject to subsidence for many years as organic material degrades, and they may generate harmful gases and odors. Former landfills can be used for many purposes but sites must be prepared with great care.

Americans deposit large, but unknown, amounts of household and commercial solid wastes as litter on picnic and campgrounds, on beaches and highways, and in vacant lots. Such litter is ugly and lacerates bare feet. Some remains where it is deposited and some is removed by governments. One reason for the volume of litter is that the United States is a high-income country where packaging materials are cheap. It is thus tempting to leave containers and packages at recreational sites where they are used instead of hauling them back to places where they can be disposed of harmlessly. But another part of the problem appears to be that residents of some countries such as America or Mexico lack the sense of duty to keep public places tidy that people have in Europe, Japan, and elsewhere. It does not appear that antilittering laws are either more or less strong or more or less well enforced here than elsewhere.

Techniques of Abating Pollution from Solid Wastes

As with air and water pollution, there are two ways to reduce pollution from solid wastes: Methods and locations of disposal can be improved or discharges can be reduced. Each will be discussed in turn.

Upgrading solid-waste disposal in mineral extraction is mainly a matter of reclaiming land after extraction. Surface mining illustrates the possibilities and problems. When mining starts, topsoil must be removed carefully and stored. After mining is finished, topsoil must be replaced and graded, and vegetation must be planted and tended until it can sustain itself. Reclamation is a technically straightforward process, but it requires care and can add substantially to the cost per ton of mineral extracted. The cost and difficulty of reclamation depend very much on soil condition, rainfall, the intended use of the reclaimed land, and the topography. The benefits may, for some locations, be less than these costs.

Agricultural wastes are mostly organic, and upgrading disposal is much the same as with any other organic waste. Animal wastes from feedlots or slaughter houses can be treated by the techniques used for municipal wastes. Treatment costs money and can be expensive if carried out on a small scale.

Industrial, household, and commercial solid wastes are often similar material and upgrading disposal involves much the same problem for most kinds of wastes. Most attention has been focused on closing open dumps and substituting for them sanitary landfills or incineration. Both dumps and landfills require large amounts of land and landfills are economical where land is cheap. Incineration is, of course, feasible only for organic wastes. If organic wastes are mixed with metals, plastics, and glass, as they are in municipally collected wastes, then organic materials must be separated before incineration. Inorganic wastes must be disposed of in another way. In addition, incineration leaves ash that must be disposed of as solid waste. Most important, incineration can cause air pollution, especially from particulates and sulfur oxides. Incineration in a modern plant is much less polluting than a smoldering dump. But air pollution can be substantial unless the system is designed and operated carefully.

Until now, attention has been concentrated on reducing pollution from solid-waste disposal by upgrading disposal techniques. The remainder of this section focuses on the more interesting and complex alternative of reducing solid-waste pollution by reducing the volume of solid wastes discharged. The popular idea is that materials should be recycled, not discharged to the environment. In fact, the issues are complex and careful distinctions must be made.

Most fundamentally, solid-waste discharges can be reduced by decreasing production of goods and services or by decreasing materials withdrawn from, and therefore discharged to, the environment per unit of output. Although the former action is advocated by some, there is little to be said for it. Some people urge that actions be taken to reduce living standards, returning to a simpler way of life, in order to reduce the volumes of wastes discharged to the environment. Of course any action to upgrade or reduce discharges requires productive resources. If such resources were not used to upgrade or reduce discharges, they could be used to produce commodities and services. Therefore any action to upgrade or reduce discharges has the incidental effect of reducing commodities and services production. This is quite different from an intentional program to reduce commodities and services production in order to abate discharges to the environment. That could be done only by government actions to stimulate unemployment, curtail capital investment, slow down or reverse technical progress, and so forth. References to such ideas will be made again in a later chapter dealing with global issues. Within the context of twentieth-century America, none of the evidence encountered in this or the last two chapters suggests that environmental damages justify such drastic actions. They would result in large-scale unemployment and widespread and well-founded social and political discontent.[2]

If it is accepted that government actions to reduce living standards are unjustified, then what can be done to reduce materials withdrawn from the environment per unit of output produced? The first thing to note is that materials withdrawal and use per unit of output have been reduced steadily for decades as a result of technical progress. Production in extractive industries, mainly mining and agriculture, has fallen steadily relative to total production in the economy. As technology improves, people learn to use materials more efficiently, so that less is wasted in production. In addition, people learn to use materials that were previously returned unused to the environment. For example, uses have been found for many parts of animals slaughtered for food that were previously discarded as waste. As a second example, many chemicals, plastics, and other products, as well as fuel, are now made from petroleum. The result is that little of the petroleum extracted goes unused. There is every reason to expect the process of gradually economizing on materials to continue into the indefinite future.

The historical process of economizing on materials has taken place

2. Such actions were advocated by many people in the late 1960s. The best-known advocates of slowdown or reversal of economic growth were those concerned with the Club of Rome project at the Massachusetts Institute of Technology. See Meadows et al., *The Limits to Growth*, and other sources from Chapter 1.

almost entirely in the production sector, as people have learned how to make more effective use of materials withdrawn. A second way to economize on materials is to reuse them. Production incorporates materials into commodities, such as food, cars, TV sets, and frying pans. As has been shown, consumption changes the form of materials so that they are no longer able to satisfy human needs and wants. But all the materials incorporated in products continue to exist after products are used and many remain more or less intact in the commodity. After consumption, materials must either be returned to the environment or recycled back into the economic sausage machine to make more commodities. In fact, the popular term *recycle* is too narrow, since it means to reuse for the original purpose. To recycle junk automobiles means to reuse the materials to make new automobiles. But materials may be reused for a different purpose from the original one. For example, old newspapers can be burned as fuel in a thermal electric plant. In this case the original use of the tree was to make newspapers, but the reuse of the paper is to make electricity. The term *reuse* includes reuse of materials for either the original or a different purpose.

Almost all materials withdrawn from the environment and incorporated in commodities can be reused, at least in principle. Some materials are easy and cheap to reuse and are reused routinely. Others are extremely difficult and costly to reuse and are never reused. Most are between the extremes. Among materials, reuse varies greatly depending on the cost and difficulty of collecting, separating, transporting, and reprocessing the material. For a given material, reuse depends on the relative prices of new and used materials. Some examples will illustrate the possibilities. As automobile tires are used, that is, consumed, the hydrocarbons of which they are made wear off and are returned to the environment, mostly to the air. It would be extremely difficult and costly to retrieve and reuse materials worn from tires, and it is not done. It is much cheaper to extract new materials from the environment. As a second example, copper is often used in relatively pure form, for instance, in wiring, because of its desirable properties. Additionally, it is not dissipated in most uses. Thus recovery for reuse is often easy and cheap. Furthermore, copper newly extracted from the environment is very expensive. The result is that there is a highly organized scrap market for copper and most of the copper incorporated in products is reused again and again. As a final example, newspapers are between these extremes. The paper is combined with other things, for example, ink. It can be recycled at some cost. Part of the cost is cost of separation and collection. Used newspapers are dispersed among millions of households and, unless handled with care, are mixed with other household refuse in trash cans. If so, they must be separated from other refuse before recycling. Newspapers must be treated chemically before reuse as paper. Furthermore, paper made from newly extracted materials is quite cheap in the United States, with the result that most newspapers are not recycled. Used paper prices fluctuate with great speed and amplitude, and paper recycling fluctuates in corresponding fashion.

Apparently, the trend of materials reuse was down in the United States for many decades preceding the 1970s. There was at least a century of gradual decline in the relative prices of extracted materials. Extraction is inevitably less labor intensive and easier to mechanize than is materials recovery. Thus rapidly rising real wage rates discourage materials recovery. The early 1970s were years of pervasive materials scarcity and rapidly rising prices. Reuse of many materials grew rapidly. There can be little doubt that materials reuse responds to relative prices of new and used materials. As prices of some materials stabilized or receded in the mid-1970s, materials reuse steadied or declined.

It seems obvious that it is worthwhile to reuse some materials but not others. How can one decide how much of which materials should be reused? The right way to formulate this question is to ask why, in the absence of specific government policies to encourage reuse, private incentives might lead to too little materials reuse. The basic answer is the same as that to the question why private incentives lead to excessive air- and waterborne discharges, namely that disposal leads to external diseconomies, that is, to costs that markets cannot adequately impute. The last two chapters have discussed such costs in detail for air and water pollution. The view expressed in this chapter is that external diseconomies are less important for solid-waste disposal than for air and water discharges, but are not unimportant. If strip mining takes place on private property and has no effects off the property, the materials disposal it entails leads to no resource misallocation regardless of how much of a mess it makes of the land. But if the resulting erosion causes water pollution elsewhere, or if the ugliness must be observed by passers-by, resource misallocation occurs. Likewise, if owners dispose of cars by abandoning them on streets, they impose costs on other users for which the car's owner is not charged. If picnickers dispose of soft-drink bottles by abandoning them on beaches, they impose costs on others and cause resource misallocation.

Thus, to the extent that materials users pay the full costs of their disposal—including both costs incurred in disposal and costs imposed on others by poor disposal—they have appropriate incentive to reuse materials when it is desirable for them to be reused. The next section will summarize what is known about the magnitudes of external diseconomies in solid-waste disposal. This section concludes with a discussion of two important materials reuse problems: junk automobiles and municipal solid wastes.

Automobiles are a major problem of materials disposal and reuse in the United States and, increasingly, elsewhere. There are more than 140 million motor vehicles in the United States, including more than 100 million automobiles. The average car lasts about 10 years, which means that about 10 percent of the stock, nearly 10 million cars, is junked each year. An automobile is a complex product, containing hundreds of materials that are combined in complex ways. Therefore separation of materials is a serious problem. Cars are registered and licensed by states, and it is therefore easy to identify ownership. Cars are disposed of in many ways when their useful lives have ended. About 15 percent are abandoned on city streets, in fields, in streams, and elsewhere. Almost all abandoned vehicles are harmful aesthetically and in other ways. Most such abandonment is illegal. In large cities, the police spend large amounts of time and money identifying abandoned cars, removing them, and, finally, disposing of them. Apparently, it is more expensive or more trouble to find the owner and force him to dispose of the car legally than it is for the police to get rid of abandoned vehicles themselves.

The other 85 percent of cars go through a relatively highly developed market system of materials retrieval and reuse. They are sold or given to dealers who cannibalize them, that is, remove usable parts for resale to owners of similar cars who need to replace parts. Then some parts are removed manually and the remaining materials are separated in one of several ways. The most sophisticated means is a large shredder which shreds the hulk into small pieces. Materials can then be separated magnetically and in other ways. After separation, most of the metal is sold as scrap and reused to make vehicles or other products. When scrap-metal prices are high, this market system works quite well. But when scrap-metal prices are relatively low, dealers are loath to accept more cars and inventories pile up at each stage of the process. The main external diseconomy is visual, but people are periodically gripped by the specter of the country being smothered in junked cars.

Municipally collected refuse has received more attention than any other kind of solid waste in recent years. Local governments collect from all sources about six pounds of solid wastes per resident per day, and the total rises steadily. Many materials are collected, mostly thrown together in refuse bins. Paper is more than one-third of the total, with it and other organic wastes making up 75 percent of the total. The remainder consists mostly of glass, metal, and plastics.

If municipally collected wastes are to be reused, the first problem is separation. Some municipalities try to persuade households and other sources to separate wastes before collection into various categories. But it is expensive and unreliable. Inexpensive mechanical and electrical devices are available that are much more satisfactory. Scrap metal can be reused at some cost since it rarely appears in pure form. Glass is technically easy to recycle, but glass made from newly extracted materials is so cheap that used glass cannot be recycled without large subsidies. Aluminum is increasingly being recycled, due mostly to the higher energy costs of newly produced aluminum versus recycled aluminum. Most plastics are difficult to reuse.

Much collected organic waste is difficult to reuse, and much is discharged after inorganic materials have been separated for reuse. Organic wastes can be burned, and in the mid-1970s the notion became popular that collected organic wastes should be used as fuel in thermal electric plants. The plant must be built or altered specifically for the purpose, and mixing organic wastes with fossil fuels poses technical problems. Using organic wastes is attractive not only as a conservation measure, but also because municipal refuse trucks can deliver the separated organic wastes directly to the local thermal electric plant without further processing. Several plants have operated effectively using both fossil-fuel and organic wastes. The idea was encouraged by high fossil-fuel prices and by difficulties cities have in solid-waste disposal. It is too soon to know if it is an effecient reuse process. Of course, using organic wastes for fuel in electricity generation converts solid wastes into airborne discharges. Burning organic wastes in a thermal electric plant causes just as much air pollution as burning them in an incinerator. The only difference is that the thermal electric plant uses the heat generated by combustion whereas the incinerator normally does not. It should be noted that the external damages associated with incineration are large enough to justify far longer distances to dumpsites than could be justified on the basis of private costs alone. To illustrate, consider a large city hemmed in by independent suburbs that are unwilling to accept the city's trash. The recourse of transporting the trash to distant rural areas where dumpsite damages would be lower might seem very expensive to the city; yet a decision having, in some cases, lower apparent costs, namely incineration, may involve far larger full social costs when pollution damages are considered. Even government officials who are presumably interested in the welfare of their citizens engage in nonoptimal behavior when faced with budget constraints!

Benefits and Costs of Solid-Waste-Pollution Abatement

The two important means of solid-waste pollution abatement that have been identified in this chapter are upgrading of disposal systems and increased reuse of materials. As was found to be true of means of air and water pollution abatement in earlier chapters, much more is known about costs of solid-waste pollution abatement than about the benefits therefrom. Not surprisingly, the best-studied subject is costs of upgrading municipal solid-waste-disposal methods.

The costs of upgrading disposal systems are conceptually straightforward. Solid-waste-disposal systems consist of collection, transportation, processing, and disposal operations. The costs of the system are competitive market values of inputs required. High-quality disposal systems normally require more, or more expensive, inputs than low-quality systems. Materials reuse involves the collection, transportation, and processing, but not the disposal, activities. Frequently, different and more expensive processing is required of solid wastes if they are to be reused than if they are to be returned to the environment. For example, much more careful separation of materials is required for reuse than for disposal.

The Council on Environmental Quality estimates (Table A-79, p. 327 of the 1983 edition) of solid-waste-disposal costs in 1981 were just shy of $10 billion. This compares to comparable figures, also in this table, of $24.5 billion for air-pollution control and $22 billion for water-pollution control in 1981. Solid-waste-control costs are not large relative to costs expended in other media and have declined as a percentage of total pollution control effort (from less than 19 percent in 1972 to 16.5 percent in 1981). In all years about two-thirds of total solid-waste disposal costs are private.

The benefits of upgrading or relocating disposal systems are reduced disamenities from low-quality or badly located disposal systems. Landfills and incinerators have less visual disamenity than dumps and many produce less air and water pollution. If its use as a landfill increases the value of the land, for example, because it makes the land usable as a park, the gain is properly counted as a benefit. It simply records the discounted value of future productivity gains from upgrading the land. Benefits from materials reuse include the resulting reduction in disposal costs and the reduced disamenities from disposal. They also include savings resulting from reduced need for newly extracted materials. For example, a benefit from using organic wastes for fuel in thermal electric plants is the resulting savings in fossil-fuel use.

The cost in the early 1980s for solid-waste disposal in urban areas is hardly a crushing burden on the population. These costs are less than $0.50 per day per family served. Eighty percent of the total solid-waste costs is spent for collection and transportation of wastes, almost entirely in the large, noisy compaction trucks that are common in American cities. Costs are much lower in the growing number of municipalities in which wastes are collected by private contractors than in communities in which it is done by the local government's sanitation department. Only 20 percent of total expenditure is spent on operation of processing and disposal facilities.

Almost the only cost of an open dump is the cost of the land. Assuming that current costs are roughly twice those existing in the late 1960s and early 1970s, operating costs are $.10 to $.50 per ton. Again excluding land costs, operating costs of sanitary landfills were about $1.50 to $4.00 per ton. Incinerator costs are about $10.00 per ton and are less than landfill costs only where land is expensive.[3] Of course, such costs should be about the same for similar kinds of industrial wastes.

3. The figures in this paragraph are inflation-adjusted versions of data presented by Jack DeMarco et al., *Incinerator Guidelines, 1969*, Public Health Service Publication no. 2012, 1969, and Thomas Song and H. L. Hickman, *Sanitary Landfill Facts*, Public Health Service Publication no. 1792, 1970.

There have been many studies of costs of land reclamation after surface mining, but there is little agreement as to their magnitude. Much depends on how the land was mined and on how high the quality of the reclaimed land is to be. Vegetation can be grown by modest leveling and by topsoil replacement. Other kinds of reclamation may require more leveling and much more careful replacement of topsoil. An interesting proposal is to use surface mine sites for sanitary landfills or for treated sludge from sewage-treatment plants. Depositing organic wastes would help to restore fertility and bulk to the land. The cost would depend greatly on distances of sites from population centers.

Unfortunately, there appears to be almost no hard evidence as to the benefits of these kinds of disposal upgrading. Take the common issue of converting a dump to a sanitary landfill. In the early 1980s, operating the landfill might have cost $2 more per ton of waste disposed of, or about $7.00 per year per family served than the dump. Is it worth it? A 15-foot-deep landfill of one acre serves about 2,500 families for one year. Using the acre as a landfill instead of as a dump for one year might cost $7.00 × 2,500 = $17,500. There must be many locations near metropolitan areas where the land would be worth that much more at the end of the year as a result of its being used as a landfill than if it were used as a dump. If so, the benefits of upgrading exceed the costs, not even taking account of reduced disamenities which might raise prices of neighboring land, or which might not be reflected in land values.

The projections in the preceding paragraph suggest, but do not prove, that benefits from upgrading disposal from dumps to landfills probably would exceed costs in and near metropolitan areas. If that is so, why is it not in communities' interests to upgrade disposal? The dump or landfill site belongs to the local government, and if upgrading increases land values by more than the extra operating cost, a local government that wants to minimize disposal cost should upgrade regardless of whether it can estimate the amenity benefits of upgrading. Some local governments do use sanitary landfills. But many, even in large metropolitan areas do not. One cannot exclude the possibility that the political process provides inadequate incentives to minimize full social costs.

What are the benefits and costs of materials reuse? To be specific, take the case of municipally collected solid wastes and compare reuse with disposal in a sanitary landfill. Wastes must be collected whether they are reused or disposed of in the landfill. If reused, they must be separated, processed, and transported to the user. If disposed of in the landfill, they must be transported to the landfill and disposed of there. Finally, there are disamenity costs of the landfill. To avoid details, suppose the wastes are collected in a metropolitan area and that transport costs are about the same to the landfill and to the potential user, as is likely if both are in the metropolitan area. Municipal wastes could be separated for $6 to $10 per ton in the early 1980s. Take $8 per ton as an average. Assume landfill operating costs were near the middle of the range quoted above, say $3.00 per ton. Then reuse would be desirable if

$$P_m + D + 3.00 > 8 + C$$

Here p_m is the price of new materials of the type in question, C is the cost per ton of special processing required of waste materials if they are to be reused, and D is the disamenity cost of disposal. The left side of the inequality measures the benefits of reuse: the saved cost per ton of new materials plus the avoided disamenity and disposal costs. The right side is the cost of reuse: the cost of separation plus the cost of special processing. Disamenity costs are difficult to estimate and processing costs depend on the material in question. If a private firm were offered the municipality's wastes free, it would accept them for reuse if

$$p_m > 8 + C$$

This inequality holds if the price the firm could get for the used materials exceeds the cost of separating and processing them. Comparison between the two inequalities shows that private incentives to reuse waste materials are deficient to the extent that private parties who make disposal and reuse decisions do not pay disposal and disamenity costs. In other words, the price of the materials must be larger relative to the cost of processing used materials if the second inequality is to hold than if the first is to hold. It is not possible to say how great the deficiency of incentives to reuse materials is, but the inequalities indicate that private incentives result in at least moderate underutilization of used materials.

There is little evidence about disamenity costs of landfills, but suppose they are $1.00 per ton of waste disposed of. Then the first inequality shows that reuse is socially efficient if $p_m - C > 4$, that is, the value of a ton of separated material exceeds any reprocessing costs by more than $4. The second inequality shows that it is privately profitable to separate and reuse materials only if $p_m - C > 8$, that is, the excess of value over reprocessing costs exceeds $8. Thus, in this example, $p_m - C$ must be twice as great to make reuse profitable as it must be to make it socially efficient.

Other Environmental-Quality Dimensions

Taking externalities as our focus for defining environmental problems, a great many problems are seen to emerge. This section presents a sampling of some recent environmental concerns, although they are not necessary the most important. For example, traffic congestion in major cities around the United States at rush hour is probably as important, in terms of wasted resources, as any other pollution problem. In this case, the decision to enter the freeway is based on private calculations of benefits and costs rather than on social costs, which are substantially higher: if an individual enters the freeway he or she may slow up hundreds of drivers by some small amount. It is easy to show in such cases that the social cost of a trip can become twice the private cost of a trip, indicating that many trips are made that should not be made. Urban blight and thermal pollution are other examples of important externality problems, but we shall focus here on noise, radioactivity, and hazardous substances as illustrative.

Consider first noise pollution. This is no less of a pollution problem than air or water contaminants. First, an externality is present in that those damaged by excessive noise are seldom compensated for those damages. Second, the damages are highly annoying to individuals and many individuals are affected. Table 7.2 shows the sources of noise that are reported as "highly annoying" by the American public. Note that what is considered annoying varies, as expected upon reflection, with population per square mile. While noise sources of all types were less troublesome in less dense areas, the second most frequently cited irritant was helicopters in locations having density less than three thousand people per square mile. Large trucks were second for middle-density areas, but were seventh in low-density areas and third in high-density areas. In all cases motorcycles were cited as most annoying.

Damages from excess noise take the form of hearing loss, some impairment of functioning, and (it is suspected) death. Some believe

TABLE 7.2

Population Reporting "Highly Annoying" Noise Sources

| | More than 20,000[1] | | 3,000–20,000[2] | | Less than 3,000[3] | |
Source	Rank[4]	Percent of respondents highly annoyed by source	Rank[4]	Percent of respondents highly annoyed by source	Rank[4]	Percent of respondents highly annoyed by source
Motorcycles	1	12.7	1	13.2	1	9.4
Autos	2	9.4	3	7.4	3	4.2
Large trucks	3	7.3	2	10.0	7	2.6
Construction	4	6.5	4	7.2	4	3.7
Sports cars	5	5.9	5	7.0	6	3.1
Constant traffic	6	4.7	6	5.5	10	1.5
Buses	7	4.7	8	3.5	11	1.1
Small trucks	8	4.1	7	4.1	9	1.5
Helicopters	9	3.9	10	3.1	2	5.3
Airplanes	10	3.6	9	3.4	5	3.2
Power garden tools	11	1.2	11	2.1	8	1.8
		(66.0)		(62.2)		(55.9)

Areas surveyed were away from the direct impact of freeway or aircraft noise.

[1] Represents 12% of the population sample surveyed.

[2] Represents 51% of the population sample surveyed.

[3] Represents 37% of the population sample surveyed.

[4] Rank = Rank order of noise sources that highly annoy respondents.

SOURCE: Council on Environmental Quality, *Environmental Quality*, 1979, p. 542.

that deaths that are officially classified as heart attacks are sometimes due to the shock of noise. But this is really beside the point in that the *irritation* one feels at being exposed to high noise levels is pervasive and a very real damage.

What can be done about noise? Are there policy options having benefits greater than costs? Certainly garbage cans can be made quieter, mufflers on motorcylce exhausts can (and have) become quieter, dirt birms or walls can reduce traffic noise (or highways can be recessed), and so on. But sometimes solutions that were impractical or undesirable for air or water pollution of the usual sort are worth exploring in the case of noise. It is sometimes far less costly to protect with ear plugs or covers those who could be damaged in certain situations than to make the noise polluter more quiet (an example that comes to mind are airport employees who wear noise-protective devices).

Also of concern in recent years is exposure to radioactive substances. Table 7.3 depicts a mixed case of dramatic environmental improvement in terms of nuclear fallout from atmospheric weapons testing, but a steady increase in exposures to radioactivity associated with nuclear-power generation. At this point one might speculate that on net we are at least somewhat better off today than we were two decades ago in our exposure to radioactive substances. However, the future might not be so bright. That there is reason for concern is made clear in Table 7.4, which shows steady increases, until most recent periods, in the volume of radioactive wastes disposed of, since the early 1960s. Should these buried wastes seep into underground water sources very serious local problems could emerge, although strict efforts are being devoted to avoid that occurrence.

TABLE 7.3

Radioactive Levels from Nuclear Fallout and Power Generation, as Measured by Ambient Concentrations of Pollutants, 1960–1982

Year	Strontium-90[1] (in pico curies/liter)	Cesium-137[1] (in pico curies/liter)	Krpton-85[2] (in pico curies/cubic meter)
1960	8.6	18	—
1961	8.0	11	—
1962	13.4	44	7.5
1963	23.5	108	9.0
1964	23.8	109	9.5
1965	17.6	58	10.0
1966	13.3	29	11.0
1967	10.2	16	11.5
1968	8.9	11	12.5
1969	7.5	9	13.5
1970	7.3	8	15.4
1971	6.8	9	14.8
1972	5.6	6	14.9
1973	4.4	5	16.7
1974	4.7	8	17.0
1975	3.9	9	17.5
1976	3.5	7	17.3
1977	3.6	6	17.4 ± 1.7
1978	3.8	7.3	NA
1979	3.5	4.2	21.8 ± 2.2

TABLE 7.3 (*continued*)

*Radioactive Levels from Nuclear Fallout and Power Generation, as
Measured by Ambient Concentrations of Pollutants, 1960–1982*

Year	Strontium-90 [1] (in pico curies/liter)	Cesium-137 [1] (in pico curies/liter)	Krpton-85 [2] (in pico curies/cubic meter)
1980	2.8	3.5	NA
1981	3.0	2.8	NA
1982	2.7	3.8	NA
1983	2.3	1.43	27.4

Data aggregated in network averages.

NA—Not available.

[1] Strontium-90 and cesium-137: were measured in pasteurized milk. They were
initially released into the atmosphere from weapons testing, distributed
worldwide, and then deposited.

[2] Krypton-85 was measured in ambient air. This radionuclide is produced as a
by-product of the nuclear power industry.

Sources:

Strontium-90 and cesium-137: U.S. Environmental Protection Agency, Eastern
Environmental Radiation Facility, unpublished data. Data from individual
network stations in Eastern Environmental Radiation Facility, Environmental Radiation Data Report, various quarterly issues.

Krypton-85, 1962–1969: Based on U.S. Environmental Protection Agency,
Radiological Quality of the Environment in the United States, 1977 (Washington:
USGPO, 1977), Fig. 2-9, p. 44. *1970–1979:* U.S. Environmental Protection Agency, Eastern Environmental Radiation Facility, unpublished data.
1983: Data from individual network stations in Radiation Data Report, various quarterly issues.

SOURCE: Council on Environmental Quality, *Environmental Quality*, 1983, Table
A-54, p. 314.

Damages from radioactivity include mutagenic and carcinogenic
effects on the entire ecosystem, and avoiding such effects is virtually
impossible should high levels of radioactivity exist at a location. On
the other hand, while not minimizing the dangers of radiation, it is
the case that those living at high altitudes receive substantially more
radiation than those living at sea level, with no apparent ill effects.
Similarly, natural radiation present in granite renders Grand Central Station in New York City, for example, more radioactive than
the walls of a nuclear power plant. Still, the large volumes to be
stored in the future are a serious problem in light of the very long
life of radioactive materials; currently unforseen events (e.g., an
earthquake) can have traumatic effects at nuclear-waste dumpsites.

TABLE 7.4

Low-Level Radioactive Wastes Disposed of, 1962–1982[1]
(thousand cubic meters buried)

Year	Annual addition			Cumulative buried		
	Commercial	U.S. Department of Energy[2]	Total	Commercial	U.S. Department of Energy[2]	Total
1962	1.9	—	—	1.9	—	—
1963	6.2	—	—	8.1	—	—
1964	13.1	—	—	21.2	—	—
1965	13.1	—	—	34.3	—	—
1966	16.2	—	—	50.5	—	—
1967	19.3	—	—	69.8	—	—
1968	20.3	—	—	90.1	—	—
1969	21.6	—	—	111.7	—	—
1970	26.0	—	—	137.7	—	—
1971	30.6	—	—	168.4	—	—
1972	37.3	—	—	205.7	—	—
1973	47.0	—	—	252.7	—	—
1974	53.6	—	—	306.3	—	—
1975	57.6	—	—	363.9	1,518	1,882
1976	74.2	56.2	130.4	438.2	1,574	2,012
1977	71.2	44.3	115.5	509.4	1,618	2,127
1978	79.6	60.1	139.7	588.9	1,678	2,267
1979	82.5	84.0	166.5	671.5	1,762	2,434
1980	106.8	57.9	164.7	778.2	1,820	2,598
1981	87.8	62.1	149.9	866.0	1,882	2,748
1982	75.9	89.1	165.0	941.9	1,971	2,913

[1] Changes have been made in the year prior to 1982 due to reclassifications, errors, and roundoff effects.
[2] Wastes generated by other federal agencies are buried at commercial sites.
SOURCE: U.S. Department of Energy, Office of Nuclear Energy, *Spent Fuel and Radioactive Waste Inventories, Projections and Characteristics*, DOE/NE-0017-2, January 1983.
SOURCE: Council on Environmental Quality, *Environmental Quality*, 1983, Table A-65, p. 320.

Following recent events at the Love Canal in New York, Times Beach in Missouri, and elswhere, much attention has been focused on the disposal of hazardous substances by industry. The 1976 issue of *Environmental Qualtiy* has a very nice twenty-page discussion of the problem and data have been getting progressively better in this underinvestigated area. Dozens of substances made or used by industry are extremely hazardous, sometimes in even minute quantities. PCBs, arsenic, lead, dioxin, mercury, and Kepone are examples that have appeared in the media in recent years. Sometimes they, or substances containing them, are discharged to water bodies, sometimes to the air, and sometimes to land. In the last case, they may find their way into streams through groundwater or to the air by evaporation or combustion. In some cases, death and disability have been established and the path of the substance from factory to those damaged has been found. Sometimes human health damage is known or suspected, but the path of the substance is unclear. Often, discharge of the substance is inadvertent, sometimes resulting from irresponsible handling. Sometimes discharge is intentional, when it is mistakenly thought that quantities are too small to be harmful.

The Kepone case is tragic and instructive. Kepone was used in ant and roach poisons and was made in a small plant in Virginia. Much was discharged, apparently through incredibly sloppy handling. Some evaporated and some ran into nearby streams. Seventy victims have been identified, some of whom have suffered untreatable ailments including brain damage and sterility. It is likely that most of the damage resulted from exposure within the plant or from ingestion of poisoned shellfish. The plant was closed in 1975.

New chemicals are constantly being invented, often to replace older chemicals that are found to be damaging, such as DDT. Many of these chemicals are deliberately introduced *because* they are toxic to certain organisms: these include insecticides, rodenticides, herbicides, fungicides, and bactericides. Some of these chemicals are not highly selective of the target organisms and if misused may have harmful effects on unintended organisms. Since so many varieties of substances are in use (about one and a half million tons of pesticides alone, representing 500,000 tons of active ingredients, are used annually in the United States alone), we will speak in a general way about treatment possibilities and benefits of reduced exposure. Recall from Chapter 2 that the benefits of reduced exposure are the damage reductions that result.

There are basically two types of hazard-reduction technologies: disposal and treatment. Under the disposal category, the two commonly discussed alternatives are landfills/impoundments and injection wells. As to effectiveness, the former are not very good for volatile compounds and are dubious for liquids based on laboratory and field tests, while injection wells should prove quite effective in theory, although limited field data exist. Siting, construction, operation, and geology all enter into the issue of reliability, and should disposal methods prove poor, the environmental media most affected will be ground and surface water. There is no resource-recovery potential for the disposal methods and the only recommendation for them is their relatively low cost. For certain chemicals that are not highly reactive, toxic, or persistent, they might be fine.

Treatment technologies include incineration and other high-temperature decomposition methods and chemical stabilization. The effectiveness of these methods is quite high, with the latter being particularly valuable for many toxic metals. Reliability issues revolve around monitoring uncertainties, limited experience with the technologies, and general ignorance about which chemicals and metals can be rendered harmless these ways. The incineration or high-temperature decomposition methods would, if improperly conducted, affect air quality in potentially very harmful ways, while chemical stabilization would affect groundwater. The high-temperature approach is good for organic compounds and some inorganics and the chemical stabilization method works best on metals but not well on organics. High-temperature approaches can result in resource recovery of energy, acids, and some metals. The chemical stabilization approach may result in some recovery of building materials. Costs for the two approaches tend to be moderate to high.

Clearly, a role would appear to exist for each of the disposal/treatment methods. The large variety of hazardous contaminants suggests that a large variety of control approaches should be entertained, including careful attention to the spatial location of any of the approaches taken.

How damaging have hazardous substances actually been? Media accounts would suggest steadily increasing exposure to damaging substances, with large potential health and ecological effects likely to result. In fact, the evidence is somewhat surprisingly to the contrary. Table 7.5 shows toxic residues found in humans during the decade of the 1970s. Except for PCBs, which exhibit a slight upward trend, residues of monitored toxic substances have shown steady decline. Similar findings, except that declines are recorded for all toxics measured, exist for toxic residues in waterfowl and starlings. The problem with drawing reassuring conclusions from these observations is that we are continually switching from substances that are

TABLE 7.5

Toxic Residues in Humans, 1970–1979

Toxic Substances

			Parts per million, geometric mean, lipid basis				
Year	N[1]	DDT[2]	Heptachlor epoxide	Oxychlordane	Dieldrin	BHC[3]	PCBs[4]
1970	1386	8.07	.14	NA	.23	.47	NA
1971	1560	8.24	.11	NA	.26	.42	NA
1972	1886	7.06	.11	.14	.22	.33	90.4
1973	1092	6.09	.11	.14	.22	.32	79.8
1974	901	5.33	.10	.14	.18	.28	91.3
1975	779	4.97	.11	.14	.17	.25	94.0
1976	683	4.68	.10	.14	.15	.26	98.1
1977	789	3.47	.09	.12	.12	.20	99.7
1978	827	3.91	.09	.13	.12	.20	98.8
1979	795	3.14	.10	.14	.11	.22	98.2

NA—Not available.

Data are for fiscal years.

Pesticides residues associated chemicals were measured in 48 states as part of the National Human Adipose Tissue survey. Specimens were collected each year by medical pathologists from selected cities. Individuals with known or suspected pesticide poisoning were excluded.

[1] Number of samples.

[2] DDT includes its metabolites.

[3] BHC includes the alpha-, beta-, gamma-, and delta- isomers of benzene hexachloride. All residue values are in parts per million, geometric mean, lipid basis except PCBs where percent population with detectable levels is given.

[4] Percent population with PCBs detected.

Sources:

DDT, heptachlor epoxide, oxychlorodane, dieldrin, BHC, 1970–1975: F. W. Kutz, S. C. Strassman, and J. F. Sperling, "Survey of Selected Organochlorine Pesticides in the General Population of the United States: Fiscal Years 1970–75," Annals of the New York Academy of Sciences 320: 60-68 (May 31, 1979). *1976–1977:* S. C. Strassman and F. W. Kutz, "Trends in Organochlorine Pesticide Residues in Human Tissue." *1978–1979:* U.S. Environmental Protection Agency, National Human Adipose Tissue, Survey, unpublished data.

PCBs, 1971: F. W. Kutz, A. R. Yobs, and S. C. Strassman, "Organochlorine Pesticide Residues in Human Adipose Tissue," 4:19 (1976). *1973–1979:* U.S. Environmental Protection Agency, National Human Adipose Tissue Survey, unpublished data.

SOURCE: Council on Environmental Quality, *Environmental Quality*, 1983, Table A-52, p. 313.

perceived as dangerous to others about which not so much is known. Hence the evidence over time may be a bit misleading, as we have switched to other chemicals that may be building up in our tissues and throughout the ecological system. The positive feeling we possess regarding hazardous substances stems from the strong regulatory approaches undertaken in recent legislation combined with far greater attention to the treatment and disposal of such wastes. Also, efforts to reduce nonpoint pollution sources of surface water will have substantial benefits in reducing hazardous substances as well as the nutrients and so on that are of primary concern in measured water-quality parameters.

DISCUSSION QUESTIONS AND PROBLEMS

1. How would you apply the analysis of materials reuse to reprocessing of uranium fuel in atomic electric plants?

2. Oregon and other states have compulsory deposits on certain bottles and other containers. The deposit is refunded when the container is returned to a seller. Evaluate it as an incentive to reuse materials. Can you think of a better incentive? Bottling companies charged deposits volunatarily in earlier years. Why did they stop?

3. How would you estimate the benefits and costs of a proposal to use sludge from a city's sewage-treatment plant to help reclaim land after strip mining? (Hint: See Table 2.4, p. 67 of *Environmental Quality*, 1983).

4. Even a moderately large city may require only one landfill. That is a justification for government ownership since a private owner would be a monopolist. But why should the local government not leave collection of solid wastes to private business and simply charge them for use of the landfill?

5. Property-value studies would seem to be an ideal method of determining the damages associated with dumps and landfills. How would you conduct such a study? You may wish to refer back to earlier chapters.

6. Referring to the solid-waste problem posed by automobiles, what do you think of the notion of having a deposit paid when a new car is purchased, which could be returned with interest upon proof of proper disposal? How would you organize such a program?

7. In a September 7, 1984 article in the *Wall Street Journal*, the toxic-dump cleanup effort was reported to be lagging, with EPA being blamed for the delays. How might you create an environment that would result in more rapid cleanup? Can dumps be cleaned up too fast?

8. How might you want to reorganize the EPA (which has essentially separate approaches to air, water, and solid-waste pollution problems) to incorporate in regulations the problems of the "displaced externality" or the

"interface" between environmental media that was highlighted in the latter part of this chapter?

REFERENCES AND FURTHER READING

Council on Environmental Quality. *Environmental Qualtiy.* Washington, D.C.: U.S. Government Printing Office, published annually. A large number of sources for further reading are contained in the various *Environmental Quality* reports. Reading through a few of the recent reports, which vary somewhat in coverage each year, will give the reader an excellent feel for the nature of the environmental problems discussed in Chapters 5, 6, and 7 of Part II of this book.)

Part III

ENVIRONMENTAL POLICY IN THE UNITED STATES

Part I presented some overview of environmental pollutants and the bare bones of the economic theory of environmental pollution and government policy. Part II put additional flesh on the bones by presenting some facts—and some conjectures—about discharges, effects of pollution on people and property, and techniques of pollution abatement. Part III analyzes government programs to control pollution in the United States.

All societies have government pollution-control programs of one kind or another, although many do not think of them in that way. Even laws or enforced traditional controls on nuisances are important pollution-control programs. Since World War II, many societies have introduced government programs specifically labeled pollution-control programs. The United States was among the first countries in the world to implement important programs that could justifiably be called comprehensive pollution-control programs. In Part III, these programs are described, analyzed, and criticized in the light of the theoretical material presented in Part I and the factual material presented in Part II.

Chapter 8

A Historical Sketch of Environmental Policy in the United States

In the broadest sense, all laws are part of governments' environmental policies. Almost all laws affect public or private resource allocation and, as was seen in Part I, almost all resource uses have environmental effects. But since the mid-1950s, and especially during the 1970s, many laws have been passed at all levels of government with the explicit intent of establishing government programs toward the discharge of materials to the environment. The most important of these laws are surveyed in this chapter. The purpose of the chapter is to describe the historical evolution of government environmental policy in the United States. Criticisms and possible reforms of environmental policy are presented in the next two chapters.

As has been shown in previous chapters, most materials can be discharged to the air, water bodies, or land. Where materials are discharged depends on technical and economic considerations and on the nature of government policies toward discharges to each medium. Furthermore, many discharges to air and land eventually end up in water bodies, and for most the sea is the ultimate sink. Logically, there should be a unified set of government policies that pertain to residuals discharged to all three media. But human affairs are rarely so logically ordered. Historically, the tendency in the United

States has been to enact separate laws regarding discharges to air, water, and land. The laws have been enacted at different times and have different provisions. It is therefore necessary to discuss separately public policies toward the three classes of discharges.

In Chapter 3 the distinction was made between direct and indirect discharges of residuals. Direct discharges are those discharged by the organization that generates them, whereas indirect discharges are collected and, possibly, treated or processed by another organization before discharge. Most indirect-discharge organizations are government agencies. This suggests that a natural classification of government policies toward the environment is between government actions to control direct discharges and government provision of indirect-discharge services. The distinction is important not only regarding environmental policies but also regarding many other government programs. For example, urban transportation is sometimes provided by a government-owned bus company and sometimes by a privately owned company subject to government regulation. Whether the subject is environmental protection or bus service, the issues are the same. Under what circumstances should services be provided by the government sector and under what circumstances by the private sector? If they are provided by government, how should the agency be organized, managed, and financed? If they are provided by the private sector, should private organizations be regulated by government agencies and, if so, in what ways? These questions will be the focus of the discussion in Part III.

In addition to direct- and indirect-discharge-control programs, a third environmental activity in which the federal government has been engaged is improving our information about the environment, ways to protect it and the consequences of damaging it. Under this heading are included research, development, monitoring, and data collection. Little has been said about these activities in previous chapters, and relatively little will be said about them in this and subsequent chapters. Relatively few people doubt that government should undertake these activities. Governments are rightly given responsibility for collecting and publishing many kinds of basic data that society needs. Census data, vital statistics, and national income accounts are examples. There is equally good reason for governments to collect environmental data. Government officials, private environmental groups, businesses, and scholars need such data to formulate, evaluate, and administer environmental programs. Much of the needed data can be collected only by governments. Although somewhat more controversial, research and development are thought by most economists to be proper functions of government. Businesses and other private organizations undertake large amounts of research. But the more basic the research, the smaller the part of the social benefits that can be captured by the group that undertakes the research. Such research is, in part, a public good just as a high-quality environment was shown to be a public good in Chapters 2 and 4. Therefore, profit-making firms lack incentive to undertake as much as is socially efficient.

The main controversies regarding research, development, and data collection are not about whether the government should undertake them, but instead about how much and what kind should be under-taken and how the activities should be organized and managed.

Until the mid-1950s the tradition was that under our federal form of government, responsibility for pollution control lay with state governments and their creations, local governments. The Constitu-tion gives the federal government jurisdiction over interstate and navigable waterways, but responsibility was interpreted to refer mainly to the promotion and protection of navigation. Local water supply, sewer systems, waste treatment and trash collection were all local government responsibilities. Much pollution was confined, as it still is, within state boundaries. But the history of the twentieth century has been one of gradually broadening federal responsibilities under the Constitution's interstate-commerce clause, and a corre-sponding contraction of state responsibilities. Once the country became seriously concerned about environmental problems, it was inevitable that major responsibility for government programs would be lodged in the federal government. Many polluting discharges cross state boundaries. As was explained in Chapter 3, the result is that state governments lack incentive to require optimum abatement. They lack jurisdiction to collect data pertaining to damages in downwind or downstream states, and they lack incentive to induce their citizens and firms to undertake expensive abatement activities that mostly benefit voters living in other states.

Before 1970, federal environmental programs were administered by several agencies. The Department of the Interior, as the govern-ment's agency to administer natural-resource programs, had first administered pollution-control programs. The 1960s were character-ized by bureaucratic infighting between Interior and the Department of Health, Education and Welfare for control of environmental programs. Many people felt that Interior's orientation was toward resource development and extractive industries, whereas HEW's orientation was toward programs that promoted human welfare. The issue of who was to have jurisdiction over environmental programs was settled in 1970, when the Council on Environmental Quality and the Environmental Protection Agency were created. The CEQ is in the president's Executive Offices. It advises the president on environmental policy and publishes *Environmental Quality* each year. The EPA is an operating agency charged with administering all the important federal programs.

The peak of the environmental movement in the United States was 1970. It was the year of Earth Day, formation of hundreds of citizen-action groups, publication of tons of popular literature, and passage of major federal legislation. It was easy to get the impression that the country was seething with idealism and concern, yet subsequent evidence makes it clear that serious interest was restricted to a rather narrow high-income and highly educated segment of the population.

Water-Quality Legislation

The earliest environmental laws in the United States were those setting and protecting drinking-water standards. Although other early laws also contained environmental provisions (e.g., the 1899 Refuse Act, which made it necessary to get a permit from the Army Corps of Engineers to discharge refuse into navigable waters), the first comprehensive act was the Federal Water Pollution Control Act of 1948. Along with its amendments during the 1950s, 1960s, and, most importantly, in 1972, it is the core of our present national water-pollution-control program in each of the three areas indicated in the introduction: regulation of direct discharges, provision of indirect-discharge services, and research and development. Each program will be discussed in turn.

Direct-Discharge Regulation   National policy in this area has been characterized by increasing boldness and stridency, if not wisdom, since 1956. Under the 1956 Amendments to the Federal Water Pollution Control Act, a federal agency was empowered to make studies of water quality in interstate water bodies. If a study concluded that a stream was polluted, that the pollution was interstate in character, and that it endangered human health or welfare, then a series of actions could be initiated. First a federal-state conference could be called and it could recommend specific actions to abate polluting discharges into the water body. For example, a common recommendation was that all major dischargers of organic wastes in the water body install secondary waste treatment or its equivalent. Second, after a delay, the federal government could hold public hearings to determine what actions were being taken. Third, after another delay, the federal government could file suit in federal court to force dischargers to take needed actions.

In 1961, the act was amended to enable the federal government to take these actions in all navigable waters, and in intrastate waters if requested to do so by the state governor.

By 1965, many studies had been made and many important river stretches had been found to be polluted. Conferences and hearings had been held and later reopened. None of the cases that had been opened had been terminated. There had been virtually no use of the courts, the only step in the complex process that could require pollution-abatement measures to be taken. The evidence suggested that water quality had continued to deteriorate, and there was little evidence that water quality had improved even in the water bodies that were the subjects of important cases. Congress, in passing the Water Quality Act of 1965, amended the law to establish ambient quality standards in interstate streams. State governments were asked to set water-quality standards in each stretch of each interstate waterway. If the states did not establish standards within a responsible time, or if the standards were not acceptable to the federal government, a federal agency was empowered to set them. The goal of the amendment was that a finding that water quality was below the standard set should be prima facie evidence that dischargers were violating the law. Thus it was hoped that polluters could be taken quickly into court without the cumbersome procedures of conferences and hearings, and without the government's being required to prove that specific discharges endangered the health and welfare of people.

By the end of the 1960s, Congress and many members of the public became convinced that the 1965 procedure was not working much better than the 1956 procedure had. States were slow to set acceptable standards, in part because they lacked guidelines, data, and technical expertise to estimate benefits and costs of various possible stream-quality levels. More important, legal authorities raised doubts whether it would be possible to identify a particular discharger as the cause of a standard violation in a way that would be acceptable to the courts. The water quality in a particular river stretch is the result of many discharges, some occurring many miles away, and it is arbitrary to sue any particular firm or municipality for discharges that violate the standard. The point is that the 1965 act did not really avoid the problem with the 1956 act. The problem with the 1956 act was that it required the government to show in court that a particular discharge imperiled health and welfare. The 1965 act required the government to show in court that a particular discharge caused a violation of a stream standard. The problem under both acts was basically the same, the identification of damage with particular discharges.

One can only be amazed that fifteen years were required to learn this elementary legal lesson. By 1970 it was clear that discharge regulation required a stronger tool than was provided by existing legislation to affect the actions of individual dischargers. In 1970 the federal government rediscovered the provision of the 1899 Refuse Act that prohibited discharges to navigable waterways without a permit issued by the U.S. Army Corps of Engineers. This appeared to be a way out of the enforceability dilemma, and the government began to accept applications for permits and issued a few. But the 1899 act was an amendment to a navigation act and was not an environmental act. Dischargers sued the government to prevent them from issuing permits under the 1899 act that were intended to meet environmental standards.

Inspired by this episode, the wave of environmental concern that culminated in 1970, and the widespread dissatisfaction with existing law, Congress further amended water-quality legislation in 1972. This eighty-nine-page bill, passed overwhelmingly over President Richard Nixon's veto, is one of the most complex ever passed by Congress. It repeals the 1899 provision and establishes a permit system based on environmental grounds. Once all permits have been issued, it will be illegal to discharge wastes to a navigable water body from a point source without a permit. Dischargers must apply to a state agency or to a designated interstate agency for a permit. After the state or interstate agency approves the permit application, it must be reviewed and approved again by a federal agency. By 1976, forty-six thousand permits had been issued, but one-third of the dischargers identified had not yet received permits.

The 1972 law lays down guidelines for EPA to use in granting discharge permits. It says that dischargers should be required to use the "best practicable discharge control technology" by 1977, and the "best available technology economically achievable" by 1983. The act also says that it is national policy to eliminate discharges to navigable waterways by 1985. This astonishing statement appears in the objectives of the act and does not have the force of law. Instead, it is an expression of congressional sentiment.

By 1976, forty-one thousand industrial and twenty-one thousand municipal dischargers had been identified. The law placed upon EPA's shoulders the burden of extremely detailed regulation of these and other institutions. To ascertain what discharge abatement is "economically achievable," EPA must investigate available production technologies, waste treatment and disposal technologies, and investment and expansion plans for each discharger. In addition, EPA must evaluate the profitability and foreign and domestic competition of each applicant. Since passage of the 1972 act, EPA has become a large bureaucracy that has undertaken large-scale studies of polluting industries and is publishing numerous lengthy regulations in the *Federal Register* for permit-issuing procedures and guidelines for discharges to be permitted. The complexity of the task is staggering. Many important cases were appealed to the courts. The resulting cases were among the most technical that courts must deal with. Given the vagueness of the law, appeals to courts are inevitable. Such cases are a major part of the business of a growing cadre of environmental lawyers.

The Clean Water Act of 1977 was a response to vague and unrealistic features of the 1972 law. This law anticipated the large recent concern over toxic substances by applying more stringent controls on designated toxic pollutants, while relaxing the limits (to "best conventional technology") on conventional pollutants. In addition to the 1977 law dealing specifically with water, many other laws have impacts on water quality in this country. Among these are the Safe Drinking Water Act of 1974 (which set national standards for maximum contaminant levels of pollutants), the Toxic Substances Control Act of 1976 (which regulated some toxic pollutants that end up in drinking and recreational waters), the Resource Conservation and Recovery Act of 1976 and its 1980 amendments (which took account of the hydrological characteristics of municipal and hazardous-waste-disposal sites), and the Surface Mining Control and Reclamation Act of 1977 (which dealt with the implications for surface and ground-water quality of coal mining and land reclamation efforts). The quest in this legislative history is for zero discharge of pollutants, employing nationally uniform effluent standards, pollution permits, and added construction grants (discussed below).

Provision of Indirect-Discharge Services   Local governments have always been responsible for water supply and the collection and treatment of sewage in their jurisdictions. The 1956 act provided for the federal government to make grants to local governments for construction of sewage-treatment plants. Local governments apply to EPA for a grant. The federal government can approve the application if it believes the proposed plant is needed, sound, and consistent with federal pollution-control policies. Federal grants are on a cost-sharing basis, under which the federal grant pays a percentage of the cost if state and local governments agree to pay the rest. The percentage of total construction cost the federal government can pay depends on circumstances, and has been increased gradually since 1956. Under the 1972 act, and continued in the 1977 act, the federal government can pay up to 75 percent of construction cost. The 1981 Clean Water Act Amendments reduced the subsidy to 55 percent and cut funding authorizations from $4.5 billion to $2.4 billion, effective in 1985.

EPA cannot make grants in excess of annual appropriations by Congress, and grant expenditures have been subject to intense political controversy on several occasions. Congress appropriates money for grants, but the executive branch is responsible for evaluating grant applications and spending the money. Not surprisingly, expenditures lag behind appropriations, and the lag is greatest when appropriations rise rapidly. It takes time for communities to plan waste-treatment plants and for grant applications to be written and evaluated. The 1972 act provided for rapid increases in grant appropriations and the large sum was President Nixon's reason for vetoing the bill. After the bill was passed over his veto, he impounded part of the funds on the grounds that the appropriations were unneeded and inflationary. The executive branch can legally refrain from spending funds if, for example, not enough applications are received that satisfy the requirements of the law. But the courts have held consistently that the president may not refuse to spend legally appropriated funds because he believes that to spend them would be bad national policy. Nevertheless, it is difficult to force the executive branch to spend a specific amount of money. It is easy to slow down the application evaluation and approval processes and the speed with which checks are written. Political infighting over such matters provides grist for headline writers, but tells us nothing about the basic desirability of the grant program or its level of financing. These issues will be discussed in the next chapter. But federal funding of munic-ipal waste-treatment-plant construction is now a multibillion-dollar business.

Research and Development   Research and development and related activities have been an important part of the federal water-pollution-control program since its beginning. Research is conducted both in federal research establishments and on contract with private insti-tutions. EPA funds several research centers around the country. Contract research is undertaken in private research firms and in uni-versities. Most of the government's water research budget is devoted to study of the effects of pollutants on water and water uses and of methods of pollution abatement. Related to the latter, the govern-ment has a demonstration program under which new techniques of pollution abatement are demonstrated in facilities of operational scale. The government's monitoring program provides most of the data available about the water quality in the United States. Finally, the federal government provides money for education and training in fields related to water quality.

Most of the research is of course scientific and technical. But EPA increasingly performs and supports some social-science research, particularly on the economic impact of pollution-control programs. In large part this stems from an Executive Order appearing in the Federal Register in 1981, which required that government programs affecting resource allocation consider the benefits *and* the costs of those programs. This has led to much improvement in the methods used in determining what environmental quality gains are worth to society. The EPA has shown less (but increasing) interest in research on data collection, alternatives to direct regulation, or institutional arrangements for improving environmental quality.

Like the waste-treatment-facility subsidy program, the research-and-development program has grown rapidly, from a few million dollars a year in the late 1950s to hundreds of millions of dollars today. With the huge budget deficits of the mid-1980s, the future of these research programs is unclear. It is noteworthy that the 1972 act provided not only substantial sums for research but also provided fifteen pages of detailed instructions as to the use of the research money. These instructions convey the attitude that pervades recent environmental legislation: Congress is determined to state its intentions in such detail that neither the executive branch, state and local governments, nor the private sector can avoid carrying them out.

Air-Quality Legislation

The national air-pollution-control program has paralleled the water program in most respects. As with water, there were local nuisance laws pertaining to air pollutants long before there was a national program. The first comprehensive national air-pollution-control law was the Clean Air Act of 1963. It closely paralleled the 1956 Water Pollution Control Act. Like the water act, the Clean Air Act has been amended several times. The most important amendment was that of 1970. Along with the 1972 water act, it constitutes the basis of our national environmental policy.

Direct-Discharge Regulation   The 1963 act contained provisions almost identical to those in force at the time for water-pollution control. The government was empowered to make studies of air pollution and its effects. If the government found that interstate air pollution was endangering health or welfare, or if requested by a governor to intervene in an intrastate case, then certain steps, could be set in motion. These steps consisted of hearings, conferences, and, finally, appeals to the courts. Discharge regulations under the 1963 act pertained only to stationary sources. Despite the fact that California had passed a law the same year to regulate automobile effluents, the national law provided only for further study of the problem.

In 1965 the Clean Air Act was amended to include discharge regulation of automobiles. In contrast with the 1963 act, which empowered the government to request abatement only if it found that discharges endangered health or welfare, the 1965 act instructed the government to set maximum permissible discharges from automobiles beginning with 1968-model-year cars. The act itself did not specify the standards. Instead, it instructed the government to determine standards that would be technically and economically feasible and would protect health and welfare. The standards actually chosen entailed modest abatement of carbon-monoxide and hydrocarbon discharges from 1968-model-year cars. Increasingly stringent standards were announced for future years, so that 1970-model-year cars could emit no more than about half the weight of the two pollutants per vehicle mile that were emitted by the last uncontrolled cars, in 1967. The act also set standards for crankcase evaporation. Curiously, it set no standards for nitrogen oxides, despite the availability of strong laboratory evidence that they were a major element in the smog-producing process. Heavy-duty gasoline trucks were first subject to emission standards in 1970.

It should be emphasized that the standards applied only to new cars. Cars were required to meet only the standards in effect in the year they were made. Thus, with an average life of about ten years per car and a moderate growth rate of the stock, it was at least four years after 1968 before the majority of cars on the road were made to meet any standard at all. Furthermore, emissions tend to increase as cars age, whether they were manufactured to meet emission standards or not. There was no provision in the 1965 law to maintain used cars so they would continue to meet emission standards during their useful lives. It was estimated that, despite the gradual tightening of standards, total auto emissions in 1970 were still 80 or 90 percent of their 1967 levels.

In 1967 Congress amended the Clean Air Act in a way that almost precisely paralleled the 1965 water amendment. The federal government was to issue a set of studies of the effects of various air pollutants on health and property. It was also to designate a set of air-quality regions throughout the country. Based on the studies, states were asked to set and implement ambient air-quality standards in the regions within their borders. If the standards set, or the measures proposed to implement them, were unsatisfactory to the federal government, then the federal government could do the job itself. The 1967 amendment left unchanged the procedure for setting auto-emission standards.

By the end of the 1960s, much of the same disillusionment was felt about the air-pollution-control program as about the water program. The federal government had been slow to issue its studies and the states had been slow to set standards and implementation programs. Furthermore, doubts about enforceability of ambient water-quality standards applied equally to air-quality standards. Popular concern about environmental quality was at its peak and Congress was under pressure to promulgate a tough new air-quality program. The result was the 1970 Clean Air Act amendment.

The 1970 air amendment was similar to the 1972 water amendment in that it placed major responsibility for setting tough ambient and discharge standards from stationary sources on EPA, and major responsibility for implementing them on the states. It continued federal responsibility for new-car emission standards, but placed responsibility for used cars on the states.

The 1970 amendment directed EPA to determine ambient air standards that would be below the threshold at which human health would be protected. These were called primary standards, and federal and state agencies were directed to implement them on very short time schedules. EPA was also directed to set secondary standards that would be more stringent than the primary standards and that would protect property and welfare, and they were to be implemented on somewhat more flexible schedules. The act directed that new stationary sources were to be required to use the "best adequately demonstrated control technology." This legal requirement was regardless of costs and benefits.

Thus for stationary sources the federal government decided to undertake the same kind of detailed regulation of production for air-pollution control that it undertook for water-pollution control in the 1972 water amendment. EPA was obliged to undertake detailed study of the technology and costs of alternative production and control methods in each industry. It then decided exactly what modifications in production and control would be required in each case. It designated controls for each configuration of existing as well as new plants. Since existing plants were constructed, expanded, and modernized at various times, each employed an almost unique technology and produced an almost unique set of commodities. Therefore much of EPA's regulatory activity had to be designed specifically for individual sources. The body of regulatory rules became extremely large.

For mobile sources, the 1970 act did something no environmental act had done before: It stated the standards in the act instead of stating guidelines for EPA to use in setting the standards. The standards were the new cars could not be sold in 1975 if they emitted more than 10 percent as much hydrocarbons and carbon monoxide as the 1970 standards permitted, equivalent to about 5 percent of the emissions of 1967 cars. In addition, 1976 cars were required to meet a similar standard for nitrogen oxides. The act provided that the EPA administrator could postpone the 1975 and 1976 standards for one year each, setting interim standards instead, if he found that technology was not available to meet the standards in the act (the administrator exercised his option in 1973). The certification procedure is as follows: A sample of each kind of new car (make, engine type, and so forth) is submitted to EPA for certification testing. The test starts with a cold engine and is a rigidly specified thirty-five-minute driving sequence during which emissions are collected. If the collected emissions do not exceed the standard, the car can be produced (or imported) and sold. A requirement for certification is that the producer guarantee the pollution-control system for fifty-thousand miles or five years, provided the owner complies with maintenance and replacement instructions in the manual. But the owner lacks incentive to comply since the car is likely to have better gas mileage and drivability if the control devices fail. Therefore the 1970 act provides for the states to test emissions as part of annual safety inspection and to require that used cars meet a standard set by the state, not necessarily as high as that for new cars, before they can be registered. After a long period of resistance (by 1976 only New Jersey tested emissions), a large number of states have annual emissions inspections, with or without a safety inspection.

Congress foresaw that it was unlikely that ambient standards set under the act's guidelines could be met by installation of pollution-control devices on stationary and mobile sources. They therefore indicated in the act a variety of other steps that states could take to achieve the ambient standards, including land-use controls, closing facilities, transportation controls (such as gasoline rationing), encouraging public transit, and so forth. Taken literally, these requirements mandate that almost every part of the production, transportation, and disposal of goods, as well as the movement of people, must be regulated in detail by a complex combination of state and federal agencies. In the mid-1970s local resentment resulted as transportation-control plans began to come into effect, mostly under court orders. Citizens and local government officials resented the federal government telling them when and where they could permit cars to travel and park, feeling the federal government was intruding on local prerogatives. That is, in the federal government's rush to impose uniform requirements throughout the country, important differences in local circumstances of benefit or cost were ignored.

Other lessons learned during the 1970s that are being incorporated into the laws of the mid-1980s are that 1) mandated arbitrary deadlines that cannot be met tend to undermine the confidence needed for steady, lasting environmental improvements where they are justified; 2) the legislative emphasis on detailed, specific controls often causes society to ignore low-cost alternative approaches; 3) federal involvement has, in some cases, hindered solutions to *local* environmental problems (for example, the federal grant subsidies encouraged many communities to buy wastewater treatment systems that were too complex and expensive to be properly managed); and 4) the uncoordinated approach of controlling each medium separately fails to deal effectively with the interactions implied by the law of conservation of matter.

Provision of Indirect-Discharge Services   Unlike liquid and solid wastes, airborne wastes are not collected, treated, or discharged by governments. But as has been mentioned several times, governments do discharge air pollutants in providing indirect-discharge services for solid and liquid wastes. Sewage-treatment plants require energy whose conversion generates air pollution. And sludge from sewage-treatment plants is sometimes burned. Likewise, solid wastes are sometimes burned in dumps or incinerators.

Since no indirect-discharge services are performed by governments for airborne wastes, there is no federal subsidy program analogous to that for sewage-treatment-plant construction.

Research and Development   As with the water program, research, development, demonstration, monitoring, and data collection have been an important part of the air program since its beginning. Much of the money has been used to study, design, and demonstrate devices to abate air pollution. But relatively more than in the water area has been used to study health effects and property damage from air pollution. Although ambient air-quality data still leave much to be desired, the quantity and quality of such data have improved greatly since the early 1960s. Dramatic increases in spending for air-quality research has occurred as a result of legislation of the 1970s, but it is too early to determine whether this is a lasting trend.

Land Quality and Other Environmental Legislation

There is a distinct pattern to the development of our national air- and water-pollution-control programs. In each area, the first laws were timid declarations of a federal role, and provided for research, development, demonstration, monitoring, data collection, planning, and cooperation. Next came a modest national program of discharge regulation. The dates were 1956 for water and 1963 for air. Subsequent laws became more strident in tone and vindictive in content, providing close and detailed government regulation of investment, production, and waste treatment. In the mid-1970s national solid-waste programs were at a stage analogous to the water program just before 1956 and the air program just before 1963. The national program consisted of modest expenditures to improve and spread technology, data, and planning. The indications are of an almost inexorable tendency for the development of a national solid-waste program along the lines of the other two programs. Indeed, this process is already well underway with the Resource Conservation and Recovery Act (1976) and its 1980 amendments, the Toxic Substances Control Act (1976) and the Comprehensive Environmental Response, Compensation, and Liability Act of 1980 (better known as the "Superfund"). The major legislative thrust into this waste-management area stems from popular concern about toxic substances, along with the recognition that poorly run dumps resulted in air- and, especially, water-pollution problems. Hazardous wastes will be discussed in greater detail later in this chapter.

A primary difference between the solid-waste program and the air and water programs at comparable stages of development is the association in Congress and in popular discussions of materials reuse with solid wastes. As was pointed out in Chapter 7, materials are and can be recovered that would otherwise be discharged to air and water. But the tonnage of solid-waste materials in much greater than of those discharged to air and water, and much of the effort toward materials reuse has been concerned with solid wastes. Thus materials reuse has come to be associated with solid wastes and for that reason it will be discussed in this section.

Direct-Discharge Regulation   There are at present few general federal programs to regulate solid-waste disposal, although the Solid Waste Disposal Act of 1965 was passed to improve state and local capabilities of disposing of municipal solid wastes. Many state and local governments of course have nuisance and litter laws that prohibit the disposal of wastes in public places. Casual disposal of containers, wrappings, and used consumer goods on streets, parks, beaches, and elsewhere is of course a common and much discussed annoyance. It is what many people think of when they think of pollution and it is the object of many recycling campaigns of local enthusiasts.

Local governments are responsible for collection and disposal of solid wastes in their jurisdiction. This will be discussed below in the section on indirect-discharge services. States often regulate local-government solid-waste-disposal practices. Such regulations may stipulate that solid-waste-disposal practices must be safe and sanitary, or they may give a state agency, such as a health department, power to approve specific practices. There does not seem to be a usable compilation or analysis of such regulations. It is widely believed, and confirmed by casual observation, that state laws are violated with impunity by local governments. A state may require that a local dump be upgraded to a sanitary landfill. But if the local government is financially pressed, the state has almost no way to force it to upgrade the facility. It can provide advice, technical assistance, and money, and it can sue in court. But it is difficult to force an impoverished local government to spend the money or pay fines. And the state can hardly imprison the mayor or town council.

Such difficulties were the stimulus for a number of provisions of the Resource Conservation and Recovery Act of 1976. The primary goal, for nonhazardous waste, was to encourage states to develop comprehensive programs controlling solid-waste-disposal practices and encouraging resource recovery, recycling, and conservation, whenever possible. Paralleling the early laws on air and water, the federal role is currently limited to establishing guidelines for solid-waste plans to be developed by states, to providing criteria for classifying land disposal facilities in terms of environmental impact, and to publishing a national inventory of open dumps that fail to meet minimal environmental standards. As of early 1983, twenty-one states had EPA-approved solid-waste-management plans, two other states had partially approved plans, eighteen states had adopted plans and have submitted them to EPA for review, and twelve states have draft plans under review at various levels. Alaska, New Mexico, and the District of Columbia had not formulated plans at that time.

Provision of Indirect-Discharge Services Local governments are responsible for the collection and disposal of solid wastes from homes and, to a limited extent, from commercial and industrial establishments. But 90 percent of commercial and industrial solid wastes is collected privately. In fact, about half of household solid waste is collected by private companies. There has been a trend toward private collection in recent years, probably because it is less expensive than when local governments do the job. In some communities, private firms contract with the local government to collect wastes and in others they contract directly with households, with or without regulation by local government. Private ownership of disposal facilities is less common than of collection. Mostly dumps, landfills, and incinerators are owned by local governments even where collection is by private firms. Privately owned disposal facilities are found mainly in rural areas.

Many people are shocked that 75 percent of municipal solid waste is still disposed of in dumps. A large part of the so-called solid-waste crisis consists of the simple fact that open dumps become increasingly intolerable, at least in metropolitan areas. The alternatives are materials reuse, landfills, and incinerators. Each costs money. Undoubtedly, it will be necessary to spend a good deal more in the future than was spent in the past on solid-waste reuse and disposal. But even a high-quality sanitary landfill involves disposal costs of only a few dollars a ton, as was shown in Chapter 7. It is a small addition to the costs of extracting and processing the materials.

State governments have programs to encourage and assist local governments to close many of the estimated fourteen thousand dumps in the country. Moreover, the national programs have led the federal government to make, largely unsubstantiated, claims that its program has resulted in the closing of several thousand dumps. But there is no evidence that the amount of solid wastes disposed of in dumps is less than it was a few years ago.

Undoubtedly, as some urban areas grow, it will become increasingly necessary to haul solid wastes substantial distances to find satisfactory disposal sites. And as larger parts of urban populations are outside central cities, disposal of one jurisdiction's wastes in another jurisdiction will become increasingly necessary. Interjurisdictional transfers have not worked well in the past. Citizens resent their community being the repository for other people's wastes. There is presumably a role for state and federal governments to play in helping to negotiate such agreements. But a large part of the solution must be money. Many low-density and rural communities would presumably be willing to have carefully operated sanitary landfills in which wastes from outside the jurisdiction were deposited provided the community was paid enough to meet a substantial part of the local governments' revenue needs, just as they are willing to have industry in the community because of its real-estate-tax payments.

Research and Development   The Solid Waste Disposal Act of 1965 and the Resource Recovery Act of 1970 and the subsequent amendments already mentioned contain the federal government's present policy toward solid wastes. The 1965 act authorized the government to undertake research, development, and demonstration projects regarding solid-waste-disposal methods and the effects of poor disposal. It also authorized similar activities regarding materials recovery and reuse. The 1970 act expanded the authority in both areas. The two acts also provide for technical assistance to state and local governments in planning and improving disposal and recovery activities. This research and development program has grown like the others, but is the smallest of the three.

There has clearly been technical progress in solid-waste recovery since the early 1960s. Most prominent have been devices for separating the materials in household waste cans. Equally important have been machines that shred junk automobiles to facilitate material separation and reuse. But it is not clear that the federal role has been important in promoting new technology. Industry, motivated by rising fuel and materials prices, has also undertaken research and development on separation and recovery devices.

Apparently there has been no significant technical progress in solid-waste collection and disposal since the introduction of the compaction truck in the 1950s.

Materials Reuse   As was stated in Chapter 7, materials reuse refers to the collection, separation, and reprocessing of used materials so they can be reused to make commodities instead of being discharged to the environment. Encouragement of materials reuse is the main purpose of the Resource Recovery Act of 1970 and the 1976 RCRA amendments. It encourages reuse by providing federal money for development and demonstration of new technology for separation and recovery of materials. Local and, especially, state governments have developed programs to encourage materials reuse in recent years.

A trend has been for states to build large-scale solid-waste-recovery-and-reuse centers with federal financial assistance. For example, New York and Connecticut have constructed regional centers to which wastes can be hauled from far away. There wastes are separated and prepared for reuse. An important component of such centers is separation and compaction of organic wastes for use as fuel in thermal electric plants. Such centers have been advocated and started with enthusiasm and idealism. They may well prove a good idea. But their limitations should be faced. Their basic task is to organize and administer centers to supply solid wastes for reuse. But it is not supply-side deficiencies that have prevented reuse of solid wastes in the past. Had there been demand for the materials, firms could easily have persuaded communities to give up their solid wastes. Instead, the problem has been a lack of demand for used materials, because newly extracted materials were cheaper and/or of higher quality. Organizing supply facilities does not change that situation. To the extent that governments subsidize processing and transportation, used materials may be made competitive with new materials. But it will then be the subsidy, not the state-run facility, that makes the difference. The question then becomes whether state-run facilities are the best way to subsidize materials reuse. That subject has not been studied carefully. Instead, state governments have followed the instinct governments usually have, to build and operate facilities themselves. A good guess is that state-operated centers will appear to be successful while raw material and fuel prices are high, but that their customers will disappear and they will face financial problems the first time materials and fuel prices slump. If relative prices of fuels and other materials again rise in the 1980s, state-run solid-waste-recovery centers may even turn out to be profitable. But it is a speculative activity for states to engage in.

The reuse of junk automobiles has received a great deal of attention. Several states levy fees on cars at registration, and use the revenues to remove abandoned cars or to encourage processing and reuse of junk cars. All such schemes are administratively complex. Subsidies to the collection or processing of junk cars do not guarantee that the materials will not merely pile up at the stage following the subsidized process. Alternatively, subsidies for reuse of scrap steel in production may go to scrap from sources other than cars. The purpose of such programs is to lower the relative price of used, compared with newly extracted, materials. A theoretically tidier program to accomplish the goal would be to tax materials as they are extracted from the environment. Extraction is administratively easier to identify than reuse, there are fewer institutions to deal with, and it would affect all uses of given materials, not merely uses in particular products. Steel is, after all, used in many products other than cars, and a ton of steel in a junk automobile is no more a disamenity than a ton of steel in any other scrapped product. Finally, it is doubtful that states can administer such programs effectively. A state that subsidized reuse of junk automobiles would encourage their importation from other states to obtain the subsidy. In 1970, President Nixon proposed a tax on new cars to be used to encourage reuse of junk autos. Legislation has not been enacted.

Hazardous Substances

A most recent concern extends beyond disposal of ordinary solid wastes. A number of highly publicized mishandlings of toxic, mutagenic, or carcinogenic materials, which we shall lump together as hazardous substances, have resulted in dramatic legislative efforts. While the Toxic Substances Control Act and the Resource Conservation and Recovery Act, both of 1976, and the Superfund legislation (1980) most obviously address this problem, a large number of other laws have direct or indirect bearing on the generation and handling of hazardous substances. Among these are the Federal Insecticide, Fungicide, and Rodenticide Act (1972, amended in 1975 and 1978), the Safe Drinking Water Act (1974, amended on 1977), the Marine Protection, Research, and Sanctuaries Act (1972), and the Occupational Safety and Health Act (1978).

Focusing on the most important legislation to date (more legislation will no doubt be forthcoming), the Toxic Substances Control Act requires premanufacture notification for the manufacture or importation of new chemicals, authorizes controls on handling of chemicals ranging from complete prohibition to required labeling, authorizes testing requirements, and requires that chemical processors or manufacturers maintain records and report to EPA the identities and quantities of chemicals they produce, including by-products.

With more than sixty thousand chemicals currently in use and with about a thousand applications to EPA each year for approval of new chemicals, the administrative burden of TSCA is large. EPA has, however, engaged in a number of rulemaking procedures under this law, including controls on polychlorinated biphenyls (PCBs), asbestos, and formaldehyde. Two hundred and three cases have been completed of the 311 complaints filed between 1979 and 1982 as of this writing and penalties of about $1.5 million have been assessed.

The RCRA was, in large part, concerned with the general treatment of solid wastes of all kinds, prohibiting open dumping and the like. Provisions dealing with hazardous wastes regulated the treatment, storage, transportation, and disposal of any wastes having deleterious impact on public health or the environment more broadly. Standards have been promulgated (in 1982) regarding how hazardous wastes are incinerated (99.99 percent destruction and removal effeciency), how they are stored (required liners and leachate collection systems), and how to deal with possible groundwater contamination (required detection, evaluation, and correction measures). In another regulatory action in the same year, EPA required a nationally uniform manifest for the transportation of hazardous waste. Progress has also been made in accumulating extensive data on hazardous waste (e.g., permit applications indicate that 9,163 hazardous-waste facilities existed as of January, 1983 to handle the wastes generated by about fifty-four thousand generators and transporters). Additional information has been gathered on the type of process employed by hazardous-waste facilities (injection well, landfill, land treatment, surface impoundment, waste pile, incinerator, storage containers, storage tanks, or treatment tanks).

The third piece of legislation dealing with hazardous substances, the "Superfund," imposed "environmental taxes" on the petroleum and chemical industries to set up a Hazardous Substance Response Trust Fund. Additionally, taxes on owners and operators of hazardous-waste-disposal facilities were imposed to create the Post-Closure Liability Trust Fund. While there are many specific details as to when and how the funds are to be used, the basic provisions involve clean-up efforts directed at top-priority hazardous-waste targets. There were to be at least four hundred such targets with the top one hundred composed of at least one facility from each state that was deemed the greatest risk to inhabitants of that state. At this writing, there were well over five hundred priority targets among the nation's more than fifteen thousand hazardous-substance sites.

In principle, almost nothing an industrial firm does is outside the purview of EPA at this time. Its activities are limited mainly by the budget Congress provides. Major industrial decisions were formerly made on the basis of competitive and profitability considerations; they are now made jointly with government lawyers and technicians. In part, the historical reason for this outcome—whether it is good or bad—stems from confusion generated by the act discussed in the following section.

National Environmental Policy Act

On January 1, 1970, President Nixon signed a six-page bill designated the National Environmental Policy Act (NEPA). Whereas the 1972 water act and more recent air-quality and other legislation are long, complicated environmental acts, NEPA receives the prize for the vaguest and most obscure. In flowery language, it declares environmental protection to be a major goal of national policy. Substantively, the act does two things. First, it established the Council on Environmental Quality in the Executive Office of the president. Second, it requires federal government agencies to prepare environmental-impact statements concerning proposed legislation and "other major federal actions significantly affecting the quality of the human environment." Congress's idea was that the federal government does many things that have environmental impacts. It builds dams, leases timber rights on federal lands, permits offshore oil drilling, and licenses atomic electric plants, for example. It is certainly desirable that the environmental impacts of such actions be taken into account. But the act says nothing specific about what kinds of federal actions require environmental-impact statements or what effect environmental considerations should have on federal actions. The result is that the act has generated a tremendous amount of litigation—so much so that it is humorously referred to as the lawyers' relief bill—which has forced the courts, in part, to write the law for Congress.

Almost every federal action has some environmental effects and the law placed almost no limits on the kinds of environmental effects that required impact statements. As a result, the courts have had to accept the claims of environmental groups who have sued to require impact statements. An important case occurred when the Interstate Commerce Commission was sued to prevent it from permitting a routine increase in railroad freight rates. Plaintiffs claimed that the ICC-regulated rates discriminated against the movement of recyclable scrap and that the ICC was therefore required by NEPA to prepare an impact statement. After litigation, courts have interpreted the requirement for impact statements broadly. Not only direct federal activities require statements, but also activities regulated or financed by federal agencies, although performed by private institutions or by state and local governments.

Much litigation has also been generated over the issue of the effect that impact statements are to have on federal actions. Federal agencies claim that the law only requires that a statement be prepared, not that it must influence their actions. They thus view NEPA as a full-disclosure requirement. Environmental groups, at the other extreme, have sometimes claimed that the act requires consideration of environmental protection almost to the exclusion of other goals of federal actions. The courts have sensibly tended to take a middle ground, but much expense and confusion could have been prevented if NEPA had instructed agencies to "give due weight to environmental considerations in relation to other benefits and costs of federal actions."

A final intriguing aspect of NEPA litigation has been the issue of who has standing to sue for whom. An inevitable aspect of many environmental effects is that they are diffuse and ill-defined in their severity and extent. Who will be hurt by the environmental impact of excessive freight rates for scrap steel? And who will be hurt by construction of a Walt Disney resort in a spectacularly beautiful, but isolated, valley in California? Deeply involved here is the issue of class-action suits, in which a small group of people sues on behalf of a large group of people. Who can sue for whom? Must the larger group approve? Must they be notified? Can anyone sue for the unborn? These issues will occupy lawyers and judges for many years.

The most important confusion surrounding NEPA is its relationship to other environmental acts. Federal and federally regulated activities are subject to the water, air, and solid-waste policies discussed in earlier sections of this chapter. Theoretically, they require that environmental impacts of such activities be taken into account. If so, why was it necessary to require environmental-impact statements under a separate act? There are many possible answers to that question, but NEPA provides none of them. In practice, NEPA simply adds another layer of regulation to federal environmental policies. Written in the near-crisis atmosphere of the time, NEPA illustrates the adage that crises bring forth bad legislation.

After the oil embargo and the dramatic increase in oil prices by the Organization of Petroleum Exporting Countries (OPEC) in the fall of 1973, Congress decided to postpone deadlines for mobile and stationary pollution-control standards. One-year delays in meeting the original 1975 auto standards were granted in 1974 and 1975.

Congress did not want to risk imposing fuel penalties on cars by tight emission standards when fuel was scarce and expensive and the economy was in recession. In the spring of 1977 the debate was whether the original standards would ever come into effect. But standards in the law meant that 1978 cars, at least when new, would emit no more than about 15 percent as much pollutants as the last uncontrolled cars.

By the mid-1970s the energy crisis had made people painfully aware that pollution control entails use of scarce and valuable resources, especially energy. The political process finally began to ask how much sacrifice of living standards was worthwhile to raise environmental quality. As we move into the latter half of the 1980s the experiences of the 1970s are beginning to bear fruit in the form of better legislation; recognition is becoming more widespread that costs must be justified by benefits and that economic incentives are more effective than direct controls in achieving goals.

DISCUSSION QUESTIONS AND PROBLEMS

1. What effect do you think the energy crisis has had, will have, or should have on national environmental policy?

2. National policy to encourage materials reuse has focused entirely on increasing the supply of used materials by collecting, sorting, and processing used materials. But declines in materials reuse in recent decades have resulted from leftward shifts in demand curves for used materials. In fact, the supply has been growing. What does this suggest about desirable directions for government policy to encourage materials reuse?

3. Do you think state governments should set air- and water-quality standards within their borders, without federal government interference?

4. River-basin commissions have been established, mostly by interstate compacts, on many rivers. Should they administer water-pollution-control laws? If so, would you recommend that metropolitan air commissions be established to administer air-pollution-control laws?

5. Proper handling of hazardous substances is viewed by many at the EPA as being *the* issue of the coming decade. How do you feel about this? Does the historical lack of legislation in the handling of solid waste generally suggest that hazardous substances may be easier and less expensive to control than is commonly supposed?

REFERENCES AND FURTHER READING

Anderson, Frederick. *NEPA in the Courts.* Baltimore: Johns Hopkins University Press for Resources for the Future, Inc. 1973.

Environmental Quality, 1982. Washington, D.C.: U.S. Government Printing Office. Chapter 3 discusses the status of all major environmental regulatory programs.

Freeman, A. Myrick, III. "Air and Water Pollution Policy." In Paul R. Portney, ed. *Current Issues in U.S. Environmental Policy.* Baltimore: Johns Hopkins University Press, for Resources for the Future, Inc., 1978. Gives a good discussion of existing policy toward air and water pollution, including the 1977 amendments.

Friedlaender, Ann, ed. *Air Pollution and Administrative Control.* Cambridge, Mass.: MIT Press, 1978.

Kneese, Allen, and Schultze, Charles. *Pollution, Prices and Public Policy.* Washington, D.C.: The Brookings Institution, 1975.

National Academy of Sciences. *Report by the Committee on Motor Vehicle Emissions.* Washington, D.C.: National Academy of Sciences, 1973.

Chapter 9

A Critical Evaluation of Environmental Policy in the United States

Environmental issues have led to dramatic political confrontations, in the United States and elsewhere, in recent years. Most dramatic has been the conflict between private environmental groups and environmentally inclined members of Congress on the one hand, and business and some public officials on the other, over how tough our environmental standards should be.

Such political struggles are grist for the headline writer's mill. They are important in that they determine how seriously environmental laws are taken. There are many examples in the United States of laws that are written vaguely and left unenforced for years. The public naturally tends to ignore them. The Sherman antitrust law is a good example. It contained a stirring declaration of national policy to oppose monopoly, but its substantive provisions were so vague that the courts have, in effect, written and rewritten it generation after generation. Environmental laws were a second example during the late 1950s and 1960s. They declared a clean, even pristine, environment to be a national goal, but said almost nothing about what was to be done to achieve that goal. Then, when Congress or the administration decides the laws should be enforced, they have to "get tough" to show they "mean business." But of course the fault is the way the laws were written and enforced to begin with. Political power struggles also determine what groups will design and enforce environmental policies. That is important because concern over the environment varies among groups within and among governments in the United States. Environmental programs designed and administered by state governments would be quite different from programs designed and administered by the federal government. And environmental programs would be administered quite differently by client-oriented agencies of the federal government, such as the Interior or Agriculture Departments, from the way they are administered by the Environmental Protection Agency.

But government environmental programs are basically about resource allocation, and political power struggles tell us little about the way programs affect resource allocation. The basic goal of environmental laws is to induce people to withdraw, use, reuse, and discharge materials in amounts and ways that take proper account of damages that discharges can do to human welfare. This requires decreases in materials discharged to the air and water environments and increases in materials returned to the land. It also requires adjustments in the times, forms, and places of discharges to each of the three environmental media. Thus, in evaluating environmental programs in this chapter, it is necessary to step back from the power struggles and other political aspects of the programs and ask whether the programs have the desired effects on resource allocation and whether they are administered efficiently and economically.

Although the notion that the purpose of environmental programs is to shift resource allocation is obvious to students of economics, it has a profound effect on the way such programs are viewed. In fact, the history of environmental programs has been to regard the problem as one of police power. Legislators and their staffs are accustomed to handling problems of the following kind: There is a surge of airplane hijackings so legislatures pass laws designating it as a specific offense and providing large fines and long jail sentences for conviction. In addition, money is appropriated to provide security forces and perhaps to subsidize security measures by airlines. This is the police-power approach and is appropriate when a certain kind of behavior is perceived as a terrible social threat and it is felt the behavior must be stopped even at great cost. Of course the goal here is really to affect resource allocation, that is, to reduce resource allocation to hijacking and to increase resource allocation to its prevention. But there is a world of difference between hijacking and pollution.

Hijacking is a threat to life and property without redeeming features, whereas pollution is a by-product of thousands of individual decisions in the course of very desirable activities: production and consumption of commodities and services. Hijacking should be prevented if possible, whereas with pollution, the goal is to induce people to continue the desirable activities in ways that reduce and alter environmental discharges. It is no exaggeration to say that our anti-pollution programs have been increasingly dominated by the police-power mentality, leading to a "get-the-so-and-sos" attitude. Make the undesirable activity illegal and if that does not work, make the prohibitions and regulations more stringent and pervasive, at the same time increasing fines and other penalties. The police-power attitude leads government officials away from resource-allocation considerations, away from the weighing of the benefits and costs of a little more or a little less, away from attempts to restructure incentives so as to give more weight to environmental considerations in production and consumption decisions. Perhaps most important, the police-power approach to environmental problems fosters the notion that those who produce commodities are criminals, or at least anti-social, whereas in fact they perform an extremely valuable social function.

Basic economic analysis has played only a small part in the formulation of our important environmental programs. Until quite recently when economists were called in, it was with regard to secondary issues, such as whether the country can afford a clean environment, or whether environmental regulations will excessively burden certain industries. No serious economic analysis of alternative programs has yet been undertaken for the government at the stage of basic program formulation. Instead, the programs are the work of lawyers and political staffs whose talents are in the brokering of political power. There is, however, increasing consensus that the role of economic analysis in our environmental programs should be emphasized.

Regulatory Programs

Regulation of discharges to air and water is the heart of our national environmental program. If the program of direct controls cannot limit discharges to justifiable amounts and in economical fashion, it must be regarded a failure, whatever else it does. It must, however, be remembered that regulation is not just a matter of government regulation of industry. Large amounts of wastes are discharged to water bodies by local government sewage systems. Thus a major part of the regulatory program consists of state and federal governments regulating local governments.

Ideally a program of direct regulation would work as follows. The EPA would estimate the volume of each discharge from each source that is justified on the benefit-cost analysis developed in Chapter 4. Then it would give each source a quota or permit that specifies the allowed discharge of each residual. Of course, a new permit would be needed after each change in output, product mix, technology, input prices, or other variables affecting a source's discharges.

In fact, EPA cannot hope to do the benefit-cost analyses for all discharges from all sources. For practical purposes, the following procedure must be used: A target ambient air or water quality is chosen for the important quality dimensions of an estuary or metropolitan air mantle. The target quality is one estimated to protect health or to achieve another goal affected by environmental quality. Then a discharge volume that will achieve the target ambient air or water quality is estimated, using an explicit or implicit dispersion function, equation (3.16). This provides a permissible total discharge volume and the remaining problem is to allocate the discharge quantity among sources.

The most straightforward way to allocate permissible discharges among sources is to permit a constant discharge per unit of output from each source. For example, each steel producer on an estuary might be permitted so many pounds of discharge of a certain waste per ton of steel produced. But the straightforward procedure is undesirable for several reasons. First, it does not provide a rule for allocating permitted discharges between producers of different products. For example, both oil refineries and food processors discharge organic wastes, but there is no common output unit between them to use to measure permissible discharges. Even among apparently similar producers, there is great variability of product mix and of the costs and techniques available for pollution control. Two steel mills on the same estuary may produce quite different product mixes and their pollution-control costs may be quite different. Second, polluting discharges depend not just on output but also on technology employed. For example, two steel mills producing the same output may generate very different waste loads if one is vertically integrated and the other is not. There are many industrial processes between iron-ore extraction and a steel toaster. A plant is vertically integrated if it performs many successive processing functions. Third, pollution-abatement costs may vary greatly between plants producing the same output if one plant is much older than the other. The newer plant may have been built since all or some discharge controls came into effect. Should the two plants be permitted the same discharge per unit output? Fourth, the law requires that the cost and availability of discharge-control technology be taken into account in some cases. In the previous chapter, it was shown that the 1972 water-pollution law sets guidelines for discharge volumes in the 1980s that require EPA to take account of cost and availability of technology. Thus the law prohibits the straightforward approach to some extent. Finally, it is likely that, under any program of direct regulation, the courts would require that gross disparities in costs be taken into account in allocating discharge permits.

For all these reasons, direct-discharge regulatory programs inevitably come eventually to the point of allocating permits on the basis of the cost and availability of control methods. At this point the camel's nose is in the tent. Government officials are inevitably tempted, and the courts inevitably require them, to make regulations more pervasive, more detailed, and more comprehensive. The costs of a range of pollution-control techniques are literally specific to particular plants. The uncertainties and magnitude of this task are such that the outcome is little more than the result of a bargaining session between government and industrial management. Almost any outcome can be challenged in the courts and delayed for years. The situation is worst for new plants. Until a plant is built, the range of options and uncertainty regarding pollution control is enormous. Government officials inevitably end up taking part in the most detailed aspects of plant design.

As was suggested earlier, the result of this complex process is an approximately uniform percentage discharge abatement from previous discharges among existing sources, and a uniform percentage abatement from a hypothetical discharge level for new sources. It is accomplished only after months or years of costly and demoralizing negotiation and litigation with government officials. In addition, it has a subtle effect on industry. It implies that profits depend a great deal on the effectiveness of firms in negotiating with government and in circumventing complex rules. Inevitably, managers are brought to high positions because they are skilled at dealing with Washington or have political influence because they are good at making, improving, and selling products.

But the most serious consequence of the program of direct regulation is that it is wasteful. Costs of pollution abatement vary greatly among sources, and a requirement of uniform percentage abatement is bound to be more costly than a policy that equates abatement costs from all sources at the margin. In Chapter 6, it was shown that the Delaware estuary study found that uniform-percentage abatement from all sources of organic discharges would be about twice as expensive in achieving a given water quality as a system of effluent fees which would equate marginal abatement costs among dischargers.

Since stringent pollution control is a relatively new national policy, much new technology is being developed. There is always uncertainty about the cost and effectiveness of new technology, in pollution control or any other application. Since direct regulation inevitably leads to the government approving specific techniques of production and pollution control, it must inevitably decide whether to require particular items of new technology. In the 1970s, fierce battles were fought between government and industry regarding installation of electrostatic precipitators by thermal electric companies. The government claimed that the technology was adequately proven so that installation should be required, whereas industry claimed that precipitators would work only erratically and would be expensive. This is a judgment that government would not have to make under a sensible pollution-control program. The only way the government can make the judgment is to require use of the technology after it has been used successfully by two or three firms. That raises complex issues as to criteria of success and as to whether other plants are sufficiently similar to those in which the technology worked so that it will be successful there as well. But the most serious consequence is that it provides industry with a powerful incentive not to develop new technology. It may be worth a great deal to the potential users of new technology to ensure that it is not developed, because they will be forced to install it at high cost once it is proven. The strategy of retarding new technology requires at least tacit collusion among firms, and cannot be successful very long. Patent protection may be obtainable by the first firm to develop a new device, making it profitable to be first. But in general, the government policy provides socially unproductive incentives to firms.

Direct controls on discharges provide other basically inappropriate incentives for dischargers. Once a permitted discharge quantity is set, dischargers must reduce discharges to the permitted level even at high cost, but they have no incentive to abate discharges further even at low cost (recall Figures 4.5 and 4.6 of Chapter 4). Compare the incentive with the working of an input market. A function of high wages is to induce employers continuously to seek ways of economizing on society's most valuable resource, its skilled labor force. How well would labor markets work if government decided how much of each kind of labor was needed by each employer and issued permits for the employment of labor? That is exactly what is done under the system of direct-discharge regulation.

The final criticism of direct-discharge regulation is that it heightens the danger of favoritism and corruption of public officials. No government program is impossible to corrupt, but the danger is greatest when officials are instructed to make subjective judgments on matters that involve large sums of money. Federal housing programs were scandalized by corruption in 1971 in good part because of the subjective nature of the judgments officials were asked to make. On the other hand, our federal income tax is relatively free of corruption because the rules are tolerably clear, making it relatively easy to identify abuse. Our pollution-control program is as subjective as any that the federal government runs, and large fortunes are at issue. In the first edition of this book, it was said: "Although it has not yet happened, it is predictable that the program will be scandalized in coming years." The much-publicized apparent corruption in the handling of toxic substances under the Superfund legislation of the early 1980s now makes clear that we should avoid the substantial temptations that inevitably exist when large amounts of money depend on the subjective decisions of a few government officials. A system of charges according to publicly available schedules would be much less subject to corruption.

All these general criticisms apply specifically to our national discharge-regulation program. The first indication that direct regulation might not be the best basis for a national policy was clear evidence that improvements in environmental quality were slow in coming under the program. Evidence presented in Part II shows that until about 1970, there was pervasive deterioration in both air and water quality. This was fully fourteen years after the beginning of the national regulatory program for liquid-waste discharges and seven years after the beginning of the program to regulate airborne discharges. Congress's reaction was merely to increase the severity and pervasiveness of the regulatory program. Since 1970 there have certainly been some improvements in air and water quality. But the evidence is that these improvements have resulted mainly from simple and unsophisticated measures. Improvement in water quality has come mostly from the program of local sewage-plant construction, which is simply an improvement in the public provision of indirect-discharge services. Improvement in air quality has come mostly from substitution of clean for dirty fuels, that is, increased use of natural gas and low-sulfur fuel oil and decreased use of coal. Such trends were occurring anyway and accelerating them hardly required a large national program of discharge regulation. And high oil prices are reversing the trend away from coal, particularly as a fuel for the generation of electricity.

That the federal-state regulatory program has by now become extremely complex, detailed, and bureaucratic can be seen by anyone with the patience to wade through the volumes of guidelines and regulations in the *Federal Register*. The most-costly and best-documented fiasco in our discharge-regulation program is that pertaining to motor-vehicle emissions. The history of this program illustrates many of the criticisms made above.

As was stated in the previous chapter, modest reductions were required in auto emissions starting with 1968-model-year cars. By 1970 evidence indicated that post-1967 cars on the road were not noticeably cleaner than earlier models. In fact, there was no reason for them to be cleaner in actual operation. New-car standards have been met by minor engine modifications that would not keep emissions low very long unless the car was maintained by at least a careful annual tune-up. But the law placed no obligation on manufacturers or owners to keep cars in good condition while on the road. In 1970 Congress decided to get tough with the automobile companies and that year's Clean Air Act amendments instructed EPA to set standards that would reduce new-car emissions of hydrocarbons (HC) and carbon monoxide (CO) to 10 percent of their 1970 levels by 1975, and would reduce emissions of nitrogen oxides (NO_x) to the same percentage by 1976. These figures imply that 1976 cars would emit only 4 percent as much of the three pollutants per mile as the last uncontrolled cars in 1967. The following table summarizes the standards set:[1]

	HC	CO	NO$_X$
1967 (uncontrolled)	8.70	87.0	· 4.0
1973–74	3.00	28.0	3.1
1975	0.41	3.4	2.0
1976 and beyond	0.41	3.4	0.4

In order to ensure that cars on the road would continue to be clean, the amendments also required durability testing of cars, contained inducement for states to institute annual emissions tests of cars on the road, and required manufacturers to warrant emission-control devices for fifty thousand miles of use. The figures in the table represent by far the most ambitious program of pollution abatement ever undertaken. In 1970 there was almost no information about whether it would be possible to make cars that would meet the 1975 and 1976 standards, what it would cost, or what the benefits of the improved air quality would be. The NO$_x$ standard raised a fundamental problem of technology. HC and CO are products of incomplete combustion and the natural way to reduce their volume is to design engines that burn fuel more completely. But NO$_x$ is the normal product of combusion and most modifications that reduce HC and CO emissions increasee NO$_x$ emissions.

The 1970 amendment permitted EPA to delay by one year each application of the 1975 and 1976 standards, setting interim standards instead, if EPA concluded that the legislated standards were technically infeasible. Taken literally, that provision is absurd. It was certainly known in 1970 how to make a small battery-powered car that could achieve about 35 miles per hour, go 100 or more miles between recharges, and have no emissions. The issue clearly was how many cars could be produced to meet the standards, at what costs, and with what performance characteristics. But the law precluded considerations of these issues.

1. The figures are grams per mile collected during the 1975 federal test procedure, a rigorously specified test involving a cold start and about thirty-five minutes of driving under stimulated urban conditions. The 1976 HC and CO figures are less than 5 percent of the 1967 figures. The 1976 NO$_x$ figure is larger because, when the 1976 standard was set, there was uncertainty about NO$_x$ emissions of uncontrolled cars.

The provisions of the law directed the industry's energies to the political arena instead of to competition to produce clean cars. It was unthinkable to shut the automobile industry down. A sudden cessation of automobile production for one year would produce massive unemployment and chaos in the country's transportation system. It must have been clear to both the industry and Congress that delay would be politically inevitable if the prospect were that 1975 and 1976 cars would be unavailable, extremely expensive, or unreliable. It is impossible to say objectively whether the industry made a reasonable effort to develop a technology that would permit cars to meet the standards. However, it was certain that the industry stood to lose a great deal if the technology became available, because they would then be forced to manufacture costly cars that embodied the technology. The point is that the government was forced to monitor the industry's research and development program because of the disincentives the law provided the industry to develop new technology. Under a sensible auto-emissions program, the incentives would have been in the opposite direction and the government would not have needed to monitor the industry's activity. The industry lobbied hard to obtain a delay and a change in the law.

In fact, EPA granted a delay in 1973 and Congress changed the law in 1974 and 1975, in response to the energy crisis. In the spring of 1977, the standards were:

	HC	CO	NO_x
1975 & 1976	1.50	15.0	3.1
1977	0.41	3.4	2.0
1978	0.41	3.4	0.4

The stage was thus set for a further focus of energies in the political arena. Once again, the industry was uncertain whether it would be forced to meet the stringent standards. It was motivated to delay development of control technology to increase the chance of obtaining delays in standard enforcements and it was motivated to concentrate its energies on securing delays in standards and further changes in the law. It was encouraged by its knowledge that delay and changes in the law were obtained previously. Any company that assumed that standards would be imposed on schedule and developed cars to meet them would be seriously penalized if further delays were granted because it would be forced to sell a more expensive car, no more valuable to its owner, than cars designed to meet lower standards. The experience of the Honda company just before the 1973 delay was granted in the 1975 and 1976 standards illustrates the problem. Honda was the first company to make a car that EPA certified as meeting the 1975 standards. Shortly after that, EPA relaxed the standards, which must have taught Honda a lesson about how the American environmental program rewards imaginative research and development. Indeed, the standards have been relaxed further, with the table below giving the most current standards (though these are hardly set in concrete!):

TABLE 9.1

Exhaust Emission Standards for Autos and Light Trucks, 1968–1985

Autos						
	Standards for new autos (grams per mile)			Percent reduction of standards from pre-control vehicles		
Year	Hydro-carbons	Carbon monoxide	Nitrogen oxides	Hydro-carbons	Carbon monoxide	Nitrogen oxides
1968	4.1	34.0	NA	*50*	*62*	*NA*
1969	4.1	34.0	NA	*50*	*62*	*NA*
1970	4.1	34.0	NA	*50*	*62*	*NA*
1971	4.1	34.0	NA	*50*	*62*	*NA*
1972	3.0	28.0	3.1	*63*	*69*	*9*
1973	3.0	28.0	3.1	*63*	*69*	*9*
1974	3.0	28.0	3.1	*63*	*69*	*9*
1975	1.5	15.0	3.1	*82*	*83*	*9*
1976	1.5	15.0	3.1	*82*	*83*	*9*
1977	1.5	15.0	2.0	*82*	*83*	*41*
1978	1.5	15.0	2.0	*82*	*83*	*41*
1979	1.5	15.0	2.0	*82*	*83*	*41*
1980	0.41	7.0	2.0	*96*	*92*	*41*
1981	0.41	3.4	1.0	*96*	*96*	*76*
1982	0.41	3.4	1.0	*96*	*96*	*76*
1983	0.41	3.4	1.0	*96*	*96*	*76*
1984	0.41	3.4	1.0	*96*	*96*	*76*
1985	0.41	3.4	1.0	*96*	*96*	*76*

TABLE 9.1 (*continued*)

Exhaust Emission Standards for Autos and Light Trucks, 1968–1985

Light Trucks

Year	Standards for new light trucks (grams per mile)			Percent reduction of standards from pre-control vehicles		
	Hydro-carbons	Carbon monoxide	Nitrogen oxides	Hydro-carbons	Carbon monoxide	Nitrogen oxides
1968	4.1	34.0	NA	50	62	NA
1969	4.1	34.0	NA	50	62	NA
1970	4.1	34.0	NA	50	62	NA
1971	4.1	34.0	NA	50	62	NA
1972	3.0	28.0	3.1	63	69	9
1973	3.0	28.0	3.1	63	69	9
1974	3.0	28.0	3.1	63	69	9
1975	2.0	20.0	3.1	76	78	9
1976	2.0	20.0	3.1	76	78	9
1977	2.0	20.0	3.1	76	78	9
1978	2.0	20.0	3.1	76	78	9
1979	1.7	18.0	2.3	79	80	32
1980	1.7	18.0	2.3	79	80	32
1981	1.7	18.0	2.3	79	80	32
1982	1.7	18.0	2.3	79	80	32
1983	1.7	18.0	2.3	79	80	32
1984	0.8	10.0	2.3	90	89	32
1985	0.8	10.0	0.9	90	89	74

NA—Not applicable.

All standards are based on the current test procedure.

Standards for hydrocarbons and carbon monoxide were not established until 1968; for nitrogen dioxides, not until 1972.

SOURCES: National Commission on Air Quality, *To Breathe Clean Air* (Washington: USGPO, 1981), p. 194.

SOURCE: Council on Environmental Quality, *Environmental Quality*, 1982, Table A-60, p. 294.

The worst part of the auto-emissions fiasco concerns NO_x. The basic role of NO_x in smog formation was established in laboratory experiments at the California Institute of Technology in 1951. As much was known about the polluting effects of NO_x as about those of any auto emissions. Yet by 1975, twenty-four years after the scientific research, and ten years after the first auto-emission standards have been set, NO_x was virtually uncontrolled. Having goofed so badly, Congress decided it would require a reduction in NO_x emissions in excess of 85 percent in one year. That posed a serious dilemma for automobile manufacturers. A major dilemma in automobile-pollution abatement has always been whether to try to clean up the conventional internal-combustion engine (ICE) or to develop and produce alternative power sources. Alternative power sources that have been produced and studied are Wankel engines, stratified-charge engines (both modifications of the ICE), diesels, electric cars, gas turbines, as well as others.

The American manufacturers have devoted almost all their efforts to cleaning up the ICE. They have developed improved carburation, exhaust-gas recirculation, and other modifications. Imaginative development of alternative power sources, especially the stratified-charge engine and the diesel, has been done mostly in Europe and Japan. In part, the American manufacturers stuck to the ICE because of their tremendous accumulated expertise with it and their unfamiliarity with alternative power sources. But in part, they made a difficult calculation that they should not have been forced to make.

In the early 1970s, it appeared that the only way to meet the 1976 NO_x standard could be with catalytic converters that would be placed on the exhaust system of an ICE. Of course the other modifications to the ICE mentioned above would also be needed. The stratified-charge and the diesel engines could be manufactured to produce less NO_x than the 1975 standard, but could probably not meet the 1976 standard. Catalysts would require a large development effort, would be expensive to produce, and would substantially increase fuel consumption compared with a similarly designed engine without the catalyst. Most important, catalysts require low-lead fuel, considerable care in automobile operation to avoid burning them out, and probably two or three replacements during the car's useful life. The owner lacks incentive to replace the catalyst because the car's fuel consumption and drivability are likely to improve if it burns out.

Catalyst-equipped ICEs will do little to reduce auto emissions, and will add considerably to car costs, unless cars are subject to annual emissions testing by states. While a number of states have instituted annual emissions tests, a large number have not, and there is at this writing some trend to no longer enforce these annual inspections in some of the states which nominally require them.

The National Academy of Sciences estimated that the ownership costs of a catalyst-equipped car designed to meet the 1976 standards would be about \$270 (in 1970 prices) more than the cost of a car that met the 1970 standards. After enough years had passed so that virtually all cars were catalyst-equipped, the result would be a staggering annual national expenditure in excess of $25 billion. Unless most states have annual emission tests, owners will not replace and maintain emission-control devices. (Indeed, about 10 percent of cars having catalytic converters are being filled with regular, leaded gasoline: while saving 4 cents a gallon, two tankfuls of leaded gasoline ruin the converter and make the car about one hundred times more polluting than it would have been!) Annual costs will be reduced considerably by failure to replace catalysts, but there will be very little reduction in auto emissions.

The stratified-charge and diesel engines, on the other hand, could not quite meet the original 1976 NO_x standards as far as is known. But they added only about $100 per year to the ownership cost of a car designed to meet the original 1975 standards. Most important, they would continue to meet high standards for years with only the maintenance the owner is motivated to have done to keep the car's performance high.

Thus manufacturers were forced to develop complex and expensive catalyst systems in order to meet the extremely stringent 1976 NO_x standard. If the American auto-emission-control program permitted flexibility in emission standards, cars could have been produced and sold that would meet very high emission standards, for years. The program's rigidity required manufacturers to concentrate on cars that meet extremely high standards when new, but that will be quite dirty during most of their lives under the inspection requirements they will be subject to in the foreseeable future. It would not have been possible to produce ten million stratified-charge- or diesel-engine cars for the American market in 1976, and it is uncertain how quickly American manufacturers would have developed production capacity for such engines. But it is certain that foreign manufacturers would have begun to ship them to the United States in large numbers, and that would provide American manufacturers with strong incentives to shift a large part of their capacity quickly. A socially efficient auto-emission-control program would provide manufacturers and owners with continuing incentives to produce and drive cleaner cars, and it would reward those that do and punish those that do not. But it would avoid arbitrary and stringent standards and deadlines that compel manufacturers to focus their energies on devices so complex and unreliable that they provide very little emission abatement in actual use. It would encourage experimentation with a variety of power systems and control devices that have low emissions, but it would avoid specific standards that must be met.

The auto-emission-control fiasco will certainly cost the American public many billions of dollars. In that respect it is unique. Such large sums are involved in the production and operation of automobiles in the United States that one should not expect mistakes of similar magnitude in discharge regulation of other industries. But there is no reason to think that the automobile muddle is unique in any other way. It results from the rigidity, stringency, and poor incentive effects of the national environmental programs. Such properties pervade the program. The pervasive fault is that the program tries to do too much. It tries to decide in Washington exactly how much of what may be discharged each year and exactly what investments and production technologies are acceptable. A better program would simply provide strong and continuing incentives to reduce the polluting effects of production and consumption.

The Federal Waste-Treatment Grant Program

The crowning irony of our national environmental program is that the one aspect of the program in which economic incentives have been used on a large scale is perhaps the least successful part of the program.

As has been seen above, the economist's classical prescription is that if government wants to discourage an activity, it should either tax the activity or subsidize its abatement. In the case of polluting discharges, the government can either levy effluent fees or pay dischargers for discharge abatement. Even at the level of basic theory, the two policies are not equivalent, as William Baumol and Wallace Oates have shown in their *Theory of Environmental Policy* and as was demonstrated in Chapter 4. Taxes and subsidies have equivalent effects on the price or cost of the activity relative to other activities the discharger might undertake, but they have different effects on the "total" conditions for firm equilibrium and on the wealth or income positions of consumers. If abatement is subsidized, the discharger ends up with more money in the bank than if discharges are taxed, which affects the amounts of various activities, including those that result in discharges, that are undertaken. For example, subsidizing firms' discharge abatement leaves them with a rosier profit picture than does taxing discharges. Competition induces firms to pass part of the subsidy on to consumers, thus lowering the price and increasing the demand for the product of the polluting activity. Thus the subsidy results in less discharge abatement than the tax, even though the marginal effect on profit of an increment in discharges may be the same under the two policies.

At the practical level, subsidizing abatement is much less desirable than taxing discharges. An efficient subsidy is proportional to the amount by which discharges are abated. But that rule requires that the government estimate how much would have been discharged in the absence of the subsidy. It is impossible for governments to make such estimates accurately. Dischargers are motivated to exaggerate how much they would have discharged in order to collect large subsidy payments. Especially when a new product is introduced or a plant is built or expanded, there is no way to estimate the hypothetical discharge levels.

When governments think of subsidizing an activity they almost always think of equity rather than efficiency effects. In the case of the waste-treatment grant program, the motivation was that local governments are financially pressed and raise most of their tax receipts by the regressive property tax. It thus seemed equitable for the federal government to pay part of the cost of the treatment plants that its stringent environmental program was forcing localities to build. The equity motivation means that Congress rarely considers carefully exactly how the subsidy should be structured. In addition, there is a bias in government activities toward building things. Governments are much more inclined to build new highways than to improve traffic control on old ones, much more inclined to build new hospitals than to improve operation of old ones. Thus Congress simply decided to pay part of the cost of building treatment plants as a way of subsidizing discharge abatement of localities.

In fact, it is a poor subsidy. As has been pointed out earlier, residents of a local government jurisdiction typically receive only a small part of the benefits of water-quality improvement. If the locality is on a flowing stream most of the benefits are received downstream. If the locality is on an estuary, it is probably only one of many dischargers that affect water quality in the estuary. Thus even a large percentage subsidy provides little incentive to treat wastes. If the residents receive little benefit from treatment of their wastes, a

50 percent subsidy simply reduces the cost of a losing activity by 50 percent. But it is still a losing activity. This point is even more important in considering subsidies for private firms. To subsidize half the cost of a firm's waste-treatment operation simply reduces the losses from what remains a losing activity. The likelihood is that most of the increases in local waste-treatment-plant construction in recent years have come about because of federal discharge regulation. The large federal subsidy has merely reduced the intensity of local political opposition to compliance.

Evidence for the above claims comes from both government and private studies. References, more detail, and a fine survey of the problems are in Allen Kneese and Charles Schultze, *Pollution, Prices and Public Policy*. Government studies show that construction grants have been given almost without regard to the benefits and costs of discharge abatement. Subsidies are allocated to states mostly on the basis of population and income, and political favoritism plays a large role in the allocation of subsidy funds within states. A disportionately large percentage of federal grant money has gone to small communities instead of to large metropolitan areas, many of which are on estuaries where water pollution is most serious.

Because subsidies are for treatment-plant construction, but not operation, localities lack incentive to operate plants efficiently. Water-pollution-control engineers invariably report that local treatment plants are poorly operated, often being run by political appointees without technical qualifications. A government study reported that fully a quarter of treatment plants in metropolitan areas were operated below 50 percent of capacity. The response of federal officials to this situation is usually to propose additional subsidies that can be used to train personnel to operate treatment plants. But the problem is not a shortage of personnel; it is a lack of incentive to employ them efficiently. If the federal government wants to subsidize localities to abate discharges, the subsidy should be proportional to localities' abatement of discharges below some norm; it should not depend on construction expenditure. Better yet, municipalities should be subject to effluent fees and subsidies should be related to overall need, as with some forms of revenue sharing, not to discharges.

Concern of elected officials with equity leads them to think carefully about which groups will be helped or hurt by specific proposals. They rarely study carefully the incentive effects of subsidies they propose. But all subsidies are granted as functions of some variables and all affect the kinds and amounts of activities undertaken by recipients. Subsidies designed mainly with a view to equity almost never have desirable resource-allocation implications. They are usually related to inappropriate variables. Our waste-treatment-construction grant program is as good an illustration of this moral as can be found.

Government Institutions

The analysis of government institutions and political behavior may be the most challenging problem facing social scientists in the last part of the twentieth century. Debate over the relative merits of alternative forms of government has of course occupied political philosophers at least since Socrates. During the last century, countless studies have been undertaken of the behavior and mores of bureaucracies, of political parties, and of particular government offices such as the national presidency. Until the 1950s, economists took almost no part in these developments. They devoted great efforts to analyzing which activities can best be carried on by the private sector and which, by subtraction, can be done well only by government. In their scholarly work economists were content to assume that the function of government in a democracy is to maximize social welfare and that the economists' responsibility ends with the demonstration that some government program, such as effluent fees, will contribute to that end.

Since the 1950s all that has changed. Social scientists have become increasingly willing to assume that government officials are motivated by self-interest to about the same extent that private citizens are, that self-interest leads to different kinds of government activity depending on how government is structured, and that some kinds of government institutions may go much further in improving people's welfare than others. Many inquiries have applied these ideas to study of the behavior of legislative bodies and of candidates for elective office. Such studies have shed light on the measurement and use of power by congressional committees and on logrolling and related legislative activities.[2]

Increasingly, this "economic theory of government" is being applied

2. A good survey is in the paper by Haefele, "Environmental Quality as a Problem of Social Choice."

to the study of appointive bodies in the executive branch of government. It can be used to understand otherwise puzzling phenomena. For example, it is puzzling that although major business and environmental groups have urged adoption of effluent fees, EPA officials have steadfastly defended the existing regulatory program. But substitution of effluent fees for direct regulation would dramatically reduce the needed size of EPA. Effluent fees are rightly viewed as a threat to the jobs of EPA employees. Perhaps more important, effluent fees would make a large part of EPA more like the Internal Revenue Service. Much IRS activity is clerical and dull, involving tax collection, auditing of returns, and so forth. With a regulatory program, EPA's activities involve complex, controversial, and discretionary activities in standard setting, negotiating with polluters, confrontation with industry, organizing support in Congress and the executive for proposed actions, and so forth. It is unrealistic to expect senior EPA officials to be willing to give up such power, excitement, and discretion in exchange for the dull routine of fee collection.

Perhaps most important, the new approach of government is being used to compare the advantages of appointive and elective offices for particular programs. Should judges be elected or appointed? Should heads of executive agencies, such as comptrollers, be appointed or elected in state governments? Should vice-presidents, deputy mayors and deputy governors be elected and, if so, should they be elected separately from the president, mayor, or governor?

Almost all such issues arise with environmental programs. Should they be designed and operated at the federal, state, or local level? Should they be operated by an agency headed by an appointed or by an elected official? How broad should the powers of the agency be? Should it be allowed to set effluent-fee rates? What range of responsibilities should an environmental agency have? These are provocative questions to which there are few definite answers. It should at least be possible to clarify some issues in this section.

It seems almost inevitable that the federal government formulate at least the broad outlines of our environmental policy. There are two reasons for this: First, environmental policy must be set by a government that has jurisdiction over the people affected by its actions. The purpose of democratic government is to motivate public officials to respond to the interests of the electorate. Environmental policies in New Jersey affect the welfare of New York City residents because New York is downwind from northern New Jersey. But New York residents do not vote in New Jersey elections and New Jersey officials are therefore not motivated to represent New Yorkers' interests. Local governments are too small to set environmental policies in the United States. Environmental effects frequently spill over state lines, especially in the East, where states are small, industrialized, and densely populated. Second, aside from size, state boundaries are poorly placed for environmental programs. Because they were easily identifiable, water bodies were frequently chosen as state boundaries. Thus the two sides of a stream are frequently in different states, which makes most water pollution interstate. From an environmental point of view, ridge lines would be much better state boundaries than water bodies. Likewise, a remarkably large number of metropolitan areas, which are natural units for air-pollution programs, are in two or more states.

These seem to be persuasive reasons for the federal government to determine at least the broad outlines of environmental policy. But the most frequent argument for federal leadership in environmental policy seems to be without merit. It is that states cannot have tough environmental laws because they must compete with each other for industry and other jobs. The range of alternatives regarding environmental protection is much broader than the extremes of giving up either industry or environmental quality. But, to the limited extent that there is a trade-off between industrialization and environmental protection in states, it is an advantage, not a disadvantage, to lodge environmental policy at the state level. It is desirable to permit the people in each state to decide whether they want well-paid jobs or high-quality environment instead of imposing the choice on them from Washington. If the choice is made at the federal level, pressure is created, and to a great extent the courts require, that the same environmental quality be achieved in each state. That cannot possibly be better than permitting each state to choose its combination of economic development and environmental protection, provided one state's choice does not affect another state's environment.

It is not even clear that strong environmental controls will unambiguously cause a loss of jobs, of tax base, and of population. Since polluting areas, notably cities, are both production areas *and* consumption areas, cleaning up might well be in the interests of local areas; would, for example, one-eighth of the United States population reside in California if it were heavily polluted? Cleaning up pollution in Los Angeles will make that location more attractive for people and better for some firms. Certainly it is the case that some types of employment would be reduced by stringent controls, but this suggests that perhaps that type of employment does not belong in highly populated areas. At any rate, these examples clarify that emphasizing only possible employment losses from environmental controls overlooks the desirable impacts on local areas from those controls.

The conclusion that the federal government should be responsible for establishing at least the broad outlines of environmental policy does not tell us specifically what the federal government should do and who should do what the federal government does not do. Existing law seems designed to maximize nothing but confusion. Its underlying idea is that the federal government should set ambient air- and water-quality levels and the states should decide, subject to federal approval, the best way to achieve the target quality. But the federal government has established discharge standards for automobiles and is doing so increasingly for thermal electric plants and other dischargers. We are moving rapidly toward a situation in which dischargers are required to go through two permit application procedures, one to a state government and one to the federal government.

Thus the federal government has been niggardly and ambiguous about the extent of environmental control it permits the states to have. But the situation is much worse. There are many actions that affect overall ambient quality, especially in water bodies, over which states have little control. In many states, the state government has exercised little control over the design, placing, and construction of waste-treatment plants by municipalities. More important, as was shown in Chapter 6, dams are sometimes built to improve downstream water quality by augmenting low flow. On navigable rivers, dams are planned and built by the federal government (by the Corps of Engineers in the East and by the Bureau of Reclamation in the West). Strong state governments influence this complex process by lobbying with congressmen from the state and with the executive branch of the federal government. But it is a cumbersome process and dam construction proposals are often subject to political infighting for decades before the decision is made one way or the other. The divided responsibility makes it difficult to have a coordinated water-pollution-control program.

Perhaps most important, some new ideas have been proposed to improve water quality, and it is unclear who has responsibility for evaluating and implementing them. In-stream reaeration, also discussed in Chapter 6, is a good example. In many streams, the benefit would occur to residents of several states, so states are poorly placed to take responsibility for evaluating and installing such devices. Yet no federal agency has responsibility to consider them. EPA does not construct or operate facilities. The Corps of Engineers and the Bureau of Reclamation are construction agencies and have very narrowly prescribed options. In any case, pollution control is not their main concern.

The foregoing considerations have led many economists and political scientists to conclude that there should be a single government agency responsible for the planning and implementation of environmental programs in a river basin or metropolitan air-quality region. The optimum combination of government actions to improve environmental quality undoubtedly varies considerably from one air or water region to another. Thus, it is thought, a single agency is needed that can consider a wide range of alternatives and implement a program tailored to the needs of the region. Such an agency might levy and collect effluent fees, or administer a program of direct-discharge control. It might allocate federal waste-treatment-plant construction grants. It might have responsibility for planning instream facilities such as dams and reaeration systems.

In the past, several special government agencies have been established to plan certain aspects of water use. Most such agencies have narrowly circumscribed powers and are referred to as special districts or commissions. The best-known such agency is the Delaware River Basin Commission, created by a compact among the states of Delaware, New Jersey, New York, and Pennsylvania and the federal government. The Delaware Commission has been analyzed in detail by Allen Kneese and Blair Bower in *Managing Water Quality: Economics, Technology, Institutions*, and by Bruce Ackerman et al. in *The Uncertain Search for Water Quality*. None of the existing agencies has a broad a range of powers as has been urged by advocates of this approach.

Existing federal air- and water-pollution legislation provides a mild stimulus to states to form such agencies. But the stimulus has had no effect and it is fair to say that the federal government has no established policy on the subject.

Advocates of the commission approach have concentrated on the need for a government agency that has the capability to consider and implement a wide range of approaches to water use and water quality. There can be little doubt that some such agency is desirable. But the new approach to government tells us that we must ask not only about the capabilities of commissions but also about their incentives. Exisiting commissions are run by appointees of governors of member states and, in the case of the Delaware Commission, an appointee of the national president. The alleged advantage of this arrangement is that appointees can be technical experts rather than politicians who must run for office. A disadvantage is that such "independent" commissions tend to become unresponsive to the wishes of the electorate whose interests they are intended to further. It would of course be possible for some or all of the heads of commissions to be elected. A second disadvantage of commissions is precisely their single-function constitution. A desirable purpose of government is to put before the electorate a set of options as to the levels and uses of tax collections. One mayoral or gubernatorial candidate can campaign on a platform of more money for schools and less for highways and another can promise the reverse priority, thus permitting voters to reflect their priorities. But a candidate for office in a single-purpose agency can advocate only more or less for the activity of the agency. Elections of heads of special districts tend to be dull and unfocused, with the result that voters lose interest.

It may not be clear what the appropriate regional pollution-control agency should be, but it is clear that the federal government has paid almost no attention to the subject except insofar as recent expressions of state and local resentment have forced its consideration. An enormous variety of federal and state agencies has responsibility for aspects of pollution control. Often, responsibilities are confused, overlapping, and duplicated. Not infrequently, dischargers must obtain approval of plans from two or more agencies. Sometimes, the agencies have very different and even inconsistent requirements. Recent environmental legislation has made the situation worse by its designation of complex and poorly specified state and federal responsibilities for discharge regulation. In the next chapter we shall consider a number of ways of improving environmental policy as currently practiced.

DISCUSSION QUESTIONS AND PROBLEMS

1. Should the federal government permit river-basin commissions to set effluent fees in their basin? Should they permit commissions to set direct-

discharge controls? Should limits be placed on the fees or controls they set?

2. How many river-basin commissions would you establish in the Mississippi River system? How would you prevent an upstream commission from permitting large discharges at places where they would mostly affect residents in downstream jurisdictions?

3. If a river-basin commission collected effluent fees, what should happen to the revenues? Think of the incentives that the use of the money would provide the commission to set high or low fee levels.

4. Could local governments be forced to pay effluent fees on sewage discharge to streams? Should they?

5. While perhaps not as immediately obvious, each of the preceding questions could be reworded to apply to air—indeed, the original intent of clean-air legislation was to identify the airsheds in the United States and to have each region determine appropriate air quality within the AQCR (Air Quality Control Region). How would the answers to the above questions be similar and different in the air case?

6. What are the spatial implications of uniform controls on the automobile? That is, even uniform controls, such as required catalytic converters on all new cars, do not have benefits that are uniform; are big cities helped relative to rural areas? Are cities in the Southwest and West helped relative to those in the Midwest or East? What does this suggest about ways to improve control policy for automobiles?

REFERENCES AND FURTHER READING

Ackerman, Bruce; Rose-Ackerman, Susan; Sawyer, James; and Henderson, Dale. *The Uncertain Search for Water Quality*. New York: Free Press, 1974.

Baumol, William, and Oates, allace. *The Theory of Environmental Policy*. Englewood Cliffs, N.J.: Prentice-Hall, 1975.

Enthoven, Alain C., and Freeman, A. Myrick, eds. *Pollution, Resources and the Environment*. New York: Norton, 1973.

Freeman, A Myrick III. *Air and Water Pollution Control: A Benefit-Cost Assessment*. New York: Wiley, 1982.

Friedlaender, Ann, ed. *Approaches to Controlling Air Pollution*. Cambridge, Mass.: MIT Press, 1978.

Haefele, Edwin. "Environmental Quality as a Problem of Social Choice." In Allen Kneese and Blair Bower, eds. *Environmental Quality Analysis*. Baltimore: Johns Hopkins University Press, for Resources for the Future, Inc., 1972.

Kneese, Allen, and Bower, Blair. *Managing Water Quality: Economics, Technology, Institutions*. Baltimore: Johns Hopkins University Press, for Resources for the Future, Inc., 1968.

Kneese, Allen, and Schultze, Charles. *Pollution, Prices and Public Policy*.

Washington, D.C.: The Brookings Institution, 1975.

Lave, L. B. and Omenn, G. S. *Clearing the Air: Reforming the Clean Air Act*. Washington, D.C.: The Brookings Institution, 1981.

National Academy of Sciences, *Report by the Committee on Motor Vehicle Emissions*. Washington, D.C.: National Academy of Sciences, 1974.

National Commission on Air Quality. *To Breathe Clean Air*. Washington, D.C.: U.S. Government Printing Office, 1981.

Portney, Paul R. "Toxic Substance Policy and the Protection of Human Health." In Paul R. Portnoy, ed. *Current Issues in U.S. Environmental Policy*. Baltimore: Johns Hopkins University Press, for Resources for the Future, Inc., 1978.

Rothfelder, M. "Reducing the Cost of Water Pollution Control under the Clean Water Act." *Natural Resources Journal* 22 (April 1981): 407–21.

Chapter 10

Restructuring Environmental Programs

The last two chapters have presented and criticized the national pollution-control program. Chapter 8 traced the development of the federal government's attempts to limit polluting discharges. It emphasized that the natonal program has relied on discharge regulations and on subsidies to local governments for the construction of waste-treatment plants to abate discharges. It was shown that the federal government has been led to increasingly detailed, pervasive, and stringent regulations and to larger subsidies during the nearly two decades of our national pollution-control program.

Chapter 9 contained many specific criticisms of the pollution-abatement program, but the basic criticism is that the government tries to do too much. It tries to regulate the kinds and amounts of air- and waterborne discharges from each source, which inevitably leads it to regulate detailed characteristics of plant design and production technology, product design, and methods of waste treatment. The result has been less pollution abatement than is called for in the law, costly programs to administer, and, perhaps most important, a reduction in the adaptability and flexibility of the private economy.

In Chapters 3 and 4, the case for effluent fees was made on the most fundamental theoretical grounds that even ideal direct regula-

269

tion leads to overproduction in industries that generate polluting discharges. But that is only a small part of the case for effluent fees. Nobody knows how important the resulting resource misallocation is, and it may be unimportant. The strongest part of the case for effluent fees is at a more practical level of analysis.

A step down from the abstract level is the notion that choosing a target environmental quality is the most difficult and subjective part of environmental politics. Even benefit-cost analysis considerably better than that available might not persuade the political process that it could help much. Once the political process has chosen a target environmental quality, an effluent fee that results in discharges to achieve the target quality induces dischargers to allocate the discharges among them in the way that achieves the target quality at least cost. Direct regulation can accomplish the same goal only if the regulatory body knows in detail the abatement cost schedule of each discharger. It is this self-enforcing aspect of effluent fees that economists find most attractive.

Perhaps the strongest argument for effluent fees is at the most practical level. After more than two decades of experience with direct-discharge controls, it can be seen that they lead to increasingly stringent and detailed controls on every aspect of production from design of plants and products to day-to-day production decisions to waste treatment and disposal decisions. What is most needed in our environmental program is to induce producers to experiment imaginatively with many different products and production processes in a broad effort to learn to operate an affluent economy without endangering the environment. Meeting precisely specified goals for precisely specified discharges at precisely specified times is unimportant. Effluent fees would encourage such experimentation in the search for profitable ways to satisfy consumer demands while keeping fee payments low. Dischargers would continue to seek economical ways to abate discharges as long as any fee was being paid. Direct regulation does the opposite. It stifles experimentation by placing all the emphasis on use of approved devices simply because they have been approved as meeting the requirements of the regulatory agency. Approved devices may be expensive, unreliable, or cumbersome, but they will avoid trouble with the regulatory agency. The environmental program is the latest example of the proposition that detailed direct regulation stifles initiative and innovation.

This chapter places most of its emphasis on the practical aspects of an effluent-fee program. There are many ways to structure environmental programs based on effluent fees. Some alternatives are presented here. Within any program, many practical issues must be settled. First and most important, how would effluent fees work? What would have to be measured? Who would do it? Who would collect the money? Who would audit records? And how would the money be used? Second, on what would fees be levied? One may be persuaded that effluent fees are a good idea without believing that they should be used to control all discharges. Third, what insitiutional arrangement would be desirable to administer effluent fees and other pollution-abatement policies?

Following this discussion, a host of other recommended changes in environmental policy, some of which have already been at least partially implemented, are discussed. These reforms would, in the main, occur automatically in the presence of a soundly devised effluent-fee program; hence the discussion presumes that actual policies will not fully incorporate the economic incentives discussed in the bulk of this chapter. Reforms in the control of stationary-source air pollution include offset programs, bubble policies, and emissions banking. For mobile-source pollutants, a two-car strategy is duscussed. In the area of water pollution, little in the way of innovative reforms has been forthcoming, although much potential exists: more emphasis on nonpoint pollution, nonuniformity through separation of use, and so on. Finally, the "waste interface" or "displaced externality" problem needs to be incorporated into all environmental policy; this is now being most clearly realized in the case of hazardous-substance control, but the lesson is far-reaching.

General Comments on Effluent-Fee Programs

The theoretically correct set of effluent fees would equate costs and social benefits of abatement at the margin for each substance at each time and place of discharge. Opponents of effluent fees often argue that they are useless as a practical tool of public policy because most information needed by government to set the correct fee schedules is unavailable. Advocates of effluent fees should never permit adversaries to get away with this argument. It was shown in Chapter 4 that the information required to set optimum effluent fees is precisely that required to issue optimum discharge permits or to carry out any other effective pollution-control policy. No more and no less. In fact of course, governments never have all the information needed to solve any social problem, environmental or otherwise, in optimum fashion. Government programs, like private decisions, are always made on the basis of incomplete information. Whatever policy tool is used, effluent fees, permits, or anything else, some mistakes will be made. But there is no reason to think that more serious mistakes will be made if effluent fees are used than if permits are used. In fact, the presumption is the reverse, if permits cannot be transferred among firms.

The political process, advised by whatever studies of benefits and costs are available, must choose a target ambient environmental quality for major river basins or for the air mantle over a metropolitan area. Then a discharge volume must be chosen and discharges must be allocated among sources so as to achieve the targeted ambient quality at minimum cost. The advantages are with effluent fees because they can be adjusted to achieve the appropriate total discharge and, unlike permits, they allocate discharges among sources at least cost without further government action. All the information available to the government about abatement costs and benefits can be used at least as effectively to set effluent-fee levels as to set permit levels.

It follows from the previous paragraph that a theoretically correct set of either effluent fees or of permits would be extremely complex. An optimum fee or permit depends not only on the substance discharged but also on the time and place of discharge. For example, the optimum permit or fee for heat discharge from a thermal electric plant in a metropolitan area is different in winter from summer. Likewise, the optimum fee or permit for the discharge of organic wastes to a stream is different thirty miles upstream from a metropolitan area than it is only five miles upstream.

Whether effluent fees or permits are used, the subtlety of the system should depend on the amount of information available. If there is no information about how damages to water quality in a metropolitan area vary with distance of discharges above the metropolitan area, then there is little point in varying effluent fees or permit levels by stream mile above the metropolitan area. The subtlety of the abatement program should also depend on the costs of administering subtle programs. It is much more expensive to administer an effluent-fee or permit program if fees or permits vary by stream mile than if they are uniform throughout a long river stretch. The national permit program has tried to be more subtle than was justified by available information or by the costs of administering a subtle program. As has been pointed out, an effluent fee that is uniform throughout a river stretch achieves an ambient quality more cheaply than a uniform permit program achieves the same ambient quality. The reason is that the effluent-fee program induces sources to allocate discharges among themselves so as to achieve the ambient quality at minimum cost, whereas the permit program does not permit this flexibility. The conclusion holds whether permits are issued for total discharges or for discharges per unit of output; the crucial issue is whether permits can be bought and sold.

As a practical matter, an effluent-fee program should probably set uniform fees for discharges of a given substance throughout a metropolitan air-quality region or throughout a river basin or long river stretch. It would be important for an effluent-fee program to avoid the unproductive complexity that has plagued the permit program. As experience accumulated with the program, both its administrators and dischargers would gain expertise and information. It may be that more subtle fee schedules would be found workable after some years of experience.

Almost identical comments apply to the timing of discharges. In temperate climates, most discharges are more harmful in summer than in winter. Heat discharges not only warm up uncomfortably warm air in summer, but also uncomfortably cold air in winter; and organic discharges to streams do most harm when the water is warm and the flow is low, both of which occur in late summer in the United States. These facts imply that permit levels or effluent fees ought in principle to vary with the season. Once again, the issue is a practical one. How much information is available about seasonal variations in costs and benefits of discharge abatement and how much more costly is it to administer effluent fees or permits that vary seasonally? In fact, relatively little use has been made of seasonal variation in discharge volumes under the existing permit program, presumably because government officials have decided that the benefits of seasonal variation in permit levels would be less than the costs. Even if that is correct, it does not follow that it would be correct under an effluent-fee program. But again the presumption is that an effluent-fee program should be started in a relatively simple fashion. This suggests that seasonally uniform fees would be best. As experience and expertise accumulated, it might be decided that seasonal variations should be introduced in fee schedules.

The desirable content of an effluent-fee bill is extremely simple. It should say that any source can discharge any amounts of certain substances to air or water, but that a fixed fee per unit discharged must be paid to a government agency. All dischargers should be required to meter discharges of the substances by means acceptable to the government. Then a report of the amount discharged would be sent, along with a check for the fee, at the end of each month or quarter of a year. Acceptable metering procedures would vary by substance, but in most cases metering would be on a sample basis. If a discharger claimed metering its discharges was impossible, the government agency could estimate them for the discharger, basing its estimate on simple norms that would be certain not to underestimate discharges. If the discharger believed the government's estimate was too high, it would be free to make its own estimate. A goal of an effluent-fee program should be to motivate dischargers to use ingenuity in metering discharges, not to lay down complex rules that had to be followed.

It is important that an effluent-fee program motivate dischargers to meter their discharges. Many states issued permits for waterborne discharges after 1972 to firms and municipalities who had never metered their discharges. Permits were issued on the basis of norms for the kind and size of operation covered. It is this fact that inspires complaints by proponents of permits that effluent fees would require more metering than is carried out in practice under the permit system, but not more than is required to make the permit system effective. Permits issued to sources that never meter discharges are a sham. Auditing is impossible and a source can hardly make appropriate resource reallocations if it has never metered its discharges.

Periodic effluent-fee reports would have to be audited by the government just as tax forms are. A government agency would have to sample discharges itself periodically but unpredictably. Unpaid or underpaid fees would be subject to interest and penalty charges, and intentionally false reports would be subject to criminal prosecution, as with tax returns.

If an effluent fee were introduced as described above, it would avoid most of the complexity of the existing permit program. People who distrust market incentives sometimes suggest combining effluent fees and permits. Under this proposal, fees would be paid only on discharges in excess of amounts covered by permits. There is almost nothing to be said for this proposal, except during a transitional period in going from permits to fees. Combining the two policies would require retention of the cumbersome bureaucracy and administration procedures required by the permit program, and the addition of more bureaucracy to collect the fees. More important, the presence of the permit program would prevent the fees from performing their resource-allocation function.

It might, however, be desirable to phase effluent fees in during a period of several years while permits were phased out. During this time, dischargers would be subject in some degree to both permits and fees. At all times, fees should be announced well in advance and should be unchanged during a substantial time. Their purpose is to permit dischargers to make advance plans of abatement in a predictable economic environment. If fees were changed suddenly or capriciously, they could not perform this function. However, it is important to provide that fees be changed periodically. Experimentation with fee levels would be important during the first few years. In addition, fees would probably have to be raised gradually, relative to other prices, as the economy and materials use grew.

The following is an example of a procedure that might satisfy the above requirements: Announce at the beginning of a year that fees would be introduced one year hence and would become fully operative three years hence. The first year after the announcement would be for planning and the permit system would remain in force. The first year fees would be introduced at one-third of their full values. The second year they would be two-thirds and the third year they would be at their full values. At the beginning of each year, fees would be announced that would come into effect three years hence.

The law should state simply that anyone who discharged the substances covered to the atmosphere or to natural water bodies had to pay the fee. It is sometimes suggested that local governments who discharge sewage, and perhaps air pollutants from burning solid wastes, be exempt from an effluent-fee bill because they are financially hard pressed. The main argument against exempting them is that municipal sewage is a large part of the organic waste discharged to many rivers and estuaries and no pollution-control program can succeed if it excludes municipalities. In addition, excluding local governments would demoralize those who were forced to pay the fees. Finally, it is sometimes claimed that local governments will not respond to economic incentives since they are not profit-oriented, and that they should therefore continue to be subject to permits. This argument is ironic in view of the fact that they have responded rationally to existing incentives in the form of waste-treatment-plant construction subsidies. It was pointed out in the last chapter that they have responded to construction subsidies by constructing many new plants. But they lack incentive to operate them efficiently and do not do so. An effluent fee would provide them an incentive to do exactly what needs to be done: operate them efficiently. In fact, the fees would not be much of a burden on local governments since the federal government pays a large part of sewage-plant construction costs.

Forcing local governments to pay effluent-fee bills is no easy matter. Imprisonment is the ultimate sanction for a private party who violates the law, but the federal government cannot, and should not, imprison a mayor and city council for nonpayment of effluent fees. An easily available sanction, frequently used to enforce civil-rights laws against private institutions, is the threat to withhold all federal funds in event of noncompliance. That would be a powerful incentive for payment of effluent fees by local governments.

More difficult is the issue of nonpoint sources, to be discussed in more detail later. As was shown in Part II, large amounts of pollutants wash into waterways from farmland, construction sites, and storm drains on streets and highways. The law should not be written so as to exclude such discharges. Instead, it should be enforced against them whenever they can be identified and metered. The law should not, and the courts would not permit it to, be enforced against farmers whose fertilizer runs off into streams unless there is some reasonable way to estimate runoff. Our knowledge about the fate of such substances improves gradually and the law should enable fees to be charged for such discharges whenever reasonable ways to meter them become available.

Environmentalists sometimes advocate a program consisting of both fees and permits, as suggested earlier. That would be legally difficult because permit violations carry criminal penalties, so payment of the fee would be an admission of guilt. Much more important, retention of the permit system would prevent fees from accomplishing their goal of converting the environmental program from a police-power matter to a resource-allocation issue.

Scope and Magnitude of Effluent Fees

On what substances should effluent fees be levied and how large should they be? The answer in principle to the first question is that any harmful substance discharged to air or water should be subject to the fee. A more practical answer is that whatever substances are covered by the existing permit system can instead be subject to fees. If enough information on discharges is available to operate a permit system, the same information can be used to operate a fee system. Those most practical answer to the question is that legislatures are unlikely to be willing to make a wholesale switch from the permit system to an effluent-fee system. Instead, the most they are likely to do is to authorize experiments with effluent fees on a few substances to try to gain information as to how well they will work. Why legislatures should be so cautious about economic incentives and require so much evidence about their likely effects, whereas they adopted the permit system with no study of its effects whatsoever, is a good question. It is also a good question why legislatures should be so cautious about effluent fees, given that they levy other taxes almost at random and with almost no thought as to their effects. Nevertheless, it is desirable and reasonable to ask what are the strong candidate substances for experimental use of effluent fees and what is known about appropriate magnitudes of fees.

The strongest candidates for experiments with effluent fees are substances that are discharged in large quantities and whose unrestricted discharge does considerable harm, but not so much that it is desirable to prevent all discharges. Substances so toxic that discharges in the smallest measurable quantities should be prevented are not good candidates. Radioactive materials and heavy metals are probably poor candidates for effluent-fee experiments. Discharges of highly toxic substances should be prohibited.

Perhaps the strongest candidate for effluent-fee experiments is biochemical-oxygen-demand (BOD) discharges to water bodies. As was seen in Chapter 6, large BOD discharges come from municipal sewage systems and a variety of industrial sources. Much is known about the harmful effects of organic wastes on the receiving water bodies. Furthermore, several studies have analyzed the effects of effluent fees on BOD discharges. The most ambitious such study[1] investigated the effect of effluent fees on BOD discharges to the Delaware estuary. It concluded that an effluent fee of 10 cents per pound of BOD discharge would result in a substantial and pervasive

1. By Edwin Johnson, summarized in Kneese and Bower, *Managing Water Quality*, pp. 158–64.

improvement in the estuary's water quality. George Löf and Allen Kneese, in their *Economics of Water Utilization in the Beet Sugar Industry*, estimated the marginal abatement-cost function for organic wastes in the beet sugar industry. Their data imply that a similar effluent fee would cause substantial abatement. Allen Kneese and Blair Bower, in *Managing Water Quality*, review the evidence about the responsiveness of BOD discharges to sewer charges. Finally, bills that would levy effluent fees of about 10 cents per pound of BOD discharged have been introduced in, but not passed by, the national and several state legislatures. There has not yet been a careful study of the BOD effluent-fee level that would balance benefits and costs of abatement at the margin, but available studies suggest strongly that a BOD effluent fee of about 10 cents per pound would have achieved substantial abatement of discharges under conditions prevailing about 1970. It should be higher by about the intervening inflation rate in subsequent years, running perhaps a quarter in the mid-1980s.

A second strong candidate for effluent fees is sulfur-oxide discharges to the atmosphere. As was shown in Chapter five, large volumes of sulfur oxides are discharged, much of it from the combustion of coal and oil in thermal electric plants. Health and property damages from ambient sulfur-oxide concentrations are tolerably well documented. Appropriate levels for effluent fees on sulfur oxides have been studied by the government and by private scholars since President Nixon proposed a sulfur tax in 1972.[2] Such studies suggest that an effluent fee of 10 to 20 cents per pound of sulfur emitted would have been appropriate in the early 1970s. A sulfur effluent fee would end the intensive warfare between EPA and the power companies about the effectiveness of stack gas scrubbers in removing sulfur before discharge. Sulfur discharges can be metered either directly or by subtracting amounts recovered from measures of sulfur content of fuels. The latter is justified by the materials balance, which implies that sulfur not recovered must be discharged to the atmosphere.

Effluent fees on several other pollutants have been studied or suggested.[3] These include discharges of suspended solids to water bod-

2. See *Environmental Quality, 1972*, and the EPA document *Legal Compilation: Air*, vol. 5, 1973.

3. A good industry study is Clifford Russell, *Residuals Management in Industry: A Case Study of Petroleum Refining*. Baltimore: Johns Hopkins University Press, for Resources for the Future, Inc., 1973.

ies, of heat to air or water, and of particulates to the air. It would be an exaggeration to say that optimum effluent-fee levels are known for these discharges. But it would not be hard to calculate fee levels for these substances that would be at least as good approximations to optimality as the permits being issued or the direct controls required under existing programs.

Motor Vehicle Effluent Fees

Special attention to effluent fees for motor vehicles is justified by the fact that they emit large amounts of pollutants at about nose level in crowded areas, that motor-vehicle pollution abatement has been studied extensively, and that motor-vehicle pollution control has been so controversial. Effluent fees have not been discussed prominently in connection with automobiles, but a strong case can be made for their use.

Because of motor vehicles' mobility and small size, continuous metering of auto emissions is not feasible. But, as has been pointed out above, data collected by sampling emissions can be used just as well to collect effluent fees as to administer standards. The purpose of this section is to describe a system for motor-vehicle effluent fees in practical detail.

The last chapter presented a detailed criticism of the motor-vehicle emissions-control program. The requirement that autos meet stringent and arbitrary emissions standards at a rigid deadline has forced automobile companies to adopt expensive and clumsy devices, which have raised car ownership costs greatly. Replacing standards with effluent fees would permit flexibility on the part of manufacturers and owners as to exactly what effluents were discharged, exactly when and how particular standards were met, and exactly which cars were cleaned up when and how much, while providing strong incentives continuously to produce and drive cleaner cars. The advantages of effluent fees over standards are overwhelming for auto emissions.

There is virtue in an auto effluent fee that parallels the existing standards program. As with the standards program, an effluent fee should be administered in two stages, for new and used cars.

An effluent fee for new cars would be very simple. A sample of each kind of new car could be tested by the federal test procedure, exactly as at present. Emissions would be collected and measured.

Based on the sample emissions, a fee for each car sold domestically would be computed as follows:

$$T = \Sigma_i t_i r_i \qquad (10.1)$$

Here r_i is the amount of the ith emission collected during the test, t_i is the fee rate per unit discharge of the ith emission, and T is the total fee levied per car. At present, standards are set for only three emissions from cars: carbon monoxide, hydrocarbons, and nitrogen oxides. For this set, the sum would be over the three pollutants. But diesel engines may emit particulates and there is reason to believe that some methods of auto-emission control may result in other emissions such as sulfur oxides. It would be desirable to include these, and any other pollutants that might conceivably be discharged from motor vehicles, in equation (10.1). Of course, if a vehicle were free of a particular pollutant, the corresponding r_i would be zero and no fee would be paid on that component of T. Thus there is no harm in including in equation (10.1) pollutants never discharged from motor vehicles.

The fee rates t_i should be set at the best estimates of the rates that will induce emissions that equate the costs and social benefits of abatement at the margin. Since the harm done by a unit discharge of a pollutant is the same regardless of the source, the effluent-fee rates, t_i, should be the same, at a given time and place, as those applied to stationary sources.[4]

The r_i are sample emissions, for example, in grams per mile, during the test procedure. Then the units for t_i should be damage per unit of the ith emission multiplied by the average number of miles driven by the car in question during its first year of life. t_i should be the same for all new cars regardless of make, model, or size, since a gram of emissions does the same harm regardless of the car from which it comes.

Of course supply and demand considerations would determine the imputation of T to car buyers and sellers, as they do with a sales tax. It would be desirable to require that the tax paid appear on the sticker to each car. The information would be valuable to buyers in

4. Mills and White have reviewed estimates of appropriate fee rates for automobiles, and presented their estimates, in their paper in Friedlaender, ed., *Air Pollution and Administrative Control*. References to studies of the benefits of automobile-pollution abatement are in Chapter 5.

predicting the future cost of owning the car, because cars that are dirty when new are likely to be dirty when old, and therefore subject to large used-car effluent fees described below.

If an automobile effluent fee were introduced, the present certification procedure should be abolished. The purpose of certification is to permit production and sale of vehicles found to meet required standards. Under an effluent-fee program, producers are permitted to sell vehicles however dirty they are, but are strongly discouraged from selling, and buyers from buying, dirty cars by the high fees paid on them. But there would be no car so dirty it would be illegal to produce and sell it, and therefore no need for certification. Abolition of certification would be a great gain since it is the source of the atmosphere of confrontation under the existing program. It is the fact that factories must shut down if vehicles fall just a little short of the certification standard that results in political action to change the standard, threats to close down, and the like. An effluent fee would substitute for this unproductive focus on an arbitrary number a system that provides rewards proportionate to success in producing clean cars.

Under an effluent-fee program, the requirement that manufacturers guarantee control devices for fifty thousand miles should also be abolished. As was said in Chapter 9, owners lack incentive to take cars in for necessary maintenance and replacement, especially since gasoline mileage may improve if devices fail. Requiring manufacturers to guarantee emission-control devices for fifty thousand miles makes less sense than requiring them to guarantee brakes for fifty thousand miles. In both cases, the guarantee removes incentive for owners to operate the car so as to increase the life of the devices. The owner's life and car are endangered if the brakes fail, but not if pollution-control devices fail. Of course manufacturers could still guarantee pollution-control devices, and might be induced to do so by competitive pressures, just as they guarantee other parts on cars for various periods. The guarantee would be replaced by a used-car effluent fee, to be described next.

Because emissions from cars on the road depend on maintenance and replacement of control devices as well as on the way the car is made, it is important that cars be subject to periodic emissions tests. Present law assigns this task to the states, with the instruction that cars be kept off the road if they do not meet appropriate standards. It would be natural to administer a used-car effluent fee by the same mechanism. States would test emissions at the time of annual safety inspection. To the registration fee would be added a used-car effluent fee computed by equation (10.1). In principle, the fee rates t_i should be computed in the same way for used as for new cars: damage per gram per mile times average miles driven per year by cars of the age in question. The damage done by a gram of pollutant does not depend on the age of the car that discharges it. It is likely that legislatures would insist on lower tax rates for older cars. Older cars are, of course, more expensive to keep up to a high emissions standard than new cars, and they are predominantly owned by lower-income people. Thus there is an equity reason for charging somewhat lower rates on older cars. But there is no case for removing cars more than five years old entirely from the program, as does the existing law. It is likely that much more than half of all auto emissions now comes from cars more than five years old.

The availability of well-publicized used-car effluent-fee rates would motivate owners to maintain and replace control devices and engine parts in order to avoid high fee payments. Yet they would not be faced with the prospect of being prohibited from driving their cars if emissions fell slightly short of an arbitrary standard.

It was pointed out in Chapter 9 that many states have done little to implement the provision in existing law that they test emissions on used cars. A large number of states do not even have annual safety inspections. If they do not institute emissions tests, they cannot implement either the existing used-car emission-control program or a used-car effluent fee.

As with the new-car effluent fee, the t_i for used cars would presumably be set equal to damage done per gram of discharge times the average number of miles driven per year by cars of the age in question. The used-car effluent fee could be made to depend on the number of miles driven since the last test. The advantage would be that the owner's tax payment would depend on his miles driven instead of on the average miles driven in cars the age of his. Disadvantages of the proposal are that it would require additional record keeping, it would raise complications when cars were sold or moved from one state to another, and it might induce owners to tamper with odometers. On the other hand, since the marginal cost of traveling another mile would be higher, the average number of miles driven each year would fall.

An important issue regarding both new- and used-car effluent fees, as well as the existing effluent standards program, is whether regional variation should be permitted. Marginal damages from additional pollution are greater in parts of the country with poor air quality and many people than elsewhere. Thus there is a case for permitting or encouraging dirtier cars in regions with high-quality air than in those with low-quality air. Drivers object to paying for expensive pollution-control devices in regions without an air-pollution problem. Existing law recognizes this fact by requiring new cars sold in California to meet higher emission standards than those sold elsewhere. However, it is undesirable to require excessive diversity. Scale economies in automobile production undoubtedly make it unduly expensive to manufacture cars that meet different standards in each state. Diversity can be permitted at the new- or used-car stages, or at both. It would be possible to have nationally uniform effluent-fee rates for new cars, but to permit states to set used-car rates that reflect local conditions. This would be desirable if scale economies in manufacturing were great and variations in maintenance and replacement had a large effect on used-car emissions. Alternatively, both the new- and used-car fees could vary by the state in which the car was sold and registered. Regional variation in new-car fees, or in standards, would, however, impose substantial costs on manufacturers. Whatever diversity is built into the system must be by state, even though fees would optimally be higher in, say, Denver or Phoenix than elsewhere in those states. States register cars and states must do emissions tests on used cars.

Sometimes concern is expressed that manufacturers will make new cars that meet high emissions standards but whose emission control will deteriorate rapidly if the requirement that control devices be guaranteed fifty thousand miles is abandoned. That concern underestimates the incentive manufacturers have in their self-interest to make durable products. Manufacturers make durable engines because poor engines are quickly discovered and sales and profits suffer. The same is true of pollution-control devices. If a manufacturer made a car that was subject to very high used-car effluent fees, its sales would quickly suffer. Of course, both government and private organizations would publish results of their tests of the efficacy and durability of pollution-control devices on various cars, as they do now on other aspects of cars' performance. Owners would be motivated to read such studies because poor emission-control performance would be reflected in high used-car effluent fee bills.

The advantages of an automobile effluent-fee system over the existing standard system would be enormous. Most important, the government would get out of the business of deciding exactly what emission level is permitted for each year. There would be an end to the threat that large manufacturing facilities would have to close down because cars barely missed an arbitrary standard. And manufacturers could no longer threaten to close down if standards were not changed. Manufacturers would no longer be forced to place clumsy devices on cars just because they appeared to be the only devices that would just meet an arbitrary, stringent standard as the car rolled off the assembly line. Instead, market incentives would induce manufacturers to seek continuously new and inexpensive ways to produce clean cars. States would be permitted to allow relatively dirty cars to register if their air-pollution problem was small or if they were willing to put up with dirty air to keep automobile ownership costs down. Owners would be faced with the true cost to society of their use of cars, and they could make socially rational decisions about the kinds of cars to buy and about maintenance and replacement of control devices.

Perhaps as important as anything else, the cost to car owners of pollution control would become evident. Existing legislation has tried to hide from car owners the fact that pollution control is expensive to them (almost 10 percent of the cost of a new car is due to environmental controls). It has required the manufacturer to be responsible for all pollution-control costs for the first fifty thousand miles the car is driven. It is an absurd provision since the manufacturer has no control over the way the car is treated and cannot compel the owner to accept even free servicing. Its only purpose is to persuade owners, that is, voters, that somebody else is paying for pollution control. Voters would be much better able to decide rationally through the democratic process how much pollution control they want if the costs of abatement were made clear to them. An effluent fee would do this in two ways. The fees charged on new and used cars would be known to owners, and they would decide for themselves how much servicing to buy for their cars to keep future fee payments low. They could also evaluate the costs to them of votes for political candidates who proposed further pollution abatement.

There was much discussion of a higher federal gasoline tax after President Jimmy Carter proposed it as part of his energy program in spring 1977. The proposal, which was allowed to lapse when the energy crisis waned, was mostly advocated to reduce petroleum imports. Would it also have been an efficient effluent fee? If so, it would have been a desirable proposal, since it would have been inexpensive to administer. In this book it has been emphasized that it is important to control discharges, not other variables. A gasoline tax induces people to economize on gasoline by driving less and by driving small cars. But harmful emissions are not proportionate to gasoline burned. As a result of the emissions-control program since the late 1960s, much has been learned about reducing harmful emissions per gallon of gasoline burned. A gasoline tax is levied on inputs, not emissions. It could possibly be justified as an approximation to the extent that harmful emissions are nearly proportionate to fuel burned. A final comment concerns the amount. It was shown in Chapter 5 that the cost of the national auto-emission-control program is probably about the same as its benefits, certainly not more than 1 cent per mile of driving. Gasoline taxes are already near that level, about 12 cents per gallon, or somewhat less than 1 cent per mile (in the mid-1980s all cars average about 16 miles per gallon).

Solid Wastes and Effluent Fees

Until now, nothing has been said about the use of effluent fees for solid-waste disposal. The primary pollution problems result from waste disposal to air and water. Effluent fees or permits on these disposals would increase disposal to land. This raises the question whether there should also be effluent fees on materials disposed of on land.

The conclusion of Chapter 7 was that solid-waste disposal causes external diseconomies, but that they are less serious than those from water- and airborne disposal. Perhaps the most obvious externality from solid-waste disposal is from litter in public places. An effluent fee on litter would be ineffectual for the same reason that laws prohibiting litter are ineffectual. Some states have responded to the situation by compulsory deposits on returnable beverage containers, coupled with a ban on nonreturnable containers. It is an indirect effluent fee equal to the forfeited deposit if the container is not returned. A disadvantage is that it charges the effluent fee whether the container is put in the trash or thrown on the beach. Also avoidance of the fee is coupled with reuse of the material instead of with proper disposal even in cases where recycling is not desirable (when full social costs of recycling exceed benefits). Finally, such fees have been levied only on a narrow and arbitrary set of materials. But they raise the question whether indirect levies can be found that can approximate effluent fees.

Most solid wastes are disposed of by industries and by local governments. Disposal methods cause externalities, sometimes when solid wastes pollute streams or when they burn and pollute the air. It is anybody's guess what is the magnitude of externalities from solid-waste disposal that could not be captured by effluent fees on air and water discharges. It is therefore uncertain whether effluent fees are justified for solid-waste disposal. A poorly administered effluent fee on solid wastes might even worsen the environment. For example, the easiest activity on which to levy an effluent fee would be disposal in a poor-quality dump. But the result might be that residents would throw their trash over the edge of a road on a dark night to avoid paying the fee.

Many people believe that materials reuse should be encouraged for conservation as well as for environmental reasons. As was seen in Chapter 3, increased reuse would reduce the volume of materials extracted from the environment to produce given amounts of commodities and services, thus conserving more materials for future use. Despite decades of writing on the subject, the basis for the belief that markets withdraw excessive amounts of materials is unclear. Of course external diseconomies from disposal are one reason. An optimum set of effluent fees on air and water disposal would mostly shift disposal to land but might also induce some materials reuse and correspondingly reduced withdrawals. A set of effluent fees that uniformly raised the cost of air, water, and land disposal would hardly alter the relative amounts of materials disposed of in the three media, but would raise the cost of discharges relative to reuse of materials and would result in less of the former and more of the latter.

Suppose there were effluent fees (certainly not uniformly raising the cost across media) that optimally accounted for external diseconomies from discharges to air, water, and land. They would cause some increased reuse of materials and therefore some decreased withdrawal of materials from the environment. Is there reason to believe that natural resources would be adequately conserved for future use? The issue is controversial and a thorough analysis is beyond the scope of this book, but the most advanced treatment would still leave grounds for honest disagreement about the answer. The strongest grounds for believing that withdrawals would nevertheless be faster than is socially optimum is that market interest rates may be greater than rates at which citizens want to discount future events, mainly because of high marginal taxes on property income. Many reforms are certainly needed in taxation of property income in the United States, but equity would require substantial taxes on property income even if the tax system were much better than it is. Thus there may be justification for government programs specifically to stimulate materials reuse and therefore to discourage withdrawals.

Is it possible to provide a pervasive economic incentive to abate polluting discharges and to increase materials reuse without the need for direct metering of discharges? The materials balance provides an intriguing means of doing so, at least in principle. As was shown in Chapter 3, the materials balance implies that for the economy as a whole, withdrawals equal discharges (apart from capital accumulation). Therefore a fee on withdrawals is a fee on discharges.

Although the foregoing sounds paradoxical, it is correct. If the goal were to reduce total discharges for environmental reasons, or to reduce total withdrawals for conservation reasons, a fee on withdrawals would be an efficient way to do so. It would be better than a fee on discharges because withdrawals are easier to measure than discharges. Most withdrawals are performed by mining, farming, forestry, and fisheries firms. Thus withdrawals are concentrated in a relatively small number of institutions and places, whereas discharges are dispersed among all firms, nonprofit institutions, and households in the economy. Fees on withdrawals would have the automatic effect of making used materials cheap relative to withdrawn materials and would therefore encourage materials reuse.

A withdrawal fee should be specific to the material withdrawn. Then, for example, if the combustion of coal did more harm than the combustion of oil, the coal fee could be higher than the oil fee. But a uniform withdrawal fee on each material would not take account of two considerations that are crucial to environmental effects: the ways materials are processed and the ways they are discharged. A barrel of petroleum withdrawn from the environment may have different environmental effects depending on whether it is processed into plastics by the petrochemical industry or into gasoline by the refining industry. Likewise, a gallon of gasoline may have different environmental effects depending on the kind of car engine in which it is burned. Or a ton of beef may have different environmental effects depending on whether the resulting raw sewage is dumped into a stream or treated carefully and the sludge returned to the land.

In principle, these problems can be solved as follows: Set the withdrawal fee at the level equal to the marginal damage done when the material is processed and discharged in the most harmful way. Then pay refunds to dischargers equal to the amount by which their discharges of the material do less harm, because processing results in less harmful products, because materials are treated before discharge, or because they are discharged at a time or place at which they do less harm. The result is that the net fee, that is, the withdrawal fee minus the refund, equals marginal damages for each material discharged, as required by the conditions for optimum resource allocation.

The following example illustrates the working of the withdrawal-fee-refund proposal. Suppose there are two materials that can be used to make two kinds of containers, call them paper and plastic. Each can be recovered and reused at a cost, and each can be disposed of in a poor way (dumped on the landscape as litter), a normal way (put in a public dump), or a good way (put in a sanitary landfill). The following table shows hypothetical marginal damages from health hazards and eyesores for each material and each disposal method:

Marginal damage

Material	Poor disposal	Normal disposal	Good disposal	Reuse
Paper	10	6	2	0
Plastic	20	13	5	0

The appropriate withdrawal fee would be 10 for paper and 20 for plastic. Appropriate refunds are as follows:

Refund

Material	Poor disposal	Normal disposal	Good disposal	Reuse
Paper	0	4	8	0
Plastic	0	7	15	0

Thus each disposal method would cost the discharger a net fee equal to the damage from disposal. For example, normal disposal of the plastic container would cost a net fee of $13 = 20 - 7$, which equals marginal damage from that form of disposal of that material. Under this program, each material user would be motivated to use each disposal method whenever it was in the social interest for him to do so. For example, suppose that for a certain user of the plastic material, poor disposal costs nothing but that normal disposal costs 5 in treatment or transportation costs. Then the user would be motivated to choose normal over poor disposal because the refund of 7 would exceed the cost incurred of 5. But the full social cost of poor disposal is 20, whereas the full social cost of normal disposal is 18, 13 for environmental damage plus 5 for disposal costs. Thus the material user is motivated to choose the disposal method that is socially efficient. Likewise, people would be motivated to switch from one material to the other when it was socially efficient to do so.

Not quite so obvious is the fact that users would be motivated to reuse materials when it was socially efficient. Reused paper would have a price advantage of 10 over new paper because only new paper would be subject to the withdrawal fee of 10. Then paper users would choose used paper whenever the cost of transporting and processing used paper was less than 10, which is exactly what society saves in environmental damages if the paper is reused instead of being disposed of in the poor fashion. Thus the appropriate policy is to pay no refund on reuse of materials because the tax on withdrawals of materials gives used materials the appropriate price advantage.

The basic advantage of the withdrawal fee over the effluent fee is that with a withdrawal fee, the government does not have to require dischargers to meter discharges, to treat wastes or process materials in certain ways, or to record reuse of materials. Dischargers would be motivated to record amounts and kinds of waste treatment in order to obtain the refunds. But they would do it in their self-interest, whereas they must be coerced to do it under an effluent-fee program. In addition, the total amount of metering would be much less than under an effluent-fee program. Many materials users would simply not find it worthwhile to meter discharges. Likewise, there would be no need for the government to collect data on materials reuse or to regulate or encourage reuse except insofar as the withdrawal fee did so automatically. Finally, a withdrawal fee would have some effect in discouraging harmful nonpoint discharges. They are especially difficult to deter directly and therefore to control by direct regulations or effluent fees.

A withdrawal fee could be designed to encourage conservation. For that purpose, it would have to be set at a level equal to the material's environmental damage plus an amount to correct for artificially high market interest rates. Then only the part of the withdrawal fee that was for environmental damage would be subject to refunds.

It is worth pointing out that much of the refunds would go to local governments who perform indirect-discharge services such as sewage treatment and solid-waste disposal. It would remove most of the cost of financing these public services from taxpayers and place the burden on users of polluting materials. Thus, whereas the effluent fee would worsen the financial plight of local governments, the withdrawal fee would improve it.

The withdrawal fee is a generalization of a variety of special environmental incentive schemes that have been tried or proposed. It generalizes beverage-container-deposit plans by applying them to other materials than those used in reusable containers, applying them at the extraction stage instead of the retailing stage, and by removing the coercive element of deposit plans. Under the withdrawal fee, the price of a beverage would go up by the amount of the fee on the container. Vendors would not be required to offer refunds on containers, but they would be motivated to switch to reusable containers and to offer refunds since used containers would become cheaper than new containers by the amount of the fee. In similar fashion, the withdrawal fee is a generalization of proposed and actual bounties to those who reuse or properly dispose of automobile hulks.

Would a withdrawal fee work? If is is worthwhile to have a comprehensive government policy toward withdrawals and discharges, encompassing many materials and discharges to water, air, and land, for environmental and conservation purposes, then a withdrawal fee is better than a similarly comprehensive effluent fee or permit policy. But if it is worthwhile to have government policies on the discharges of only a few substances to air and water, then effluent fees are better. At least until considerable experience is gained in the administration of well-planned economic-incentive programs, it would be a mistake to undertake such a comprehensive program.

Institutional Arrangements and Other Problems

This chapter has concentrated on the issue of effluent fees versus permits because discharge regulation is at the heart of the pollution-control program, because effluent fees are so controversial and so misunderstood, and because economics has important things to say on the subject. But it is only one of several important issues concerning government policy toward the environment. As has been pointed out in earlier chapters, governments undertake a variety of indirect-discharge services and other programs to protect the environment. The invariable conclusion of independent studies of such activities is that they are performed poorly. Government response to criticisms is usually to provide money for a particular input thought to be underutilized: subsidies for waste-treatment plants, training grants for waste-treatment-plant operators, money for dams, and so forth. Although some such expenditures may be justified, the conclusion of Chapter 9 was that the basic problem is the absence of public institutions that have the appropriate range of power and responsibilities and the appropriate incentives to choose among options in the public interest. Thus this section discusses public institutions for pollution control and indicates how particular activities could be assigned to appropriate institutions.

The need for public institutions is greatest with water-pollution programs, next greatest for solid waste disposal, and least for air-pollution programs. As was pointed out in Chapter 9, governments have been assigned responsibility for important indirect-discharge services for liquid wastes, and there are many activities governments can undertake to improve stream quality. Governments also have responsibility for indirect-discharge services for solid wastes, but the range of options is narrower. Governments perform no important indirect-discharge services for airborne wastes and there are almost no ways to improve ambient air quality other than to reduce discharges of pollutants to it. Hence, most of the debate about government institutions has focused on water quality.

As was indicated in the last chapter, the consensus among those who have studied the subject is that there should be a single government agency responsible for choosing among a wide range of options to improve water quality throughout a substantial river basin. At present many government agencies are responsible for planning, constructing, financing, and operating waste-treatment plants, building and operating dams, issuing discharge permits, controlling discharges, and regulating specific discharges. These institutions are the creations of several levels and agencies of our complex system of governments. In addition, as was also pointed out earlier, some options, such as in-stream reaeration, seem to be beyond the purview of all relevant agencies. It is difficult to resist the conclusion that a river basin should be treated as a unit for planning purposes and that a single agency should be responsible for choosing the policy instruments best suited for each basin.

In addition to having a broad range of options, the river-basin agencies should be responsive to the wishes of the electorate affected by their decisions. The debate among political scientists and public-administration specialists as to how to constitute an agency for his purpose was discussed in Chapter 9.

Whether permits or effluent fees are used to regulate discharges, administering the program should be among the responsibilities of the river-basin agency. Fee or permit levels should vary from basin to basin and it is best to have the levels chosen by those most familiar with local conditions. The federal government should, and inevitably will, take responsibility for the broad outlines of pollution-control policy, so it would certainly place limits on ranges of fee or permit levels that river-basin agencies could set. For example, federal law might say that the effluent fee for organic discharges must be between 6 and 15 cents per pound of BOD and that each agency could set the fee in its basin subject to federal approval.

In a sense the method of financing river-basin agencies is the key to their success. Substantial amounts of money would have to come from the federal government, partly as seed money to induce state governments to take part in the formation of the river-basin agencies and to surrender power to them. In part, federal money would also be needed to help agencies finance continuing operations. A promising possibility would be for the federal government to use the large sums now provided for local waste-treatment-plant construction subsidies to help finance river-basin agencies. If formation of such agencies were a condition for receipt of such money it would be a powerful inducement to state and local governments to cooperate. If subsidy funds were used to help finance river-basin agencies, it would be appropriate to broaden the purposes for which the funds could be used beyond the construction of sewage-treatment plants. For example, it might be desirable to permit river-basin agencies to use funds for in-stream reaeration, dam and reservoir construction, recreational facilities, and other activities, as well as for sewage-treatment plants. A further financial inducement to the formation of appropriate agencies would be to permit them to use all or part of their effluent-fee collections for operation of the agency. It would, however, not be desirable to restrict use of effluent-fee collections to a narrow range of activities, such as sewage-plant construction.

Federal money for river-basin agencies would be to perform functions now performed by EPA. Thus some federal money could represent a transfer of functions from EPA to the agencies.

Some Alternative Reforms

In spite of the clear advantages of the economic incentives provided by effluent fees discussed earlier, the predominant approach of actual environmental programs has been direct regulation. Requiring catalytic converters on cars, electrostatic precipitators and wet limestone scrubbers on utility smokestacks, and the like are examples of this approach. Indeed, the regulations are becoming increasingly detailed for a broad range of industries, almost to the point where firms in these industries can do nothing new without a disturbingly large number of highly subjective approvals. Why has the approach of direct regulation been so relentlessly pursued in light of its inflexibility, high costs, and frequently negligible environmental benefits?

The most basic and quite important answer to this question is that an effluent-fee approach often involves greater *monitoring costs*. That is, it is much easier to ascertain that a catalytic converter is being placed on a new car than it is to be certain that the new car emits pollutants at a certain level; similarly, one can know more readily whether scrubbers and precipitators are on smokestacks than one can know the volume of flue gases emitted at these smokestacks. This is, it should be emphasized, largely an historical problem; were environmental policy to be developed today for the first time, effluent-fee and other approaches based on economic incentives rather than police control would be advocated by most observers. (There are those who say "Charging an effluent-fee is selling the environment," but this rather irrational view can be seen for what it is when one recognizes that it is surely better to sell the environment than to give it away free!) Modern monitoring devices are available that can monitor emissions or effluent with considerable accuracy either continuously or intermittently. The point really is that while it is not feasible to adopt a pollution tax unless emissions can be monitored, this is equally true of an income tax: it is not possible to raise revenue with an income tax if one cannot determine an individual's income. But, like income, it is now the case that discharges can be measured with a fair degree of accuracy—and, of course, more accurate methods would become readily available as environmental policy moved increasingly toward an economic-incentive approach.

Still, it is unlikely that the current direct-regulation approach will melt away in the near future, as it is quite well entrenched. While we wait for initial applications of the economic-incentive approach (taxes, salable emissions rights, and so on) in areas where monitoring costs are low, what other reforms might we wish for? A first recommendation would be to make, as suggested in the preceding sentence, pollution permits transferable; this would enable those with very high costs of clean-up to purchase rights to pollute from those willing to sell them, namely those with low costs of clean-up. This would overcome the major disadvantage to the permit system as currently employed and would have an important advantage even over the effluent-fee system: with, say, emissions of only 70 percent of the previous year's amount being allowed, society will achieve a *known* future air or water quality, and what is unknown is what the equilibrium price will be for the pollution permits. With the effluent-fee approach, there would be a known tax but an uncertain environmental-quality improvement. The former outcome, greater certainty of environmental results, may well be preferred by decision-makers. The same issues, of course, about location or time of release of pollution surround the salable-permit system as they do effluent fees or direct regulation. The salable-permit system may well be more politically attractive than effluent fees, but it is really quite similar and the earlier discussion could have been conducted in terms of such a system.

Other reforms are more in the spirit of the current direct-regulation approach and are designed to reduce some of the most undesirable features of the existing environmental programs. For example, *variances*, which allow air or water polluters to violate environmental requirements under specified conditions (e.g., when costs or benefits do not justify the requirements), have the potential to offset the most undesirable aspects of uniform standards. Such variances have been used for years on a temporary basis, but they could be made permanent (although the moral impact of ignoring even unrealistically high standards should not be taken lightly—the attitude of Italian taxpayers comes to mind in this regard!). *Emission density zoning* also comes to mind as a way of giving greater locational flexibility to environmental controls than is allowed in current uniform standards. This approach would have standards varying by location (e.g., by acre or quarter square mile), and the stringency of the standards would be determined by the health, materials, and other damages discussed in Chapter 2. Population density would in most cases be a primary determinant of stringency and firms would have an incentive to move to locations where damages were lower. Another approach to this same problem would require *siting permits for major polluters*, under which new facilities were located not only with private costs in mind but also incorporating environmental damages. A new facility would be allowed in a high-damage area only if the private cost advantage of that location were clearly demonstrated to more than offset the environmental effects. This approach is more practical than it would first seem, in that there are actually a very small number of major polluters in even large metropolitan areas (for example, fewer than two dozen firms emit 90 percent of the industrial pollution of Chicago).

Other reforms would involve relaxation of *new-source performance standards*, which require much stronger emission limits on all new or substantially modified industrial sources of controlled air pollutants. If justified on cost grounds, as is sometimes the case, such differentially stringent requirements make sense. But in practice they operate much like tariffs in that they protect older firms from competition. Moreover, NSPS encourage firms to continue to operate their old, high-polluting facilities rather than move to newer plants that would be both technologically superior and environmentally cleaner. This is particularly important in light of the fact that most older firms are located in denser, higher-damage central areas, while the new plants that are discouraged are more likely to be located at suburban, lower-damage locations.

This point relates to a more general problem with existing legislation, the concept of *prevention of significant deterioration* (PSD). Throughout much of this book we have stressed the locational dimension of environmental quality. It makes a great deal of difference whether a ton of SO_2 is emitted in a corn field in the Midwest or in downtown New York City. Yet a 1974 court ruling (Sierra Club *vs.* EPA) required the 1977 Clean Air Act Amendments to guarantee that a pristine area having high air quality should not be allowed to deteriorate toward the level of the national standards. Certainly, in some cases this is justified, as for example the Everglades or certain other rare wildlife or scenic areas. But in general PSD is wildly inefficient, consigning the almost three-fourths of the population that live in urban areas to breathe dirtier air than they would if polluters were allowed to relocate to cleaner areas. The following quote from Harrison and Portney perhaps makes most clear the nature of the problems introduced by PSD requirements:

> The Byzantine system that resulted is a maze of maximum allowable increments, preconstruction reviews, background modeling of base-line air quality, and determination of best available control technology. It is roundly condemned by industrialists, state control authorities, and indeed many environmentalists as unworkable, unwieldy and, perhaps most damning of all, apparently unnecessary. It has been accused of inhibiting energy development in the coal- and mineral-rich western states and of intensifying the bias against new industrial growth there and in other clean-air regions. The effect has been to exacerbate the already bitter interregional conflicts arising out of differential energy and labor costs and the natural ebb and flow of population.
>
> There is little reason to retain the special protection the Clean Air Act affords to or imposes upon all unpolluted sections of the country. Air-quality standards in these regions should, like those elsewhere, be based on comparisons of benefits and costs, the benefits including not only health, materials damage, and ecological effects but also enhanced visibility. The latter is a particularly important benefit of pollution control around national parks and is likely by itself to justify discouraging industrial activity near the parks. Lowering the cost of locating in clean but unexceptional areas, while preserving strict controls in or near parks, will steer development into areas where it will harm neither people nor important environmental resources. That ought to be one of the major goals of air-quality policy, even if one side effect is to make some areas dirtier.[5]

Other points regarding current legislation and possible reform are that the distinction between "primary" and "secondary" standards makes absolutely no sense (as already mentioned in Chapter 2). The rational policy compares marginal benefits to marginal costs of clean-up and proceeds when the former exceed the latter. To look only at health effects on humans, as is done with the "primary" standards, is to ignore the host of other effects that accompany those health effects—the aesthetic, materials, and ecological effects, which are of increasing relative importance. The point, in short, is that marginal benefits of clean-up will be understated by standards that look only

5. D. Harrison, Jr., and P. R. Portney, "Making Ready for the Clean Air Act," p. 30.

at human health effects. Also related to standards is the issue of whether a single standard is appropriate for each criteria pollutant; there is considerable evidence that the marginal damage associated with, for example, particulates depends on the amount of SO_2 in the atmosphere. The potential exists to calculate schedules of various combinations of pollutants having equivalent marginal damages (perhaps to be called "isodamage" curves). With such curves, least-cost ways of obtaining equivalent air quality could be recommended. The process would be just like ordinary cost minimization subject to an output constraint or maximizing utility subject to a budget constraint (see Chapter 3). It is probable, however, that at this time or in the near future too little is known about interactions among pollutants to yield accurate isodamage curves; hence the recommendation that the implications of those interactions be explored is perhaps premature.

A number of policy improvements have emerged in recent years as a result of certain negative features of past legislation. The *emissions offset policy* gave somewhat greater flexibility to polluters, while guaranteeing that dirty air in the so-called "non-attainment" areas (areas not meeting national environmental standards) not get dirtier. The idea, in brief, is that rather than prohibit industrial growth altogether in such areas, EPA would permit additional emissions as long as the firms involved arranged for *more* than offsetting reductions in the same pollutants from existing sources in the area. The popular *bubble policy* has not as yet amounted to too terribly much, although several million dollars have been saved under its provisions. The basic notion is that although some overall emission limit is to apply to each polluter, the specifics of how that overall limit is to be attained are left up to the producer. The advantage is that costs are lowered by letting the firms find the least-cost ways of meeting requirements, rather than (as in the past) requiring detailed specific controls at each point of emission throughout a plant. Indeed, the bubble notion has a great deal of potential and is being expanded to large numbers of firms, so that they can transfer among themselves the pollution-control effort, leading to control effort being conducted by those firms that are relatively most efficient at cleaning up. Of course, these elaborate programs would not be necessary if the effluent-fee approach discussed earlier were adopted; many of the recommendations given in this section are in the nature of "second-best" solutions.

Most of the preceding discussion has, at least implicitly, been concerned with air quality. But most of the recommended options, such as bubbles, offsets, and the like, apply equally to water. There are a couple of differences, however, and they stem from the differences between the air and water media. Most obviously we have much greater flexibility in dealing with water since we do not breathe it. There is even less reason why all watersheds should be of uniform quality than there is in the case of air. In fact, experiments in Europe indicate that both substantial cost savings *and* perceived improvements in environmental quality can be obtained through separation of use. In the case of air, the principle is similar to having separate smoking and non-smoking areas in a restaurant. A uniform standard, say allowing only one cigarette with your meal, satisfies neither the non-smokers nor the smokers. The separation of use, not usually available in the case of air but nearly always available in the case of water, is far superior: some streams could be specialized into pollution receptors with no recreation allowed while others could be specialized into recreational areas with no pollution allowed. Both groups in society that benefit from the use of water could benefit without conflict, much like having smoking and non-smoking areas. If the polluted stream extended into a larger stream as a tributary, or if damage to the ocean were an issue, then the entire polluted stream could be treated, usually much more inexpensively than if each polluter cleaned up at the plant.

Another difference between air and water policy relates to the distinction between point and nonpoint sources for water. Existing controls have dealt predominantly with point sources, while at current levels of control it is now the case that marginal costs of further such controls are very high and the potential environmental gains are low. Nonpoint sources, such as urban runoff, agricultural runoff of fertilizers and pesticides, and so on should clearly be controlled relatively more and point sources relatively less. As it becomes realized that current standards are often violated by nonpoint sources, even if point sources emitted nothing at all, the direction of policy will no doubt change.

In closing this chapter, we would like to reiterate our strong belief that we should move toward policy approaches that are based upon economic incentives. If one does not think carefully about them, they may appear to be quite complicated and perhaps "just another tax," yet the convoluted, often inconsistent, and extremely detailed direct-control approach has been, and will continue to be, a cripplingly inefficient means of attaining the high level of environmental quality demanded in a wealthy nation such as ours.

DISCUSSION QUESTIONS AND PROBLEMS

1. What kind of government institutions would you propose for solid-waste disposal and reuse? How would the institution's directors be chosen and what would be its power and responsibilities?

2. Estimate government revenues that might result from a set of reasonable nationwide effluent fees on a few important pollutants.

3. In what ways should pollution-control policies toward the electricity-generating industry differ from those toward other industries?

4. One way to make river-basin agencies responsive to the electorate is to make them go to elected legislatures for their annual budgets. Another way is to require that they raise funds by selling environmental services to the public. A third way is to permit them to levy taxes and make the directorship an elective office. Which way do you think would be best?

5. Economists mostly oppose designation of particular government revenue sources for particular expenditures should be subject to the political process, not to the vagaries of revenue sources. What use should be made of effluent-fee collections?

REFERENCES AND FURTHER READING

Baumol, William, and Oates, Wallace. *The Theory of Environmental Policy.* Englewood Cliffs, N.J.: Prentice-Hall, 1975.

Dorfman, Robert, and Dorfman, Nancy, eds. *Economics of the Environment.* 2nd ed. New York: Norton, 1977.

Friedlander, Ann, ed. *Air Pollution and Administrative Control.* Cambridge, Mass.: MIT Press, 1978.

Harrison, D., Jr., and Portney, P. R. "Making Ready for the Clean Air Act." *Regulation* 5, no. 2 (Mar.-April 1981): 24–31.

Kneese, Allen, and Bower, Blair. *Managing Water Quality: Economics, Technology, Institutions.* Baltimore: Johns Hopkins University Press, for Resources for the Future, Inc., 1968.

Löf, George, and Kneese, Allen. *Economics of Water Utilization in the Beet Sugar Industry.* Baltimore: Johns Hopkins University Press, for Resources for the Future, Inc., 1968.

Mäler, Karl-Göran. *Environmental Economics.* Baltimore: Johns Hopkins University Press, for Resources for the Future, Inc., 1974.

Tolley, G. S., Graves, P. E., and Blomquist, G. C. *Environmental Policy: Elements of Environmental Analysis.* Cambridge, Mass.: Ballinger, 1981. Chapter 8.

Tolley, G. S., Graves, P. E., and Cohen, A. S. *Environmental Policy: Air Quality*. Cambridge, Mass.: Ballinger, 1982. Chapter 17.

Tolley, G. S., Blomquist, G. C., and Yaron, D., *Environmental Policy: Water Quality*. Cambridge, Mass.: Ballinger, 1983. Chapter 10.

Part IV

FOREIGN AND GLOBAL PROBLEMS

This book is mainly concerned with pollution problems in the United States and the programs to control them. There was a time when one could study pollution problems abroad, but the only interesting government pollution-control programs were those in the United States. That time is now past. Most European and many other countries now have elaborate pollution-control programs. Each country's program borrows some elements from abroad but has its own local flavor. Although countries borrow from each other's environmental programs, they rarely precede program formulation with careful study of what is best borrowed from whom. At this point in history, the United States can learn a great deal about pollution control from abroad. Chapter 11 begins that task by examining case studies from other countries.

In many ways, the most intriguing and complex pollution problems are those that spill across national boundaries. Of these, the most interesting are those that affect many or all countries in more or less the same way. These global problems are scientifically subtle and are frustrating from the point of view of international controls. Chapter 12 discusses several such global environmental problems.

Chapter 11

Environmental Problems and Policies Abroad

Contrary to the impression conveyed by some popular writers on the subject, Americans did not invent pollution. Other countries have pollution problems, and in many they are more serious and of longer duration than those in the United States. Nor did the United States invent national pollution-control programs, although we pioneered the early stages of national program development and influenced many countries in the development of their programs.

The first pollution caused by human activity probably resulted from planting crops and grazing, both of which can cause soil erosion. The earliest important effects may have been on the supply of arable land rather than water and air pollution. But eroded soil washes into streams and overgrazing worsens dust storms. Later, anecdotal evidence indicates that air- and water-pollution problems were severe in preindustrial European cities. Indeed, sanitation probably placed severe limits on city sizes and life expectancy in medieval cities was far below that in the surrounding countryside. The Industrial Revolution introduced new environmental problems resulting from rapid growth of materials use and energy conversion. Nineteenth-century English and European cities had severe air- and water-pollution problems.

All countries have environmental problems, but their nature and severity vary greatly from one country to another. Broadly speaking, pollution problems are more severe the greater the discharges of wastes relative to the capacity of the receiving media to absorb them without impairing the quality of the media. Thus, other things equal, high-density countries have more serious pollution problems than low-density countries. Japan and Western European countries such as France, England, and the Netherlands have serious pollution problems. In this respect, the United States us unusually well placed. Among industrialized countries, our population density is as low as almost any, with the exceptions of Canada and Australia, and even there people are concentrated in small parts of the countries.

A perennial source of controversy and confusion is the relationship between pollution and industrialization. Some naíve enthusiasts believe that pollution problems are exclusive to highly industrialized countries and that they would go away if we returned to a simpler agrarian economy. The view is badly distorted and leads to dramatically incorrect conclusions. Discharges to the environment equal withdrawals, and both are about proportionate to production of commodities and services, except for reuse of materials. Total production and income per capita are certainly much greater in industrialized than in other economies, and discharges to the environment are correspondingly greater. In that sense, industrialized countries have the most serious pollution problems. But environmental quality depends on the time, form, and location of discharges far more than on their volume. Industrialized countries are high-income countries, and residents of high-income countries wish to devote large amounts of resources to environmental protection. Discharges can be made much less polluting if resources are devoted to making them innocuous, as has been seen throughout this book. All high-income countries devote substantial resources to the removal, treatment, and disposal of wastes that low-income countries view as having opportunity costs, in terms of forgone other goods, that are too high. A simpler, though slightly misleading, way to express this point is to say that poor countries "can't afford" a clean environment, while rich countries can.

The most dramatic difference in environmental quality between high- and low-income countries concerns the public water supply. High-income countries devote resources to treating sewage and drinking water, to withdrawal of drinking water in safe places, to protecting watersheds upstream of drinking water withdrawals, and to removal of treated or untreated wastes to safe places. Poor countries "cannot afford" such activities. The result is that their populations (and many tourists) are afflicted with amoebic dysentery, diarrhea, and other serious ills conveyed through drinking water. Such diseases are debilitating and impair people's ability to produce and otherwise function normally. Unsafe public water supplies are endemic in poor countries, but are rare in rich countries.

Measured by damage to human health, poor countries have more serious pollution problems than rich countries. Many people, including some in poor countries, resist the notion that poor countries have serious environmental problems, because they think of environmental problems in terms of solid wastes and air pollution. Solid wastes are about proportionate to commodity production and are, indeed, a much bigger problem in rich than in poor countries, although litter is very much apparent in many poor countries. As was seen in Chapter 5, airborne discharges are closely related to energy conversion which, in turn, is strongly correlated with GNP. It is therefore more serious in high- than low-income countries. Furthermore, air pollution has disproportionate effects on old people. It is therefore logically of greater concern in high-income countries where the life expectancy exceeds seventy years than in low-income countries where it may be less than forty years.

Environmental problems, like all other problems, are more serious in poor than rich countries. But they are different, and require a different focus of analysis and different solutions.

Not only did the United States not invent pollution, we did not invent national pollution-control programs. In the 1960s and early 1970s, American pollution-control programs were already among the most elaborate and far-reaching, if not among the most imaginative, in the world. Officials from many countries studied our programs in the course of designing their own. By the mid-1970s many countries had developed pollution-control programs, some good and some bad. But almost all pollution-control programs have unique national flavors, depending on national customs, ways of thought, institutions, and legal structures. For example, the West German program has always placed greater emphasis on hazardous chemical substances than have we, although this is rapidly changing in the United States. The American program is now no more imaginative or effective than several others, and it is more bureaucratic and plodding than the best programs elsewhere.

This chapter illustrates environmental problems and programs abroad by three case studies: Sweden, Japan, and South Korea. The countries are by no means randomly selected or representative. They were selected in part because each is representative of a particular kind of problem and program. But they were selected in part because their environmental problems and programs are unusually well documented. Beyond a doubt, their national pollution-control programs are more thorough and effective than those of most other countries. The three economies differ dramatically from each other: Sweden's has living standards which are among the highest in the world, Japan's are somewhat greater than half those in the United States, and Korea's are roughly 10 percent those in the United States. But all three are rapidly growing countries.

Sweden

Sweden is a small country of about eight million people, somewhat more than the state of New Jersey. Its overall population density is somewhat less than that in the United States. Most people live in the southern part of the country, but even there density is less than on the East Coast of the United States. Sweden is a very high-income country, with income per capita about the same as that in the United States. The economy is highly industrialized, with about the same percentage of GNP originating in manufacturing as in the United States. It has a broad spectrum of heavy and polluting industries, including metals and chemical industries.

Like other Scandinavian countries, Sweden has a population that is educated, public spirited, and responsible. Many decisions are made by formal and informal cooperation and consultation between government and private representatives of business and labor. It is the envy of those who favor a society based on consultation and cooperation instead of on competition and a careful distinction between the rights and responsibilities of the government and the private sector. Swedish law and practice give great discretion to government officials on the confident assumption that it will be employed with integrity and judgment. It is a society in substantial contrast with the American ideal of a government of laws, not of men. The sense of trust, responsibility, and consultation pervades the Swedish approach to environmental protection.

Prior to 1969, Swedish environmental measures were scattered among public health and other laws and regulations. In 1969, the Environmental Protection Act and a related ordinance formulated a broad program to protect and enhance all aspects of the environment, including air, water, and solid waste discharges. It is not possible to date the birth of the American program so definitively, but our national air- and water-pollution-control programs predate the Swedish legislation by at least six and thirteen years, respectively. In contrast with the twists and turns of American legislation, the Swedish program was laid down once and has remained in place since.

The Environmental Protection Act states that polluting discharges are to be limited to the extent feasible, taking into account the nature and extent of likely damages, technology available for discharge abatement, and costs of abatement. This broad principle is in contrast with similar statements in American legislation which limit or preclude consideration of costs in deciding how much abatement is to be required. In carrying out the provisions of the act, plant locations, as well as the technology of production and discharge abatement, may be controlled. Both existing and new facilities are required to make modifications to control polluting discharges. It is more expensive to control discharges in an existing facility than in one designed and built to control discharges, and it was felt that existing facilities should not be penalized by laws passed after they were built. Subsidies were paid for five years after the act was passed, but terminated in 1975. Note how this approach differs from the new-source performance standards discussed in Chapter 10.

Environmental legislation in the United States either specifies discharge standards in complex laws or narrowly limits the standards that administrative bodies can set. The Swedish act is in dramatic contrast, merely specifying in broad terms the criteria to be used in setting discharge requirements. American laws, and their legislative history, show a deep distrust by Congress of administrative agencies, whereas the Swedish approach is based on the confident assumption that the administrative agencies will interpret the criteria responsibly and consistently. The American situation reflects the constitutional and political separation between the legislative and executive branches of government, in contrast with the parliamentary system in which executive department heads are elected members of parliament.

Every Swedish facility likely to cause serious pollution must apply for a discharge permit to the National Franchise Board of Environmental Protection. In this regard, the Swedish program was a model for the American permit system established for discharges to water in 1973. The board functions like a court of law. Permit applications must contain complete information and must be published so that interested parties can testify at a public hearing. A permit decision has the force of law and can be appealed only to the government. In the United States, in contrast, permits are granted by administrative bodies with few judicial requirements but can be, and frequently are, appealed to state and federal courts.

The act also contains a provision for those damaged by pollution to sue polluters for damages. In principle it is undesirable to permit suits for damages if the government regulates discharges optimally. If discharge regulations permit discharges that equate marginal benefits and marginal costs, the remaining discharges are a desirable deterrent to people from activities that would cause them to be injured by the pollution. Compensation would reduce the deterrent and thus cause excessive damage from pollution. For example, remaining smoke from an optimally controlled smokestack provides a desirable deterrent to downwind residential locations. If people are compensated for smoke damage, they are indifferent to locating there or elsewhere; then too many people do locate there and hence excessive smoke damage results. In the absence of discharge regulations, provision for damage suits can accomplish much the same goal. Damage suits might be an alternative to regulations or effluent fees. In practice, estimating damages on a case-by-case basis is beyond the capability of courts. Damage suits tend to be successful when there has been a gross violation of the letter or spirit of laws controlling pollution.

The board gradually established guidelines for discharges, usually after careful consultation with industry representatives. The guidelines take account of damage done, costs of pollution abatement, technology available, and Sweden's international competitive position. The board normally stays close to the guidelines in issuing permits, but sometimes modifies them for individual circumstances. Nevertheless, an average permit application requires a year. During the first five years of its life, the board granted seven hundred permits. About three times that number were granted by a less thorough administrative process to less polluting facilities. As was reported in Chapter 6, the American water-pollution program has generated about forty thousand permit applications.

The Swedish program seems to have worked well. It has been administered conscientiously and objectively. There has been no evidence of corruption or other scandal. At least in the case of waterborne discharges, the total has been reduced during the life of the act. The most difficult task for a discharge-setting agency is to permit discharge levels that equate marginal abatement costs among sources. There is no way to know how close the board has come to achieving that end. The ultimate goal of any pollution-control program is improvement in ambient environmental quality. The Swedes long debated whether they needed to monitor ambient concentrations, and established a comprehensive monitoring system in the mid-1970s, now firmly in place in the 1980s.

The Swedish environmental protection program applies to both government and private dischargers. As in other countries, local governments are responsible for sewage-treatment plants. Also as in other countries, the national government has provided large subsidies to local governments for sewage-treatment-plant construction. The result has been that, as in the Unized States, most of the urban population was served by secondary treatment plants by the mid-1970s.

The Swedish and American pollution-control programs differ in ways that are characteristic of the two countries. The basic Swedish legislation is simple and procedural, merely assigning responsibility for discharge regulation to an agency and specifying procedures for setting standards. In contrast, American national environmental legislation is long and detailed, specifying tortuous layers of overlapping and vague responsibilities among agencies and levels of government and detailed instructions intended to force the executive to carry out Congress's intentions exactly. Both countries rely for water effluent on a discharge-permit system. In Sweden, guidelines for permits are formulated with closer and more explicit consultation with affected private groups than in the United States. Application for and issuing of permits is done in quasi-judicial hearings in Sweden, whereas it is an administrative activity in the United States. Appeals to the courts are common in the United States, but unheard of in Sweden.

It is impossible to tell which system has been more effective. In previous chapters, it was shown that the American program has reduced the discharges and ambient concentrations of pollutants it has controlled, but the program was criticized as being unimaginative and clumsy. The Swedish program is undoubtedly administratively simpler than the American program. The presumption must be that the Swedish quasi-judicial permit program finds it difficult to equate marginal abatement costs among discharge activities. At least, the board does not appear to devote much effort to careful balancing of marginal costs. In neither country has benefit-cost analysis played much of a role in discharge regulation. And neither country has shown much interest in using economic incentives as part of its pollution-control program, although the United States is moving in this direction in the 1980s.

Japan

Japan has among the world's most serious potential environmental problems. Its population is half that of the United States, whereas its land areas is smaller than California. Its overall population density is more than ten times that in the United States. Much of the country is too mountainous for farming or cities, so its people are crowded on its small amount of relatively flat land.

Japan has a large and high-income economy. It has the world's third largest GNP, after the United States and the Soviet Union. During the quarter-century following World War II, it had as high a growth rate as has ever been recorded by any country during a comparable period. Japan transformed itself from a desperately poor, war-ravaged country into a modern, wealthy, industrialized society. Japan could be classified among developing countries in the 1950s. Its period of extraordinary growth has meant that it is among the world's industrial giants in the 1980s.

Japan has the potential for almost every environmental problem known to humanity. It has large amounts of heavy industry and other polluting activities. Population and industrial output per square mile on a stretch of land along the Pacific Ocean from Tokyo to Osaka, about the same distance as from New York to Washington, are probably as great as anywhere in the world. Activity in the region places great stress on the capacity of the ambient environment to absorb wastes. Japan now has more than twenty motor vehicles per one hundred population, near the ratio found in many Western European countries. Japan has hot, sultry summers, with cities subject to frequent inversions. Its rivers are short and small, with only limited capacity to absorb wastes. Waterborne discharges quickly end up in estuaries or in the surrounding sea, the source of Japan's traditional seafood protein supply. Japanese agriculture is rice-based, carried on at extreme intensity and with large amounts of chemical fertilizer. The only important environmental problems not potentially present in Japan are those resulting from the mining of fuels and metals. Japan has only meager known deposits of metals and fossil fuels; most are imported. The massive solid-waste-disposal activities associated with mining are therefore unknown in Japan.

Japan's population is among the world's most highly educated. Like most Western European countries, it is a parliamentary democracy. As Sweden, Japan has a tradition of a sophisticated, highly educated, and responsible civil service. But government is a much smaller part of the labor force and of the economy in Japan than it is in Sweden or the United States. The Japanese government has only limited functions. It owns, regulates, and controls business activity to a much smaller extent than in Sweden or the United States. Relationships between government and business tend to be less formal and less institutionalized in Japan than in Sweden. The quasi-judicial Environmental Board that administers Swedish discharge permits would be quite foreign to the Japanese. They tend to avoid explicitly adversary proceedings, instead settling issues by discussion and negotiation among relevant parties.

Like the Swedes, the Japanese formulated a national environmental program somewhat later than the Americans. The first comprehensive environmental law was passed in 1967. It was extensively revised in 1970, and an administrative body, the Environment Agency, was established in 1971. The environmental movement has been highly political in Japan and the United States. In both countries national pollution-abatement programs have been adopted after intensive lobbying by citizen groups. In neither country has environmental protection been a partisan issue in the sense of one political party favoring a program and another opposing it. Important national programs have been legislated with the strong support of major political parties in both Japan and the United States.

Like those in Sweden and in contrast with those in the United States, Japanese pollution-control laws are simple and procedural. They assign responsibility for setting environmental standards to the Environment Agency, giving it broad discretion as to the pollutants for which standards are to be set and as to the stringency of the standards. The agency has concentrated its efforts on a relatively small number of pollutants. It has set air-pollution standards for particulates, sulfur oxides, and nitrogen oxides. It has set water-pollution standards for heavy metals and a few toxic agents. Little attention has so far been paid to organic discharges to water bodies. No careful benefit-cost studies appear to have been undertaken to decide which pollutants to control in light of known or suspected health damages and in light of known technology and costs of discharge abatement.

For the pollutants it chose to concentrate on, the agency first set ambient standards. Ambient standards are goals that administrative agencies aspire to achieve in both Japan and the United States. The ambient standards set by the Japanese have been very ambitious, indeed. They represent even higher ambient environmental quality than corresponding American standards, although the initial ambient quality was worse in Japan than in the United States for most pollutants.

In the United States, state and local governments have on the whole preferred less stringent ambient standards than the federal government, fearing loss of local employment and controls on local transportation. In Japan, on the contrary, local governments tend to set more stringent ambient standards than the uniform nationally set ambient standards.

Ambient standards have been taken very seriously in Japan. The Environment Agency has used them to determine discharge standards for industries. Discharge standards vary depending on a host of details specific to particular industrial plants. The standards finally set appear to result from prolonged negotiation between agency officials and managers from private industries. But the standards appear to be very stringent and to be taken very seriously as goals to be achieved by the industries. The procedure by which standards are set is administrative and confidential, with only rare public exposure and hardly any appeal to judicial or quasi-judicial bodies. In this respect, the Swedish procedure, with its public quasi-judicial emphasis, is at the opposite extreme from the Japanese procedure.

There is no reason to believe that the informal and confidential Japanese procedure has resulted in less stringent emissions controls than the Swedish or American procedures. The easiest comparison is with automobile-emission standards. Japanese cars sold in the United States must of course meet the American emissions standards. The

Japanese therefore decided in 1969 that cars made and sold in Japan should be tested with the American test and should meet the standards required by cars sold in the United States. Because Japanese companies had to manufacture cars to meet American standards anyway, it was decided that they should beet the same standards in Japan. It was mentioned in Chapter 9 that a Japanese company was the first to meet the original American 1975 emission standards. By the mid-1970s the Japanese government decided that cars sold in Japan should meet more stringent emission standards than cars sold in the United States. It therefore set emission standards for 1978 cars that were much stricter than even the original American 1976 standards. It was shown in Chapter 10 that the American companies perhaps never will be required to meet the original American 1976 standards, particularly since the NO_x standard appears to be permanently relaxed. Indeed, it is doubtful that the benefits exceed the costs of going to the 1985 standards (which have not changed since 1981), at least in the United States. At first Japanese manufacturers complained that they could not meet the more stringent 1978 Japanese standards. But by 1976 all the major Japanese automobile manufacturers agreed that they would be able to meet the 1978 Japanese standards with no more than modest cost increases.

There is no publicly available evidence that the Environment Agency did careful benefit-cost analysis of alternative standards in choosing the 1978 Japanese auto-emissions standards. It may be that they are somewhat more stringent than is justified. But the speed, versatility, and boldness of the Japanese manufacturers in meeting the extraordinary technological challenge of the 1978 standards is extremely impressive. Since about 1973, the Japanese have been the world leaders in automobile-emission-control technology. Also impressive is the ability the Environment Agency has shown to choose extremely stringent standards that would challenge the manufacturers to a strong technological effort, yet would not be so stringent that the agency would have to relent and thus undermine its credibility.

In the United States environmental laws have become extremely complex and have imposed rigid actions on the executive branch of the government because Congress does not trust the administrative agency to enforce reasonably stringent standards. In Japan, the law gives the administrative agency much more flexibility than does American law, yet the Japanese have set and enforced far more stringent standards than the Americans. That would not be possible without a high-quality, dedicated, and responsible group of government officials in charge of the program. They must have intimate and confidential discussions with industry officials, yet maintain their independence.

As a technical and administrative feat, the Japanese auto-emissions-control program is a marvel. Although less fundamental technological advances are involved, the other aspects of the Japanese pollution-control program are equally impressive feats of speed, flexibility, and determination. But no careful benefit-cost analysis appears to have underlain any aspect of the Japanese pollution-control program. The setting of emissions standards has resulted from judgment, determination, and careful negotiation between government and industry officials. Furthermore, the Japanese have shown hardly any more interest in economic incentives in pollution abatement than have the Americans. Finally, at least with respect to automobiles, the Japanese emissions-control program has paid no more attention to cars on the road than has the American program. The basic emission-control technology developed by the Japanese, the stratified-charge engine, is inherently more durable than the devices on which American companies rely. But it is hard to imagine that Japanese cars will meet standards very long after they are manufactured unless vehicles are driven, inspected, and maintained carefully. It will be interesting to observe how the Japanese solve this problem.

Throughout the Japanese pollution-control program, standards are enforced by detailed negotiation between government and industry officials. Standards are set for particular plants according to the plant's existing technology, its economic viability, and the cost and available technology of alternative control systems. Government officials play active parts in planning new industrial plants and in modifying existing plants. Negotiations are publicly exposed only in the face of the most serious disagreement between government and private officials. The result is extreme embarrassment on all sides, public apologies, and sometimes disgrace. Administrative penalties for standards violations are imposed only rarely and as a last resort. Disagreements are almost never permitted to go to the courts.

An American can only marvel at the Japanese system. He would predict that it would lead to corruption of government officials, endless and futile negotiation, and little concrete improvement. None of these things has happened in Japan. Instead, ambient concentrations of most pollutants on which the Japanese have focused their efforts have declined steadily since the early 1970s. Sulfur-oxide concentrations, which were very high in Tokyo and elsewhere in Japan, have fallen more than 50 percent. Ambient carbon-monoxide concentrations have also fallen steadily since 1970. Likewise, concentrations of heavy metals and toxic substances in water bodies have decreased substantially. As in the United States, little progress has been made in reducing concentrations of nitrogen oxides and the resulting smog. Likewise, dissolved oxygen is still low in Japanese water bodies, since the government has not made major efforts to abate organic discharges to water bodies.

In the previous section, the Swedish program of compensating victims of pollution was discussed, and the theoretical issue of compensation was analyzed. The Japanese have by far the most elaborate program of compensation of pollution victims in the world. They use three kinds of compensation for environmental damage.[1]

First is private compensation. When pollution can be attributed to a particular source and when those damaged are well organized, there are sometimes negotiations between the two parties that result in compensation for damages. Tanker oil spills that damage fishing grounds where the fishermen are organized in a cooperative are the best example. Such compensation may be an out-of-court settlement if liability is specified by the law. But it is rare for such cases to go to court in Japan and laws do not state clearly under what circumstances compensation must be paid. Private compensation can hardly work well as a general remedy for pollution damage. Most commonly those damaged cannot identify particular sources of offending discharges. And those damaged are often not organized, unless they constitute, for example, an occupational group with many common interests.

Second is judicial compensation. In Japan, as elsewhere, laws provide liability for nuisances. In a few cases, Japanese courts have awarded compensation for environmental damages. Such cases are tried under general nuisance laws not written with specifically environmental damages in mind. Judicial compensation suffers from the defects of private compensation: The source must be identifiable and those damaged must be organized. Such court cases have been rare in Japan, although those that have been tried have been successful

---

1. See the OECD report, *Environmental Policy in Japan*, for a fuller discussion.

for plaintiffs. The most dramatic and tragic cases, which galvanized the Japanese environmental movement, have involved heavy-metals discharged into water bodies from industrial plants. The metals entered the food chain and were ingested by humans eating seafood. Dozens of victims died or were maimed. The most tragic and best-known case is that in Minimata, where citizens were poisoned by mercury ingested by eating polluted fish.

The third type of compensation is administered by the government. A 1973 law provides that those living or working in areas designated by the government as high-pollution areas can be compensated if they suffer from disabilities that might be pollution-related. For example, a victim of emphysema who lives in a neighborhood where sulfur-oxide levels are high can apply for compensation. Compensation is financed by a tax on polluters, but it is not closely related to actual discharges and cannot therefore be thought of as an effluent fee. This program is superior to private and judicial compensation in that it is not necessary to identify the specific discharges that caused damage, which is normally not possible with air pollution. Victims do not have to prove that disabilities were caused by pollution. It is rarely possible to establish, for example, to what extent emphysema is caused by air pollution or by smoking. It is politically difficult to refuse to compensate those who suffer disabilities that might to some extent have been caused or exacerbated by pollution. There is danger that such a program might become a political grab bag under which any group that suffers from any disability that might be pollution-related would demand compensation. There are few disabilities that could not be pollution-related. There is also the theoretical problem that compensation will not give people an incentive to avoid damages, even when they could at relatively low cost.

The Japanese pollution-control program is like the Swedish and American programs in that it relies on direct controls instead of economic incentives. It is in contrast with the Swedish program in that it relies heavily on administrative bodies with broad discretion and few elements of due process. The Japanese program is characterized by unpublicized negotiations between government and industry officials, whereas the Swedish program is characterized by quasi-judicial proceedings and publicly made decisions. It is remarkable that two such different programs work so well. The Japanese system has characteristics that in the United States lead to prolonged decision-making, few positive results, and corruption of public officials. Yet in terms of results it must be judged the world's most successful pollution-abatement program.

South Korea

South Korea is a poor and very rapidly developing country. Income per capita is as noted at the outset about 10 percent of that in the United Stated, less than one-fifth of that in Japan. Since the early 1960s, real income and output have grown about 8 percent per year in Korea. This extremely rapid growth rate implies that living standards are rising more than twice as fast as in the United States and many other developed countries. At the end of the Korean War in 1953, South Korea was a devastated and desperately poor country, with living standards hardly above those in the world's poorest countries in South Asia and Africa. Korea's recent period of extremely rapid growth has almost eliminated the most desperate poverty and has created large groups of prosperous working- and middle-class citizens.

Korea is a very crowded country. Among countries larger than city-states, only Taiwan has a greater population density than Korea. Korea's density is 15 times that of the United States, 1.2 times that of Japan, and 4.2 times that of mainland China. The country is mostly mountainous, and most of its people and industry are crowded in the Seoul-Inchon area and along the southern rim of the country on the Sea of Japan. Korea faces all the environmental problems of poor countries including those of sanitation and public-water supply. As a rapidly industrializing and urbanizing country, it also faces the air- and water-pollution problems characteristic of industrialized countries. All its environmental problems are worsened by its concentration of people on a small peninsula.

Poor countries lack the government structure, data, and communication system that rich countries use to administer elaborate pollution-control programs. Korea's government has been dedicated to the industrialization of the country. It promotes industrialization by a large number of formal and informal controls, subsidies, and stimuli for economic activity. Until recently, the government and people of Korea have felt that industrialization was a much higher national priority than environmental protection.

There is a tendency in poor countries to believe that environmental protection is a luxury they cannot afford. People feel it is much more important to build factories that can produce things people need desperately than to worry about the wastes that factories discharge. There is something to this view, but some distinctions need to be made. In a very poor country such as India, where life expectancy is hardly more than half that in rich countries, it makes little sense to worry greatly about air pollution. Relatively few people survive to an age at which the debilitating effects of air-pollution-related disease are important. In a country that can afford almost no provision for the elderly, concern about the effects of air pollution on them is probably not the place to start.

Water quality, however, is a different matter. As was stated in the introduction, drinking-water pollution in poor countries causes serious health problems that affect people's welfare and productivity.

By the mid-1970s, South Korea was out of the category of very poor countries, and officials had to begin to think carefully about priorities in pollution control. Beyond a doubt, Korea's most serious environmental problem is pollution of municipal water supplies by domestic sewage. The traditional means of disposal of domestic sewage in Korea and other developing countries was to collect it daily from households in tanks and haul it to farms where it was used as fertilizer. Eating uncooked vegetables that have been fertilized by human wastes causes diarrhea and other intestinal disorders. But rice and other traditional Korean vegetables are always cooked before eating. Westerners who like raw vegetables in salads are the main sufferers from this source.

Some of the sewage used as fertilizer washed into streams. In addition some part of urban sewage was always dumped directly into streams. In recent years, fertilization of crops by human wastes has given way to chemical fertilizers. At the same time, Korea urbanized at a phenomenal rate, resulting in a major problem of sewage collection and disposal. Gradually sewers have been built. Ninety percent of Seoul's population, and much of that in other large cities, is now sewered. Seoul's first sewage-treatment plant, serving about one-fifth the city's population, only opened in 1976, but most Korean cities are still without treatment plants. Thus the main function of urban sewer systems is to collect sewage and discharge it to the nearest river or estuary.

In a densely populated country such as Korea, it is inevitable that many communities withdraw drinking water downstream from discharge points of other communities' sewage. Some communities discharge sewage upstream from Seoul and others withdraw water downstream from Seoul on the Han River, Korea's largest and most important river. In fact, Seoul withdraws some of its water downstream from where some of its wastes are discharged.

Serious debilitating diseases such as the diarrhea or amoebic dysentary already mentioned are spread by the pollution of drinking water from untreated or incompletely degraded sewage. Typhoid is even more important in some countries. In Korea such diseases have become less common in recent years because of investments in water-supply and sewage systems. Withdrawals have been moved upstream, water is treated before use, and wastes are treated more than before. But waterborne intestinal diseases are still an important health problem in Korea and in other poor countries. Water quality in urban estuaries and river stretches is low. Stretches of the Han and its tributaries in Seoul are anaerobic during some months each year. At such times they stink and merely convey wastes to the ocean while hardly degrading them. Some stretches of the Han never reach the four to six parts per million (ppm) of dissolved oxygen necessary to support most kinds of fish life.

In contrast with the United States, most organic discharges to Korean water bodies are from municipal sewage, not from industry. In Chapter 6, it was shown that only a small part of American organic discharges come from municipal sewage. In Korea, the proportion is much higher; industrial organic discharges are less than 20 percent of the total. Two facts account for the difference. First, Korea is less industrialized than the United States, so municipal wastes are larger relative to industrial wastes than in the United States. Second, almost all municipal wastes are subject to secondary treatment in the United States, whereas in Korea they are mostly untreated. The Korean situation has and will continue to become more like the United States as the country industrializes and as municipal wastes are better treated.

Improved water-supply and sewage-treatment systems are high-priority investments in Korea. Once a country's living standards are above the level of destitute poverty, substantial investments in public water supply and sewage systems are likely to have high benefit-cost ratios. But Korea is not yet free of public-health damages from water pollution.

Air pollution has received relatively little government attention in Korea because it is felt, probably correctly, to be a lower priority problem than many others. Nevertheless, the Koreans have collected substantial amounts of data on the subject. Discharge data have mostly been inferred from data on fuel use, but some ambient air-quality measurements have been made directly. Total tons of airborne discharges are in about the same proportion to GNP in Korea as in the United States. Ambient air quality depends in part on discharges per unit of land area. Korean discharges per unit of land area are about half those in the United States, mainly reflecting much lower Korean living standards and energy use than in the United States. The foregoing suggests that ambient air quality should not be much worse in Korea than in the United States. But nationwide ambient air-quality data are unavailable in both countries. Most ambient data pertain to a few cities, and Korean production and population are heavily concentrated in a few dense cities.

The transportation sector accounts for less than one-fifth of airborne discharges in Korea, whereas it was shown in Chapter 5 that it accounts for more than half of American airborne discharges. Cars are uncommon in Korea; most transporattion takes place in diesel buses and trucks, which emit relatively few pollutants. Discharges from industry and from thermal electric plants have grown rapidly in recent years, accounting together for more than half of all airborne discharges at this time. Continuing rapid industrialization will further this trend. Traditional home heating in Korea is done by burning coal briquettes, which discharge large quantities of sulfur oxides and carbon monoxide to the winter air in residential areas. Hot air is circulated through the house by flues under floors, and pollutants frequently leak into houses from cracks in flues, causing death or disability, especially from carbon monoxide. Indoor pollution problems are of increasing importance in the United States as well, particularly as a result of the higher energy costs leading to almost completely insulated homes.

Limited data on ambient concentrations show high and rising sulfur oxide levels in the air around Korean cities. Sulfur oxide levels appear to be below the peak levels recorded in Japanese cities during the late 1960s, but Japanese levels have currently fallen well below those in Korean cities. There have been no Korean studies of health damages from sulfur oxides similar to those described in Chapter 5. But ambient concentrations in Korea are well above those that appear to have caused serious health damage in the United States and Western Europe.

The Korean government has no comprehensive program to abate

air pollution. It has devoted enormous effort and resources to helping build industries in Korea that can compete with those in Japan and elsewhere. Koreans see the addition of pollution-control costs as a threat to the competitive advantage they have built up. Nevertheless, it will be desirable to devote gradually increasing efforts to air-pollution control in coming years as incomes rise and as industrial emissions increase.

Korea has a broad antipollution law, covering both air and water pollution, that gives the government broad authority to force discharge abatement. Polluting firms have been induced to build plants away from population centers. By the mid-1970s cars were required to limit discharges to 65 percent of those of the last uncontrolled cars. The Korean government does not hesitate to use its authority to influence firms' behavior when it perceives a national interest in doing so. It will be interesting to observe the development of a national pollution-control program in coming years.

Conclusions

The three case studies discussed in this chapter illustrate the range of pollution problems and national control programs throughout the world. The problems depend on the level of development, the structure of production, the density of population, and on climate and other natural conditions. The programs adopted have characteristics that reflect the nature of government, the sophistication of officials, and customary approaches to national problems.

The one thing virtually all national pollution-control programs have in common is the neglect of economic analysis and of economic incentives. All programs take costs and benefits of abatement into account informally, and experienced, intelligent, and educated officials with good data undoubtedly make better informal estimates than others. But few countries collect or make publicly available careful estimates of costs of alternative pollution-control programs. In fact, the United States has collected as much pollution-abatement-cost data as any country. But no national program appears to have been based on explicit benefit calculations of alternative abatement programs, on comparisons of benefits and costs, or on careful program analysis. And no country has introduced economic incentives as central parts of its programs. One must study a subject like pollution control to realize what a small part of the population of even highly educated countries has any understanding of basic economic concepts.

DISCUSSION QUESTIONS AND PROBLEMS

1. Do you think effluent fees would be more or less advantageous in a poor country like Korea than in a rich country like Sweden?

2. Suppose a country's only environmental law was one that permitted people to sue for pollution damages in courts. Would that program produce effective pollution abatement?

3. What should be the role of the United Nations in pollution abatement? Should the UN discourage movement of polluting industries from industrialized to developing countries?

4. Rich countries show much greater concern with air pollution abatement than poor countries. It suggests that the benefits of air pollution abatement increase rapidly with income. Is that correct? How would you test the suggestion? Would it be possible to estimate an income elasticity of demand for clean air? (You may wish to refer back to Chapter 2).

REFERENCES AND FURTHER READING

Kneese, Allen, and Bower, Blair. *Managing Water Quality: Economics, Technology, Institutions.* Baltimore: Johns Hopkins University Press, for Resources for the Future, Inc., 1968. See especially Chapter 12 for discussion of environmental programs in Germany.

Mills, Edwin S., and Song, Byung Nak. *Korea's Urbanization and Urban Problems.* Cambridge, Mass.: Harvard University Press, 1978.

Organization for Economic Cooperation and Development. *Environmental Policy in Japan.* Paris, 1976.

Organization for Economic Cooperation and Development. *Environmental Policy in Sweden.* Paris, 1976.

Chapter 12

The Global Environment

Previous chapters have analyzed environmental issues of a local or regional character. Deleterious effects of dumping raw sewage into a flowing stream are limited geographically to the stretch of the stream a few miles below the discharge point. Harmful effects of carbon-monoxide discharges from motor vehicles are limited to the immediate vicinity of the road. A smoldering town dump may make life uncomfortable for nearby residents, but it should be of little concern to people more than a mile or two away. Most geographical linkages of environmental problems, and all those that are easy to measure and analyze, are limited. But some environmental problems have, or are thought to have, much more pervasive geographical linkages. Even those whose obvious effects are localized may have international or global effects. A thermal electric plant may affect the environment in its immediate neighborhood in calculable ways. But worldwide fossil-fuel combustion may have subtle effects on worldwide climate. An oil spill may make a mess of a nearby beach, but the global effect of all the oil discharges to the oceans may be to alter its fundamental ecological structure. The purpose of this chapter is to step back from the local and regional problems heretofore analyzed, and to consider problems that may have widespread and even worldwide effects. In some cases, different discharges need to be considered when analyzing global effects, as for example carbon dioxide, which is harmless locally but which may lead to the much-discussed "greenhouse effect." In other cases, it is a matter of looking at the same discharges, but of seeking damages on a global scale, to the neglect of local effects.

The problems to be analyzed in this chapter will be referred to as *global*, although the term is somewhat fanciful in many applications. Geographical linkages are always matters of degree. Heat discharges have different effects on climate near the equator from those on climate near the poles. Pollution of oceans by oil is worse in the North Atlantic than in the Pacific, since the North Atlantic is smaller and has much more shipping, oil drilling, and other sources of oil discharges than the Pacific. Acid rain extends over large regions and *might* be of very broad geographic scope. But some problems discussed in this chapter are genuinely worldwide in scope and all have effects that show up over a larger area than a region of a country such as the East Coast of the United States.

Separate analysis of global problems is justified because of two basic characteristics. First and most obvious, they transcend the boundaries of sovereign government jurisdictions. There are many problems in cajoling the people of New Jersey to take account of the effects of their actions on New Yorkers, or of persuading the people of Colorado to take account of the effect of their withdrawals from the Colorado River on the residents of Los Angeles. But all these residents are subject to the laws and police power of a single sovereign national government. National governments have many instruments to influence actions whose effects cross regional or state boundaries. But actions whose effects cross national boundaries are a completely different matter. There is no institution whose power to police resource allocation crosses national boundaries. If massive combustion of fossil fuels, largely in industrialized countries, indirectly heats up the earth's atmosphere, it affects people all over the world. But there is no international institution that can set and enforce discharge standards or effluent fees on a worldwide basis. Thus the mechanisms of control are much more limited and insecure for global than for local and regional problems. And attitudes toward pollution vary greatly from one part of the world to another. Many people in poor countries believe, with some justification, that they cannot afford to sacrifice resources for environmental protection. In Communist countries, the view is sometimes held that pollution is entirely a problem of capitalist countries. Varying basic attitudes toward pollution make international cooperation difficult.

Second, the time and uncertainty involved in global problems may be great. In part, the reason is simply that the world is a big place. An effect that moves across a country in weeks may take years to move around the world. More important, the linkages that are worldwide are subtle and poorly understood. The two most important linkages are the stratosphere and the oceans. Little is known about how substances move and interact in these media, and they are sinks into which substances move slowly but from which there may be little movement. It may take years to discover that discharges are damaging the stratosphere or the oceans in ways that may ultimately prove harmful to man. By the time the damage is manifest, it may be irreversible if the harmful substances take many months or years to reach the sink.

The subject of this chapter is environmental discharges that may affect people's welfare over all or a large part of the world. The first step, taken in the next section, is to put the subject in a basic framework of the interaction between people and the environment in the extraction of resources, the production and consumption of commodities and services, and the return of materials to the environment.

Resources, Production, Population, and Environment: A Global View

The earth consists of finite amounts of many substances. Human life and welfare require that materials be extracted from the environment, that usable products be produced from them, that products be consumed, and that the materials be returned to the environment.

Production of commodities and services is limited by the amounts and quality of human, capital, and raw-material inputs and by the state of technology. The ratio of production of wanted commodities and services to population is the standard of living of the population. Societies vary enormously as to the living standards they achieve. The countries with the world's highest living standards are mostly in Northern Europe and North America. Those with the lowest living standards are mostly in Asia and Africa. Living standards in the highest-income countries are about twenty times those in the lowest-income countries. To most people, the differences represented by such extremes of living standards are more important than anything else. People at the low end of the range live only half as long as those at the high end, and existence consists mainly of a desperate struggle to stay alive.

What determines the success of societies in producing high living standards? That is the most important and difficult question economists can ask. In the eighteenth and nineteenth centuries, much of economists' efforts was devoted to a special aspect of the problem: Under what circumstances can living standards be permanently above the subsistence level? Smith, Ricardo, Malthus, Marx and others devoted much of their professional lives to this basic problem. The debate has continued during the twentieth century, most recently in efforts to ascertain the limits to economic growth. The issues are extremely complex, but much needless and emotional controversy can be avoided by a careful statement of the problem.

The first thing to say is that a major determinant of economic development is noneconomic conditions. There is much debate about the proper role of governments in promoting economic development. Some people believe that a poor country can raise its living standards quickly only if its government takes the main responsibility for investment, planning, or ownership of production. Others believe that economic growth is most rapid if government assumes only a minor role in the economy. But whatever the proper role of government in promoting economic development, a sufficiently bad government can certainly stop or impede development. Otherwise most simple statements on the relationship between politics and economic development are refuted by the facts. There are both democratic and totalitarian countries that are highly developed. Likewise, some countries with high living standards have violent, dishonest, or oppressive governments, as have some countries with low living standards. Nevertheless, sufficiently bad government can make economic development virtually impossible. Likewise, sufficiently devastating warfare can retard development and reduce living standards.

As to economic determinants of living standards, the basic insights are obtained by considering conditions of production. A society's production function can be written

$$Y = f(L, K, M, t) \qquad (12.1)$$

Here Y equals total output of commodities and services, and L, K, and M are inputs of labor, capital, and materials. t stands for time and represents the fact that technology enables more output to be produced from given inputs as time passes. Technical change can certainly be affected by the way resources are allocated, but there is a stringent upper limit to how rapidly new technology can be implemented, and it can usefully be assumed to depend on the passage of time in the present context. Thus Y should be assumed to increase, for fixed input volumes, as t increases. The composition of output is unimportant in this section, and total output can be thought of as a single variable, designated *output* or *income*.

If production is subject to constant returns to scale in the three inputs, division of both sides of equation (12.1) by L gives

$$\frac{Y}{L} = f\left(1, \frac{K}{L}, \frac{M}{L}, t\right) = F\left(\frac{K}{L}, \frac{M}{L}, t\right) \tag{12.2}$$

The left side of equation (12.2) is output per worker. The ratio of workers to population is the labor-force participation rate. It changes only slowly and has a stringent upper limit, since about half the people in most countries are too young or too old to work. For present purposes, the labor-force participation rate can be assumed constant. Then output per worker is proportionate to output per capita, or the average living standard. Equation (12.2) then expresses the average living standard as a function of capital and material inputs per capita and of time.

Production functions with constant returns have the advantage that output per capita can be expressed as an explicit function of inputs per capita. But all production functions normally used by economists imply that living standards are high if inputs per capita are great and are aribtrarily low if inputs per capita are sufficiently small.[1]

The foregoing implies that at any state of technology, a sufficiently large population relative to capital and material inputs must result in arbitrarily low living standards. Malthus and others believed that at least in the absence of widespread use of birth control, population growth would inevitably outstrip the growth of inputs, and living standards would be reduced to the subsistence level. The question that must be asked is why capital and material inputs can-

---

1. Sufficient conditions are that equation (12.1) be continuous and have positive marginal products and convex isoquants, and that $f(0, K, M, t) = 0$. The last condition is that some labor be required to produce any output.

not increase indefinitely at least as fast as population and thus, with improving technology, enable living standards to improve forever, regardless how large population is.

The answer is that there must ultimately be limits to the population and living standard the earth can support, just because available substances are finite. Both capital and raw materials consist of substances extracted from the environment. Since there are only finite amounts of substances, only finite amounts can be extracted. Therefore, a sufficiently large population must outstrip capital and raw-material inputs, causing low living standards. That there are limits to population and living standards the earth can support, there can be no doubt. But enormous uncertainty prevails as to what the limits are and how quickly they may be approached. In fact, until two or three centuries ago, most of the people in the history of the world must have lived at or near a subsistence living standard. Since then the Industrial Revolution has permitted dramatic increases in production and has been accompanied by sharp decreases in birth rates throughout the presently developed world. The result is that people in the developed world have living standards at least twenty-five times the subsistence level. Nevertheless, people in many parts of the world still live close to the subsistence level. Although overpopulation is by no means the sole cause of extremely low living standards, it must be true that living standards would be higher if population were smaller in Bangladesh and elsewhere in the underdeveloped world.

Malthus and others stressed arable land as the material that would limit population and keep living standards at subsistence levels. Malthus understood that fixed birth and death rates lead to a constant annual percentage growth of population. There is only a finite amount of arable land and, in a given state of technology, there are severe limits to the food that can be grown on it. He believed that food production could not increase at a constant percentage rate indefinitely; rather he believed it would grow arithmetically (e.g., 1, 2, 3, 4, . . . rather than 1, 2, 4, 8, 16, . . . as would be the case for things, like population, which he believed grew geometrically. But he lacked a clear concept of a production function and had no perception that birth control might reduce birth rates to a level at which population remained constant. Writers since Malthus have forecast that other materials would limit population and living standards. Many writers have forecast more or less imminent depletion of world fuel supplies such as coal and oil. There certainly is only a finite amount of coal and oil in the ground and they are being depleted more rapidly than new supplies are being formed, so we will run out of them some day. The important questions are, when and with what consequences? The report of the National Commission on Supplies and Shortages has an excellent discussion of the difficulties in answering such questions.[2]

Almost all writers on the subject of resource limitations have underestimated the importance of capital formation and, most important, technical change. Malthus certainly underestimated the extent to which technology would permit increased food production in the two centuries following his birth just before the American Revolution. Countless writers have underestimated the importance of technology for increasing energy supplies. Europe's timber supplies were much too limited to supply energy for the Industrial Revolution. But the technology of coal extraction and combustion improved dramatically, and coal and iron became the basic material inputs of the Industrial Revolution. In the twentieth century, coal supplies dwindled in many European countries. But technical progress has permitted extraction of vast amounts of energy from petroleum. Oil was useless until technology enabled it to be used as fuel and, more recently, to make many other products.

The point is that all constraints on population and living standards are conditional on the state of technology. As technology advances, constraints are pushed outward so that a larger population and higher living standards are possible than previously. But the fact that constraints are conditional on technology does not mean that they are unimportant. At any time, it is possible for the world's population to be so large that it can achieve only a low living standard. That has happened in the past in many countries and is true now in some countries.

People cannot resist asking what will be the ultimate constraint that limits population and living standards. Will it be food supplies, pollution, minerals, energy, or something else? The question has not been carefully formulated. Ultimately, the sun's energy will be exhausted and the earth will be a cold, lifeless planet. In many countries, perhaps all, any increase in population now or in the foresee-

2. National Commission on Supplies and Shortages, *Government and the Nation's Resources*.

able future will cause living standards to be lower than they would be had population not increased. In terms of equation (12.2) many countries are at points at which it is difficult to increase material inputs proportionately with population. Therefore, M/L falls as L increases, with the implication that Y/L must decrease unless K/L or technology increases enough to offset the lower M/L. For the next century to two, the issue is not ultimate limits to population and living standards, but instead the fact that, in the poorest third or so of the world, population growth may result in decreases in extremely low living standards. At least 10 percent of the earth's population suffers from severe malnutrition. Population growth in many countries appears to make reduction of malnutrition very difficult. There is no reason to doubt that the earth's present population can be supported at gradually rising living standards for centuries. But if the world's population grows 3 percent per year, the average living standard will be lower at the end of the twentieth century than if it grows 1 percent per year. Beyond such statements as these, few categorical statements can be made with confidence.

Predictions of resource depletion and food shortage have been made for centuries. But predictions that population and living standards will be constrained first or mainly by environmental conditions have become frequent only during the second half of the twentieth century. Writers emphasize that the earth is a closed system with only a limited capacity to absorb polluting discharges without degradation that might impair the quality of life and perhaps endanger life itself. Many writers are vague as to the specific worldwide environmental dangers they foresee. But several specific issues have been identified and studied so that problems and possibilities can be discussed systematically. The remainder of this chapter discusses the global environment problems that have been raised most prominently. We shall return briefly to overall issues of scarcity in the closing Chapter 13.

Heat

The notion of the earth as a closed system is dramatically wrong as it pertains to heat. Massive amounts of heat arrive from the sun at the earth's atmosphere. About half of this heat is absorbed at the earth's surface. The temperature balance at the surface is maintained by release of the heat, mostly by evaporation of water. Evaporation carries the heat back to the atmosphere, where it is released by precipitation and returned to outer space.

Virtually all the energy that people release by combustion emerges as heat, much of it as waste heat during combustion, and much from friction as energy is used. Exactly where and how heat is discharged is important, but all is eventually dissipated to the atmosphere. Much is discharged directly to the atmosphere, but even that discharged elsewhere ends up in the atmosphere. For example, heat discharged to a stream from a thermal electric plant's cooling system causes increased evaporation from the receiving water body, even though it may occur at some distance from the point of discharge. Evaporation returns the heat to the atmosphere.

All heat released by man to the atmosphere is eventually returned to outer space. Meanwhile, it makes the atmosphere warmer than it would otherwise be. How much? In terms of effects on climate, the relevant comparison is between heat released by man's energy conversion and that reaching the earth's surface from the sun. On a worldwide basis, heat released by man's energy conversion is negligible compared with that coming from the sun. But it is not negligible around large cities. In the 1980s energy conversion releases about 5 percent as much heat as comes from the sun in the Los Angeles basin. In the entire industrial Northeast of the United States, the figure is as large as 1 percent. Urban areas are already made several degrees warmer than nearby places by man's energy conversion, and the local climate is affected.

During the first half of the twentieth century, the earth's atmosphere heated up about 0.5°C, and many people attributed it to fossil-fuel combustion. Recent research makes clear that the alleged cause was too small to explain the effect. The atmosphere has been cooling very gradually in recent decades, and the entire process is natural. But what about the future? Heat from energy conversion can certainly affect climate; it does now in cities and may in densely populated regions by the end of the century. Scientists doubt that heat released by man's activities will be enough to have global climatic effects by the end of the century. How much energy conversion will it take and what might the effects be? Nobody knows. The most obvious possible effect would be if heating the atmosphere melted the polar ice caps. It is now known that previous ice ages entailed remarkably small differences in average global temperatures compared with other historical periods. It is therefore not inconceivable that modest increases in the temperature of the atmosphere might cause substantial melting. Before that possibility is dismissed out of hand, it should be noted that one reason the polar regions remain so cold is that ice is highly reflective, so little of the sun's heat is absorbed. If the ice melts somewhat, reflectivity decreases in the area, which causes more of the sun's heat to be absorbed, and hence further melting. Some people become overly anxious at the thought of such global instabilities, but the fact is that little is known about how they work and how unstable various natural systems may be. The natural temperature increase during the first half of the twentieth century apparently caused some shrinkage of the ice caps and some advance of the oceans up the beaches. It is unlikely that man's heat discharges will affect this situation during the next half a century. But it could at some future time, and meanwhile the system is, quite properly, being studied intensively.

It should be noted that more efficient use of energy is no direct help in reducing heat discharges. All energy conversion ends up as heat, whether it is used efficiently or not. More efficient use of energy is, however, of important indirect help in that the more efficiently it is used the less energy conversion is necessary to satisfy people's needs and wants. For example, better insulated houses will not reduce the heat discharged per gallon of oil burned. It is all discharged. But it will reduce the oil that must be burned to keep the house at 70°F, and therefore the amount of heat that is discharged to the atmosphere.

Carbon Dioxide

Like heat, carbon dioxide is discharged to the atmosphere by combustion of fossil fuels. Carbon dioxide appears naturally in the atmosphere, constituting about 3 hundredths of a percent of the atmosphere by volume. During the time since accurate measurements were started, in the late 1950s, combustion has increased substantially the carbon dioxide content of the atmosphere (see Table 12.1) The increase in atmospheric carbon dioxide has been about half that discharged by combustion. The other half is apparently absorbed by the oceans and by photosynthesis in plant life. It is not known in what proportions the oceans and plant life have absorbed the carbon dioxide. More important, it is not known whether the 50 percent absorption experience can be extrapolated to the future. An increase in the car-

TABLE 12.1

Carbon Dioxide Concentrations in Air, 1958–1981
(parts per million)

Year	Mauna Loa, Hawaii	South Pole, Antarctica	Year	Mauna Loa, Hawaii	South Pole, Antarctica
1958	NA	315	1970	325	324
1959	316	316	1971	326	325
1960	317	316	1972	327	326
1961	317	317	1973	329	327
1962	318	318	1974	330	328
1963	319	318	1975	331	329
1964	319	319	1976	332	330
1965	320	319	1977	334	332
1966	321	320	1978	335	333
1967	321	321	1979	337	335
1968	322	322	1980	338	337
1969	324	322	1981	339	338

Concentrations are average annual concentrations.

NA—Not available.

SOURCE: 1958–1980: R. B. Bacastow and C. D. Keeling, "Atmospheric Carbon Dioxide Concentration, the Observed Airborne Fraction, the Fossil Fuel Airborne Fraction, and the Difference in Hemispheric Airborne Fractions," *in Scope* 16: *Global Carbon Modelling*, B. Bolen, ed. (London: John Wiley and Sons, 1981).

1981: Private communication with Dr. C. D. Keeling, Scripts Institute of Oceanography, LaJolla, California.

SOURCE: Council on Environmental Quality, *Environmental Quality*, 1982, Table A-77, p. 304.

bon-dioxide concentration in the atmosphere should stimulate plant growth and therefore carbon dioxide absorption around the world. But increases in population and economic activity induce people to clear forests, which reduces plant life. Furthermore, plants live a few decades at most, and when they die and rot they release carbon dioxide.

Atmospheric carbon dioxide increases heat retention close to the earth's surface. The SCEP report[3] projects that combustion may increase the concentration of carbon dioxide in the atmosphere by about 18 percent between 1970 and 2000. Scientists estimate that the effect might be to raise the temperature of the atmosphere by

3. Carroll Wilson, *Man's Impact on the Global Environment*.

0.5°C. That is about the same as the naturally caused increase in the atmosphere's temperature during the first half of the twentieth century. It is unlikely to have a significant effect on weather or on the ice caps, especially if the recent trend toward natural cooling continues. Continued growth of fossil-fuel combustion into the twenty-first century might, however, increase the atmosphere's temperature by 1 or 2°C. The result might be the risk of undesirable weather changes.

It is not appropriate to extrapolate rapid growth of fossil-fuel combustion indefinitely. Nobody knows the earth's reserves of fossil fuels, but we have already used a substantial part of them. It is likely that the earth's oil reserves will be mostly used in another century. Coal will last longer; how long depends very much on the rate at which it is burned. Using the 50 percent retention factor, it is conceivable that combustion of all the world's fossil-fuel reserves could multiply current atmospheric carbon dioxide by a factor of four. That could be a very serious problem, indeed, but the uncertainties of the underlying scientific calculations are enormous. Presumably, during the next century or so, fossil fuels will gradually give way to atomic fuels as the principal source of energy. Atomic energy has at least as serious heat-discharge problems as do fossil fuels, but it does not cause release of carbon dioxide to the atmosphere. Alternatively, solar energy, or some other energy source, could become important during the twenty-first century. Solar energy would solve the carbon-dioxide problem, but in the 1980s its prospects as an inexpensive source of large amounts of usable energy are not good.

The pronounced recent antipathy towards fission nuclear energy in the United States has a number of interesting implications and clarifies the far-reaching nature of externalities. The United States uses more than a third of the world's fossil fuels, and our failure *not* to "go nuclear" will result in global externalities on a very large scale, should the preceding discussion of the effects of CO_2 build-up be even approximately correct. As in the United States where about half of the population lives near oceans or large lakes, much of the world's population is so located. Our decision to limit local external effects of nuclear power plants at the expense of increased global effects will involve the sinking of most of the world's greatest treasures, from Saint Mark's Cathedral (and most of the rest of Venice) to the relics which abound in all of the world's great harbor cities. Similar comments will apply to later discussion of certain other global problems (e.g., our desires to have spray deodorants propelled by chlorofluorocarbons might have caused an increased skin cancer risk for the four and a half billion people on earth).

Oil in the Oceans

Accidental oil spills are among the great rallying issues of the environmental movement. People are moved by pictures of student volunteers mopping oil from beaches with straw or of an ecologist holding a bird whose feathers are soaked with oil. Dramatic events such as the breakup of the oil tanker *Torry Canyon* off the south coast of England and the blowout of the offshore oil well at Santa Barbara, California, have galvanized legislatures into action and have resulted, as frequently happens in crises, in poor legislation. In the winter of 1977, a blowout of a North Sea oil rig dominated the headlines for days. Table 12.2 gives a perspective on the size and trends in oil and other spills in U.S. waters, and this would be a relatively small part of the global problem.

Global estimates are much more difficult to find, particularly since petroleum hydrocarbons enter the oceans from so many sources. Table 12.3 presents two estimates of worldwide totals from the early and mid-1970s. Each estimate refers to a typical year in the early 1970s.

The dramatic difference between the two estimates is in hydrocarbons from the atmosphere, the National Academy of Sciences estimate being 0.6 million tons and the Kash estimate being 9 to 90 million tons. The sources of atmospheric hydrocarbons are those shown in Chapter 5. The enormous difference results from the fact that no one really knows what happens to hydrocarbon discharges to the air. The Kash estimate assumes that the oceans are the sink for them. That is correct to the extent that hydrocarbons settle out of the atmosphere into the oceans or settle out onto land and are washed into the oceans or into waterbodies that empty into the oceans. More recently published data showing declines in American hydrocarbon emissions make it clear that the upper end of the Kash interval for atmospheric hydrocarbons is too large. The upper end of the Kash interval implies that all atmospheric hydrocarbon discharges end up in the oceans. That is unlikely, but even half the total, about 45 million tons, would dwarf all other sources of hydrocarbon discharges to the oceans.

In terms of total discharges to the oceans, everything depends on

TABLE 12.2

Oil and Hazardous Spills in U.S. Waters, 1971–1981 and by Location, 1981

Year	Total		Oil		Hazardous		Other	
	Number of incidents	Million gallons	Number of incidents	Million gallons	Number of incidents	Million gallons	Number of incidents	Million gallons
1971	8,736	8.840	7,522	8.635	NA	NA	1,214	0.204
1972	9,931	18.806	8,380	16.765	NA	NA	1,551	2.041
1973	13,232	22.108	10,995	15.353	237	.435	2,000	6.321
1974	14,432	19.422	11,902	16.710	220	.909	2,310	1.803
1975	12,781	22.243	10,868	21.724	239	.462	1,674	.056
1976	13,930	36.608	11,700	24.352	299	2,135	1,931	10.121
1977	15,330	11.248	12,605	9.979	289	1.433	2,436	.835
1978	14,495	17.557	11,950	14.343	261	2.164	2,284	1.050
1979	13,134	13.661	10,990	10.500	239	.434	1,905	2.727
1980	9,578	15.093	7,837	10.171	133	4.589	1,812	.333
1981[1]	10,072	19.638	8,376	17.668	91	1.051	1,605	.917
1981 by location								
Inland	4,140	17.332	3,435	16.291	55	.706	650	0.335
Atlantic	2,449	1.248	1,913	.629	21	.334	565	.285
Pacific	1,214	.444	1,063	.189	5	.001	146	.253
Gulf	1,846	.471	1,674	.435	7	.010	165	.026
Great Lakes	308	.137	232	.118	3	.001	73	.017

Areas affected include the Great Lakes, ocean waters within 200 miles of the coast, and inland waters (rivers channels, harbors, etc.). Sources of spills include vessels, land vehicles, nontransportation-related facilities, pipelines, marine facilities, and land facilities.

Data are compiled from the U.S. Coast Guard's Pollution Incident Reporting System (PIRS).

[1] Data for 1981 are preliminary.

Sources: *1971–1972:* U.S. Department of Transportation, Coast Guard, *Polluting Incidents In and Around U.S. Waters, Calendar Year 1977* (Washington: USGPO, 1978), pp. 7, 23. *1973:——— Calendar Year 1978 and 1979* (Washington: USGPO, 1980), p. 16. *1974–1980:——— Calendar Year 1979 and 1980* (Washington: USGPO, 1981), pp. 3, 16. *1981:——— Calendar Year 1980 and 1981* (Washington: USGPO, 1982), pp. 3, 16.

Source: Council on Environmental Quality, *Environmental Quality*, 1982, Table A-48, p. 287.

the solution of the mystery of the fate of atmospheric hydrocarbons. Otherwise the two estimates are similar and the National Academy of Sciences estimates will be referred to in what follows. About half the nonatmospheric total results from marine operations. Most is intentional discharges of waste oil and oil products from oil tankers and barges and from other cargo ships. Of discharges from marine

TABLE 12.3

Oil Pollution of the World's Waters (in millions of metric tons per year)

| National Academy of Sciences[a] | | Kash[b] | |
Source	Volume	Source	Volume
		Marine operations	2.3
Marine operations	2.13	LOT tankers (ballast cleaning)	0.27
LOT tankers[c]	0.31	Non-LOT tankers (ballast cleaning)	0.70
Non-LOT tankers	0.77	Discharge (bilge, pumping, leaks, etc.)	0.12
Bilges bunkering	0.5	Tankers and tank barges	0.60
Terminal operations	0.0003	Other vessels	0.09
Dry docking	0.25	Terminal operations	0.27
Tanker accidents	0.2	Tanker and tank-barge casualties	0.25
Nontanker accidents	0.1	All other vessel casualties	
Nonmarine operations	2.7	Nonmarine operations	2.5
Coastal refineries	0.2	Refineries and petrochemical plants	0.30
Coastal, nonrefining, industrial wastes	0.3	Industrial machinery	0.75
Coastal municipal wastes	0.3	Highway motor vehicles	1.44
Urban runoff	0.3	Offshore production	0.20
River runoff	1.6	Normal operations	0.10
Offshore production	0.08	Blowouts and accidents	0.10
Total direct pollution	4.91	Total direct pollution	5.0
Natural seeps	0.6	Natural seeps	$\ll 0.1$[d]
Atmosphere	0.6	Atmosphere	9.0–90.0
TOTAL	6.11	TOTAL	14.0–95.0

[a] National Academy of Sciences, *Petroleum in the Marine Environment* (Washington, D.C., 1975).

[b] Kash, Don, et al., *Energy Under the Oceans: A Technology Assessment of Outer Continental Shelf Oil and Gas Operations* (Norman, Okla.: University of Oklahoma Press, 1973).

[c] "LOT" means "loan-on-top."

[d] $\ll$ means "very much less than."

SOURCE: Council on Environmental Quality, *Environmental Quality*, 1975, p. 602.

operations, only about 14 percent results from accidents of all kinds, including those to tankers and to other cargo ships. Accidental spills are probably recorded accurately because a dramatic spill is difficult to conceal. But intentional marine discharges are mostly illegal and are very difficult to detect outside harbors. It is likely that the estimate of intentional marine discharges in Table 12.3 is too small and Table 12.2 largely ignores them.

Of the 2.7 million tons of estimated discharges from nonmarine operations, most is runoff of waste petroleum products. Much is grease and crankcase oil that is drained from vehicles and discarded or leaks onto streets and is washed into sewers and thence to nearby streams by rainwater. Another large part is discharges to water bodies from refineries and other manufacturing industries.

A small amount of total discharges comes from offshore drilling, and much of that is from small leakages in normal operations. Discharges from large accidental spills have been small. But until the mid-1970s, most offshore drilling has been in relatively shallow and tranquil water. Drilling in the North Sea and elsewhere where seas are deep and rough may result in more accidental spills.

What damages are done by the discharges recorded in Tables 12.2 and 12.3? Much of the damage is local and regional. Most of the marine discharges and those of offshore production, and all of the discharges from nonmarine operations occur at or near the water's edge. Beautiful beaches may be made unusable for long times by oil caked on them. Harbors and estuaries and their shorelines are made ugly. Most important, oil discharges in and near estuaries damage the breeding grounds of most kinds of aquatic life. Careful studies have shown that oil spills kill mollusks, fish, and marine birds in large numbers. Furthermore, sudden spills may be much more damaging than similar amounts of oil that leak slowly into the water. The ocean, like any other environmental medium, can absorb limited amounts of oil and other discharges without degradation. Unfortunately, little is known about safe discharge quantities. But large spills certainly exceed the capacity of the receiving water body to handle them. Local and regional damages from oil pollution may be large, indeed, especially relative to abatement costs. But they do not qualify as global effects on any reasonable definition.

Nothing is known with certainty about the global effects of oil pollution in the oceans. The principal concern among scientists is that it may interfere with the foundation of the aquatic food chain.

Phytoplankton is the basic green plant life in the oceans. Through photosynthesis, it provides the base of the food chain for higher forms of aquatic life and governs the oxygen balance in the oceans. In concentrations in excess of 60 parts per billion, oil interferes with photosynthesis. Much of the phytoplankton is contaminated with oil off the East Coast of the United States, and contamination may extend elsewhere. Widespread contamination could cause severe disruption of the aquatic ecological structure, with unknown consequences to people.

The more widespread are hydrocarbon discharges to the oceans, the greater is the likelihood of fundamental damage to the ocean's food chain and ecology. Atmospheric hydrocarbons are probably much more dispersed than other hydrocarbon discharges to the oceans. Therefore the probablity of fundamental ecological damage to the ocean probably depends on how great the atmospheric source of hydrocarbon discharges is.

What can be done to reduce hydrocarbon pollution of oceans? The technically easiest sources of pollution to deal with are the dramatic spills, but they are probably less important than many other sources. Most tanker disasters could be prevented by better constructed, maintained, and operated ships. The worst disasters have been the result of unimaginably sloppy navigation. Captains simply did not know where they were, or took absurd risks to save a few hours travel time. Statistically, more accidents must occur as ocean traffic increases. But inexpensive ways of reducing accident probabilities are simply not used. That is the inescapable conclusion from the facts; it also follows from the existing incentive structure. At present there is almost no way to make those who control tanker operations liable for environmental damages from accidents. To improve the incentive structure all that is needed is a requirement that a tanker cannot unload oil in an American port (or, better yet, an agreement among importing nations that they cannot unload in a port of any major importing country) unless it is covered by adequate insurance or a bond to cover environmental damages from an accident the tanker might be involved in. The cost to operators of tankers of bonds or insurance would be much less if the ship were built, maintained, and operated with care. Owners would thus be motivated to reduce probabilities of accidents.

The same is true of discharges of bilge and other routine discharges from tankers. Techniques are available for acceptable disposal in ports. But there are only inadequate means of forcing tanker operators to use them. All that is required is a rule that tankers cannot use ports unless they present proof that they have used acceptable means of waste disposal.

Accidental and intentional spills from tankers are examples of the proposition stated at the beginning of the chapter, that police powers do not exist for international waterways. Technical means of controlling such discharges, at least in a statistical sense, are hardly more complex than for controlling domestic discharges. But extending police powers to international waterways is a complex and fundamental change, indeed. There are important steps that a single country such as the United States could take to reduce substantially oil spills on the oceans. But many of the costs of discharges are external to particular countries. Countries therefore lack motivation to incur the costs that would be necessary to control discharges, much of whose benefits would accrue elsewhere.

But from a global point of view it may be that the hydrocarbon discharges that are relatively easy for countries to control are less important than others. Atmospheric hydrocarbon discharges to the oceans may be most important in terms of chronic effects. If so, individual countries lack the means and motivation to take account of the international damages in controlling sources within their boundaries.

If chronic pollution of the oceans from atmospheric hydrocarbons should prove important, the time scale may prove to be crucial. Little is known about how long hydrocarbons discharged to the oceans in a given year may remain to damage the ecology of the oceans. Hydrocarbons probably decay only slowly in the oceans and they may do damage for years after they enter the ocean. Thus the effects of hydrocarbon discharges to the oceans may build up over many years. By the time serious ecological damage has occurred and been recorded, damages may be irreversible for many years. The alternative to learning from such field observations is careful scientific research on the likely effects of hydrocarbon pollution of the oceans on the food chain. Such laboratory and other scientific studies are never conclusive; a laboratory experiment is never a perfect replication of the ocean environment as to scale, time span, or complexity. But careful research over a period of years results in a buildup of scientific results that is invaluable. The only alternative to learning from scientific study is to learn from experience on a global basis. The costs of one such bad experience could be enormous.

Chlorofluorocarbons

The chlorofluorocarbon (hereafter CFC) issue is one of the best examples of the subtleties, complexities, and uncertainties of global environmental problems. It also illustrates the sense of drama, crisis, and detective mystery that people find to be such a compelling part of environmental problems.

CFCs are gases used as propellants in aerosol cans and as the coolant in refrigeration and air-conditioning systems. Their use increased dramatically in the 1960s and continued to grow in the early 1970s (see Table 12.4), mainly because of growth in air conditioning and a tremendous growth in use of aerosols for spray paints, deodorants, household cleaners, and many other products. CFCs are discharged to the atmosphere as the aerosol is used, as they leak from cooling systems, and as cooling systems are repaired or replaced. CFCs apparently do no harm in the lower atmosphere.

However, over a period of years, CFCs work their way up to the stratosphere, beginning about forty thousand feet above the earth. The stratosphere is quite different from the lower atmosphere, and is characterized by extremely low air pressure, constant low temperatures, absence of water vapor, and an apparently slow mixing with the heavy atmosphere below, although recent evidence suggests more mixing than had been suspected. The slow vertical mixing means

TABLE 12.4

World Chlorofluorocarbon Production, 1970–1981
(millions of pounds)

Year	World production[1]	Year	World production[1]	Year	World production[1]
1970	1232.9	1974	1791.3	1978	1501.2
1971	1333.2	1975	1532.3	1979	1425.6
1972	1514.0	1976	1654.7	1980	1360.6
1973	1702.9	1977	1550.5	1981	1407.1

[1] Data are the total of the compounds F–11, F–12, which are about 94% of the chlorofluoromethanes produced. Chlorofluoromethanes are a group of chlorofluorocarbons.

SOURCE: Chemical Manufacturer's Association, *1981 World Production and Sales of Fluorocarbons FC–11 and FC–12* (Washington, D.C., August 25, 1982), pp. 7, 8.

SOURCE: Council on Environmental Quality, *Environmental Quality*, 1982, Table A-76, p. 304.

that residence times of gases in the stratosphere may be very long. Little is known about the physical and chemical properties of the stratosphere, and therein lies the mystery.

The stratosphere contains an ozone layer, one of whose functions is to reduce the penetration of ultraviolet radiation from the sun to the earth's surface. An increase in the penetration of ultraviolet radiation would increase the incidence of skin cancer in people and might cause changes in the earth's ecological system and climate. Scientists believe that the concentration of CFCs in the stratosphere would modify the ozone layer in such a way as to increase the penetration of ultraviolet radiation to the earth's surface.

The CFC danger was first recognized in 1974. There followed two years of frenetic government and private research on the subject, propaganda, anxiety in companies that manufacture fluorocarbons, and lobbying on all sides. In mid-1976 the National Academy of Sciences published a report[4] that carefully laid out the issues and uncertainties. No one knows how long it takes CFCs to reach the stratosphere, but it may take years. No one knows the residence time of fluorocarbons in the stratosphere, but it may be a year or so. No one knows with certainty the effect of CFCs on the ozone layer, but it may be substantial enough to do serious damage.

The best evidence is that there is no imminent danger of damage to the ozone layer. But it would take a bold person to guarantee that present and likely future growth of CFC use will not do serious damage to the ozone layer that could have dire consequences on earth. The worst aspect of the problem is that damage to the ozone layer in one year may depend on CFC discharges during the previous ten or more years. If CFC use were suddenly stopped at the first sign of harm on earth, the situation might continue to worsen for a decade.

The CFC crisis has passed and the communications media have moved on to other issues. The subject is now being studied carefully by scientists. It is likely that the conclusion will be that the risks of indefinitely continued uncontrolled fluorocarbon use are not worth taking. Meanwhile, the government first introduced controls on fluorocarbon use in 1977, and as of April 15, 1979, products using aerosol applications of CFCs were banned from interstate commerce

4. National Academy of Sciences, Committee on Impacts of Stratospheric Change, "Halocarbons: Environmental Effects of Cholrofluoromethane Refuse" (Washington, D.C., 1976).

by the FDA. Their use continues, however, in foreign countries.

Fluorocarbons are valuable as propellants and coolants; such a large industry does not grow up quickly unless the products satisfy strong human wants. But serious risk of long-term damage to the ozone layer is a price humanity should not pay. There are other ways to propel aerosols in cans, other ways to apply paint, and so forth. Many alternatives to fluorocarbons have been used before and others could be found. But the problem is not restricted to the United States. A large though unknown part of the world's fluorocarbon production and consumption is in the United States. In the absence of controls, fluorocarbon use will grow in other countries. Eventually controls on production or consumption will have to be international if they are to be effective, as seen in the 1981 production figures shown in Table 12.4.

Conclusions

Previous sections have discussed four examples of global environmental problems. One, heat discharges, is both a local problem of modest dimensions and a potential global problem. The second, carbon dioxide, is not actually or potentially a local problem, but is a potential global problem. The third, oil on the oceans, is mostly a local or regional problem, but could become a serious international if not global problem. The fourth, CFCs, can hardly cause local damages, but could have serious global effects. Other examples could be found. Both peaceful and wartime uses of atomic energy entail environmental dangers on which much has been written. Persistent pesticides such as DDT were among the earliest environmental problems to be studied carefully, first by Rachel Carson in her classic, *Silent Spring*. But the four examples discussed here illustrate the kinds of global problems that have been studied and, most important of all, the uncertainties and subtleties of the subject.

What lessons can be learned from the examples of global environmental problems that have been discussed? Is the world about to come to an end? Or is concern with the global environment a conspiracy among elitist ecologists? Answers that can be given with confidence are scarce and leave much room for honest differences of opinion, judgments, and fantasy. It is useful to keep in mind the three R's of global environmental studies:

Robust The world's environment and most of the world's inhabitants are robust and resilient. The global environment is not a delicate, unstable system that will collapse the first time it is altered or abused. Chicken Little is wrong; the sky is not falling. The history of writing on global environmental and resource problems is replete with hyperbole, speculation stated as fact, and forecasts of doom, and it is easy to dismiss the subject out of hand. Raising worldwide living standards is a serious and extraordinarily difficult matter. There is no way to do it without massive impacts on the environment, some of them good and some of them bad. Among the gravest injustices of our time is the tendency among some to treat anyone who tries to produce goods and services as an enemy of the people.

Respect It is important that a fundamental respect for the environment be reflected in both private and government actions. People have constructed a massive industrial machine during the last two or three centuries. We have clearly acquired the capability to impose fundamental and destructive changes on the environment. Both collectively, through governments and international organizations, and privately, through corporations, families, and other groups, we should acquire the habit of thinking carefully about the environmental implications of production, consumption, and waste disposal. Providing a high-quality environment, both locally and globally, can add greatly to people's health and welfare. Global environmental problems are potentially serious and difficult to solve in both technical and institutional senses. The prophets of imminent doom have been wrong every time. But they will be right only once!

Research Our ignorance about the global environment, what we might do to it and what it might do to us, is profound. Until the second half of the twentieth century there hardly existed a concept of the global environment, let alone serious research on the subject. Even now we have little idea just what happens in the oceans and the stratosphere and how people's actions affect them. Research on the global environment is much more important than research on local environmental matters. We can learn from our own and others' experiences regarding local environmental problems. But we have only one global environment to work with. Our first serious mistake with it may be our last.

DISCUSSION QUESTIONS AND PROBLEMS

1. What global environmental problems result from peaceful uses of atomic energy?

2. Why do high-income countries have much lower birth rates than low-income countries?

3. Why are supersonic planes of greater global environmental concern than subsonic planes? Is it possible that they can be made differently to reduce or eliminate any additional concern?

4. Explore the notion that the global environment may be a more severe constraint on world population than global natural resources.

REFERENCES AND FURTHER READING

Commoner, Barry. *The Closing Circle*. New York: Knopf, 1971.

Council on Environmental Quality. *Environmental Quality*. Washington, D.C.: Environmental Protection Agency, published annually.

Meadows, Donnella, et al. *The Limits to Growth*. New York: Universe Books, 1972.

National Commission on Supplies and Shortages. *Government and the Nation's Resources*. Washington, D.C.: U.S. Government Printing Office, 1976.

Nordhaus, William. "Economic Growth and Climate: The Carbon Dioxide Problem." *American Economic Review* 67 (February 1977): 341–46.

Wilson, Carroll. *Man's Impact on the Global Environment*. Cambridge, Mass: MIT Press, 1970. (Study of Critical Environmental Problems [SCEP] report).

Chapter 13

The Future of Environmental Economics: Epilog

Since we have no crystal ball, much of this chapter will be somewhat speculative. One thing that we are quite certain about is that concern for the environment is not something that will, for any significant period, fade into obscurity. There will be periods, to be sure, during which other issues (such as energy or unemployment) will take precedence and during which environmental concerns will appear to be on the wane. But considerable evidence suggests that environmental quality is a superior and certainly a normal good; with rising real incomes likely into the foreseeable future, demands for improved environmental quality will grow.

We are also confident that growing demands for environmental quality will be met with resistance and that there will continue to be strong disagreement about what are appropriate levels of environmental quality. This is not just because equity owners of polluting firms (or individuals) will suffer losses (or see utility levels fall) as they are forced to clean up (although much future discussion will focus on these very real facts): it is also the public-good nature of environmental quality that will lead to strong disagreement about appropriate levels. The case is really very much like national defense, in which real differences in individual demands cannot be simultaneously met: the defense that exists, exists for all. This aspect of the

346

argument will be downplayed, however, because, unlike national defense, few people will openly argue for lower environmental quality. Nevertheless, the underlying distribution of costs and benefits of environmental programs will importantly shape future environmental policy.

In the future many more countries will become involved with environmental policy and those that are currently actively involved will be in the forefront of efforts to coordinate policies aimed at global environmental problems. France began a new air-quality agency in 1979, recent controls in Italy (while based on emissions rather than on air quality) exhibit considerable regional flexibility, and Germany has experienced a 65 percent emission reduction in lead since the Petrol Lead Act (this amid a strong general emphasis on hazardous substances). Sweden, discussed in Chapter 11, has moved slowly and steadily in its air-quality program, while the United States' effort has slowed somewhat since the energy crunch of 1973. Various environmental policies will no doubt spread to a host of countries currently without programs as incomes continue to grow and as new and old environmental problems become of concern. International cooperation will grow, stimulated by the acid-deposition controversies of the 1980s, and the United States is likely to take the lead in this effort.

One direction that future environmental policy will take is likely to be met with considerable public resistance. There is likely to be greater control placed on the behavior of individuals, as compared to firms, in the future. To a large extent this is because firms have become relatively highly controlled and, as a consequence, marginal costs of obtaining environmental improvements are lower if those controls are placed on individuals: the likely regulation of wood-burning stoves and fireplaces in the near future comes to mind as an example of life-style changes that will not prove popular. These sources of heat are quite environmentally damaging and are becoming important contributors to Denver's winter haze and to air-quality problems in the Northeast as well. Similar controls will be likely to be introduced on liquid wastes that are run through garbage disposals. While it is unclear what role should be played by government, recent concerns about indoor exposures to air pollution (radon, carbon monoxide from ranges, and so on) are likely to find expression in future legislation. Another example, already being instituted in Colorado, is "no-drive days" on which (depending on what number your license plate ends with) individuals are asked not to drive.

These controls will probably begin as voluntary programs, with reliance on moral suasion. As in the case of the no-drive days, it is likely that the voluntary programs will be ineffectual—the vast majority of people tend not to cease behavior that is perceived as having benefits greater than costs. As a consequence, various regulations will emerge to alter the life-styles of Americans. It is hoped that the regulatory approaches will be flexible, taking the economic-incentive approach advocated throughout this book.

We would hope that a number of myths and environmental fallacies will be exposed for what they are in the coming years. Examples would be: (1) defining pollution in arbitrary physical terms rather than in terms of externalities, (2) believing that the dollars usually used in benefit-cost analyses render those analyses shallow or base, (3) believing that everyone should have the right to experience the same level of environmental quality regardless of where they live, (4) thinking that we all benefit equally from environmental policy since we all breathe the air (hence ignoring the very real distributional issues that surround environmental policy as currently practiced), (5) believing that the "priceless" nature of human health means that we should not accept trade-offs in our demands for environmental quality, and so on. Perhaps the most disturbing myth, at least from our perspective, is the widespread belief that direct controls are somehow more "dependable" than are economic incentives, when in fact all the evidence suggests exactly the reverse.

How likely are the preceding beliefs (and others that will occur to the reader of this book) to become recognized as myths? The answer to this question depends in the main on which of two very different views of the world comes to dominate the public mind in the future. The first view, which we will call the "Doomsday Scenario," is represented by the many *Limits to Growth* type of analyses that have emerged in recent years and has its roots in a mix of Malthusian and ecological theory. Among recent proponents of this scenario are Paul Ehrlich, Amory Lovins, and Ralph Nader. The second view, labeled here the "Brighter-Future Scenario," is represented by recent thinkers such as Herman Kahn or Julian Simon and also has long historical roots. We shall consider each view in turn. The reader may wish to refer back to the first section of Chapter 12, which considers some of these same issues more formally.

The Doomsday Scenario

In its simplest form, the doomsday model merely says that since we live in a finite world, geometric growth rates are impossible to maintain indefinitely. This is, of course, in some sense obvious, although the arithmetic of some of the examples used to clarify the nature of geometric growth rates can be quite scary to the uninitiated. For example, if a bacterium were placed in a bucket and that bacterium doubled in number every hour (1, 2, 4, 8, 16, and so on), it would take surprisingly little time for the bucket to become full—perhaps 100 hours, to pursue an example from *The Ninety-Ninth Hour*. The startling and disturbing aspect of geometric growth is that the bucket would only be half full at the ninety-ninth hour and many might be quite complacent about the ability of the bucket to hold the bacteria for a long time to come, when in fact the bucket will be overflowing a mere hour later.

The analogy to the bucket in the real world is, of course, the earth, and we are the bacteria that are filling it at geometric growth rates. To be sure, the earth's population is not doubling every hour, but at 2 percent growth rates it would double every thirty-five years (although in some locations and at some times populations have not grown). Moreover, the exponential growth of income (which you will recall is equal to output) is proceeding in addition to the population growth in most countries of the world. What are the implications, especially for the environment which is our main concern here, of this exponential growth of population and income in a finite environment?

The beliefs that stem from the doomsday scenario are that we are running out of the scarce natural resources and energy necessary for human beings to live enjoyable lives. Only by controlling our drives for more people and goods now can we postpone, and possibly prevent, a period of horrible adjustment, with massive population die-offs and famine as the food supply (which grows arithmetically) fails to keep pace with the exploding population. With the increase in people and their goods has come, and will continue to come, in this view, increased environmental pollution in every form.

Let us expand a bit on the environmental implications, as they are the central focus of the present book. The notion, in brief, is that the increase in human activity will result in loss of ecosystem diversity (e.g., monoculture farming) as we drive various other species to extinction. The loss of ecosystem diversity leads, it is argued, to a less stable ecosystem. Moreover, less stable ecosystems are felt to be more at risk to pollution damage; hence high levels of human activity (population or income) exceed the "assimilative capacity" of the ecosystem and, in the process, lower future assimilative capacity by lowering species diversity.

This ecological view has existed for at least seventy years and is viewed as controversial by many ecologists. It is based on the notion that an evolving natural ecosystem begins simply (e.g., lichens on a wet rock) and steadily increases in complexity, and biomass, through an orderly natural succession until a so-called "climax state" is reached. In the climax state (for example, the forest), there is great diversity and the ecosystem is argued to be at constant, maximum biomass. Moreover, the soil structures are believed to have maximal retention of nutrients at the climax state. Disruptions in this system reduce its ability to capture the nutrients to maintain itself. The controversy among ecologists about these points relates to whether plant succession is orderly or random and the extent to which diverse ecosystems are more stable than simpler ecosystems.

The policy implication of the preceding scenario is that we should be very careful not to exceed the assimilative capacity of the environment by producing either too many offspring or too many goods. If we overproduce or overpopulate, we may think we are better off in the short run but we must of necessity be worse off in the long run, since the diminishing assimilative capacity will render our population or income levels non-maintainable. Hence, many biologists recommend biologically based environmental standards (for example, dissolved oxygen levels that are high enough to support trout) rather than economically based standards (those that set marginal benefits equal to marginal costs from our human perspective). While both ecologists and economists would agree that the uncontrolled case results in non-optimally large levels of pollution, the optimum from an economist's perspective may still leave environmental damage that is unacceptably large and, indeed, that cannot be maintained in any event. If the ecologist's view is accurate, and if we are at our global assimilative capacity, efforts to keep people from starving today only mean that more people must starve tomorrow: some of the apparently callous statements one hears in casual conversation almost appear humanitarian!

The important issue is whether we are currently exceeding assimilative capacity or whether the concern of the economist for best allocation of resources from our human perspective also guarantees high environmental quality to other species. We turn now to a quite different scenario.

The Brighter-Future Scenario

Doomsday predictions always make good press, and much of the preceding story will have been familiar to the reader (see, also, the preceding chapter). But there is another, very different, view of the interaction among income, population, and the environment. We shall draw upon the provocative book by Julian Simon to paint a quite different picture. The doomsday models rely on simulation models of varying complexity (the original *Limits to Growth* version has now been disavowed by its sponsors) and merely let them run: starting with any initial population or income level, any finite world ultimately becomes either inundated by people and pollution or runs out of critical resources. Moreover, decreases in population or income growth rates (if they remain positive) or discoveries of larger reserves (if they remain finite) of the critical resource only postpone the unavoidable disaster.

In *The Ultimate Resource*, Simon argues from actual data, not relying extensively on simulations of the usual sort (although some interesting simulations are conducted). He makes the following arguments:

• Natural resources and energy are getting *less* scarce (we have entered an age of essentially limitess substitutability, and resource prices have steadily fallen).

• Population growth has substantial long-term benefits and fairly small short-term costs, more in the nature of inconveniences (larger numbers of people mean more potential for solutions to problems, more great artists and inventions).

• The world's food supply is improving (there is less famine and hunger than ever before, with rising *per capita* food production over the period for which UN or U.S. data are available).

and, of specific interest here,

• Pollution in the United States has been decreasing (this is likely to be the case elsewhere but data are scant. The argument, familiar to readers of this book, is that rising incomes increase the demands for environmental quality and the ability to exercise those demands).

The detailed presentation that accompanies these arguments is of book length and can hardly be presented here. The conclusions rest largely upon the best data available (often the only data available). But the spirit of the book is analytical, for Simon is clearly aware that a history of, say, falling resource prices does not mean that they must inevitably continue to fall. The driving force behind the optimistic conclusions is ultimately human ingenuity.

All doomsday models ignore or downplay technology and advances in human knowledge. But what is invented or learned in the future is hardly an accident. The economic system has powerful, though poorly understood, incentives to develop appropriate kinds of knowledge in much the same way that it gives incentives to produce the proper amount of goods. If there is an anticipated shortage in some resource, there is profit to be made by finding a substitute or a way to use a lower grade of the resource (for example, as copper prices rise we turn to optic fibers, which are made of very cheap ingredients, or we come to use space stations and microwave beams rather than string even these cheaper cables across the land).

The discussion of the interaction between population and environmental quality is perhaps the weakest link in the Simon argument. While some convincing evidence was presented regarding, for example, average life expectancy (which has increased steadily, and is surely a reasonable overall gauge of environmental quality), there is some muddling of the separate effects of income and population. To be sure, some of the best environmental experiences, such as a view of the Grand Canyon or a wilderness excursion in a scenic area, would be unavailable to nearly everyone if we were few in number (there would be no interstate highway or airport system—or infrastructure generally—if we did not have a large population base). But, and Simon is clearly aware of this point, the very crowding of people on the planet may be viewed by many as "environmental pollution." This brings us back to an earlier point in the book: economists tend to take individual tastes as given and indeed as valuable. We would not like to trample upon your tastes, unless your tastes, say a taste for murder, had substantial external effects on others. And Simon in his book is really attacking those who try to "educate" the tastes that others have for children; he argues rather convincingly that people who want to have more children, whether they are in developed or in undeveloped countries, are not socially inconsiderate, as often implied.

Who is right? A careful reading of both doomsday and brighter-future scenarios suggests that the truth, as is so often the case, lies between extreme positions. We feel that the truth is somewhat closer to being represented by the Simon position, summed up in the following quote:

> Is a rosy future guaranteed? Of course not. There always will be temporary shortages and resource problems where there are strife, political blundering, and natural calamities—that is, where there are people. But the natural world allows, and the developed world promotes through the marketplace, responses to human needs and shortages in such manner that one backward step leads to 1.0001 steps forward, or thereabouts. That's enough to keep us headed in a life-sustaining direction. The main fuel to speed our progress is our stock of knowledge, and the brake is lack of imagination. The ultimate resource is people—skilled, spirited, and hopeful people who will exert their wills and imaginations for their own benefit, and so, inevitably, for the benefit of us all. (p. 348)

REFERENCES AND FURTHER READING

Commoner, Barry. *The Closing Circle: Nature, Man, and Technology.* New York: Bantam Books, 1972. A classic statement of the environmentalist position.

Ehrlich, Paul R. *The Population Bomb.* New York: Ballantine Press, 1968. Had perhaps the most significant impact on attitudes regarding population growth of any single writing; against continued population growth.

Fuller, Buckminster. *Utopia or Oblivion: The Prospect for Humanity.* New York: Bantam Books, 1969.

Goeller, H. E., and Weinberg, A. M. "The Age of Substitutability." *Science* 191 (1978): 683–89. Argues against the relevance of effective resource constraints.

Kahn, Herman; Brown, William; and Martel, Leon. *The Next 200 Years: A Scenario for America and the World.* New York: Morrow, 1976. Provides an optimistic scenario that nicely complements the Simon book.

Malthus, Thomas R. *An Essay on the Principle of Population, or a View of Its Past and Present Effects on Human Happiness.* 1798. Reprint, edited by Philip Appleman. New York: Norton, Norton Critical Editions. 1976; see, however, the following: Malthus, T. R.; Huxley, J.; and Osborn, F. *On*

Population: Three Essays by Thomas Malthus, Julian Huxley, and Frederick Osborn. New York: New American Library (Mentor Books), 1960.

Meadows, D. H.; Meadows, D. L.; Randers, J.; and Behrens, W. W., III. *The Limits to Growth.* New York: Potomac Association, 1972. Very instrumental book, sponsored by the Club of Rome, which later reversed their position on population growth.

Olson, Mancur, Jr., and Landsberg, Hans, eds. *The No-Growth Society.* New York: Norton, 1974. Discusses the great many undesirable aspects of a no-growth system.

Rosenberg Nathan. *Technology and American Economic Growth.* New York: Harper and Row, 1972. An interesting economic historian's account of the dramatic role technology can indeed have in "saving" us and in our prosperity more generally.

Simon, Julian. *The Economics of Population Growth.* Princeton: Princeton University Press, 1977. An analytical treatment. For a more accessible and more general statement, see the following:

Simon, Julian. *The Ultimate Resource.* Princeton: Princeton University Press, 1981. A fascinating, eye-opening book that will very much jar those who have accepted the apparently inescapable logic of the limits-to-growth approach. See also the large number of references, both pro and con, contained in this book.

Index